D0241576

# Paper P2 (INT and UK)

## Corporate Reporting

## EXAM KIT

KAPLAN
PUBLISHING

**British Library Cataloguing-in-Publication Data**

A catalogue record for this book is available from the British Library.

Published by:

Kaplan Publishing UK

Unit 2 The Business Centre

Molly Millar's Lane

Wokingham

Berkshire

RG41 2QZ

ISBN: 978-0-85732-685-0

© Kaplan Financial Limited, 2013

Printed and bound in Great Britain

The text in this material and any others made available by any Kaplan Group company does not amount to advice on a particular matter and should not be taken as such. No reliance should be placed on the content as the basis for any investment or other decision or in connection with any advice given to third parties. Please consult your appropriate professional adviser as necessary. Kaplan Publishing Limited and all other Kaplan group companies expressly disclaim all liability to any person in respect of any losses or other claims, whether direct, indirect, incidental, consequential or otherwise arising in relation to the use of such materials.

All rights reserved. No part of this examination may be reproduced or transmitted in any form or by any means, electronic or mechanical, including photocopying, recording, or by any information storage and retrieval system, without prior permission from Kaplan Publishing.

*Acknowledgements*

The past ACCA examination questions are the copyright of the Association of Chartered Certified Accountants. The original answers to the questions from June 1994 onwards were produced by the examiners themselves and have been adapted by Kaplan Publishing.

We are grateful to the Chartered Institute of Management Accountants and the Institute of Chartered Accountants in England and Wales for permission to reproduce past examination questions. The answers have been prepared by Kaplan Publishing.

# CONTENTS

## Section

**Key features in this edition**

In addition to providing a wide ranging bank of real past exam questions, we have also included in this edition:

- An analysis of all of the recent new syllabus examination papers.

- Paper specific information and advice on exam technique.

- Our recommended approach to make your revision for this particular subject as effective as possible.

  This includes step by step guidance on how best to use our Kaplan material (Complete text, pocket notes and exam kit) at this stage in your studies.

- Enhanced tutorial answers packed with specific key answer tips, technical tutorial notes and exam technique tips from our experienced tutors.

- Complementary online resources including full tutor debriefs and question assistance to point you in the right direction when you get stuck.

**June and December 2011, June and December 2012 – Real examination questions with enhanced tutorial answers**

The real June 2011, December 2011, June 2012, and December 2012 exam questions with enhanced "walk through answers" and full "tutor debriefs", updated in line with legislation relevant to your exam sitting, is available on Kaplan EN-gage at:

www.EN-gage.co.uk

You will find a wealth of other resources to help you with your studies on the following sites:

www.EN-gage.co.uk

www.**acca**global.com/students/

**UK GAAP Focus**

The Examiner has indicated that, for the purposes of this exam, International Financial Reporting Standards (IFRS) are the main accounting standards examined in the preparation of financial information.

The significance of this for students preparing for the UK GAAP variant of Paper P2 are that the key differences between UK GAAP and International Financial Reporting Standards are looked at on a subject by subject basis.

The majority of the UK variant paper will be the same as the international paper, which is based on IFRS. There will be some key UK differences examined in the UK paper, but it is anticipated that the differences will account for no more than 20% in Paper P2. UK GAAP differences and/or UK legislation will appear in all exam sessions from June 2011.

There will be little overall change to the question style, although some of the written elements will focus on the legal requirements rather than accounting standard requirements. Candidates may have to discuss and show the impact of differences between UK and international GAAP.

UK GAAP variant students should refer to the article written by the F7 and P2 examiners in September 2010, together with the list of examinable documents for the UK variant of the examination which identifies the main areas of difference between IFRS and UK GAAP and the extent to which those differences are examinable at P2; both are available on the ACCA web site at www.accaglobal .com..

To assist UK GAAP variant students additional past examination questions and answers based on UK GAAP variant are also included within this Exam Kit.

# INDEX TO QUESTIONS AND ANSWERS

## INTRODUCTION

The style of current Paper P2 exam question is different to old syllabus Paper 3.6 questions and significant changes have had to be made to questions in light of changes to reporting standards. The syllabus has also been updated for the June 2011 sitting.

Accordingly, many of the old ACCA questions within this kit have been adapted to reflect the new style of paper and current reporting standards. If changed in any way from the original version, this is indicated in the end column of the index below with the mark *(A)*.

One of the fundamental alterations for the 2011 syllabus is the adoption of International Financial Reporting Standards as the principal standards for the UK stream. To reflect this the UK and INT versions of the kit have been merged. Where relevant answers have been appended to reflect where there is variance between the UK and INT versions.

Note that the majority of the questions within the kit are past ACCA exam questions, the more recent questions (from 2005) are labelled as such in the index.

The pilot paper is included at the end of the kit.

## KEY TO THE INDEX

### PAPER ENHANCEMENTS

We have added the following enhancements to the answers in this exam kit:

**Key answer tips**

All answers include key answer tips to help your understanding of each question.

*Tutorial note*

All answers include more tutorial notes to explain some of the technical points in more detail.

*Top tutor tips*

For selected questions, we "walk through the answer" giving guidance on how to approach the questions with helpful 'tips from a top tutor', together with technical tutor notes.

These answers are indicated with the "footsteps" icon in the index.

## ONLINE ENHANCEMENTS

 *Timed question with Online tutor debrief*

For selected questions, we recommend that they are to be completed in full exam conditions (i.e. properly timed in a closed book environment).

In addition to the examiner's technical answer, enhanced with key answer tips and tutorial notes in this exam kit, online you can find an answer debrief by a top tutor that:

- works through the question in full

- points out how to approach the question

- how to ensure that the easy marks are obtained as quickly as possible, and

- emphasises how to tackle exam questions and exam technique.

These questions are indicated with the "clock" icon in the index.

 *Online question assistance*

Have you ever looked at a question and not know where to start, or got stuck part way through?

For selected questions, we have produced "Online question assistance" offering different levels of guidance, such as:

- ensuring that you understand the question requirements fully, highlighting key terms and the meaning of the verbs used

- how to read the question proactively, with knowledge of the requirements, to identify the topic areas covered

- assessing the detail content of the question body, pointing out key information and explaining why it is important

- help in devising a plan of attack

With this assistance, you should then be able to attempt your answer confident that you know what is expected of you.

These questions are indicated with the "signpost" icon in the index.

Online question enhancements and answer debriefs will be available from Spring 2010 on Kaplan EN-gage at:

www.EN-gage.co.uk

## SECTION A-TYPE QUESTIONS

## SECTION B-TYPE QUESTIONS

KAPLAN PUBLISHING

KAPLAN PUBLISHING

# ANALYSIS OF PAST PAPERS

The table below summarises the key topics that have been tested in the new syllabus examinations to date.

The questions and answers in this edition of the exam kit have been amended, where appropriate, to reflect changes to the syllabus for 2011 examinations. Note that the question references are to the number of the question in this edition of the exam kit. The Pilot Paper is produced at the end of this kit and has also been amended to reflect changes to the syllabus for 2013 examinations together with changes in examinable documents; these questions have retained their original numbering in the Pilot Paper itself.

Where a past examination question is not included in this edition of the exam kit, are indicated with the prefix (E).

|  | Jun 09 | Dec 09 | Jun 10 | Dec 10 | Jun 11 | Dec 11 | Jun 12 |
|---|---|---|---|---|---|---|---|
| **Compulsory question** |  |  |  |  |  |  |  |
| Consolidated SOCI |  |  | Q10 |  |  |  |  |
| Consolidated SOFP | Q5 | Q13 |  |  | (E)Q1 | (E)Q1 | (E)Q1 |
| Combined SOFP & SOCI |  |  |  |  |  |  |  |
| Foreign subsidiary |  |  |  |  | (E)Q1 |  |  |
| Complex group |  |  | Q10 |  |  |  |  |
| Step by step acquisition | Q5 |  |  |  |  |  | (E)Q1 |
| Acquisition in the year |  |  |  |  |  |  |  |
| Loss of control in the year |  | Q13 | Q10 |  |  |  |  |
| Equity transfer in the year |  | Q13 | Q10 |  | (E)Q1 | (E)Q1 |  |
| Held for sale subsidiary |  |  |  |  |  |  |  |
| Joint arrangement |  |  |  |  |  |  | (E)Q1 |
| Associates | Q5 |  |  |  |  |  |  |
| Group cash flow statement |  |  |  | Q12 |  |  |  |
| Ethics & ethical behaviour | Q5 | Q13 | Q10 | Q12 | (E)Q1 | (E)Q1 | (E)Q1 |
| Creative accounting | Q5 |  |  | Q12 |  |  | (E)Q1 |
| Earnings management |  |  | Q10 |  |  |  |  |
| Segment reporting |  |  |  |  |  | (E)Q1 |  |
| Financial instruments |  |  |  |  |  |  | (E)Q1 |

| | Jun 09 | Dec 09 | Jun 10 | Dec 10 | Jun 11 | Dec 11 | Jun 12 | |
|---|---|---|---|---|---|---|---|---|
| **Mixed transactional questions** | | | | | | | | |
| Framework & accounting principles | | | | | | | | |
| IAS 1 | | | | | (E)Q3 | | (E)Q2 | 2 |
| IAS 2 | | | | | | | | 1 |
| IAS 8 | | | | | (E)Q3 | | | 1 |
| IAS 10 | | Q44 | | | | | | 2 |
| IAS 12 | | | Q19 | | | | (E)Q3 | 2 |
| IAS 16 | Q43 | | | | | | | 1 |
| IAS 17 | Q43 | | | | | | | 1 |
| IAS 18 | Q43 | Q44 | | | (E)Q3 | | | 3 |
| IAS 19 | | | Q19 | | (E)Q3 | | (E)Q2 | 3 |
| IAS 20 | | | | | | | | |
| IAS 21 | Q41 | | | | | | | 1 |
| IAS 23 | | | | | | | | |
| IAS 24 | | | | | (E)Q3 | | | 1 |
| IAS 27 | | | | | | | | |
| IAS 28 | | | Q19 | Q39 | | | | 2 |
| IAS 32/IAS 39/IFRS 7/IFRS 9 | Q40 | | Q25 | Q39 | (E)Q4 | | (E)Q3 | 5 |
| IAS 33 | | | | | | | | |
| IAS 36 | | Q32 | Q19 | | | (E)Q3 | | 3 |
| IAS 37 | | | | Q39 | (E)Q2 | | (E)Q2 | 3 |
| IAS 38 | | Q44 | | Q39 | (E)Q2 | (E)Q3 | | 4 |
| IAS 40 | | | | | | | | |
| IFRS 1 | | | | | (E)Q2 | | | 1 |
| IFRS 2 | | | | Q36 | | | (E)Q2 | 2 |
| IFRS3 Revised | | | | | | | | |
| IFRS 5 | | | Q19 | | | | | 1 |
| IFRS 8 | | | | | | | | |
| IFRS 10/11/12 | | Q44 | | | | | | 1 |
| IFRS 13 | | | | | | | | |
| IFRS for SME | | | | Q57 | | | | 1 |
| Entity reconstructions | | | | | | | | |
| Group reorganisations | | | | | | (E)Q2 | | 1 |

| | Jun 09 | Dec 09 | Jun 10 | Dec 10 | Jun 11 | Dec 11 | Jun 12 |
|---|---|---|---|---|---|---|---|
| **Essay question** | | | | | | | |
| Movement in harmonisation | | | | | | | |
| Conceptual framework | | | | | | | |
| Transition to IFRS & inconsistencies | | | | | | | |
| Accounting standards & disclosures | | | | | | | |
| IAS 19 Employee benefits | (E)Q4 | | | | | | |
| Financial instruments | | Q56 | | | (E)Q4 | | |
| Lease accounting | | | Q55 | | | | |
| IFRS for SME | | | | Q57 | | | |
| Revenue recognition | | | | | | (E)Q4 | |
| IAS 37 amendment | | | | | | | (E)Q4 |

# EXAM TECHNIQUE

- Use the allocated **15 minutes reading and planning time** at the beginning of the exam:
  - read the questions and examination requirements carefully, and
  - begin planning your answers.

  See the Paper Specific Information for advice on how to use this time for this paper.

- **Divide the time** you spend on questions in proportion to the marks on offer:
  - there are 1.8 minutes available per mark in the examination
  - within that, try to allow time at the end of each question to review your answer and address any obvious issues

  Whatever happens, always keep your eye on the clock and **do not over run on any part of any question!**

- Spend the last **five minutes** of the examination:
  - reading through your answers, and
  - **making any additions or corrections**.

- If you **get completely stuck** with a question:
  - leave space in your answer book, and
  - **return to it later.**

- Stick to the question and **tailor your answer** to what you are asked.
  - pay particular attention to the verbs in the question.

- If you do not understand what a question is asking, **state your assumptions**.

  Even if you do not answer in precisely the way the examiner hoped, you should be given some credit, if your assumptions are reasonable.

- You should do everything you can to make things easy for the marker.

  The marker will find it easier to identify the points you have made if your **answers are legible**.

- **Written questions**:

  Your answer should have:
  - a clear structure, including headings and paragraphs to provide focus
  - a brief introduction, a main section and a conclusion.

  Be concise.

  It is better to write a little about a lot of different points than a great deal about one or two points.

- **Computations**:

  It is essential to include all your workings in your answers – method marks are available

  Many computational questions require the use of a standard format:

  e.g. standard formats for financial statements.

  Be sure you know these formats thoroughly before the exam and use the layouts that you see in the answers given in this book and in model answers.

- **Reports, memos and other documents**:

  Some questions ask you to present your answer in the form of a report, a memo, a letter or other document.

  Make sure that you use the correct format – there could be easy marks to gain here.

# PAPER SPECIFIC INFORMATION

## THE EXAM

**FORMAT OF THE EXAM**

| | | | *Number of marks* |
|---|---|---|---|
| **Section A: 1 compulsory question** | | | 50 |
| Question 1: | Group accounts and discussion including ethics | | |
| **Section B: choice of two from three available questions @ 25 marks each** | | | 50 |
| Question 2: | Mixed transactional | 25) | |
| Question 3: | Mixed transactional | 25) | 50 |
| Question 4: | Essay style - discussion | 25) | |
| | | | ───── |
| | | | 100 |
| Total time allowed: | 3 hours plus 15 minutes reading and planning time. | | ───── |

Note that:

- Question 1 will focus on preparation of group financial statements for 35 marks. There may also be an additional element, such as calculation of the gain or loss on disposal of a subsidiary. The remainder of the question is likely to be discursive, perhaps based upon the appropriateness of a particular accounting treatment within the group accounts and will require application of ethical and professional principles to information within the question.

- Question 1 is also likely to require technical knowledge of reporting standards to be applied as part of the consolidation exercise.

- Questions 2 and 3 are likely to be multi-transactional questions. They will often be presented in the form of a scenario with an entity in the final stages of preparing their annual financial statements, with technical issues still to resolve. This may also include use of incorrect accounting treatments which will require identification, correction and explanation.

- Questions 2 and 3 are likely to require both quantitative and qualitative assessment of information provided, perhaps with a summary of corrected or adjusted amounts to include in the financial statements. Discursive explanation of relevant issues will be required and may be in the form of a report or memorandum.

- Question 4 is invariably an essay-style question, usually comprising a current issue or a theoretical or conceptual issue for discussion. This may include a relatively small computation element. The importance of awareness of current issues in accounting cannot be emphasised too much, including knowledge of articles from Student Accountant.

- Note that, for paper P2, two professional marks are available for each question in section B of the examination. As only two from the three available questions must be attempted, a maximum of four professional marks are available per examination.

## PASS MARK

The pass mark for all ACCA Qualification examination papers is 50%.

**UK GAAP FOCUS**

The Examiner has indicated that up to 20% of an examination paper may comprise specific UK GAAP content. This could consist of an individual question or elements of more than one question from either or both sections of the examination paper. It may comprise of discursive and/or numerical content and requirements. Note that the UK variant examination paper will be denominated in dollars (identified as $); this Exam Kit adopts the same notation and style for UK variant content.

# READING AND PLANNING TIME

Remember that all three hour paper based examinations have an additional 15 minutes reading and planning time.

**ACCA GUIDANCE**

ACCA guidance on the use of this time is as follows:

This additional time is allowed at the beginning of the examination to allow candidates to read the questions and to begin planning their answers before they start to write in their answer books.

This time should be used to ensure that all the information and, in particular, the exam requirements are properly read and understood.

During this time, candidates may only annotate their question paper. They may not write anything in their answer booklets until told to do so by the invigilator.

**KAPLAN GUIDANCE**

As there is some choice in Section B, there is a decision to make regarding which one of the optional questions to drop, together with the decision of which order you should attempt the questions.

Therefore, in relation to P2, we recommend that you take the following approach with your reading and planning time:

- **Skim through the whole paper**, assessing the level of difficulty of each question.

- **Write down** on the question paper next to the mark allocation **the amount of time you should spend on each part.** Do this for each part of every question.

- **Decide which optional question to drop and the order** in which you think you will attempt each question:

   This is a personal choice and you have time on the revision phase to try out different approaches, for example, if you sit mock exams.

   A common approach is to tackle the question you think is the easiest and you are most comfortable with first.

   Others may prefer to tackle the longest questions first, or conversely leave them to the last.

   Psychologists believe that you usually perform at your best on the second and third question you attempt, once you have settled into the exam, so not tackling the bigger Section A questions first may be advisable.

It is usual however that student tackle their least favourite topic and/or the most difficult question in their opinion last.

Whatever your approach, you must make sure that you leave enough time to attempt all questions fully and be very strict with yourself in timing each question.

- **For each question** in turn, read the requirements and then the detail of the question carefully.

  **Always read the requirement** first as this enables you to **focus on the detail of the question with the specific task in mind.**

  **For computational questions:**

  Highlight key numbers / information and key words in the question, scribble notes to yourself on the question paper to remember key points in your answer.

  Jot down proformas required if applicable.

  **For written questions:**

  Take notice of the format required (e.g. letter, memo, notes) and identify the recipient of the answer. You need to do this to judge the level of financial sophistication required in your answer and whether the use of a formal reply or informal bullet points would be satisfactory.

  Plan your beginning, middle and end and the key areas to be addressed and your use of titles and sub-titles to enhance your answer.

  **For all questions:**

  Spot the easy marks to be gained in a question and parts which can be performed independently of the rest of the question.  For example, noting relevant reporting standards and unusual accounting treatments, laying out basic proformas correctly etc.

  Make sure that you do these parts first when you tackle the question.

  Don't go overboard in terms of planning time on any one question – you need a good measure of the whole paper and a plan for all of the questions at the end of the 15 minutes.

  By covering all questions you can often help yourself as you may find that facts in one question may remind you of things you should put into your answer relating to a different question.

- With your plan of attack in mind, **start answering your chosen question** with your plan to hand, as soon as you are allowed to start.

 **Always keep your eye on the clock and do not over run on any part of any question!**

# DETAILED SYLLABUS

The detailed syllabus and study guide written by the ACCA can be found at:

www.accaglobal.com/students/

# KAPLAN'S RECOMMENDED REVISION APPROACH

## QUESTION PRACTICE IS THE KEY TO SUCCESS

Success in professional examinations relies upon you acquiring a firm grasp of the required knowledge at the tuition phase. In order to be able to do the questions, knowledge is essential.

However, the difference between success and failure often hinges on your exam technique on the day and making the most of the revision phase of your studies.

The **Kaplan complete text** is the starting point, designed to provide the underpinning knowledge to tackle all questions. However, in the revision phase, pouring over text books is not the answer.

**Kaplan Online progress tests** help you consolidate your knowledge and understanding and are a useful tool to check whether you can remember key topic areas.

**Kaplan pocket notes** are designed to help you quickly revise a topic area, however you then need to practice questions. There is a need to progress to full exam standard questions as soon as possible, and to tie your exam technique and technical knowledge together.

**The importance of question practice cannot be over-emphasised.**

The recommended approach below is designed by expert tutors in the field, in conjunction with their knowledge of the examiner and their recent real exams.

The approach taken for the fundamental papers is to revise by topic area. However, with the professional stage papers, a multi topic approach is required to answer the scenario based questions.

**You need to practice as many questions as possible in the time you have left.**


## OUR AIM

Our aim is to get you to the stage where you can attempt exam standard questions confidently, to time, in a closed book environment, with no supplementary help (i.e. to simulate the real examination experience).

Practising your exam technique on real past examination questions, in timed conditions, is also vitally important for you to assess your progress and identify areas of weakness that may need more attention in the final run up to the examination.

In order to achieve this we recognise that initially you may feel the need to practice some questions with open book help and exceed the required time.

The approach below shows you which questions you should use to build up to coping with exam standard question practice, and references to the sources of information available should you need to revisit a topic area in more detail.

Remember that in the real examination, all you have to do is:

- attempt all questions required by the exam

- only spend the allotted time on each question, and

- get them at least 50% right!

Try and practice this approach on every question you attempt from now to the real exam.

# EXAMINER COMMENTS

We have included the examiners comments to the specific new syllabus examination questions in this kit for you to see the main pitfalls that students fall into with regard to technical content.

However, too many times in the general section of the report, the examiner comments that students had failed due to:

- "misallocation of time"

- "running out of time" and

- showing signs of "spending too much time on an earlier questions and clearly rushing the answer to a subsequent question".

**Good exam technique is vital.**

# THE KAPLAN PAPER P2 REVISION PLAN

## Stage 1: Assess areas of strengths and weaknesses

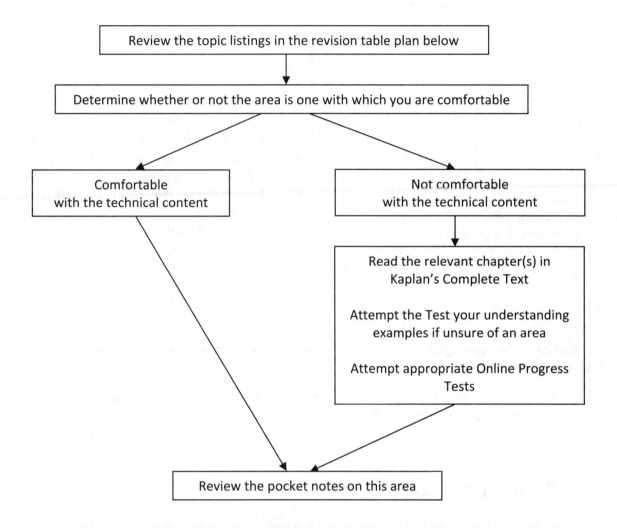

## Stage 2: Practice questions

Follow the order of revision of topics as recommended in the revision table plan below and attempt the questions in the order suggested.

Try to avoid referring to text books and notes and the model answer until you have completed your attempt.

Try to answer the question in the allotted time.

Review your attempt with the model answer and assess how much of the answer you achieved in the allocated exam time.

Fill in the self-assessment box below and decide on your best course of action.

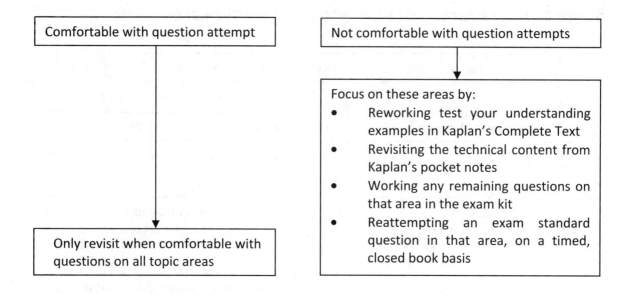

Note that :

The "footsteps questions" give guidance on exam techniques and how you should have approached the question.

The "clock questions" have an online debrief where a tutor talks you through the exam technique and approach to that question and works the question in full.

## Stage 3: Final pre-exam revision

We recommend that you **attempt at least one three hour mock examination** containing a set of previously unseen exam standard questions.

It is important that you get a feel for the breadth of coverage of a real exam without advanced knowledge of the topic areas covered – just as you will expect to see on the real exam day.

Ideally this mock should be sat in timed, closed book, real exam conditions and could be:

- a mock examination offered by your tuition provider, and/or

- the pilot paper in the back of this exam kit, and/or

- the last real examination paper (available shortly afterwards on Kaplan EN-gage with "enhanced walk through answers" and a full "tutor debrief").

# KAPLAN'S DETAILED REVISION PLAN

| Topic | Complete Text Chapter | Pocket note Chapter | Questions to attempt | Tutor guidance | Date attempted | Self assessment |
|---|---|---|---|---|---|---|
| The professional and ethical duty of the accountant | 7 | 6 | Q11(c) Q13(c) | Ensure that you can apply the ACCA Code of Ethics to a practical scenario. | | |
| The financial reporting framework | 8 | 7 | Q17 Q48 | Ensure that you are able to define, discuss and apply the elements of financial statements as identified in The Framework. Note that IFRS 13 was published in 2011. | | |
| Reporting financial performance | | | | | | |
| Performance reporting | 9 | 9 | Q15 Q18 | This could include revenue recognition per IAS 18, plus discontinued activities and non-current assets held for sale per IFRS 5 | | |
| Non-current assets | 14 | 10 | Pilot Q2 Q42 Q43 | There are several reporting standards within this heading. In particular, the accounting requirements of IAS 16, IAS 36 and IAS 38 are regularly examined. | | |
| Financial instruments | 16 | 12 | Q21 Q41 | Ensure that you understand and can apply recognition, measurement and classification rules relating to financial instruments per IAS 32, IAS 39 and IFRS 9. | | |

| Topic | | | Reference | Notes |
|---|---|---|---|---|
| Leases | 15 | 11 | Pilot Q2 Q43 | Ensure that you can classify and explain the differences between finance and operating leases per IAS 17, together with transactions not at fair value. |
| Segment reporting | 13 | 9 | Q29 | This is a P2 only topic - ensure that you can define a reportable segment per IFRS 8 and apply the definition to information provided. |
| Employee benefits | 10 | 8 | Q20 Q26 | This is a P2 only topic - ensure that you understand the differences between-accounting for defined benefit and defined contribution schemes per IAS 19. Revisions were made to IAS 19 in 2011. |
| Income taxes | 18 | 14 | Pilot Q3 Q19 | The main focus is likely to be deferred tax, with recognition of temporary differences to create deferred tax assets and liabilities per IAS 12. |
| Provisions and events after the reporting period | 17 | 13 | Q20 | Ensure that you can know when a legal or constructive obligation arises per IAS 37, and can apply the definition of an adjusting and non-adjusting event per IA 10. |
| Related parties | 12 | 9 | Q28 | This is a P2 only topic – ensure you can identify related parties per IAS 24, and the implications for any transactions which they may enter into. |
| Share-based payment | 11 | 8 | Pilot Q2 Q36 | This is a P2 only topic – ensure that you understand how to account for both cash-settled transactions and equity-settled transactions per IFRS 2. |

KAPLAN PUBLISHING

## Group financial statements

| Topic | | | Questions | Comment | | |
|---|---|---|---|---|---|---|
| Basic groups | 1 | 1 | Q5<br>Q16 | Ensure that you understand the standard workings required for subsidiaries and associates in group accounts, plus new definitions per IFRS 10/IFRS 11/IFRS 12 | | |
| Complex structures | 2 | 2 | Q9<br>Q10 | Ensure that you understand how control is exercised in complex structures, and the impact upon standard workings required. | | |
| Changes in group structure | 3,4 | 5 | Q10<br>Q13 | Ensure that you know how to account for transactions where control is either lost or retained. | | |
| Foreign currency transactions and subsidiaries | 5 | 3 | Q7<br>Q11 | Ensure that you know how to account for exchange differences arising on individual transactions, and how to consolidate a foreign subsidiary into group accounts per IAS 21. | | |
| Statements of cash flows | 6 | 4 | Pilot Q1<br>Q6 | Ensure that you know the standard proforma statement per IAS 7 and can account for changes in group structure within the statement. | | |
| Specialised entities & specialised transactions | 20 | 15,16 | Q45<br>Q54 | Ensure that you understand accounting issues associated with SMEs. In addition, entity reconstructions are examinable from 2011. | | |
| Changes in accounting regulation and reporting | 21,22 | 17,18 | Q49 | Adoption of IFRS, together with on-going convergence with US GAAP continues to be an important topic. | | |

| | | | |
|---|---|---|---|
| Appraisal of financial performance and position | 23 | 9 | Q33 | This is likely to be asked as part of a question, and may also require consideration of other accounting issues. |
| Current issues | 21,22 | 18 | Q48 Q52 | Regularly review the IASB web site for current developments, together with the ACCA web site for articles relevant to paper P2. |

Note that not all of the questions are referred to in the programme above. We have recommended an approach to build up from the basic to exam standard questions.

The remaining questions are available in the kit for extra practice for those who require more question on some areas.

# TECHNICAL UPDATE

In the period from 1 October 2010, several new and revised reporting standards have been issued by the IASB. They are examinable documents for ACCA P2 examinations in 2012, and their key points are summarised below.

## IFRS 9 FINANCIAL INSTRUMENTS (Revised)

This is part of a project to replace IAS 39 *Financial instruments – recognition and measurement*. It was published in November 2009, dealing with recognition and measurements of financial assets. Financial assets are now classified under three headings as follows:

1   **Financial assets at fair value through profit or loss (FAFVTPL).**

    This is the default classification for financial assets and will include any financial assets held for trading or speculative transactions. They will also include derivatives, unless they are part of a designated hedging arrangement. They will also include debt instruments unless they have been correctly designated to be measured at amortised cost. Initial recognition at fair value is normally cost incurred and this will exclude transactions costs which are charged to profit or loss as incurred. This accounting treatment automatically incorporates an annual impairment review.

2   **Financial assets at fair value through other comprehensive income (FAFVOCI)**

    This classification can apply to equity instruments only and requires an election for classification upon initial recognition. It will typically be applicable for equity interests which an entity wishes to retain ownership of on a continuing basis. Initial recognition at fair value would normally include the associated transaction costs of purchase. The accounting treatment automatically incorporates an impairment review, with any change in fair value taken to other comprehensive income in the year. Upon derecognition, any gain or loss is based upon the carrying value at the date of disposal; there is no recycling of any amounts previously taken to equity in earlier years.

3   **Financial assets measured at amortised cost**

    This classification can apply only to debt instruments and requires an election for classification upon initial recognition. For the election to be effective, the financial instrument must pass two tests as follows:

    (i)   *The business model test* – to pass this test, the entity must be holding the financial asset to collect in the contractual cash flows associated with the financial asset. If this is not the case, such as the financial asset being held to take advantage of changes in fair value, then the test is failed and the financial asset must be measured at FVTPL.

    (ii)  *The cash flow characteristics test* – to pass this test, the contractual cash flows collect must solely consist of payment of interest and capital. If this is not the case (e.g. with convertible bonds) the test is failed and the financial asset must be measured at FVTPL.

    This classification of financial asset requires annual review for evidence of possible impairment and, if there is evidence, there must be an impairment review.

IFRS 9 was updated in October 2010 to include recognition and measurement of financial liabilities. Essentially, the requirements of IAS 39 in relation to financial liabilities have been transferred to IFRS 9 which also retains the option for some liabilities to be measured at fair value

---

extent that part of the change in fair value of the financial liability is due to a change on own credit risk, this must be taken to other comprehensive income in the year, with the balance of any change in fair value taken to profit or loss.

Normally, financial liabilities will be measured at FVTPL, with all other financial liabilities measured at amortised cost.

The overall impact of IFRS 9 is that there is likely to be increased emphasis upon fair value accounting, rather than the use of other forms of measurement such as amortised cost or historical cost.

IFRS 9 is effective for accounting periods commencing on or after 1 January 2015 (deferred from 1 January 2013), with earlier application possible. Note that further developments are in the pipeline dealing with impairment, derivatives and hedging. To the extent that IFRS 9 does not yet deal with a particular issue, the provisions of IAS 39 continue to apply.

**Note:** Tony Sweetman of Kaplan Publishing wrote an article discussing IFRS 9 which appears in the August 2011 edition of Student Accountant. You can access this article from the ACCA web site (www.accaglobal.com).

**Note:** Tom Clendon of Kaplan Financial wrote a two-part article discussing IFRS 9 which appears in the July 2012 edition of Student Accountant. You can access this article from the ACCA web site (www.accaglobal.com).

## CONSOLIDATION AND INTERESTS IN OTHER ENTITIES

On 12 May 2011, the IASB published a collected group or package of five new or updated reporting standards which are effective for accounting periods commencing on or after 1 January 2013. Early adoption of these new and revised standards is possible but, as they have been issued together in a coordinated manner, early adoption must apply to all or none of the relevant standards, with the exception of IFRS 12 which can be applied early as a stand-alone reporting standard if required. The five reporting standards are as follows:

- IFRS 10 Consolidated Financial Statements
- IFRS 11 Joint Arrangements
- IFRS 12 Disclosure of Interests in other Entities
- IAS 27 Separate Financial Statements (revised)
- IAS 28 Investments in Associates and Joint Ventures (revised)

## IFRS 10 CONSOLIDATED FINANCIAL STATEMENTS

IFRS 10 replaces parts, but not all of IAS 27. There is now a single basis of control to determine whether consolidation of entities is required. This definition should be subject to continuous assessment, and should be considered at least at each reporting date to determine that control continues to apply. In developing the new standard, it is hoped that areas of divergent practice which had developed will be removed, such as:

- Having control with less than a majority of voting rights
- Accounting for special purpose entities
- Determining whether there is a principal or anent relationship
- Consideration of protective rights, which only become effective upon specified circumstances arising.

# Section 1

# PRACTICE QUESTIONS

## SECTION A-TYPE QUESTIONS

## GROUP FINANCIAL STATEMENTS

1  **GLOVE (JUN 07 EXAM)**  *Walk in the footsteps of a top tutor*

The following draft statements of financial position relate to Glove, Body and Fit, all public limited companies, as at 31 May 20X7:

|  | Glove $m | Body $m | Fit $m |
|---|---|---|---|
| Assets |  |  |  |
| Non-current assets: |  |  |  |
| Property, plant and equipment | 260 | 20 | 26 |
| Investment in Body | 60 |  |  |
| Investment in Fit |  | 30 |  |
| Financial assets at fair value | 10 |  |  |
| Current assets | 65 | 29 | 20 |
| |  |  |  |
| Total assets | 395 | 79 | 46 |
| |  |  |  |
| Ordinary shares | 150 | 40 | 20 |
| Other components of equity | 30 | 5 | 8 |
| Retained earnings | 135 | 25 | 10 |
| |  |  |  |
| Total equity | 315 | 70 | 38 |
| |  |  |  |
| Non-current liabilities | 45 | 2 | 3 |
| Current liabilities | 35 | 7 | 5 |
| |  |  |  |
| Total liabilities | 80 | 9 | 8 |
| |  |  |  |
| Total equity and liabilities | 395 | 79 | 46 |

The following information is relevant to the preparation of the group financial statements:

(i) Glove acquired 80% of the ordinary shares of Body on 1 June 20X5 when Body's other reserves were $4 million and retained earnings were $10 million. The fair value of the net assets of Body was $60 million at 1 June 20X5. Body acquired 70% of the ordinary shares of Fit on 1 June 20X5 when the other reserves of Fit were $8 million and retained earnings were $6 million. The fair value of the net assets of Fit at that date was $39 million. The excess of the fair value over the net assets of Body and Fit is due to an increase in the value of non-depreciable land of the companies. There have been no issues of ordinary shares in the group since 1 June 20X5.

(ii) Body owns several trade names which are highly regarded in the market place. Body has invested a significant amount in marketing these trade names and has expensed the costs. None of the trade names has been acquired externally and, therefore, the costs have not been capitalised in the statement of financial position of Body. On the acquisition of Body by Glove, a firm of valuation experts valued the trade names at $5 million and this valuation had been taken into account by Glove when offering $60 million for the investment in Body. The valuation of the trade names is not included in the fair value of the net assets of Body above. Group policy is to amortise intangible assets over ten years.

(iii) Glove has issued 30,000 convertible bonds with a three year term repayable at par. The bonds were issued at par with a face value of $1,000 per bond. Interest is payable annually in arrears at a nominal interest rate of 6%. Each bond can be converted at any time up to maturity into 300 shares of Glove. The bonds were issued on 1 June 20X6 when the market interest rate for similar debt without the conversion option was 8% per annum. Glove does not wish to account for the bonds at fair value through profit or loss. The interest has been paid and accounted for in the financial statements. The bonds have been included in non-current liabilities at their face value of $30 million and no bonds were converted in the current financial year.

(iv) On 31 May 20X7, Glove acquired plant with a fair value of $6 million. In exchange for the plant, the supplier received land, which was currently not in use, from Glove. The land had a carrying value of $4 million and an open market value of $7 million. In the financial statements at 31 May 20X7, Glove had made a transfer of $4 million from land to plant in respect of this transaction.

(v) Goodwill has been tested for impairment at 31 May 20X6 and 31 May 20X7 and no impairment loss occurred. Goodwill is to be calculated as acquired by the parent and the non-controlling interest as a proportionate share of the subsidiary's net assets

(vi) Ignore any taxation effects.

**Required:**

(a) Prepare the consolidated statement of financial position of the Glove Group at 31 May 20X7 in accordance with International Financial Reporting Standards (IFRSs). (30 marks)

(b) An unlisted company, Shine, has approached the directors of Glove wishing to acquire the group. Shine is significantly larger than Glove and wishes to obtain a stock exchange listing by acquiring Glove in a reverse acquisition.

Discuss the accounting issues that need to be considered in a reverse acquisition. (6 marks)

(c) Glove has always published an environmental report in its financial statements. It is aware that the IASB has published a Practice Statement on management commentary and would like to prepare a management commentary in its next financial report. Discuss the status of the reporting standard, together with objectives, content and benefits of a management commentary, and state whether Glove can include one in its financial statements. (14 marks)

(Total: 50 marks)

## 2 ANDASH (DEC 06 EXAM)

The following group draft financial statements relate to Andash, a public limited company:

Draft group statements of financial position at 31 October

|  | 20X6 $m | 20X5 $m |
|---|---|---|
| **Assets** | | |
| Non-current assets: | | |
| Property, plant and equipment | 5,170 | 4,110 |
| Goodwill | 120 | 130 |
| Investment in associate | 60 | – |
|  | | |
|  | 5,350 | 4,240 |
| Current assets: | | |
| Inventories | 2,650 | 2,300 |
| Trade receivables | 2,400 | 1,500 |
| Cash and cash equivalents | 140 | 300 |
|  | | |
|  | 5,190 | 4,100 |
|  | | |
| Total assets | 10,540 | 8,340 |
|  | | |
| **Equity and liabilities** | $m | $m |
| Share capital | 400 | 370 |
| Other reserves | 120 | 80 |
| Retained earnings | 1,250 | 1,100 |
|  | | |
|  | 1,770 | 1,550 |
| Non Controlling interest | 200 | 180 |
|  | | |
| Total equity | 1,970 | 1,730 |

|                              | 20X6<br>$m | 20X5<br>$m |
|------------------------------|-----------|-----------|
| Non-current liabilities:     |           |           |
| Long-term borrowings         | 3,100     | 2,700     |
| Deferred tax                 | 400       | 300       |
| Current liabilities:         |           |           |
| Trade payables               | 4,700     | 2,800     |
| Interest payable             | 70        | 40        |
| Current tax payable          | 300       | 770       |
|                              |           |           |
| Total equity and liabilities | 10,540    | 8,340     |

**Draft statement of changes in equity of the parent for the year ended 31 October 20X6**

|                             | Share<br>capital<br>$m | Other<br>reserves<br>$m | Retained<br>earnings<br>$m | Total<br>$m |
|-----------------------------|-----------------------|------------------------|---------------------------|-------------|
| Balance at 31 October 20X5  | 370                   | 80                     | 1,100                     | 1,550       |
| Profit for the year         |                       |                        | 200                       | 200         |
| Dividends                   |                       |                        | (50)                      | (50)        |
| Issue of share capital      | 30                    | 30                     |                           | 60          |
| Share options issued        |                       | 10                     |                           | 10          |
|                             |                       |                        |                           |             |
| Balance at 31 October 20X6  | 400                   | 120                    | 1,250                     | 1,770       |

**Draft group statement of profit or loss for the year ended 31 October 20X6**

|                                      | $m       |
|--------------------------------------|----------|
| Revenue                              | 17,500   |
| Cost of sales                        | (14,600) |
|                                      |          |
| Gross profit                         | 2,900    |
| Distribution costs                   | (1,870)  |
| Administrative expenses              | (490)    |
| Finance costs – interest payable     | (148)    |
| Gain on disposal of subsidiary       | 8        |
|                                      |          |
| Profit before tax                    | 400      |
| Tax                                  | (160)    |
|                                      |          |
| Profit for the year                  | 240      |
|                                      |          |
| Attributable to: Owners of the parent | 200     |
| Non-controlling interest             | 40       |
|                                      |          |
| Profit for the year                  | 240      |

There were no items of other comprehensive income.

The following information relates to the draft group financial statements of Andash:

(i)    There had been no disposal of property, plant and equipment during the year. The depreciation for the period included in cost of sales was $260 million. Andash had issued share options on 31 October 20X6 as consideration for the purchase of plant. The value of the plant purchased was $9 million at 31 October 20X6 and the share options issued had a market value of $10 million. The market value had been used to account for the plant and share options.

(ii)   Andash had acquired 25 per cent of Joma on 1 November 20X5. The purchase consideration was 25 million ordinary shares of Andash valued at $50 million and cash of $10 million. Andash has significant influence over Joma. The investment is stated at cost in the draft group statement of financial position. The reserves of Joma at the date of acquisition were $20 million and at 31 October 20X6 were $32 million. Joma had sold inventory in the period to Andash at a selling price of $16 million. The cost of the inventory was $8 million and the inventory was still held by Andash at 31 October 20X6.

(iii)  Andash owns 60% of a subsidiary Broiler, a public limited company. Goodwill, calculated on a proportionate basis, attributable to the parent company arising on acquisition was $90 million. The carrying value of Broiler's identifiable net assets (excluding goodwill arising on acquisition) in the group consolidated financial statements is $240 million at 31 October 20X6. The recoverable amount of Broiler is expected to be $260 million and no impairment loss has been recorded up to 31 October 20X5.

(iv)   On 30 April 20X6 a wholly owned subsidiary, Chang, was disposed of. Chang prepared interim financial statements on that date which are as follows:

|                                | $m |
|--------------------------------|----|
| Property, plant and equipment  | 10 |
| Inventory                      | 8  |
| Trade receivables              | 4  |
| Cash and cash equivalents      | 5  |
|                                | 27 |
|                                |    |
| Share capital                  | 10 |
| Retained earnings              | 4  |
| Trade payables                 | 6  |
| Current tax payables           | 7  |
|                                | 27 |

The consolidated carrying values of the assets and liabilities at that date were the same as above. The group received cash proceeds of $32 million and the carrying amount of goodwill was $10 million. The non controlling interest is not measured at fair value.

(Ignore the taxation effects of any adjustments required to the group financial statements and round all calculations to the nearest $million).

**Required:**

(a) Prepare a group statement of cash flows using the indirect method for the Andash Group for the year ended 31 October 20X6 in accordance with IAS 7 *Statement of cash flows* after making any necessary adjustments required to the draft group financial statements of Andash as a result of the information above.

(Candidates are not required to produce the adjusted group financial statements of Andash.) **(28 marks)**

(b) Discuss how and why the cash flow provides useful financial information. Include in your answer ways of measuring cash flow performance. **(10 marks)**

(c) Some companies 'window dress' their financial statements at the year-end. Explain what 'window dressing' is and discuss how it can be achieved and whether it is an ethical way of preparing financial statements. **(12 marks)**

**(Total: 50 marks)**

3     **EJOY (JUN 06 EXAM)**  *Walk in the footsteps of a top tutor*

Ejoy, a public limited company, has acquired two subsidiaries. The details of the acquisitions are as follows:

| Company | Date of acquisition | Equity share capital of $1 $m | Retained earnings at acquisition $m | Fair value of net assets at acquisition $m | Cost of investment $m | Equity share capital of $1 acquired $m |
|---|---|---|---|---|---|---|
| Zbay | 1 June 20X4 | 200 | 170 | 600 | 520 | 160 |
| Tbay | 1 Dec 20X5 | 120 | 80 | 310 | 216 | 72 |

The draft statements of profit or loss for the year ended 31 May 20X6 are:

| | Ejoy $m | Zbay $m | Tbay $m |
|---|---|---|---|
| Revenue | 2,500 | 1,500 | 800 |
| Cost of sales | (1,800) | (1,200) | (600) |
| | | | |
| Gross profit | 700 | 300 | 200 |
| Other income | 70 | 10 | – |
| Distribution costs | (130) | (120) | (70) |
| Administrative expenses | (100) | (90) | (60) |
| Finance costs | (50) | (40) | (20) |
| | | | |
| Profit before tax | 490 | 60 | 50 |
| Income tax expense | (200) | (26) | (20) |
| | | | |
| Profit for the year | 290 | 34 | 30 |
| | | | |
| Profit for year ended 31 May 20X5 | 190 | 20 | 15 |

There were no items of other comprehensive income in the draft financial statements of each company.

The following information is relevant to the preparation of the group financial statements:

(i) Tbay was acquired exclusively with a view to sale and at 31 May 20X6 meets the criteria of being a disposal group. The fair value of Tbay at 31 May 20X6 is $300 million and the estimated selling costs of the shareholding in Tbay are $5 million.

(ii) Ejoy entered into a joint venture with another company on 31 May 20X6. The joint venture is a limited company and Ejoy has contributed assets at fair value of $20 million (carrying value $14 million). Each party will hold five million ordinary shares of $1 in the joint venture. The gain on the disposal of the assets ($6 million) to the joint venture has been included in 'other income'.

(iii) On acquisition, the financial statements of Tbay included a large cash balance. Immediately after acquisition Tbay paid a dividend of $40 million. The receipt of the dividend is included in other income in the statement of comprehensive income of Ejoy. Since the acquisition of Zbay and Tbay, there have been no further dividend payments by these companies.

(iv) Zbay has a loan asset which is being carried at $60 million in the draft financial statements for the year ended 31 May 20X6. The loan's effective interest rate is six per cent. On 1 June 20X5 the company felt that because of the borrower's financial problems, it would receive $20 million in approximately two years time, on 31 May 20X7. At 31 May 20X6, the company still expects to receive the same amount on the same date. The loan asset has been correctly designated to be measured at amortised cost.

(v) On 1 June 20X5, Ejoy purchased an equity instrument for $50 million. Because of the size of the investment, Ejoy has entered into a floating interest rate swap. Ejoy has designated the swap as a fair value hedge of the equity instrument. At 31 May 20X6, the fair value of the equity instrument has decreased to $48.3 million. Ejoy has received $0.5 million in interest on the swap contract at 31 May 20X6 and the fair value hedge has been 100% effective in the period. No entries have been made in the statement of comprehensive income to account for the equity instrument or the hedge arrangement.

(vi) No impairment of the goodwill arising on the acquisition of Zbay had occurred at 1 June 20X5. The recoverable amount of Zbay was $630 million and that of Tbay was $290 million at 31 May 20X6. Impairment losses on goodwill are charged to cost of sales. The non-controlling interest is calculated as a proportionate share of the subsidiary's net assets i.e. with no goodwill allocated to it.

(vii) Assume that profits accrue evenly throughout the year and ignore any taxation effects.

**Required:**

(a) **Prepare a consolidated statement of profit or loss for the Ejoy Group for the year ended 31 May 20X6 in accordance with International Financial Reporting Standards.** **(35 marks)**

Related party relationships are a common feature of commercial life. The objective of IAS 24 *Related party disclosures* is to ensure that financial statements contain the necessary disclosures to make users aware of the possibility that financial statements may have been affected by the existence of related parties.

**Required:**

(b) Describe the main circumstances that give rise to related parties. **(4 marks)**

(c) Explain why the disclosure of related party relationships and transactions may be important. **(3 marks)**

(d) A public listed company, X, owns two subsidiary company investments. It owns 100% of the equity shares of A and 55% of the equity shares of B. During the year ended 31 May 20X6 B made several sales of goods to A. These sales totalled $15 million and had cost B $14 million to manufacture. B made these sales on the instruction of the Board of X. It is known that one of the directors of B, who is not a director of X, is unhappy with the parent company's instruction as he believes the goods could have been sold to other companies outside the group at the far higher price of $20 million. All directors within the group benefit from a profit sharing scheme.

Describe the financial effect that X's instruction may have on the financial statements of the companies within the group and the implications this may have for other interested parties. **(6 marks)**

Professional marks will be awarded in this question for clarity and quality of discussion **(2 marks)**

**(Total: 50 marks)**

## 4 LATERAL (DEC 05 EXAM)

Lateral, a public limited company, acquired two subsidiary companies, Think and Plank, both public limited companies. The details of the acquisitions are as follows:

| Subsidiary | Date of acquisition | Retained earnings at acquisition $m | Share capital acquired $1 shares m | Fair value of net assets at acquisition $m | Fair value of the NCI at acquisition date $m |
|---|---|---|---|---|---|
| Think | 1 November 20X3 | 150 | 200 | 400 | 90 |
| Plank | 1 November 20X3 | 210 | 300 | 800 | 330 |

The draft statements of financial position as at 31 October 20X5 are:

| | Lateral $m | Think $m | Plank $m |
|---|---|---|---|
| **Assets** | | | |
| *Non-current assets* | | | |
| Property, plant and equipment | 700 | 390 | 780 |
| Investment in subsidiaries: | | | |
| Think | 380 | | |
| Plank | 340 | | |
| Financial asset | 30 | | |
| | 1,450 | 390 | 780 |
| *Current assets:* | | | |
| Inventories | 200 | 185 | 90 |
| Trade receivables | 170 | 80 | 100 |
| Cash and cash equivalents | 40 | 30 | 50 |
| Non-current assets classified as held for sale | | 15 | |
| Total assets | 1,860 | 700 | 1,020 |

| Equity and liabilities: | $m | $m | $m |
|---|---|---|---|
| Share capital – shares of $1 | 400 | 250 | 500 |
| Retained earnings | 850 | 280 | 290 |
| | | | |
| Total equity | 1,250 | 530 | 790 |
| Non-current liabilities | 250 | 60 | 80 |
| Current liabilities | 360 | 110 | 150 |
| | | | |
| Total equity and liabilities | 1,860 | 700 | 1,020 |

The following information is relevant to the preparation of the group financial statements:

(i) There have been no new issues of shares in the group since 1 November 20X3 and the fair value adjustments have not been included in the subsidiaries' financial records.

(ii) Any increase in the fair values of the net assets over their carrying values at acquisition is attributable to plant and equipment. Plant and equipment is depreciated at 20% per annum on the reducing balance basis.

(iii) Think sold plant and equipment to Lateral on 12 November 20X5. The transaction was completed at an agreed price of $15 million after selling costs. The transaction complies with the conditions in IFRS 5 *Non-current assets held for sale and discontinued operations* for disclosure as assets held for sale. The plant and equipment had been valued at fair value less costs to sell in the individual accounts of Think. At 1 November 20X4, this plant and equipment had a carrying value of $10 million and no depreciation on these assets has been charged for the year ended 31 October 20X5.

(iv) Lateral had purchased a debt instrument with five years remaining to maturity on 1 November 20X3. The purchase price and fair value was $30 million on that date. The instrument will be repaid in five years time at an amount of $37.5 million. The instrument carries fixed interest of 4.7% per annum on the principal of $37.5 million and has an effective interest rate of 10% per annum. The fixed interest has been received and accounted for but no accounting entry has been made other than the recognition of the original purchase price of the instrument. This financial asset has been correctly designated to be measured at amortised cost

(v) Goodwill arising on the acquisition of the subsidiaries was impairment tested on 31 October 20X4 and 31 October 20X5 in accordance with IAS 36 *Impairment of assets*. Both Think and Plank are cash generating units in their own right. At 31 October 20X5, the recoverable amount of Think was $567m. The goodwill arising on the acquisition of Plank was not impaired at 31 October 20X4 and 31 October 20X5.

(vi) On 31 October 20X5, after accounting for the results of the impairment test, Lateral sold 100 million shares in Plank for $180 million. Lateral still maintains significant influence over Plank after the disposal of the shares. The receipt of the sale proceeds has been recorded in the cash book and as a reduction in the carrying value of the cost of the investment in the subsidiary. The fair value of the residual holding in Plank after the disposal is $366m.

**Required:**

(a) Calculate the gain or loss that would be recorded in the group statement of comprehensive income on the sale of the shares in Plank. **(4 marks)**

(b) Prepare a consolidated statement of financial position as at 31 October 20X5 for the Lateral Group in accordance with International Financial Reporting Standards. **(28 marks)**

(c) Discuss whether purchased goodwill meets the definition of an asset according to the IASB's *Framework for the preparation and presentation of financial statements.* **(6 marks)**

(d) The IASB has recently issued the Conceptual Framework for Financial Reporting 2010 which focuses on the objective of financial reporting and the qualitative characteristics of financial statements.

Briefly discuss the key points of this current development including the reason why a new conceptual framework is required. **(12 marks)**

**(Total: 50 marks)**

5 **BRAVADO (JUN 09 EXAM)**  *Walk in the footsteps of a top tutor*

 *Timed question with Online tutor debrief*

Bravado, a public limited company, has acquired two subsidiaries and an associate. The draft statements of financial position are as follows at 31 May 2009:

|  | Bravado $m | Message $m | Mixted $m |
|---|---|---|---|
| Non-current assets : |  |  |  |
| Property, plant and equipment | 265 | 230 | 161 |
| Investments in subsidiaries: |  |  |  |
| Message | 300 |  |  |
| Mixted | 128 |  |  |
| Investment in associate – Clarity | 20 |  |  |
| Financial assets at FV through OCI | 51 | 6 | 5 |
|  | 764 | 236 | 166 |
| Current assets: |  |  |  |
| Inventories | 135 | 55 | 73 |
| Trade receivables | 91 | 45 | 32 |
| Cash and cash equivalents | 102 | 100 | 8 |
|  | 328 | 200 | 113 |
| Total assets | 1,092 | 436 | 279 |

|                               | $m   | $m  | $m  |
|-------------------------------|------|-----|-----|
| Equity and liabilities:       |      |     |     |
| Share capital                 | 520  | 220 | 100 |
| Retained earnings             | 240  | 150 | 80  |
| Other components of equity    | 12   | 4   | 7   |
| Total equity                  | 772  | 374 | 187 |
| Non-current liabilities:      |      |     |     |
| Long-term borrowings          | 120  | 15  | 5   |
| Deferred tax                  | 25   | 9   | 3   |
| Current liabilities:          |      |     |     |
| Trade and other payables      | 115  | 30  | 60  |
| Current tax payable           | 60   | 8   | 24  |
| Total equity and liabilities  | 1,092| 436 | 279 |

The following information is relevant to the preparation of the group financial statements:

(i)    On 1 June 2008, Bravado acquired 80% of the equity interests of Message, a private entity. The purchase consideration comprised cash of $300 million. The fair value of the identifiable net assets of Message was $400 million including any related deferred tax liability arising on acquisition. The owners of Message had to dispose of the entity for tax purposes by a specified date and, therefore, sold the entity to the first company to bid for it, which was Bravado. An independent valuer has stated that the fair value of the non-controlling interest in Message was $86 million on 1 June 2008. Bravado does not wish to measure the non-controlling interest in subsidiaries on the basis of the proportionate interest in the identifiable net assets but wishes to use the 'full goodwill' method. The retained earnings of Message were $136 million and other components of equity were $4 million at the date of acquisition. There had been no new issue of capital by Message since the date of acquisition and the excess of the fair value of the net assets is due to an increase in the value of non-depreciable land.

(ii)   On 1 June 2007, Bravado acquired 6% of the ordinary shares of Mixted. Bravado had treated this investment as far value through other comprehensive income in the financial statements to 31 May 2008 but had restated the investment at cost on Mixted becoming a subsidiary. On 1 June 2008, Bravado acquired a further 64% of the ordinary shares of Mixted and gained control of the company. The consideration for the acquisitions was as follows:

|              | Holding | Consideration |
|--------------|---------|---------------|
|              |         | $m            |
| 1 June 2007  | 6%      | 10            |
| 1 June 2008  | 64%     | 118           |

Under the purchase agreement of 1 June 2008, Bravado is required to pay the former shareholders 30% of the profits of Mixted on 31 May 2010 for each of the financial years to 31 May 2009 and 31 May 2010. The fair value of this arrangement was estimated at $12 million at 1 June 2008 and at 31 May 2009 this value had not changed. This amount has not been included in the financial statements.

At 1 June 2008, the fair value of the equity interest in Mixted held by Bravado before the business combination was $15 million and the fair value of the non-controlling interest in Mixted was $53 million. The fair value of the identifiable net assets at 1 June 2008 of Mixted was $170 million (excluding deferred tax assets and liabilities), and the retained earnings and other components of equity were $55 million and $7 million respectively. There had been no new issue of share capital by Mixted since the date of acquisition and the excess of the fair value of the net assets is due to an increase in the value of property, plant and equipment (PPE).

The fair value of the PPE was provisional pending receipt of the final valuations for these assets. These valuations were received on 1 December 2008 and they resulted in a further increase of $6 million in the fair value of the net assets at the date of acquisition. This increase does not affect the fair value of the non-controlling interest. PPE is depreciated on the straight-line basis over seven years. The tax base of the identifiable net assets of Mixted was $166 million at 1 June 2008. The tax rate of Mixted is 30%.

(iii) Bravado acquired a 10% interest in Clarity, a public limited company, on 1 June 2007 for $8 million. The investment was initially accounted for as fair value through other comprehensive income and, at 31 May 2008, its value was $9 million. On 1 June 2008, Bravado acquired an additional 15% interest in Clarity for $11 million and achieved significant influence. Clarity made profits after dividends of $6 million and $10 million for the years to 31 May 2008 and 31 May 2009.

(iv) On 1 June 2007, Bravado purchased an equity instrument of 11 million dinars which was its fair value. The instrument was classified as fair value through other comprehensive income. The relevant exchange rates and fair values were as follows:

|  | $ to dinars | Fair value of instrument – dinars |
|---|---|---|
| 1 June 2007 | 4.5 | 11 |
| 31 May 2008 | 5.1 | 10 |
| 31 May 2009 | 4.8 | 7 |

Bravado has not recorded any change in the value of the instrument since 31 May 2008.

(v) Bravado manufactures equipment for the retail industry. The inventory is currently valued at cost. There is a market for the part completed product at each stage of production. The cost structure of the equipment is as follows:

|  | Cost per unit $ | Selling price per unit $ |
|---|---|---|
| Production process – 1st stage | 1,000 | 1,050 |
| Conversion costs – 2nd stage | 500 |  |
| Finished product | 1,500 | 1,700 |

The selling costs are $10 per unit and Bravado has 100,000 units at the first stage of production and 200,000 units of the finished product at 31 May 2009. Shortly before the year end, a competitor released a new model onto the market which caused the equipment manufactured by Bravado to become less attractive to customers. The result was a reduction in the selling price to $1,450 of the finished product and $950 for 1st stage product.

(vi)    The directors have included a loan to a director of Bravado in cash and cash equivalents of $1 million. The loan has no specific repayment date on it but is repayable on demand. The directors feel that there is no problem with this accounting entry as there is a choice of accounting policy within International Financial Reporting Standards (IFRS) and that showing the loan as cash is their choice of accounting policy as there is no IFRS which says that this policy cannot be utilised.

(vii)   There is no impairment of goodwill arising on the acquisitions.

**Required:**

(a)     **Prepare a consolidated statement of financial position as at 31 May 2009 for the Bravado Group.**                                                            **(35 marks)**

(b)     **Calculate and explain the impact on the calculation of goodwill if the non-controlling interest was calculated on a proportionate basis for Message and Mixted.**                                                                                **(8 marks)**

(c)     **Discuss the view of the directors that there is no problem with showing a loan to a director as cash and cash equivalents, taking into account their ethical and other responsibilities as directors of the company.**                          **(5 marks)**

**Professional marks will be awarded in part (c) for clarity and expression of your discussion.**                                                                            **(2 marks)**

                                                                                    **(Total: 50 marks)**

 *Calculate your allowed time, allocate the time to the separate parts*

## 6 WARRBURT (DEC 08 EXAM)  *Walk in the footsteps of a top tutor*

The following draft group financial statements relate to Warrburt, a public limited company:

**Warrburt Group: Statement of financial position as at 30 November 2008**

|  | 30 Nov 2008 $m | 30 Nov 2007 $m |
|---|---|---|
| Non-current assets |  |  |
| Property, plant and equipment | 350 | 360 |
| Goodwill | 80 | 100 |
| Other intangible assets | 228 | 240 |
| Investment in associate | 100 | – |
| Financial assets at FV through OCI | 142 | 150 |
|  | 900 | 850 |
| Current assets |  |  |
| Inventories | 135 | 198 |
| Trade receivables | 92 | 163 |
| Cash and cash equivalents | 312 | 323 |
| Total assets | 1,439 | 1,534 |
| Equity and Liabilities |  |  |
| Equity attributable to owners of the parent |  |  |
| Share capital | 650 | 595 |
| Retained earnings | 391 | 454 |
| Other components of equity | 25 | 20 |
|  | 1,066 | 1,069 |
| Non-controlling interest | 70 | 53 |
| Total equity | 1,136 | 1,122 |
| Non-current liabilities: | $m | $m |
| Long-term borrowings | 20 | 64 |
| Deferred tax | 28 | 26 |
| Long-term provisions | 100 | 96 |
| Current liabilities: |  |  |
| Trade payables | 115 | 180 |
| Current tax payable | 35 | 42 |
| Short-term provisions | 5 | 4 |
| Total equity and liabilities | 1,439 | 1,534 |

**Warrburt Group: Statement of profit or loss and other comprehensive income for the year ended 30 November 2008**

|  | $m |
|---|---:|
| Revenue | 910 |
| Cost of sales | (886) |
| | |
| Gross profit | 24 |
| Other income | 31 |
| Distribution costs | (40) |
| Administrative expenses | (35) |
| Finance costs | (9) |
| Share of profit of associate | 8 |
| | |
| Loss before tax | (21) |
| Income tax expense | (31) |
| | |
| Loss for the year from continuing operations | (52) |
| | |
| Loss for the year | (52) |
| | |
| Other comprehensive income for the year (after tax) which will not be reclassified to profit or loss in future years: | |
| Financial assets at FV  through OCI | 27 |
| Gains on property revaluation | 2 |
| Remeasurement component losses on defined benefit plan | (4) |
| | |
| Other comprehensive income for the year (after tax) | 25 |
| | |
| Total comprehensive income for the year | (27) |

| Profit/loss attributable to: | $m |
|---|---:|
| Owners of the parent | (74) |
| Non-controlling interest | 22 |
| | |
| | (52) |

| Total comprehensive income attributable to: | $m |
|---|---:|
| Owners of the parent | (49) |
| Non-controlling interest | 22 |
| | |
| | (27) |

**Warrburt Group: Statement of changes in equity for the year ended 20 November 2008**

| | Share Capital | Retained Earnings | Financial Assets at FVTOCI | Revaluation Surplus | Total | Non-controlling Interest | Total Equity |
|---|---|---|---|---|---|---|---|
| | $m | $m | $m | $m | $m | $m | $m |
| Bal at 1 Dec 2007 | 595 | 454 | 16 | 4 | 1,069 | 53 | 1,122 |
| Share capital issued | 55 | | | | 55 | | 55 |
| Dividends | | (9) | | | (9) | (5) | (14) |
| TCI for the year | | (78) | 27 | 2 | (49) | 22 | (27) |
| Transfer to retained earnings | | 24 | (24) | | | | |
| Bal 30 Nov 2008 | 650 | 391 | 19 | 6 | 1,066 | 70 | 1,136 |

Note to Statement of changes in equity:

| | $m |
|---|---|
| Profit/Loss attributable to owners of parent | (74) |
| Remeasurement component losses on defined benefit plan | (4) |
| Total comprehensive income for the year – retained earnings | (78) |

The following information relates to the financial statements of Warrburt:

(i) Warrburt holds financial assets at fair value through other comprehensive income (FVTOCI) which are owned by the holding company. The following schedule relates to those assets.

| | $m |
|---|---|
| Balance 1 December 2007 | 150 |
| Less sales of financial assets at FVTOCI at carrying value | (38) |
| Add gain on revaluation of financial assets | 30 |
| | 142 |

The sale proceeds of the financial assets at FVTOCI were $45 million. Profit on the sale of these financial assets is included within 'other income' in the financial statements. Deferred tax of $3 million arising on the revaluation gain above has been taken into account in 'other comprehensive income' for the year. The profit held in equity on the financial assets at FVTOCI that were sold, amounting to $24 million, has been transferred to retained earnings.

 KAPLAN PUBLISHING

(ii)    The retirement benefit liability is shown as a long-term provision in the statement of financial position and comprises the following:

|  | $m |
|---|---|
| Liability at 1 December 2007 | 96 |
| Expense for period | 10 |
| Contributions to scheme (paid) | (10) |
| Remeasurement component losses | 4 |
| Liability at 30 November 2008 | 100 |

Warrburt recognises remeasurement component gains and losses within other comprehensive income in the period in which they occur. The benefits paid in the period by the trustees of the scheme were $3 million. There is no tax impact with regards to the retirement benefit liability.

(iii)   The property, plant and equipment (PPE) in the statement of financial position comprises the following:

|  | $m |
|---|---|
| Carrying value at 1 December 2007 | 360 |
| Additions at cost | 78 |
| Gains on property revaluation | 4 |
| Disposals | (56) |
| Depreciation | (36) |
| Carrying value at 30 November 2008 | 350 |

Plant and machinery with a carrying value of $1 million had been destroyed by fire in the year. The asset was replaced by the insurance company with plant and machinery which was valued at $3 million. The machines were acquired directly from the insurance company and no cash payment was made to Warrburt. The company included the net gain on this transaction in 'additions at cost' and 'other income'.

The disposal proceeds were $63 million. The gain on disposal is included in administrative expenses. Deferred tax of $2 million has been deducted in arriving at the 'gains on property revaluation' figure in 'other comprehensive income'.

The remaining additions of PPE comprised imported plant and equipment from an overseas supplier on 30 June 2008. The cost of the PPE was 380 million dinars with 280 million dinars being paid on 31 October 2008, and the balance was paid on 31 December 2008.

The rates of exchange were as follows:

|  | Dinars to $1 |
|---|---|
| 30 June 2008 | 5 |
| 31 October 2008 | 4.9 |
| 30 November 2008 | 4.8 |

Exchange gains and losses are included in administrative expenses.

(iii)   Warrburt purchased a 25% interest in an associate for cash on 1 December 2007. The net assets of the associate at the date of acquisition were $300 million. The associate made a profit after tax of $24 million and paid a dividend of $8 million out of these profits in the year ended 30 November 2008. Assume a tax rate of 25%.

(iv)   An impairment test had been carried out at 30 November 2008, on goodwill and other intangible assets. The result showed that goodwill was impaired by $20 million and other intangible assets by $12 million.

(v)   The short term provisions relate to finance costs which are payable within six months

Warrburt's directors are concerned about the results for the year in the statement of comprehensive income and the subsequent effect on the cash flow statement. They have suggested that the proceeds of the sale of property, plant and equipment and the sale of financial assets at FVTOCI should be included in 'cash generated from operations'. The directors are afraid of an adverse market reaction to their results and of the importance of meeting targets in order to ensure job security, and feel that the adjustments for the proceeds would enhance the 'cash health' of the business.

**Required:**

(a)   **Prepare a group statement of cash flows for Warrburt for the year ended 30 November 2008 in accordance with IAS 7 *Statement of cash flows* using the indirect method.**                                                       **(35 marks)**

(b)   **Discuss, the key issues which the statement of cash flows highlights regarding the cash flow of the company.**                                                     **(10 marks)**

(c)   **Discuss the ethical responsibility of the company accountant in ensuring that manipulation of the statement of cash flows, such as that suggested by the directors, does not occur.**                                             **(5 marks)**

*Note:* **Requirements (b) and (c) include 2 professional marks in total for the quality of the discussion.**

**(Total: 50 marks)**

## 7   MEMO (JUN 04 EXAM)

Memo, a public limited company, owns 75% of the equity share capital of Random, a public limited company which is situated in a foreign country. Memo acquired Random on 1 May 20X3 for 120 million crowns (CR) when the retained earnings of Random were 80 million crowns. Random has not revalued its assets or issued any equity capital since its acquisition by Memo. The following financial statements relate to Memo and Random:

**Statements of financial position at 30 April 20X4**

|  | Memo | Random |
|---|---|---|
|  | $m | CRm |
| Property, plant and equipment | 297 | 146 |
| Investment in Random | 48 | – |
| Loan to Random | 5 | – |
| Current assets | 355 | 102 |
|  | 705 | 248 |

| Equity and liabilities | $m | $m |
|---|---|---|
| Equity shares of $1/1CR | 60 | 32 |
| Share premium account | 50 | 20 |
| Retained earnings | 360 | 95 |
| | 470 | 147 |
| Non-current liabilities | 30 | 41 |
| Current liabilities | 205 | 60 |
| | 705 | 248 |

**Statements of profit or loss for year ended 30 April 20X4**

| | Memo $m | Random CRm |
|---|---|---|
| Revenue | 200 | 142 |
| Cost of sales | (120) | (96) |
| Gross profit | 80 | 46 |
| Distribution and administrative expenses | (30) | (20) |
| Operating profit | 50 | 26 |
| Interest receivable | 4 | – |
| Interest payable | – | (2) |
| Profit before taxation | 54 | 24 |
| Income tax expense | (20) | (9) |
| Profit for the year | 34 | 15 |

There were no items of other comprehensive income in the financial statements of either entity.

The following information is relevant to the preparation of the consolidated financial statements of Memo:

(a)  During the financial year Random has purchased raw materials from Memo and denominated the purchase in crowns in its financial records. The details of the transaction are set out below:

| | Date of transaction | Purchase price $m | Profit percentage on selling price |
|---|---|---|---|
| Raw materials | 1 February 20X4 | 6 | 20% |

At the year-end, half of the raw materials purchased were still in the inventory of Random. The inter-company transactions have not been eliminated from the financial statements and the goods were recorded by Random at the exchange rate ruling on 1 February 20X4. A payment of $6 million was made to Memo when the exchange rate was 2.2 crowns to $1. Any exchange gain or loss arising on the transaction is still held in the current liabilities of Random.

(b)   Memo had made an interest free loan to Random of $5 million on 1 May 20X3. The loan was repaid on 30 May 20X4. Random had included the loan in non-current liabilities and had recorded it at the exchange rate at 1 May 20X3.

(c)   The fair value of the net assets of Random at the date of acquisition is to be assumed to be the same as the carrying value. Memo uses the full goodwill method when accounting for acquisition of a subsidiary. Goodwill was impairment tested at the reporting date and had reduced in value by ten per cent. At the date of acquisition, the fair value of the non-controlling interest was CR38 million.

(d)   Random operates with a significant degree of autonomy in its business operations.

(e)   The following exchange rates are relevant to the financial statements:

Crowns to $
| | |
|---|---|
| 30 April/1 May 20X3 | 2.5 |
| 1 November 20X3 | 2.6 |
| 1 February 20X4 | 2 |
| 30 April 20X4 | 2.1 |
| Average rate for year to 30 April 20X4 | 2 |

(f)   Memo has paid a dividend of $8 million during the financial year.

**Required:**

(a)   **Prepare a consolidated statement of total comprehensive income for the year ended 30 April 20X4 and a consolidated statement of financial position, including separate disclosure of the group foreign exchange reserve, at 30 April 20X4 in accordance with International Financial Reporting Standards.    (30 marks)**

(b)   **Define functional and presentation currency and detail how an entity decides its functional and presentation currency.    (8 marks)**

**(Total (adjusted): 38 marks)**

8   **BETH (DEC 07 EXAM)**  *Online question assistance*

Beth, a listed entity, has produced the following draft statements of financial position as at 30 November 2007. Lose and Gain are both listed entities:

| | Beth $m | Lose $m | Gain $m |
|---|---|---|---|
| Assets | | | |
| Non current assets | | | |
| Property, plant and equipment | 1,700 | 200 | 300 |
| Intangible assets | 300 | | |
| Investment in Lose | 200 | | |
| Investment in Gain | 180 | | |
| | 2,380 | 200 | 300 |
| Current assets | | | |
| Inventories | 800 | 100 | 150 |
| Trade receivables at amortised cost | 600 | 60 | 80 |
| Cash | 500 | 40 | 20 |
| Total assets | 4,280 | 400 | 550 |

|  | $m | $m | $m |
|---|---|---|---|
| Equity capital of $1 | 1,500 | 100 | 200 |
| Other reserves | 300 | | |
| Retained earnings | 400 | 200 | 300 |
| Total equity | 2,200 | 300 | 500 |
| Non-current liabilities | 700 | | |
| Current liabilities | 1,380 | 100 | 50 |
| Total equity and liabilities | 4,280 | 400 | 550 |

The following information is relevant to the preparation of the group financial statements of the Beth Group:

(i) **Date of acquisition**

|  | Holding acquired | Retained earnings at acquisition | Purchase consideration |
|---|---|---|---|
|  |  | $m | $m |
| Lose: 1 December 2005 | 20% | 80 | 40 |
| 1 December 2006 | 60% | 150 | 160 |
| Gain: 1 December 2006 | 30% | 260 | 180 |

Lose and Gain have not issued any equity capital since the acquisition of the shareholdings by Beth. The fair values of the net assets of Lose and Gain were the same as their carrying amounts at the date of the acquisitions. The fair value of the investment of the original 20% in Lose on 1 December 2005 was $70m at the date of the second acquisition

In accordance with the revised IFRS 3 *Business combinations*, the non controlling interest is to be measured at fair value i.e. including goodwill. At the date of acquisition the fair value of the non-controlling interest in Lose was $60m.

Beth does have significant influence over Gain. There has been no impairment of goodwill on the acquisition of Lose since its acquisition, but the recoverable amount of the net assets of Gain has been deemed to be $610 million at 30 November 2007.

(ii) Lose entered into an operating lease for a building on 1 December 2006. The building was converted into office space during the year at a cost to Lose of $10 million. The operating lease is for a period of six years, at the end of which the building must be returned to the lessor in its original condition. Lose thinks that it would cost $2 million to convert the building back to its original condition at prices at 30 November 2007. The entries that had been made in the financial statements of Lose were the charge for operating lease rentals ($4 million per annum) and the improvements to the building. Both items had been charged to profit or loss. The improvements were completed during the financial year.

(iii) On 1 October 2007, Beth sold inventory costing $18 million to Gain for $28 million. At 30 November 2007, the inventory was still held by Gain. The inventory was sold to a third party on 15 December 2007 for $35 million.

(iv) Beth had contracted to purchase an item of plant and equipment for 12 million euros on the following terms:

| Payable on signing contract (1 September 2007) | 50% |
|---|---|
| Payable on delivery and installation (11 December 2007) | 50% |

The amount payable on signing the contract (the deposit) was paid on the due date and is refundable. The following exchange rates are relevant:

| 2007 | Euros to 1 dollar |
|---|---|
| 1 September | 0.75 |
| 30 November | 0.85 |
| 11 December | 0.79 |

The deposit is included in trade receivables at the rate of exchange on 1 September 2007. A full year's charge for depreciation of property, plant and equipment is made in the year of acquisition using the straight line method over six years.

(v) Beth sold some trade receivables which arose during November 2007 to a factoring company on 30 November 2007. The trade receivables sold are unlikely to default in payment based on past experience but they are long dated with payment not due until 1 June 2008. Beth has given the factor a guarantee that it will reimburse any amounts not received by the factor. Beth received $45 million from the factor being 90% of the trade receivables sold. The trade receivables are not included in the statement of financial position of Beth and the balance not received from the factor (10% of the trade receivables factored) of $5 million has been written off against retained earnings.

(vi) Beth granted 200 share options to each of its 10,000 employees on 1 December 2006. The shares vest if the employees work for the Group for the next two years. On 1 December 2006, Beth estimated that there would be 1,000 eligible employees leaving in each year up to the vesting date. At 30 November 2007, 600 eligible employees had left the company. The estimate of the number of employees leaving in the year to 30 November 2008 was 500 at 30 November 2007. The fair value of each share option at the grant date (1 December 2006) was $10. The share options have not been accounted for in the financial statements.

(vii) The Beth Group operates in the oil industry and contamination of land occurs including the pollution of seas and rivers. The Group only cleans up the contamination if it is a legal requirement in the country where it operates. The following information has been produced for Beth by a group of environmental consultants for the year ended 30 November 2007:

| Cost to clean up contamination $m | Law existing in country |
|---|---|
| 5 | No |
| 7 | To come into force in December 2007 |
| 4 | Yes |

The directors of Beth have a widely publicised environmental attitude which shows little regard to the effects on the environment of their business. The Group does not currently produce a separate environmental report and no provision for environmental costs has been made in the financial statements. Any provisions would be shown as non-current liabilities. Beth is likely to operate in these countries for several years.

**Other information**

Beth is currently suffering a degree of stagnation in its business development. Its domestic and international markets are being maintained but it is not attracting new customers. Its share price has not increased whilst that of its competitors has seen a rise of between 10% and 20%. Additionally it has recently received a significant amount of adverse publicity because of its poor environmental record and is to be investigated by regulators in several countries. Although Beth is a leading supplier of oil products, it has never felt the need to promote socially responsible policies and practices or make positive contributions to society because it has always maintained its market share. It is renowned for poor customer support, bearing little regard for the customs and cultures in the communities where it does business. It had recently made a decision not to pay the amounts owing to certain small and medium entities (SMEs) as the directors feel that SMEs do not have sufficient resources to challenge the non-payment in a court of law. The management of the company is quite authoritarian and tends not to value employees' ideas and contributions.

**Required:**

(a)   **Prepare the consolidated statement of financial position of the Beth Group as at 30 November 2007 in accordance with International Financial Reporting Standards.**

(35 marks)

(b)   **Describe to the Beth Group the possible advantages of producing a separate environmental report.** (8 marks)

(c)   **Discuss the ethical and social responsibilities of the Beth Group and whether a change in the ethical and social attitudes of the management could improve business performance.** (7 marks)

*Note:* **Requirement (c) includes 2 professional marks for development of the discussion of the ethical and social responsibilities of the Beth Group.**

(Total: 50 marks)

 *Online question assistance*

9   **ROD (DEC 07 EXAM)**

The following draft statements of financial position relate to Rod, a public limited company, Reel, a public limited company, and Line, a public limited company, as at 30 November 20X2:

|  | Rod | Reel | Line |
|---|---|---|---|
|  | $m | $m | $m |
| Non-current assets |  |  |  |
| Property, plant and equipment – at cost/valuation | 1,230 | 505 | 256 |
| Investment in Reel | 640 | – | – |
| Investment in Line | 160 | 100 | – |
|  |  |  |  |
| Current assets |  |  |  |
| Inventory | 300 | 135 | 65 |
| Trade receivables | 240 | 105 | 49 |
| Cash at bank and in hand | 90 | 50 | 80 |
|  |  |  |  |
| Total assets | 2,660 | 895 | 450 |

| Equity and liabilities | $m | $m | $m |
|---|---|---|---|
| Equity capital | 1,500 | 500 | 200 |
| Share premium | 300 | 100 | 50 |
| Revaluation reserve | – | – | 70 |
| Retained earnings | 625 | 200 | 60 |
| | 2,425 | 800 | 380 |
| Non-current liabilities | 135 | 25 | 20 |
| Current liabilities | 100 | 70 | 50 |
| Total equity and liabilities | 2,660 | 895 | 450 |

The following information is relevant to the preparation of the group financial statements:

(i) Rod had acquired eighty per cent of the equity share capital of Reel on 1 December 20W9 when the retained earnings of Reel were $100 million. The fair value of the net assets of Reel was $710 million at 1 December 20W9. Any fair value adjustment related to net current assets and these net current assets had been realised by 30 November 20X2. There had been no new issues of shares in the group since the current group structure was created. For all members of the group, the non-controlling interest is to be calculated as a proportionate share of the subsidiary's net assets, i.e. not at fair value and with no goodwill attaching.

(ii) Rod and Reel had acquired their holdings in Line on the same date as part of an attempt to mask the true ownership of Line. Rod acquired forty per cent and Reel acquired twenty-five per cent of the equity share capital of Line on 1 December 20X0. The retained earnings of Line on that date were $50 million and those of Reel were $150 million. There was no revaluation reserve in the books of Line on 1 December 20X0. The fair values of the net assets of Line at 1 December 20X0 were not materially different from their carrying values.

(iii) The group operates in the pharmaceutical industry and incurs a significant amount of expenditure on the development of products. These costs were formerly written off to profit or loss as incurred but then reinstated when the related products were brought into commercial use. The reinstated costs are shown as 'Development Inventory'. The costs do not meet the criteria in IAS 38 *Intangible assets* for classification as intangibles and it is unlikely that the net cash inflows from these products will be in excess of the development costs. In the current year, Reel has included $20 million of these costs in inventory. Commercial sales of this product had commenced during the current period. The accountant now wishes to ensure that the financial statements comply strictly with IFRSs as regards this matter.

(iv) Reel had purchased a significant amount of new production equipment during the year. The cost before trade discount of this equipment was $50 million. The trade discount of $6 million was recognised in profit or loss. Depreciation is charged on the straight line basis over a six year period.

(v) The policy of the group is now to state property, plant and equipment (PPE) at depreciated historical cost. The group changed from the revaluation model to the cost model under IAS 16 *Property, plant and equipment* in the year ended 30 November 20X2 and restated all of its PPE to historical cost in that year except for the PPE of Line which had been revalued by the directors of Line on 1 December

20X1. The values were incorporated in the financial records creating a revaluation reserve of $70 million. The PPE of Line were originally purchased on 1 December 20X0 at a cost of $300 million. The assets are depreciated over six years on the straight line basis. The group does not make an annual transfer from revaluation reserves to the retained earnings in respect of the excess depreciation charged on revalued PPE. There were no additions or disposals of the PPE of Line for the two years ended 30 November 20X2.

(vi) On 1 December 20X1, the directors of Rod announced the formation of a defined benefit pension scheme for the employees of the parent company and on that date contributed cash to it of $100 million. The following details relate to the scheme at 30 November 20X2:

|  | $m |
|---|---|
| Present value of obligation | 121 |
| Fair value of plan assets | 116 |
| Current service cost | 10 |
| Past service cost | 110 |
| Discount rate for obligation – 10% | |

The only entry in the financial statements made to date is in respect of the cash contribution which has been included in Rod's trade receivables. The directors have been uncertain as to how to deal with the above pension scheme in the consolidated financial statements because of the significance of the potential increase in the amount recognised in profit or loss relating to the pension scheme. They wish to recognise any remeasurement gain in other comprehensive income in accordance with IAS 19 (revised). For the purposes of calculating the net interest component, you should treat initial recognition of the defined benefit obligation and asset as if they had been included in the financial statements for the year ended 30 November 20X1.

**Required:**

(a) **Show how the defined benefit pension scheme should be dealt with in the consolidated financial statements.** **(6 marks)**

(b) **Prepare a consolidated statement of financial position of the Rod Group as at 30 November 20X2 in accordance with the standards of the International Accounting Standards Board.** **(29 marks)**

**(Total (adjusted):35 marks)**

*Note:* **Questions in this section will have an additional discursive requirement(s) for 15 marks, making a total of 50 marks.**

## 10   ASHANTI (JUN 10 EXAM)  *Walk in the footsteps of a top tutor*

The following financial statements relate to Ashanti, a public limited company.

**Ashanti Group: Statements of profit or loss and other comprehensive income for the year ended 30 April 2010.**

|  | Ashanti $m | Bochem $m | Ceram $m |
|---|---|---|---|
| Revenue | 810 | 235 | 142 |
| Cost of sales | (686) | (137) | (84) |
|  | ──── | ──── | ──── |
| Gross profit | 124 | 98 | 58 |
| Other income | 31 | 17 | 12 |
| Distribution costs | (30) | (21) | (26) |
| Administrative expenses | (55) | (29) | (12) |
| Finance costs | (8) | (6) | (8) |
|  | ──── | ──── | ──── |
| Profit before tax | 62 | 59 | 24 |
| Income tax expense | (21) | (23) | (10) |
|  | ──── | ──── | ──── |
| Profit for the year | 41 | 36 | 14 |
|  | ──── | ──── | ──── |
| Other comprehensive income for the year, net of tax which will not be reclassified to profit or loss in future periods: |  |  |  |
| Gains (net) on PPE revaluation | 12 | 6 | – |
| Remeasurement losses on defined benefit plan | (14) | – | – |
|  | ──── | ──── | ──── |
| Other comprehensive income for the year, net of tax | (2) | 6 | -- |
|  | ──── | ──── | ──── |
| Total comprehensive income and expense for year | 39 | 42 | 14 |
|  | ──── | ──── | ──── |

The following information is relevant to the preparation of the group statement of comprehensive income:

1    On 1 May 2008, Ashanti acquired 70% of the equity interests of Bochem, a public limited company. The purchase consideration comprised cash of $150 million and the fair value of the identifiable net assets was $160 million at that date. The fair value of the non-controlling interest in Bochem was $54 million on 1 May 2008. Ashanti wishes to use the 'full goodwill' method for all acquisitions. The share capital and retained earnings of Bochem were $55 million and $85 million respectively and other components of equity were $10 million at the date of acquisition. The excess of the fair value of the identifiable net assets at acquisition is due to an increase in the value of plant, which is depreciated on the straight-line method and has a five year remaining life at the date of acquisition. Ashanti disposed of a 10% equity interest to the non-controlling interests (NCI) of Bochem on 30 April 2010 for a cash consideration of $34 million. The carrying value of the net assets of Bochem at

30 April 2010 was $210 million before any adjustments on consolidation. Goodwill has been impairment tested annually and as at 30 April 2009 had reduced in value by 15% and at 30 April 2010 had lost a further 5% of its original value before the sale of the equity interest to the NCI. The goodwill impairment should be allocated between group and NCI on the basis of equity shareholding.

2   Bochem acquired 80% of the equity interests of Ceram, a public limited company, on 1 May 2008. The purchase consideration was cash of $136 million. Ceram's identifiable net assets were fair valued at $115 million and the NCI of Ceram attributable to Ashanti had a fair value of $26 million at that date. On 1 November 2009, Bochem disposed of 50% of the equity of Ceram for a consideration of $90 million. Ceram's identifiable net assets were $160 million and the fair value of the NCI of Ceram attributable to Bochem was $35 million at the date of disposal. The remaining equity interest of Ceram held by Bochem was fair valued at $45 million. After the disposal, Bochem can still exert significant influence. Goodwill had been impairment tested and no impairment had occurred. Ceram's profits are deemed to accrue evenly over the year.

3   Ashanti has sold inventory to both Bochem and Ceram in October 2009. The sale price of the inventory was $10 million and $5 million respectively. Ashanti sells goods at a gross profit margin of 20% to group companies and third parties. At the year-end, half of the inventory sold to Bochem remained unsold but the entire inventory sold to Ceram had been sold to third parties.

4   On 1 May 2007, Ashanti purchased a $20 million bond with annual interest of 8%, which is also the effective rate, payable on 30 April. The bond is classified as fair value through profit or loss. At 30 April 2010, the carrying value of the bond is $20 million and interest has just been received as normal, but there are reports that the issuer of the bond is in financial difficulty. The market rate of interest is now 10% and Ashanti estimates that the only amounts that will be received in settlement of the bond will be as follows: $1.6 million on 30 April 2011, $1.4 million on 30 April 2012 and $16.5 million on 30 April 2013. The only accounting entries made in the financial statements for the above bond since 30 April 2009 were to correctly account for the interest received.

5   Ashanti sold $5 million of goods to a customer who recently made an announcement that it is restructuring its debts with its suppliers including Ashanti. It is probable that Ashanti will not recover the amounts outstanding. The goods were sold after the announcement was made although the order was placed prior to the announcement. Ashanti wishes to make an additional allowance of $8 million against the total receivable balance at the year end, of which $5 million relates to this sale.

6   Ashanti owned a piece of property, plant and equipment (PPE) which cost $12 million and was purchased on 1 May 2008. It is being depreciated over 10 years on the straight-line basis with zero residual value. On 30 April 2009, it was revalued to $13 million and on 30 April 2010, the PPE was revalued to $8 million. The whole of the revaluation loss had been posted to the statement of comprehensive income and depreciation has been charged for the year. It is Ashanti's company policy to make all necessary transfers for excess depreciation following revaluation.

7   The salaried employees of Ashanti are entitled to 25 days paid leave each year. The entitlement accrues evenly over the year and unused leave may be carried forward for one year. The holiday year is the same as the financial year. At 30 April 2010, Ashanti has 900 salaried employees and the average unused holiday entitlement is three days per employee. 5% of employees leave without taking their entitlement

and there is no cash payment when an employee leaves in respect of holiday entitlement. There are 255 working days in the year and the total annual salary cost is $19 million. No adjustment has been made in the financial statements for the above and there was no opening accrual required for holiday entitlement.

8    Ignore any taxation effects of the above adjustments and the disclosure requirements of IFRS 5 *Non-current assets held for sale and discontinued operations*.

**Required:**

**(a)    Prepare a consolidated statement of comprehensive income for the year ended 30 April 2010 for the Ashanti Group.                                               (35 marks)**

The directors of Ashanti have heard that the International Accounting Standards Board (IASB) has issued amendments to the rules regarding reclassification of financial instruments. The directors believe that the IASB has issued these amendments to reduce the difference between US GAAP and IFRS in respect of reclassification of financial assets. Reclassification, which was previously severely restricted under the IFRS, is now permitted in specific circumstances if the conditions and disclosure requirements are followed. They feel that this will give them the capability of managing their earnings, as they will be able to reclassify loss-making financial assets and smooth income. They feel that there is no problem with managing earnings as long as the shareholders do not find out and as long as the accounting practices are within the guidelines set out in International Financial Reporting Standards (IFRS).

**Required:**

**(b)    Describe the amendments to the rules regarding reclassification of financial assets issued in October 2008 by the IASB, discussing how these rules could lead to 'management of earnings'.                                               (7 marks)**

**(c)    Discuss the nature of and incentives for 'management of earnings' and whether such a process can be deemed to be ethically acceptable.                (6 marks)**

**Professional marks will be awarded in question 1(c) for clarity and quality of discussion.                                               (2 marks)**

**(Total: 50 marks)**

**11    RIBBY, HALL AND ZIAN (JUN 08 EXAM)**      *Online question assistance*

The following draft statements of financial position relate to Ribby, Hall, and Zian, all public limited companies, as at 31 May 2008:

|  | Ribby $m | Hall $m | Zian Dinars m |
|---|---|---|---|
| Assets |  |  |  |
| Non-current assets: |  |  |  |
| Property, plant and equipment | 250 | 120 | 360 |
| Investment in Hall | 98 | – | – |
| Investment in Zian | 30 | – | – |
| Financial assets | 10 | 5 | 148 |
| Current assets | 22 | 17 | 120 |
| Total assets | 410 | 142 | 628 |

| | $m | $m | Dinars m |
|---|---|---|---|
| Equity shares | | | |
| Equity shares | 60 | 40 | 209 |
| Other components of equity | 30 | 10 | – |
| Retained earnings | 120 | 80 | 299 |
| Total equity | 210 | 130 | 508 |
| Non-current liabilities | 90 | 5 | 48 |
| Current liabilities | 110 | 7 | 72 |
| Total equity and liabilities | 410 | 142 | 628 |

The following information needs to be taken account of in the preparation of the group financial statements of Ribby:

(i)     Ribby acquired 70% of the equity shares of Hall on 1 June 2006 when Hall's other reserves were $10 million and retained earnings were $60 million. The fair value of the net assets of Hall was $120 million at the date of acquisition. Ribby acquired 60% of the equity shares of Zian for 330 million dinars on 1 June 2006 when Zian's retained earnings were 220 million dinars. The fair value of the net assets of Zian on 1 June 2006 was 495 million dinars. The excess of the fair value over the net assets of Hall and Zian is due to an increase in the value of non-depreciable land. There have been no issues of ordinary shares since acquisition and goodwill on acquisition is not impaired for either Hall or Zian. Goodwill is to be calculated on the proportion of net assets basis i.e. without allocating any goodwill to the non controlling interest.

(ii)    Zian is located in a foreign country and imports its raw materials at a price which is normally denominated in dollars. The product is sold locally at selling prices denominated in dinars, and determined by local competition. All selling and operating expenses are incurred locally and paid in dinars. Distribution of profits is determined by the parent company, Ribby. Zian has financed part of its operations through a $4 million loan from Hall which was raised on 1 June 2007. This is included in the financial assets of Hall and the non-current liabilities of Zian. Zian's management have a considerable degree of authority and autonomy in carrying out the operations of Zian and other than the loan from Hall, are not dependent upon group companies for finance.

(iii)   Ribby has a building which it purchased on 1 June 2007 for 40 million dinars and which is located overseas. The building is carried at cost and has been depreciated on the straight-line basis over its useful life of 20 years. At 31 May 2008, as a result of an impairment review, the recoverable amount of the building was estimated to be 36 million dinars.

(iv)    Ribby has a long-term loan of $10 million which is owed to a third party bank. At 31 May 2008, Ribby decided that it would repay the loan early on 1 July 2008 and formally agreed this repayment with the bank prior to the year end. The agreement sets out that there will be an early repayment penalty of $1 million.

(v)     The directors of Ribby announced on 1 June 2007 that a bonus of $6 million would be paid to the employees of Ribby if they achieved a certain target production level by 31 May 2008. The bonus is to be paid partly in cash and partly in share options. Half of the bonus will be paid in cash on 30 November 2008 whether or not the employees are still working for Ribby. The other half will be given in share options on the same date, provided that the employee is still in service on 30 November 2008. The exercise price and number of options will be fixed by management on 30 November 2008. The target production was met and management expect 10% of employees to leave between 31 May 2008 and 30 November 2008. No entry has been made in the financial statements of Ribby.

(vi)   Ribby operates a defined benefit pension plan that provides a pension of 1.2% of the final salary for each year of service, subject to a minimum of four years service. On 1 June 2007, Ribby improved the pension entitlement so that employees receive 1.4% of their final salary for each year of service. This improvement applied to all prior years' service of the employees. As a result, the present value of the defined benefit obligation on 1 June 2007 increased by $4 million as follows:

|  | $m |
|---|---|
| Employees with more than four years service | 3 |
| Employees with less than four years service (average service of two years) | 1 |
|  | — |
|  | 4 |
|  | — |

Ribby had not accounted for the improvement in the pension plan.

(vii)  Ribby is considering selling its subsidiary, Hall. Just prior to the year end, Hall sold inventory to Ribby at a price of $6 million. The carrying value of the inventory in the financial records of Hall was $2 million. The cash was received before the year end, and as a result the bank overdraft of Hall was virtually eliminated at 31 May 2008. After the year end the transaction was reversed and it was agreed that this type of transaction would be carried out again when the interim financial statements were produced for Hall, if the company had not been sold by that date.

(viii) All financial assets, with the exception of the loan by Hall to Zian, referred to in note (ii) above are correctly stated at fair value at 31 May 2008.

(ix)   The following exchange rates are relevant to the preparation of the group financial statements:

|  | Dinars to $ |
|---|---|
| 1 June 2006 | 11 |
| 1 June 2007 | 10 |
| 31 May 2008 | 12 |
| Average for year to 31 May 2008 | 10.5 |

**Required:**

(a)  **Discuss and apply the principles set out in IAS 21 *The effects of changes in foreign exchange rates* in order to determine the functional currency of Zian.      (8 marks)**

(b)  **Prepare a consolidated statement of financial position of the Ribby Group at 31 May 2008 in accordance with International Financial Reporting Standards.**
**(35 marks)**

(c)  **Discuss how the manipulation of financial statements by company accountants is inconsistent with their responsibilities as members of the accounting profession setting out the distinguishing features of a profession and the privileges that society gives to a profession. (Your answer should include reference to the above scenario.)                                                      (7 marks)**

*Note:* **Requirement (c) includes 2 marks for the quality of the discussion.**

**(Total: 50 marks)**

 *Online question assistance*

## 12   JOCATT GROUP (DEC 10 EXAM)  *Walk in the footsteps of a top tutor*

The following draft group financial statements relate to Jocatt, a public limited company:

**Jocatt Group: Statement of financial position as at 30 November**

|  | 2010 $m | 2009 $m |
|---|---|---|
| Non-current assets |  |  |
| Property, plant and equipment | 327 | 254 |
| Investment property | 8 | 6 |
| Goodwill | 48 | 68 |
| Intangible assets | 85 | 72 |
| Investment in associate | 54 |  |
| Financial assets at FV through OCI | 94 | 90 |
|  | 616 | 490 |
| Current assets |  |  |
| Inventories | 105 | 128 |
| Trade receivables | 62 | 113 |
| Cash and cash equivalents | 232 | 143 |
| Total assets | 1,015 | 874 |

| Equity and Liabilities | $m | $m |
|---|---|---|
| Equity attributable to the owners of the parent: |  |  |
| Share capital | 290 | 275 |
| Retained earnings | 351 | 324 |
| Other components of equity | 15 | 20 |
|  | 656 | 619 |
| Non-controlling interest | 55 | 36 |
| Total equity | 711 | 655 |
| Non-current liabilities: |  |  |
| Long-term borrowings | 67 | 71 |
| Deferred tax | 35 | 41 |
| Long-term provisions-pension liability | 25 | 22 |
| Current liabilities: |  |  |
| Trade payables | 144 | 55 |
| Current tax payable | 33 | 30 |
| Total equity and liabilities | 1,015 | 874 |

**Jocatt Group: Statement of profit or loss and other comprehensive income for the year ended 30 November 2010**

|  | $m |
|---|---|
| Revenue | 434 |
| Cost of sales | (321) |
| | |
| Gross profit | 113 |
| Other income | 15 |
| Distribution costs | (55.5) |
| Administrative expenses | (36) |
| Finance costs paid | (8) |
| Gains on property | 10.5 |
| Share of profit of associate | 6 |
| | |
| Profit before tax | 45 |
| Income tax expense | (11) |
| | |
| Profit for the year | 34 |

|  | $m |
|---|---|
| Other comprehensive income after tax – items that will not be reclassified to profit or loss in future accounting periods: | |
| Gain on financial assets at FV through OCI | 2 |
| Losses on property revaluation | (7) |
| Net remeasurement component gain on defined benefit plan | 8 |
| | |
| Other comprehensive income for the year, net of tax | 3 |
| | |
| Total comprehensive income for the year | 37 |
| | |
| Profit attributable to: | |
| Owners of the parent | 24 |
| Non-controlling interest | 10 |
| | |
| | 34 |
| | |
| Total comprehensive income attributable to: | |
| Owners of the parent | 27 |
| Non-controlling interest | 10 |
| | |
| | 37 |

### Jocatt Group: Statement of changes in equity for the year ended 30 November 2010

| | Share capital | Retained earnings | Fin assets at FVTOCI | Revaluation surplus (PPE) | Total | Non-controlling interest | Total equity |
|---|---|---|---|---|---|---|---|
| | $m | $m | $m | $m | $m | $m | $m |
| Balance at 1 Dec 2009 | 275 | 324 | 4 | 16 | 619 | 36 | 655 |
| Share capital issued | 15 | | | | 15 | | 15 |
| Dividends | | (5 | | | (5) | (13) | (18) |
| Rights issue | | | | | | 2 | 2 |
| Acquisitions | | | | | | 20 | 20 |
| Total comp inc for year | | 32 | 2 | (7) | 27 | 10 | 37 |
| Balance at 30 Nov 2010 | 290 | 351 | 6 | 9 | 656 | 55 | 711 |

The following information relates to the financial statements of Jocatt:

(i) On 1 December 2008, Jocatt acquired 8% of the ordinary shares of Tigret. On recognition, Jocatt had properly designated this investment as fair value through other comprehensive income in the financial statements to 30 November 2009. On 1 December 2009, Jocatt acquired a further 52% of the ordinary shares of Tigret and gained control of the company. The consideration for the acquisitions was as follows:

| | Holding | Consideration $m |
|---|---|---|
| 1 December 2008 | 8% | 4 |
| 1 December 2009 | 52% | 30 |
| | 60% | 34 |

At 1 December 2009, the fair value of the 8% holding in Tigret held by Jocatt at the time of the business combination was $5 million and the fair value of the non-controlling interest in Tigret was $20 million. No gain or loss on the 8% holding in Tigret had been reported in the financial statements at 1 December 2009. The purchase consideration at 1 December 2009 comprised cash of $15 million and shares of $15 million.

The fair value of the identifiable net assets of Tigret, excluding deferred tax assets and liabilities, at the date of acquisition comprised the following:

| | $m |
|---|---|
| Property, plant and equipment | 15 |
| Intangible assets | 18 |
| Trade receivables | 5 |
| Cash | 7 |

The tax base of the identifiable net assets of Tigret was $40 million at 1 December 2009. The tax rate of Tigret is 30%.

(ii) On 30 November 2010, Tigret made a rights issue on a 1 for 4 basis. The issue was fully subscribed and raised $5 million in cash.

(iii) Jocatt purchased a research project from a third party including certain patents on 1 December 2009 for $8 million and recognised it as an intangible asset. During the year, Jocatt incurred further costs, which included $2 million on completing the research phase, $4 million in developing the product for sale and $1 million for the initial marketing costs. There were no other additions to intangible assets in the period other than those on the acquisition of Tigret.

(iv)    Jocatt operates a defined benefit scheme. The current service costs for the year ended 30 November 2010 are $10 million. Jocatt enhanced the benefits on 1 December 2009 however, these do not vest until 30 November 2012. The total cost of the enhancement is $6 million. The net interest cost of $2 million is included within finance costs.

(v)     Jocatt owns an investment property. During the year, part of the heating system of the property, which had a carrying value of $0.5 million, was replaced by a new system, which cost $1 million. Jocatt uses the fair value model for measuring investment property.

(vi)    Jocatt had exchanged surplus land with a carrying value of $10 million for cash of $15 million and plant valued at $4 million. The transaction has commercial substance. Depreciation for the period for property, plant and equipment was $27 million.

(vii)   Goodwill relating to all subsidiaries had been impairment tested in the year to 30 November 2010 and any impairment accounted for. The goodwill impairment related to those subsidiaries which were 100% owned.

(viii)  Deferred tax of $1 million arose on the gains on the financial assets designated as fair value through other comprehensive income in the year.

(ix)    The associate did not pay any dividends in the year.

**Required:**

(a)    **Prepare a consolidated statement of cash flows for the Jocatt Group using the indirect method under IAS 7 'Statement of Cash Flows'.**

       *Note:* **Ignore deferred taxation other than where it is mentioned in the question.**

                                                                              **(35 marks)**

(b)    Jocatt operates in the energy industry and undertakes complex natural gas trading arrangements, which involve exchanges in resources with other companies in the industry. Jocatt is entering into a long-term contract for the supply of gas and is raising a loan on the strength of this contract. The proceeds of the loan are to be received over the year to 30 November 2011 and are to be repaid over four years to 30 November 2015. Jocatt wishes to report the proceeds as operating cash flow because it is related to a long-term purchase contract. The directors of Jocatt receive extra income if the operating cash flow exceeds a predetermined target for the year and feel that the indirect method is more useful and informative to users of financial statements than the direct method.

       (i)    **Comment on the directors' view that the indirect method of preparing statements of cash flow is more useful and informative to users than the direct method.** **(7 marks)**

       (ii)   **Discuss the reasons why the directors may wish to report the loan proceeds as an operating cash flow rather than a financing cash flow and whether there are any ethical implications of adopting this treatment.** **(6 marks)**

       **Professional marks will be awarded in part (b) for the clarity and quality of discussion.** **(2 marks)**

                                                                           **(Total: 50 marks)**

**13   GRANGE (DEC 09 EXAM)**   *Walk in the footsteps of a top tutor*

Grange, a public limited company, operates in the manufacturing sector. The draft statements of financial position of the group companies are as follows at 30 November 2009:

|  | Grange $m | Park $m | Fence $m |
|---|---|---|---|
| Assets: |  |  |  |
| Non-current assets |  |  |  |
| Property plant and equipment | 257 | 311 | 238 |
| Investments in subsidiaries |  |  |  |
| Park | 340 |  |  |
| Fence | 134 |  |  |
| Investment in Sitin | 16 |  |  |
|  | 747 | 311 | 238 |
| Current assets | 475 | 304 | 141 |
| Total assets | 1,222 | 615 | 379 |
| Equity and liabilities: |  |  |  |
| Equity share capital | 430 | 230 | 150 |
| Retained earnings | 410 | 170 | 65 |
| Other components of equity | 22 | 14 | 17 |
| Total equity | 862 | 414 | 232 |
| Non-current liabilities | 172 | 124 | 38 |
| Current liabilities: |  |  |  |
| Trade and other payables | 178 | 71 | 105 |
| Provisions for liabilities | 10 | 6 | 4 |
| Total equity and liabilities | 1,222 | 615 | 379 |

The following information is relevant to the preparation of the group financial statements:

(i)   On 1 June 2008, Grange acquired 60% of the equity interests of Park, a public limited company. The purchase consideration comprised cash of $250 million. Excluding the franchise referred to below, the fair value of the identifiable net assets was $360 million. The excess of the fair value of the net assets is due to an increase in the value of non-depreciable land.

Park held a franchise right, which at 1 June 2008 had a fair value of $10 million. This had not been recognised in the financial statements of Park. The franchise agreement had a remaining term of five years to run at that date and is not renewable. Park still holds this franchise at the year-end.

Grange wishes to use the 'full goodwill' method for all acquisitions. The fair value of the non-controlling interest in Park was $150 million on 1 June 2008. The retained earnings of Park were $115 million and other components of equity were $10 million at the date of acquisition.

Grange acquired a further 20% interest from the non-controlling interests in Park on 30 November 2009 for a cash consideration of $90 million.

(ii)  On 31 July 2008, Grange acquired a 100% of the equity interests of Fence for a cash consideration of $214 million. The identifiable net assets of Fence had a provisional fair value of $202 million, including any contingent liabilities. At the time of the business combination, Fence had a contingent liability with a fair value of $30 million. At 30 November 2009, the contingent liability met the recognition criteria of IAS 37 *Provisions, contingent liabilities and contingent assets* and the revised estimate of this liability was $25 million. The accountant of Fence is yet to account for this revised liability.

However, Grange had not completed the valuation of an element of property, plant and equipment of Fence at 31 July 2008 and the valuation was not completed by 30 November 2008. The valuation was received on 30 June 2009 and the excess of the fair value over book value at the date of acquisition was estimated at $4 million. The asset had a useful economic life of 10 years at 31 July 2008.

The retained earnings of Fence were $73 million and other components of equity were $9 million at 31 July 2008 before any adjustment for the contingent liability.

On 30 November 2009, Grange disposed of 25% of its equity interest in Fence to the non-controlling interest for a consideration of $80 million. The disposal proceeds had been credited to the cost of the investment in the statement of financial position.

(iii)  On 30 June 2008, Grange had acquired a 100% interest in Sitin, a public limited company, for a cash consideration of $39 million. Sitin's identifiable net assets were fair valued at $32 million.

On 30 November 2009, Grange disposed of 60% of the equity of Sitin when its identifiable net assets were $35 million. The sale proceeds were $23 million and the remaining equity interest was fair valued at $13 million. Grange could still exert significant influence after the disposal of the interest. The only accounting entry made in Grange's financial statements was to increase cash and reduce the cost of the investment in Sitin.

(iv)  Grange acquired a plot of land on 1 December 2008 in an area where the land is expected to rise significantly in value if plans for regeneration go ahead in the area. The land is currently held at cost of $6 million in property, plant and equipment until Grange decides what should be done with the land. The market value of the land at 30 November 2009 was $8 million but as at 15 December 2009, this had reduced to $7 million as there was some uncertainty surrounding the viability of the regeneration plan.

(v)  Grange anticipates that it will be fined $1 million by the local regulator for environmental pollution. It also anticipates that it will have to pay compensation to local residents of $6 million although this is only the best estimate of that liability. In addition, the regulator has requested that certain changes be made to the manufacturing process in order to make the process more environmentally friendly. This is anticipated to cost the company $4 million.

(vi)     Grange has a property located in a foreign country, which was acquired at a cost of 8 million dinars on 30 November 2008 when the exchange rate was $1 = 2 dinars. At 30 November 2009, the property was revalued to 12 million dinars. The exchange rate at 30 November 2009 was $1 = 1.5 dinars. The property was being carried at its value as at 30 November 2008. The company policy is to revalue property, plant and equipment whenever material differences exist between book and fair value. Depreciation on the property can be assumed to be immaterial.

(vii)    Grange has prepared a plan for reorganising the parent company's own operations. The board of directors has discussed the plan but further work has to be carried out before they can approve it. However, Grange has made a public announcement as regards the reorganisation and wishes to make a reorganisation provision at 30 November 2009 of $30 million. The plan will generate cost savings. The directors have calculated the value in use of the net assets (total equity) of the parent company as being $870 million if the reorganisation takes place and $830 million if the reorganisation does not take place. Grange is concerned that the parent company's property, plant and equipment have lost value during the period because of a decline in property prices in the region and feel that any impairment charge would relate to these assets. There is no reserve within other equity relating to prior revaluation of these non-current assets.

(viii)   Grange uses accounting policies, which maximise its return on capital, employed. The directors of Grange feel that they are acting ethically in using this approach as they feel that as long as they follow 'professional rules', then there is no problem. They have adopted a similar philosophy in the way they conduct their business affairs. The finance director had recently received information that one of their key customers, Brook, a public limited company, was having serious liquidity problems. This information was received from a close friend who was employed by Brook. However, he also learned that Brook had approached a rival company Field, a public limited company, for credit and knew that if Field granted Brook credit then there was a high probability that the outstanding balance owed by Brook to Grange would be paid. Field had approached the director for an informal credit reference for Brook who until recently had always paid promptly. The director was intending to give Brook a good reference because of its recent prompt payment history as the director felt that there was no obligation or rule which required him to mention the company's liquidity problems. (There is no change required to the financial statements as a result of the above information.)

**Required:**

(a)     **Calculate the gain or loss arising on the disposal of the equity interest in Sitin.**

(6 marks)

(b)     **Prepare a consolidated statement of financial position of the Grange Group at 30 November 2009 in accordance with International Financial Reporting Standards.**

(35 marks)

(c)     **Discuss the view that ethical behaviour is simply a matter of compliance with professional rules and whether the finance director should simply consider 'rules' when determining whether to give Brook a good credit reference.**          (7 marks)

**Professional marks will be awarded in part (c) for clarity and expression.    (2 marks)**

(Total: 50 marks)

## 14 TREE

Tree, a listed entity, acquired two subsidiaries, Branch and Leaf, both listed entities. The details of the acquisitions were as follows:

| | Acq' date | Equity shares @$1 | Retained earnings | Cost of parent's investment | Equity shares acquired | Fair value of NA acquired | Fair value of the NCI at acq'n |
|---|---|---|---|---|---|---|---|
| | | m | $m | $m | m | $m | $m |
| Branch | 01/07/X6 | 800 | 400 | 1,250 | 600 | 1,400 | 400 |
| Leaf | 01/01/07 | 600 | 200 | 820 | 480 | 900 | 200 |

| | Tree $m | Branch $m | Leaf $m |
|---|---|---|---|
| Revenue | 4,000 | 3,200 | 2,500 |
| Cost of sales | (3,000) | (2,800) | (2,360) |
| Gross profit | 1,000 | 400 | 140 |
| Distribution costs | (240) | (80) | (52) |
| Admin expenses | (200) | (72) | (68) |
| Operating profit | 560 | 248 | 20 |
| Finance costs | (20) | (8) | (40) |
| Investment income | 100 | | |
| Profit before tax | 640 | 240 | (20) |
| Income tax expense | (180) | (72) | (12) |
| Profit/(loss) on ordinary activities | 460 | 168 | (32) |
| Retained earnings at 1 January 20X7 | 700 | 500 | 200 |

The draft statements of profit or loss and other comprehensive income for the year ended 31 December 20X7 were as follows:

The following information is relevant to the preparation of the group statement of comprehensive income:

(i)  On 30 June 20X7, Tree sold the following shareholdings in the subsidiary entities as follows:

| | Shares sold | Proceeds $m |
|---|---|---|
| Branch | 120m | 280 |
| Leaf | 240m | 400 |

Goodwill is calculated using the full goodwill basis. Tree exercises significant influence over Leaf after the disposal of shares. At the date of disposal of Leaf, the fair value of the remaining equity interest in Leaf was $370m.

(ii)  Branch sold $200m of goods to Tree during the year. The transfer price of inventory of such goods held by Tree at 31 December 20X6 was $40m and $20m at 31 December 20X7. The profit on these goods was sold at a sales margin of 25%.

(iii)  At the date of acquisition, the fair value of the depreciable non-current assets of Branch was $20m above the carrying value and that of the non-depreciable land was $180m. The fair value adjustment in Leaf relates to non-depreciable land. At acquisition, it was estimated that the remaining economic useful life of the depreciable non-current assets was five years.

(iv)   Tree carried out a review of the carrying value of goodwill as at 31 December 20X7. The review was based on the following information:

Branch: On acquisition, the management of Tree expected pre-tax profits in the year to 31 December 20X7 to be $230m.

Leaf: On acquisition, it was anticipated that Leaf would be profitable for at least five years. At 31 December 20X7, if regarded as cash generating unit, changes in business regulations have resulted in Leaf having a value in use of $920m and an estimated net selling price of $860m. The directors of Leaf are currently developing a new product which hopefully will increase the value in use of the business in future years.

(v)    Tree paid a dividend of $40m and Branch paid a dividend of $80m in November 20X7.

(vi)   The fair value adjustments have not been incorporated into the individual entity accounts, and the sales of shares have not yet been accounted for by Tree. Assume that profits accrue evenly throughout the year and that there are no other items of income or expense. Tax on any capital gain can be ignored

(vii)  Ignore any inter-company profits in inventory when calculating the gain or loss on disposal of shares.

(viii) Tree operates a defined benefit pension plan on behalf of its employees. The net obligation at 1 January 20X7 was $50m. The increase in the defined benefit obligation arising as a result of employee work and services provided during the year to 31 December 20X7 was $5m. On 31 December 20X7, Tree announced that increased pension benefits would be payable in respect of earlier years of service and that this additional benefit would vest on 31 December 20X9. At 31 December 20X7, the present value of this additional obligation was $3m. Cash contributed into the plan during the year was $4m. At the 31 December 20X7 the present value of the net obligation was $58.5m. During the year, pension benefits paid amounted to $1.5m. The discount rate applicable for the year was 5%. The current and past service costs, together with the finance costs associated with the net defined benefit obligation, have already been included within profit or loss for the year.

(ix)   Tree intends to buy one hundred tonnes of raw materials from an overseas entity. The materials will cost Krams 50m and will be delivered and paid for in Krams on 30 June 20X8. Tree has therefore entered into a forward contract to buy Krams 50m on 30 June 20X8 at a cost of $32m. At 31 December 20X7, 50m Krams would cost $34m. The directors have not accounted for this contract at all as it had no cost at inception. The finance director has designated and documented the contract as a hedging instrument.

(x)    During the year Tree purchased an equity investment for $20m, plus associated transaction cost of $1m. The investment is classified to be accounted for as fair value through other comprehensive income. At the reporting date the value of this financial asset had risen to $40m.

**Required:**

(a)  **Prepare a consolidated statement of comprehensive income for the Tree Group for the year ended 31 December 20X7 in accordance with International Accounting Standards.**                                                                      **(35 marks)**

(b)  **Calculate and explain the impact of the disposal of shares in Branch during the year.**                                                                                                                       **(6 marks)**

**(Total: 41 marks)**

# SECTION B-TYPE QUESTIONS

## REPORTING STANDARDS

### 15 FINANCIAL PERFORMANCE AND OCI (JUN 05 EXAM)

The International Accounting Standards Board (IASB) has recently completed a joint project with the Financial Accounting Standards Board (FASB) in the USA on the topic reporting financial performance, with particular focus on reporting of other comprehensive income (OCI). This process was completed with the publication of *Presentation of Items of Other Comprehensive Income – Amendments to IAS 1* in June 2011.

**Required:**

(a) Describe the reasons why the two accounting standards boards have decided to cooperate and produce a converged basis for the presentation of other comprehensive income in the statement of financial performance.     **(8 marks)**

(b) Explain the requirements introduced by the amendments made to IAS 1 and evaluate the extent to which they may improve the quality of information included within annual financial reports.     **(10 marks)**

(c) Discuss whether gains and losses that have been reported initially in one section of the performance statement should be 'recycled' in a later period in another section and whether only 'realised' gains and losses should be included in such a statement.     **(7 marks)**

**(Total: 25 marks)**

### 16 INVESTMENTS IN OTHER ENTITIES

In May 2011, the International Accounting Standards Board issued several new and revised reporting standards dealing with accounting for interests in other entities as follows:

- IFRS 10 – Consolidated financial statements
- IFRS 11 – Joint arrangements
- IFRS 12 – Disclosure of interests in other entities
- IAS 27 – (revised) Separate financial statements
- IAS 28 – (revised) Associates and joint ventures

**Required:**

**Explain why the new and revised reporting standards were required and explain the key requirements of each of those reporting standards.     (25 marks)**

## 17 FAIR VALUE MEASUREMENT (IFRS 13)

The International Accounting Standards Board issued IFRS 13 *Fair value measurement* in 2011 and this is likely to be relevant to entities who prepare financial statements which include the impact of measurements based upon fair value.

**Required:**

(a) **Explain why the International Accounting Standards Board has introduced IFRS 13** *Fair value measurement* **(5 marks)**

(b) **Explain how fair value is to be determined in accordance with IFRS 13** **(15 marks)**

(c) **Explain the nature of the supporting disclosures required by IFRS 13** **(5 marks)**

**(Total: 25 marks)**

## 18 ROCKBY (JUN 04 EXAM)

Rockby, a public limited company, has committed itself before its year-end of 31 March 20X4 to a plan of action to sell a subsidiary, Bye. The sale is expected to be completed on 1 July 20X4 and the financial statements of the group were signed on 15 May 20X4. The subsidiary, Bye, a public limited company, had net assets at the year-end of $5 million and the book value of related goodwill is $1 million. Bye has made a loss of $500,000 from 1 April 20X4 to 15 May 20X4 and is expected to make a further loss up to the date of sale of $600,000. Rockby was at 15 May 20X4 negotiating the consideration for the sale of Bye but no contract has been signed or public announcement made as of that date.

Rockby expected to receive $4.5 million for the company after selling costs. The value-in-use of Bye at 15 May 20X4 was estimated at $3.9 million.

Further the non-current assets of Rockby include the following items of plant and head office land and buildings:

(i) Property, plant and equipment held for use in operating leases: at 31 March 20X4 the company has at carrying value $10 million of plant which has recently been leased out on operating leases. These leases have now expired. The company is undecided as to whether to sell the plant or lease it to customers under finance leases. The fair value less selling costs of the plant is $9 million and the value-in-use is estimated at $12 million.

Plant with a carrying value of $5 million at 31 March 20X4 has ceased to be used because of a downturn in the economy. The company had decided at 31 March 20X4 to maintain the plant in workable condition in case of a change in economic conditions. Rockby subsequently sold the plant by auction on 14 May 20X4 for $3 million net of costs.

(ii) The Board of Rockby approved the relocation of the head office site on 1 March 20X3. The head office land and buildings were renovated and upgraded in the year to 31 March 20X3 with a view to selling the site. During the improvements, subsidence was found in the foundations of the main building. The work to correct the subsidence and the renovations were completed on 1 June 20X3. As at 31 March 20X3 the renovations had cost $2.3 million and the cost of correcting the subsidence was $1 million. The carrying value of the head office land and buildings was $5 million at 31 March 20X3 before accounting for the renovation. Rockby moved its head office to the new site in June 20X3 and at the same time, the old head office property was offered for sale at a price of $10 million.

However, the market for commercial property had deteriorated significantly and as at 31 March 20X4, a buyer for the property had not been found. At that time the company did not wish to reduce the price and hoped that market conditions would improve. On 20 April 20X4, a bid of $8.3 million was received for the property and eventually it was sold (net of costs) for $7.5 million on 1 June 20X4. The carrying value of the head office land and buildings was $7 million at 31 March 20X4.

Non-current assets are shown in the financial statements at historical cost.

**Required:**

(a) **Discuss the way in which the sale of the subsidiary, Bye, would be dealt with in the group financial statements of Rockby at 31 March 20X4 under IFRS 5 *Non-current assets held for sale and discontinued operations*.** **(8 marks)**

(b) **Discuss whether the following non-current assets would be classed as held for sale if IFRS 5 had been applied to:**

(i) **the items of plant in the group financial statements at 31 March 20X4;** **(7 marks)**

(ii) **the head office land and buildings in the group financial statements at 31 March 20X3 and 31 March 20X4.** **(5 marks)**

**(Total: 20 marks)**

19 **CATE (JUN 10 EXAM)**  *Walk in the footsteps of a top tutor*

(a) Cate is an entity in the software industry. Cate had incurred substantial losses in the financial years 31 May 2004 to 31 May 2009. In the financial year to 31 May 2010 Cate made a small profit before tax. This included significant non-operating gains. In 2009, Cate recognised a material deferred tax asset in respect of carried forward losses, which will expire during 2012. Cate again recognised the deferred tax asset in 2010 on the basis of anticipated performance in the years from 2010 to 2012, based on budgets prepared in 2010. The budgets included high growth rates in profitability. Cate argued that the budgets were realistic as there were positive indications from customers about future orders. Cate also had plans to expand sales to new markets and to sell new products whose development would be completed soon. Cate was taking measures to increase sales, implementing new programs to improve both productivity and profitability. Deferred tax assets less deferred tax liabilities represent 25% of shareholders' equity at 31 May 2010. There are no tax planning opportunities available to Cate that would create taxable profit in the near future.

**(5 marks)**

(b) At 31 May 2010 Cate held an investment in and had a significant influence over Bates, a public limited company. Cate had carried out an impairment test in respect of its investment in accordance with the procedures prescribed in IAS 36 *Impairment of assets*. Cate argued that fair value was the only measure applicable in this case as value-in-use was not determinable as cash flow estimates had not been produced. Cate stated that there were no plans to dispose of the shareholding and hence there was no binding sale agreement. Cate also stated that the quoted share price was not an appropriate measure when considering the fair value of Cate's significant influence on Bates. Therefore, Cate estimated the fair value of its interest in Bates through application of two measurement techniques; one based on earnings multiples and the other based on an option–pricing model. Neither of these methods supported the existence of an impairment loss as of 31 May 2010.          **(5 marks)**

(c)     At 1 April 2009 Cate had a direct holding of shares giving 70% of the voting rights in Date. In May 2010, Date issued new shares, which were wholly subscribed for by a new investor. After the increase in capital, Cate retained an interest of 35% of the voting rights in its former subsidiary Date. At the same time, the shareholders of Date signed an agreement providing new governance rules for Date. Based on this new agreement, Cate was no longer to be represented on Date's board or participate in its management. As a consequence Cate considered that its decision not to subscribe to the issue of new shares was equivalent to a decision to disinvest in Date. Cate argued that the decision not to invest clearly showed its new intention not to recover the investment in Date principally through continuing use of the asset and was considering selling the investment. Due to the fact that Date is a separate line of business (with separate cash flows, management and customers), Cate considered that the results of Date for the period to 31 May 2010 should be presented based on principles provided by IFRS 5 *Non-current assets held for sale and discontinued operations.*          **(8 marks)**

(d)     In its 2010 financial statements, Cate disclosed the existence of a voluntary fund established in order to provide a post-retirement benefit plan (Plan) to employees. Cate considers its contributions to the Plan to be voluntary, and has not recorded any related liability in its consolidated financial statements. Cate has a history of paying benefits to its former employees, even increasing them to keep pace with inflation since the commencement of the Plan. The main characteristics of the Plan are as follows:

(i)      the Plan is totally funded by Cate;

(ii)     the contributions for the Plan are made periodically;

(iii)    the post retirement benefit is calculated based on a percentage of the final salaries of Plan participants dependent on the years of service;

(iv)     the annual contributions to the Plan are determined as a function of the fair value of the assets less the liability arising from past services.

Cate argues that it should not have to recognise the Plan because, according to the underlying contract, it can terminate its contributions to the Plan, if and when it wishes. The termination clauses of the contract establish that Cate must immediately purchase lifetime annuities from an insurance company for all the retired employees who are already receiving benefit when the termination of the contribution is communicated.          **(5 marks)**

**Required:**

**Discuss whether the accounting treatments proposed by the company are acceptable under International Financial Reporting Standards.**

**Professional marks will be awarded in this question for clarity and quality of discussion.**

**(2 marks)**

**The mark allocation is shown against each of the four parts above.**

**(Total: 25 marks)**

## 20 MACALJOY (DEC 07 EXAM)  *Online question assistance*

Macaljoy, a public limited company, is a leading support services company which focuses on the building industry. The company would like advice on how to treat certain items under IAS 19 *Employee benefits* and IAS 37 *Provisions, contingent liabilities and contingent assets*. The company operates the Macaljoy (2006) Pension Plan which commenced on 1 November 2006 and the Macaljoy (1990) Pension Plan, which was closed to new entrants from 31 October 2006, but which was open to future service accrual for the employees already in the scheme. The assets of the schemes are held separately from those of the company in funds under the control of trustees. The following information relates to the two schemes:

**Macaljoy (1990) Pension Plan**

The terms of the plan are as follows:

(i)     employees contribute 6% of their salaries to the plan

(ii)    Macaljoy contributes, currently, the same amount to the plan for the benefit of the employees

(iii)   On retirement, employees are guaranteed a pension which is based upon the number of years service with the company and their final salary

The following details relate to the plan in the year to 31 October 2007:

|  | $m |
|---|---|
| Present value of obligation at 1 November 2006 | 200 |
| Present value of obligation at 31 October 2007 | 240 |
| Fair value of plan assets at 1 November 2006 | 190 |
| Fair value of plan assets at 31 October 2007 | 225 |
| Current service cost | 20 |
| Pension benefits paid | 19 |
| Total contributions paid to the scheme for year to 31 October 2007 | 17 |

**Macaljoy (2006) Pension Plan**

Under the terms of the plan, Macaljoy does not guarantee any return on the contributions paid into the fund. The company's legal and constructive obligation is limited to the amount that is contributed to the fund. The following details relate to this scheme:

|  | $m |
|---|---|
| Fair value of plan assets at 31 October 2007 | 21 |
| Contributions paid by company for year to 31 October 2007 | 10 |
| Contributions paid by employees for year to 31 October 2007 | 10 |

The discount rates for the two plans are:

|  | 1 November 2006 | 31 October 2007 |
|---|---|---|
| Discount rate | 5% | 6% |

The company would like advice on how to treat the two pension plans, for the year ended 31 October 2007, together with an explanation of the differences between a defined contribution plan and a defined benefit plan.

**Warranties**

Additionally the company manufactures and sells building equipment on which it gives a standard one year warranty to all customers. The company has extended the warranty to two years for certain major customers and has insured against the cost of the second year of the warranty. The warranty has been extended at nil cost to the customer. The claims made under the extended warranty are made in the first instance against Macaljoy and then Macaljoy in turn makes a counter claim against the insurance company. Past experience has shown that 80% of the building equipment will not be subject to warranty claims in the first year, 15% will have minor defects and 5% will require major repair. Macaljoy estimates that in the second year of the warranty, 20% of the items sold will have minor defects and 10% will require major repair.

In the year to 31 October 2007, the following information is relevant:

|  | Standard warranty (units) | Extended warranty (units) | Selling price per unit (both)($) |
|---|---|---|---|
| Sales | 2,000 | 5,000 | 1,000 |

|  | Major repair $ | Minor defect $ |
|---|---|---|
| Cost of repair (average) | 500 | 100 |

Assume that sales of equipment are on 31 October 2007 and any warranty claims are made on 31 October in the year of the claim. Assume a risk adjusted discount rate of 4%.

**Required:**

**Draft a report suitable for presentation to the directors of Macaljoy which:**

(a)   (i)   **Discusses the nature of and differences between a defined contribution plan and a defined benefit plan with specific reference to the company's two schemes.**                                                                                  **(7 marks)**

       (ii)  **Shows the accounting treatment for the two Macaljoy pension plans for the year ended 31 October 2007 under 19 *Employee benefits*.**          **(7 marks)**

(b)   (i)   **Discusses the principles involved in accounting for claims made under the above warranty provision.**                                                                 **(6 marks)**

       (ii)  **Shows the accounting treatment for the above warranty provision under IAS 37 *Provisions, contingent liabilities and contingent assets* for the year ended 31 October 2007.**                                                                       **(3 marks)**

       **Appropriateness of the format and presentation of the report and communication of advice.**                                                                                            **(2 marks)**

                                                                                                                 **(Total: 25 marks)**

 *Online question assistance*

## 21 FINANCIAL INSTRUMENTS

(a) Explain how financial instruments are classified, recognised and measured in accordance with IAS 32 *Financial instruments: presentation*, IAS 39 *Financial instruments: recognition and measurement* and IFRS 9 *Financial instruments*.

(12 marks)

(b) Explain (using calculations as appropriate) how the following financial instruments should be dealt with in the financial statements.

(i) An entity, Firth issues three debt instruments, all with a nominal value of $100,000 redeemable in two years. The effective interest rate for all three instruments is 10%.

- The first is issued at par, has a coupon rate of 0% and is redeemable at a premium of $21,000.

- The second is redeemable at par, has a coupon rate of 0% and is issued at a discount of $17,355.

- The third has a coupon rate of 2%, is issued at a discount of $5,000 and is redeemable at a premium of $10,750. (5 marks)

(ii) An entity, Thompson trades in dollars and decided in January that it will need to buy an item of plant in one year's time for €400,000. As a result of being risk adverse it wishes to hedge the risk that the cost of buying euros will rise and so enters into a forward rate agreement to buy €400,000 in one year for the fixed sum of $200,000. The fair value of this contract at inception is zero and is designated as a hedging instrument. At the year-end of 31 July the euro has depreciated and the value of €400,000 is $180,000 and is at that value when the plant is bought. (5 marks)

(iii) An entity, MacDonald buys an equity instrument for trading purposes at a cost of $25 million and incurred transactions costs of a further $1 million. At the first reporting date the asset had a fair value of $75 million. Shortly after the year-end the asset is sold for its then market value of $200 million. (3 marks)

(Total: 25 marks)

## 22 AMBUSH (DEC 05 EXAM)

Ambush, a listed entity, is assessing the impact of implementing IAS 39 *Financial instruments: recognition and measurement* and IFRS 9 *Financial instruments*. The directors realise that significant changes may occur in their accounting treatment of financial instruments and they understand that on initial recognition any financial asset or liability will normally be measured at either fair value or amortised cost. However, there are certain issues that they wish to have explained and these are set out below.

**Required:**

(a) Outline in a report to the directors of Ambush the following information:

(i) How financial assets and liabilities are measured and classified, briefly setting out the accounting method used for each category. (Hedging relationships can be ignored.) (10 marks)

(ii) Why the fair value option was initially introduced and why it has caused such concern. (5 marks)

Ambush loaned $200,000 to Bromwich on 1 December 20X3. The loan is primarily held for collection of interest and capital throughout the loan term. Additionally, the cash inflows received consist solely of repayment of interest and capital. It has therefore been designated to be measured at amortised cost. The effective and stated interest rate for this loan was 8 per cent. Interest is payable by Bromwich at the end of each year and the loan is repayable on 30 November 20X7. At 30 November 20X5, the directors of Ambush have heard that Bromwich is in financial difficulties and is undergoing a financial reorganisation. The directors feel that it is likely that they will only receive $100,000 on 30 November 20X7 and no future interest payment. Interest for the year ended 30 November 20X5 had been received.

The financial year-end of Ambush is 30 November 20X5.

**Required:**

(b)  (i)  **Outline the requirements of IAS 39 and IFRS 9 as regards the impairment of financial assets.** **(6 marks)**

    (ii)  **Explain the accounting treatment under IAS 39 of the loan to Bromwich in the financial statements of Ambush for the year ended 30 November 20X5.**

**(4 marks)**

**(Total: 25 marks)**

## 23  ARTWRIGHT (DEC 04 EXAM)

Artwright, a public limited company, produces artefacts made from precious metals. Its customers vary from large multinational companies to small retail outlets and mail order customers.

(i)  Derivatives are financial instruments that derive their value from the price of some underlying item. Examples of derivatives include options and futures. Derivatives can be entered into at little or no cost, but must always be measured on the statement of financial position at their fair value. Whatever reason the derivative is entered into it will transform the risk profile of the company.

Artwright has entered into three derivatives during the year ended 30 November 20X4, details of which are as follows:

|  | Initial recognition at fair value | Fair value at the year-end | Reason |
|---|---|---|---|
| A | Nil | $20m (liability) | Artwright believes that oil prices are due to rise in the future so during the year has entered into oil futures contract to buy oil at a fixed price. Artwright has no exposure to oil prices in the course of its business. In fact, oil prices have fallen resulting in the loss at the year-end. |
| B | $1m | $9m (liability) | Artwright has an asset that it is concerned will fall in value and it wishes to cover this risk. Thus during the year it has entered into derivative B to cover any fall in value. In fact, the asset has risen in value by $8.5 million. |

| C | Nil | $25m (asset) | Artwright is concerned about the potential for raw material prices to rise. It wishes to cover this risk that future costs will rise over the next two to three years. Thus it has entered into derivative C – a futures contract. At the year-end the raw material prices have risen, potentially giving the company an increased future cost of $24 million. Taking out this contract has been beneficial to Artwright. |
|---|---|---|---|

(ii) Artwright has a mail order business. The customers pay for their goods on a loan basis over a period which varies from six months to 24 months. The average life of a loan is 12 months and the effective interest rate on the loans is 10% per annum. Most of the loans are repaid on time and of those that do not pay on time, any delay in payment is not penalised by extra interest payments. Artwright currently has as at 30 November 20X4, loans outstanding of $2 million (principal) on which interest of $150,000 is expected to be earned from 1 December 20X4. The amounts due are $1.05 million on 31 May 20X5 and $1.1 million on 30 November 20X5. The company estimates that it will receive cash repayments of $1 million on 31 May 20X5 and $1.04 million on 30 November 20X5.

Also one of Artwright's customers had experienced financial difficulties and as at 1 December 20X3, a receivable of $200,000 had been converted into a fixed interest loan of 10%. The loan was repayable over two years and at 30 November 20X4, the customer had paid $100,000 to Artwright. The accrued interest for the year was $16,500. Because of the continuing problems of the customer, at 30 November 20X4 the loan was rescheduled over a further three years at an interest rate of 10%, and the annual repayments subsequently reduced. The management of Artwright feel that the customer will be able to meet the payments under the restructured loan agreement.

(iii) The company also trades with multi-national corporations. Artwright often has cash flow problems and factors some of its trade receivables. On 1 November 20X4, it sold trade receivables of $500,000 to a bank and received a cash settlement of $440,000 for these trade receivables. The portfolio of trade receivables sold is due from some of the company's best customers who always pay their debts but are quite slow payers. Because of the low risk of default, Artwright has guaranteed 12% of the balance outstanding on each receivable and the fair value of this guarantee is thought to be $12,000.

**Required:**

**Using the principles of IAS 39 *Financial instruments: recognition and measurement*:**

(a) Discuss how each of the derivatives would be accounted for in the financial statements for the year ended 30 November 20X4. **(10 marks)**

(b) Discuss, with suitable calculations, the potential impairment of the mail order receivables and the loan to the customer. **(10 marks)**

(c) Discuss whether the sale of the trade receivables would result in them being derecognised in the statement of financial position at 30 November 20X4 and how the sale of the trade receivables would be recorded. **(5 marks)**

**(Total: 25 marks)**

## 24    PANEL (DEC 05 EXAM)

The directors of Panel, a public limited company, are reviewing the procedures for the calculation of the deferred tax provision for their company. They are quite surprised at the impact on the provision caused by reporting standards such as IFRS 1 *First time adoption of International Financial Reporting Standards* and IFRS 2 *Share-based payment*. Panel is adopting International Financial Reporting Standards for the first time as at 31 October 20X5 and the directors are unsure how the deferred tax provision will be calculated in its financial statements ended on that date including the opening provision at 1 November 20X3.

**Required:**

(a)    (i)    **Explain how changes in reporting standards are likely to have an impact on the provision for deferred taxation under IAS 12 *Income taxes*.**    **(5 marks)**

       (ii)    **Describe the basis for the calculation of the provision for deferred taxation on first time adoption of IFRSs including the provision in the opening IFRS statement of financial position.**    **(4 marks)**

Additionally the directors wish to know how the provision for deferred taxation would be calculated in the following situations under IAS 12 *Income taxes*:

(i)    On 1 November 20X3, the company had granted ten million share options worth $40 million subject to a two year vesting period. Local tax law allows a tax deduction at the exercise date of the intrinsic value of the options. The intrinsic value of the ten million share options at 31 October 20X4 was $16 million and at 31 October 20X5 was $46 million. The increase in the share price in the year to 31 October 20X5 could not be foreseen at 31 October 20X4. The options were exercised at 31 October 20X5. The directors are unsure how to account for deferred taxation on this transaction for the years ended 31 October 20X4 and 31 October 20X5.

(ii)    Panel is leasing plant under a finance lease over a five year period. The asset was recorded at the present value of the minimum lease payments of $12 million at the inception of the lease which was 1 November 20X4. The asset is depreciated on a straight line basis over the five years and has no residual value. The annual lease payments are $3 million payable in arrears on 31 October and the effective interest rate is 8% per annum. The directors have not leased an asset under a finance lease before and are unsure as to its treatment for deferred taxation. The company can claim a tax deduction for the annual rental payment as the finance lease does not qualify for tax relief.

(iii)    A wholly owned overseas subsidiary, Pins, a limited liability company, sold goods costing $7 million to Panel on 1 September 20X5, and these goods had not been sold by Panel before the year-end. Panel had paid $9 million for these goods. The directors do not understand how this transaction should be dealt with in the financial statements of the subsidiary and the group for taxation purposes. Pins pays tax locally at 30%.

(iv)   Nails, a limited liability company, is a wholly owned subsidiary of Panel, and is a cash generating unit in its own right. The value of the property, plant and equipment of Nails at 31 October 20X5 was $6 million and purchased goodwill was $1 million before any impairment loss. The company had no other assets or liabilities. An impairment loss of $1.8 million had occurred at 31 October 20X5. The tax base of the property, plant and equipment of Nails was $4 million as at 31 October 20X5. The directors wish to know how the impairment loss will affect the deferred tax provision for the year. Impairment losses are not an allowable expense for taxation purposes.

Assume a tax rate of 30%.

**Required:**

(b)   **Discuss, with suitable computations, how the situations (i) to (iv) above will impact on the accounting for deferred tax under IAS 12 *Income taxes* in the group financial statements of Panel.** **(16 marks)**

**(The situations in (i) to (iv) above carry equal marks)**

**(Total: 25 marks)**

25   **SELTEC (JUN 10 EXAM)**   *Walk in the footsteps of a top tutor*

Seltec, a public limited company, processes and sells edible oils and uses several financial instruments to spread the risk of fluctuation in the price of the edible oils. The entity operates in an environment where the transactions are normally denominated in dollars. The functional currency of Seltec is the dollar.

(a)   The entity uses forward and futures contracts to protect it against fluctuation in the price of edible oils. Where forwards are used the company often takes delivery of the edible oil and sells it shortly afterwards. The contracts are constructed with future delivery in mind but the contracts also allow net settlement in cash as an alternative. The net settlement is based on the change in the price of the oil since the start of the contract. Seltec uses the proceeds of a net settlement to purchase a different type of oil or purchase from a different supplier. Where futures are used these sometimes relate to edible oils of a different type and market than those of Seltec's own inventory of edible oil. The company intends to apply hedge accounting to these contracts in order to protect itself from earnings volatility. Seltec has also entered into a long-term arrangement to buy oil from a foreign entity whose currency is the dinar. The commitment stipulates that the fixed purchase price will be denominated in pounds sterling.

Seltec is unsure as to the nature of derivatives and hedge accounting techniques and has asked your advice on how the above financial instruments should be dealt with in the financial statements. **(14 marks)**

(b)   Seltec has decided to enter the retail market and has recently purchased two well-known brand names in the edible oil industry. One of the brand names has been in existence for many years and has a good reputation for quality. The other brand name is named after a famous film star who has been actively promoting the edible oil as being a healthier option than other brands of oil. This type of oil has only been on the market for a short time. Seltec is finding it difficult to estimate the useful life of the brands and therefore intends to treat the brands as having indefinite lives.

In order to sell the oil, Seltec has purchased two limited liability companies from a company that owns several retail outlets. Each entity owns retail outlets in several shopping complexes. The only assets of each entity are the retail outlets. There is no operational activity and at present the entities have no employees.

Seltec is unclear as to how the purchase of the brands and the entities should be accounted for. **(9 marks)**

**Required:**

**Discuss the accounting principles involved in accounting for the above transactions and how the above transactions should be treated in the financial statements of Seltec.**

**Professional marks will be awarded in this question for clarity and quality of discussion.**

**(2 marks)**

**The mark allocation is shown against each of the two parts above.** **(Total: 25 marks)**

## 26 SAVAGE (DEC 05 EXAM)

Savage, a public limited company, operates a funded defined benefit plan for its employees. The plan provides a pension of 1% of the final salary for each year of service. The cost for the year is determined using the projected unit credit method. This reflects service rendered to the dates of valuation of the plan and incorporates actuarial assumptions (primarily regarding discount rates, expected years of service, retirement age and mortality rate).

The directors have provided the following information about the defined benefit plan for the current year (year ended 31 October 20X5):

(i)    the actuarial cost of providing benefits in respect of employees' service for the year to 31 October 20X5 was $40 million. This is the present value of the pension benefits earned by the employees in the year.

(ii)    The pension benefits paid to former employees in the year were $42 million.

(iii)    Savage should have paid contributions to the fund of $53 million. Because of cash flow problems $8 million of this amount had not been paid at the financial year-end of 31 October 20X5.

(iv)    The present value of the obligation to provide benefits to current and former employees was $3,000 million at 31 October 20X4 and $3,375 million at 31 October 20X5.

(v)    The fair value of the plan assets was $2,900 million at 31 October 20X4 and $3,170 million (including the contributions owed by Savage) at 31 October 20X5. The actuarial gains recognised at 31 October 20X4 were $336 million.

With effect from 1 November 20X4, the company had amended the plan so that the employees were now provided with an increased pension entitlement. The benefits became vested immediately and the actuaries computed that the present value of the cost of these benefits at 1 November 20X4 was $125 million. The discount rates and expected rates of return on the plan assets were as follows:

|  | 31 October 20X4 | 31 October 20X5 |
|---|---|---|
| Discount rate | 6% | 7% |

**Required:**

**(a)** **Show the amounts which will be recognised in the statement of financial position and the single statement of total comprehensive income of Savage for the year ended 31 October 20X5 under IAS 19 *Employee benefits*, and the movement in the net liability in the statement of financial position. (Your calculations should show the changes in the present value of the obligation and the fair value of the plan assets during the year. Ignore any deferred taxation effects and assume that pension benefits and the contributions paid were settled at 31 October 20X5.)**

(21 marks)

**(b)** **Explain how the non-payment of contributions and the change in the pension benefits should be treated in the financial statements of Savage for the year ended 31 October 20X5.** (4 marks)

(Total: 25 marks)

## 27 EGIN (JUN 06 EXAM)

On 1 June 20X5, Egin, a public limited company, was formed out of the re-organisation of a group of companies with foreign operations. The directors require advice on the disclosure of related party information but are reluctant to disclose information as they feel that such transactions are a normal feature of business and need not be disclosed.

Under the new group structure, Egin owns 80% of Briars, 60% of Doye, and 30% of Eye. Egin exercises significant influence over Eye. The directors of Egin are also directors of Briars and Doye but only one director of Egin sits on the management board of Eye. The management board of Eye comprises five directors. Originally the group comprised five companies but the fifth company, Tang, which was a 70% subsidiary of Egin, was sold on 31 January 20X6. There were no transactions between Tang and the Egin Group during the year to 31 May 20X6. 30% of the shares of Egin are owned by another company, Atomic, which exerts significant influence over Egin. The remaining 40% of the shares of Doye are owned by Spade.

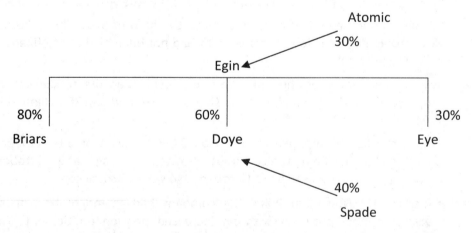

During the current financial year to 31 May 20X6, Doye has sold a significant amount of plant and equipment to Spade at the normal selling price for such items. The directors of Egin have proposed that where related party relationships are determined and sales are at normal selling price, any disclosures will state that prices charged to related parties are made on an arm's length basis.

The directors are unsure how to treat certain transactions relating to their foreign subsidiary, Briars. Egin purchased 80% of the ordinary share capital of Briars on 1 June 20X5 for 50 million euros when its net assets were fair valued at 45 million euros, with goodwill measured on a proportion of net assets basis. At 31 May 20X6, it is established that goodwill is impaired by 3 million euros. Additionally, at the date of acquisition, Egin had made an interest free loan to Briars of $10 million. The loan is to be repaid on 31 May 20X7. An equivalent loan would normally carry an interest rate of 6% taking into account Briars' credit rating.

The exchange rates were as follows:

|  | Euros to $ |
|---|---|
| 1 June 20X5 | 2.0 |
| 31 May 20X6 | 2.5 |
| Average rate for year | 2.3 |

Financial liabilities of the Group are normally measured at amortised cost.

One of the directors of Briars who is not on the management board of Egin owns the whole of the share capital of a company, Blue, that sells goods at market price to Briars. The director is in charge of the production at Briars and also acts as a consultant to the management board of the group.

**Required:**

(a)  (i)  **Discuss why it is important to disclose related party transactions, explaining the criteria which determine a related party relationship.**                    **(5 marks)**

  (ii)  **Describe the nature of any related party relationships and transactions which exists:**

  –  **within the Egin Group including Tang**                    **(5 marks)**

  –  **between Spade and the Egin Group**                    **(3 marks)**

  –  **between Atomic and the Egin Group**                    **(3 marks)**

  **commenting on whether transactions should be described as being at 'arm's length'.**

(b)  **Describe with suitable calculations how the goodwill arising on the acquisition of Briars will be dealt with in the group financial statements and how the loan to Briars should be treated in the financial statements of Briars for the year ended 31 May 20X6.**                    **(9 marks)**

                    **(Total: 25 marks)**

## 28    ENGINA (PILOT 01)

Engina, a foreign company, has approached a partner in your firm to assist in obtaining a local Stock Exchange listing for the company. Engina is registered in a country where transactions between related parties are considered to be normal but where such transactions are not disclosed. The directors of Engina are reluctant to disclose the nature of their related party transactions as they feel that although they are a normal feature of business in their part of the world, it could cause significant problems politically and culturally to disclose such transactions.

The partner in your firm has requested a list of all transactions with parties connected with the company and the directors of Engina have produced the following summary:

(a)  Every month, Engina sells $50,000 of goods per month to Mr Satay, the financial director. The financial director has set up a small retailing business for his son and the goods are purchased at cost price for him. The annual revenue of Engina is

$300 million. Additionally Mr Satay has purchased his company car from the company for $45,000 (market value $80,000). The director, Mr Satay, earns a salary of $500,000 a year, and has a personal fortune of many millions of dollars.

(b) A hotel property had been sold to a brother of Mr Soy, the Managing Director of Engina, for $4 million (net of selling cost of $0.2 million). The market value of the property was $4.3 million but in the overseas country, property prices were falling rapidly. The carrying value of the hotel was $5 million and its value in use was $3.6 million. There was an oversupply of hotel accommodation due to government subsidies in an attempt to encourage hotel development and the tourist industry.

(c) Mr Satay owns several companies and the structure of the group is as follows:

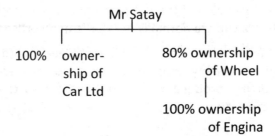

Engina earns 60% of its profit from transactions with Car and 40% of its profit from transactions with Wheel. All the above companies are incorporated in the same country.

**Required:**

**Write a report to the directors of Engina setting out the reasons why it is important to disclose related party transactions and the nature of any disclosure required for the above transactions under IAS 24 *Related party disclosures*.**

**(25 marks)**

## 29 NORMAN (JUN 08 EXAM)  *Online question assistance*

(a) Norman, a public limited company, has three business segments which are currently reported in its financial statements. Norman is an international hotel group which reports to management on the basis of region. It does not currently report segmental information under IFRS 8 *Operating segments*. The results of the regional segments for the year ended 31 May 2008 are as follows:

| Region | Revenue | | Segment results | Segment | Segment |
| | External | Internal | profit/(loss) | assets | liabilities |
| | $m | $m | $m | $m | $m |
|---|---|---|---|---|---|
| European | 200 | 3 | (10) | 300 | 200 |
| South East Asia | 300 | 2 | 60 | 800 | 300 |
| Other regions | 500 | 5 | 105 | 2,000 | 1,400 |

There were no significant intercompany balances in the segment assets and liabilities. The hotels are located in capital cities in the various regions, and the company sets individual performance indicators for each hotel based on its city location.

**Required:**

**Discuss the principles in IFRS 8 *Operating segments* for the determination of a company's reportable operating segments and how these principles would be applied for Norman plc using the information given above.** **(11 marks)**

(b)   One of the hotels owned by Norman is a hotel complex which includes a theme park, a casino and a golf course, as well as a hotel. The theme park, casino, and hotel were sold in the year ended 31 May 2008 to Conquest, a public limited company, for $200 million but the sale agreement stated that Norman would continue to operate and manage the three businesses for their remaining useful life of 15 years. The residual interest in the business reverts back to Norman after the 15 year period. Norman would receive 75% of the net profit of the businesses as operator fees and Conquest would receive the remaining 25%. Norman has guaranteed to Conquest that the net minimum profit paid to Conquest would not be less than $15 million.

**(4 marks)**

Norman has recently started issuing vouchers to customers when they stay in its hotels. The vouchers entitle the customers to a $30 discount on a subsequent room booking within three months of their stay. Historical experience has shown that only one in five vouchers are redeemed by the customer. At the company's year end of 31 May 2008, it is estimated that there are vouchers worth $20 million which are eligible for discount. The income from room sales for the year is $300 million and Norman is unsure how to report the income from room sales in the financial statements. **(4 marks)**

Norman has obtained a significant amount of grant income for the development of hotels in Europe. The grants have been received from government bodies and relate to the size of the hotel which has been built by the grant assistance. The intention of the grant income was to create jobs in areas where there was significant unemployment. The grants received of $70 million will have to be repaid if the cost of building the hotels is less than $500 million. **(4 marks)**

Appropriateness and quality of discussion **(2 marks)**

**Required:**

**Discuss how the above income would be treated in the financial statements of Norman for the year ended 31 May 2008.**

**(Total: 25 marks)**

 *Online question assistance*

## 30    WADER (JUN 07 EXAM)

Wader, a public limited company, is assessing the nature of its provisions for the year ended 31 May 20X7. The following information is relevant:

(a)    The impairment of trade receivables has been calculated using a formulaic approach which is based on a specific percentage of the portfolio of trade receivables. This general provision approach has been used by the company at 31 May 20X7. At 31 May 20X7, one of the credit customers, Tray, has come to an arrangement with Wader whereby the amount outstanding of $4 million from Tray will be paid on 31 May 20X8 together with a penalty of $100,000. The total amount of trade receivables outstanding at 31 May 20X7 was $11 million including the amount owed by Tray. The following is the analysis of the trade receivables:

|  | Balance $m | Cash expected $m | Due date |
|---|---|---|---|
| Tray | 4 | 4.1 | 31 May 20X8 |
| Milk | 2 | 2 | 31 July 20X7 |
| Other receivables | 5 | 4.6 | On average 31 July 20X7 |
|  | 11 | 10.7 |  |

Wader has made an allowance of $520,000 against trade receivables that represents the difference between the cash expected to be received and the balance outstanding plus a 2% general allowance. Milk has a similar credit risk to the 'other receivables'.    **(7 marks)**

(b)    Wader is assessing the valuation of its inventory. It has a significant quantity of a product and needs to evaluate its value for the purposes of the statement of financial position. Sales of the product are high, but it incurs high production costs. The reason for its success is that a sales commission of 20% of the list selling price is paid to the sales force. The following details relate to this product:

|  | $ per unit |
|---|---|
| List price – normal selling price | 50 |
| Allocation of customer discounts on selling price | 2.5 |
| Warehouse overheads until estimated sale date | 4 |
| Basic salaries of sales team | 2 |
| Cost of product | 35 |

The product is collected from the warehouses of Wader by the customer.    **(4 marks)**

(c)    Wader is reviewing the accounting treatment of its buildings. The company uses the 'revaluation model' for its buildings. The buildings had originally cost $10 million on 1 June 20X5 and had a useful economic life of 20 years. They are being depreciated on a straight line basis to a nil residual value. The buildings were revalued downwards on 31 May 20X6 to $8 million which was the buildings' recoverable amount. At 31 May 20X7 the value of the buildings had risen to $11 million which is to be included in the financial statements. The company is unsure how to treat the above events.    **(7 marks)**

(d)  Wader has decided to close one of its overseas branches. A board meeting was held on 30 April 20X7 when a detailed formal plan was presented to the board. The plan was formalised and accepted at that meeting. Letters were sent out to customers, suppliers and workers on 15 May 20X7 and meetings were held prior to the year-end to determine the issues involved in the closure. The plan is to be implemented in June 20X7. The company wish to provide $8 million for the restructuring but are unsure as to whether this is permissible. Additionally there was an issue raised at one of the meetings. The operations of the branch are to be moved to another country from June 20X7 but the operating lease on the present buildings of the branch is non-cancellable and runs for another two years, until 31 May 20X9. The annual rent of the buildings is $150,000 payable in arrears on 31 May and the lessor has offered to take a single payment of $270,000 on 31 May 20X8 to settle the outstanding amount owing and terminate the lease on that date. Wader has additionally obtained permission to sublet the building at a rental of $100,000 per year, payable in advance on 1 June. The company needs advice on how to treat the above under IAS 37 *Provisions, contingent liabilities and contingent assets.*                    **(7 marks)**

**Required:**

**Discuss the accounting treatments of the above items in the financial statements for the year ended 31 May 20X7.**

*Note:* **A discount rate of 5% should be used where necessary. Candidates should show suitable calculations where necessary.**

**(Total: 25 marks)**

**31  ROUTER (JUN 07 EXAM)**  *Online question assistance*

(a)  Router, a public limited company operates in the entertainment industry. It recently agreed with a television company to make a film which will be broadcast on the television company's network. The fee agreed for the film was $5 million with a further $100,000 to be paid every time the film is shown on the television company's channels. It is hoped that it will be shown on four occasions. The film was completed at a cost of $4 million and delivered to the television company on 1 April 20X7. The television company paid the fee of $5 million on 30 April 20X7 but indicated that the film needed substantial editing before they were prepared to broadcast it, the costs of which would be deducted from any future payments to Router. The directors of Router wish to recognise the anticipated future income of $400,000 in the financial statements for the year ended 31 May 20X7.                    **(5 marks)**

(b)  Router has a number of film studios and office buildings. The office buildings are in prestigious areas whereas the film studios are located in 'out of town' locations. The management of Router wish to apply the 'revaluation model' to the office buildings and the 'cost model' to the film studios in the year ended 31 May 20X7. At present both types of buildings are valued using the 'revaluation model'. One of the film studios has been converted to a theme park. In this case only, the land and buildings on the park are leased on a single lease from a third party. The lease term was 30 years in 1990. The lease of the land and buildings was classified as a finance lease even though the financial statements purport to comply with IAS 17 *Leases.*

The terms of the lease were changed on 31 May 20X7. Router is now going to terminate the lease early in 2015 in exchange for a payment of $10 million on 31 May 20X7 and a reduction in the monthly lease payments. Router intends to move from the site in 2015. The revised lease terms have not resulted in a change of classification of the lease in the financial statements of Router. **(10 marks)**

(c) At 1 June 20X6, Router held a 25% shareholding in a film distribution company, Wireless, a public limited company. On 1 January 20X7, Router sold a 15% holding in Wireless thus reducing its investment to a 10% holding. Router no longer exercises significant influence over Wireless. Immediately before that sale, the carrying value of the interest in Wireless in the group financial statements was $55 million. Router received $40 million for its sale of the 15% holding in Wireless. At 1 January 20X7, the fair value of the remaining investment in Wireless was $23 million and at 31 May 20X7 the fair value was $26 million. **(6 marks)**

(d) Additionally Router purchased 60% of the ordinary shares of a radio station, Playtime, a public limited company, on 31 May 20X7. The remaining 40% of the ordinary shares are owned by a competitor company who owns a substantial number of warrants issued by Playtime which are currently exercisable. If these warrants are exercised, they will result in Router only owning 35% of the voting shares of Playtime. **(4 marks)**

**Required:**

**Discuss how the above items should be dealt with in the group financial statements of Router for the year ended 31 May 20X7.**

**(Total: 25 marks)**

 *Online question assistance*

---

**32 KEY (DEC 09 EXAM)**  *Walk in the footsteps of a top tutor*

(a) Key, a public limited company, is concerned about the reduction in the general availability of credit and the sudden tightening of the conditions required to obtain a loan from banks. There has been a reduction in credit availability and a rise in interest rates. It seems as though there has ceased to be a clear relationship between interest rates and credit availability, and lenders and investors are seeking less risky investments. The directors are trying to determine the practical implications for the financial statements particularly because of large write downs of assets in the banking sector, tightening of credit conditions, and falling sales and asset prices. They are particularly concerned about the impairment of assets and the market inputs to be used in impairment testing. They are afraid that they may experience significant impairment charges in the coming financial year. They are unsure as to how they should test for impairment and any considerations which should be taken into account.

**Required:**

**Discuss the main considerations that the company should take into account when impairment testing non-current assets in the above economic climate.** **(8 marks)**

**Professional marks will be awarded in part (a) for clarity and expression.** **(2 marks)**

(b) There are specific assets on which the company wishes to seek advice. The company holds certain non-current assets, which are in a development area and carried at cost less depreciation. These assets cost $3 million on 1 June 2008 and are depreciated on the straight-line basis over their useful life of five years. An impairment review was carried out on 31 May 2009 and the projected cash flows relating to these assets were as follows:

| Year to | 31 May 2010 | 31 May 2011 | 31 May 2012 | 31 May 2013 |
|---|---|---|---|---|
| Cash flows ($000) | 280 | 450 | 500 | 550 |

The company used a discount rate of 5%. At 30 November 2009, the directors used the same cash flow projections and noticed that the resultant value in use was above the carrying amount of the assets and wished to reverse any impairment loss calculated at 31 May 2009. The government has indicated that it may compensate the company for any loss in value of the assets up to 20% of the impairment loss.

Key holds a non-current asset, which was purchased for $10 million on 1 December 2006 with an expected useful life of 10 years. On 1 December 2008, it was revalued to $8.8 million. At 30 November 2009, the asset was reviewed for impairment and written down to its recoverable amount of $5.5 million.

Key committed itself at the beginning of the financial year to selling a property that is being under-utilised following the economic downturn. As a result of the economic downturn, the property was not sold by the end of the year. The asset was actively marketed but there were no reasonable offers to purchase the asset. Key is hoping that the economic downturn will change in the future and therefore has not reduced the price of the asset.

**Required:**

**Discuss with suitable computations, how to account for any potential impairment of the above non-current assets in the financial statements for the year ended 30 November 2009.** **(15 marks)**

*Note:* **The following discount factors may be relevant**

| | |
|---|---|
| Year 1 | 0.9524 |
| Year 2 | 0.9070 |
| Year 3 | 0.8638 |
| Year 4 | 0.8227 |

**(Total: 25 marks)**

**33    MARRGRETT (DEC 08 EXAM)**  *Walk in the footsteps of a top tutor*

 *Timed question with Online tutor debrief*

Marrgrett, a public limited company, is currently planning to acquire and sell interests in other entities and has asked for advice on the impact of IFRS 3 (Revised) *Business combinations* and IFRS 10 *Consolidated financial statements*. The company is particularly concerned about the impact on earnings, net assets and goodwill at the acquisition date and any ongoing earnings impact that the new standards may have.

The company is considering purchasing additional shares in an associate, Josey, a public limited company. The holding will increase from 30% stake to 70% stake by offering the shareholders of Josey, cash and shares in Marrgrett. Marrgrett anticipates that it will pay $5 million in transaction costs to lawyers and bankers. Josey had previously been the subject of a management buyout. In order that the current management shareholders may remain in the business, Marrgrett is going to offer them share options in Josey subject to them remaining in employment for two years after the acquisition. Additionally, Marrgrett will offer the same shareholders, shares in the holding company which are contingent upon a certain level of profitability being achieved by Josey. Each shareholder will receive shares of the holding company up to a value of $50,000, if Josey achieves a pre-determined rate of return on capital employed for the next two years.

Josey has several marketing-related intangible assets that are used primarily in marketing or promotion of its products. These include trade names, internet domain names and non-competition agreements. These are not currently recognised in Josey's financial statements.

Marrgrett does not wish to measure the non-controlling interest in subsidiaries on the basis of the proportionate interest in the identifiable net assets, but wishes to use the 'full goodwill' method on the transaction. Marrgrett is unsure as to whether this method is mandatory, or what the effects are of recognising 'full goodwill'. Additionally the company is unsure as to whether the nature of the consideration would affect the calculation of goodwill.

To finance the acquisition of Josey, Marrgrett intends to dispose of a partial interest in two subsidiaries. Marrgrett will retain control of the first subsidiary but will sell the controlling interest in the second subsidiary which will become an associate. Because of its plans to change the overall structure of the business, Marrgrett wishes to recognise a re-organisation provision at the date of the business combination.

**Required:**

**Discuss the principles and the nature of the accounting treatment of the above plans under International Financial Reporting Standards setting out any impact that IFRS 3 (Revised) *Business combinations* and IFRS 1 *Consolidated financial statements* might have on the earnings and net assets of the group.**

*Note:* **This requirement includes 2 professional marks for the quality of the discussion.**

**(25 marks)**

 *Calculate your allowed time, allocate the time to the separate parts*

## 34 TYRE (JUN 06 EXAM)

Tyre, a public limited company, operates in the vehicle retailing sector. The company is currently preparing its financial statements for the year ended 31 May 20X6 and has asked for advice on how to deal with the following items:

(i) Tyre requires customers to pay a deposit of 20% of the purchase price when placing an order for a vehicle. If the customer cancels the order, the deposit is not refundable and Tyre retains it. If the order cannot be fulfilled by Tyre, the company repays the full amount of the deposit to the customer. The balance of the purchase price becomes payable on the delivery of the vehicle when the title to the goods passes. Tyre proposes to recognise the revenue from the deposits immediately and the balance of the purchase price when the goods are delivered to the customer. The cost of sales for the vehicle is recognised when the balance of the purchase price is paid. Additionally, Tyre had sold a fleet of cars to Hub and gave Hub a discount of 30% of the retail price on the transaction. The discount given is normal for this type of transaction. Tyre has given Hub a buyback option which entitles Hub to require Tyre to repurchase the vehicles after three years for 40% of the purchase price. The normal economic life of the vehicles is five years and the buyback option is expected to be exercised. **(8 marks)**

(ii) The property of the former administrative centre of Tyre is owned by the company. Tyre had decided in the year that the property was surplus to requirements and demolished the building on 10 June 20X6. After demolition, the company will have to carry out remedial environmental work, which is a legal requirement resulting from the demolition. It was intended that the land would be sold after the remedial work had been carried out. However, land prices are currently increasing in value and, therefore, the company has decided that it will not sell the land immediately. Tyres uses the 'cost model' in IAS 16 *Property, plant and equipment* and has owned the property for many years. **(7 marks)**

(iii) Tyre has entered into two new long lease property agreements for two major retail outlets. Annual rentals are paid under these agreements. Tyre has had to pay a premium to enter into these agreements because of the outlets' location. Tyre feels that the premiums paid are justifiable because of the increase in revenue that will occur because of the outlets' location. Tyre has analysed the leases and has decided that one is a finance lease and one is an operating lease but the company is unsure as to how to treat this premium. **(5 marks)**

(iv) Tyre recently undertook a sales campaign whereby customers can obtain free car accessories, by presenting a coupon, which has been included in an advertisement in a national newspaper, on the purchase of a vehicle. The offer is valid for a limited time period from 1 January 20X6 until 31 July 20X6. The management are unsure as to how to treat this offer in the financial statements for the year ended 31 May 20X6. **(5 marks)**

**Required:**

**Advise the directors of Tyre on how to treat the above items in the financial statements for the year ended 31 May 20X6.**

**(The mark allocation is shown against each of the above items.)**

**(Total: 25 marks)**

## 35    PROCHAIN (JUN 06 EXAM)

Prochain, a public limited company, operates in the fashion industry and has a financial year-end of 31 May 20X6. The company sells its products in department stores throughout the world. Prochain insists on creating its own selling areas within the department stores which are called 'model areas'. Prochain is allocated space in the department store where it can display and market its fashion goods. The company feels that this helps to promote its merchandise. Prochain pays for all the costs of the 'model areas' including design, decoration and construction costs. The areas are used for approximately two years after which the company has to dismantle the 'model areas'. The costs of dismantling the 'model areas' are normally 20% of the original construction cost and the elements of the area are worthless when dismantled. The current accounting practice followed by Prochain is to charge the full cost of the 'model areas' against profit or loss in the year when the area is dismantled. The accumulated cost of the 'model areas' shown in the statement of financial position at 31 May 20X6 is $20 million. The company has estimated that the average age of the 'model areas' is eight months at 31 May 20X6.  **(7 marks)**

Prochain acquired 100% of a sports goods and clothing manufacturer, Badex, a private limited company, and on 1 June 20X5.  Prochain incurred legal fees of $2 million in respect of the acquisition.  Prochain intends to develop its own brand of sports clothing which it will sell in the department stores. The shareholders of Badex valued the company at $125 million based upon profit forecasts which assumed significant growth in the demand for the 'Badex' brand name. Prochain had taken a more conservative view of the value of the company and estimated the fair value to be in the region of $108 million to $120 million of which $20 million relates to the brand name 'Badex'. Prochain is only prepared to pay the full purchase price if profits from the sale of 'Badex' clothing and sports goods reach the forecast levels. The agreed purchase price was $100 million plus two potential further payments. The first being $10 million in two years on 31 May 20X7. This is a guaranteed payment of $10 million in cash with no performance conditions. The second payment is contingent on certain profits target being met. At the date of acquisition it was assessed that the fair value of such consideration was $5 million.  **(8 marks)**

After the acquisition of Badex, Prochain started developing its own sports clothing brand 'Pro'. The expenditure in the period to 31 May 20X6 was as follows:

| Period from | Expenditure type | $m |
|---|---|---|
| 1 June 20X5 – 31 August 20X5 | Research as to the extent of the market | 3 |
| 1 September 20X5 | Prototype clothing and goods design | 4 |
| 1 December 20X5 – 31 January 20X6 | Employee costs in refinement of products | 2 |
| 1 February 20X6 – 30 April 20X6 | Development work undertaken to finalise design of product | 5 |
| 1 May 20X6 – 31 May 20X6 | Production and launch of products | 6 |
| | | 20 |

The costs of the production and launch of the products include the cost of upgrading the existing machinery ($3 million), market research costs ($2 million) and staff training costs ($1 million).

Currently an intangible asset of $20 million is shown in the financial statements for the year ended 31 May 20X6.  **(6 marks)**

Prochain owns a number of prestigious apartments which it leases to famous persons who are under a contract of employment to promote its fashion clothing. The apartments are let at below the market rate. The lease terms are short and are normally for six months. The leases terminate when the contracts for promoting the clothing terminate. Prochain wishes to account for the apartments as investment properties with the difference between the market rate and actual rental charged to be recognised as an employee benefit expense.

**(4 marks)**

Assume a discount rate of 5.5% where necessary.

**Required:**

**Discuss how the above items should be dealt with in the financial statements of Prochain for the year ended 31 May 20X6 under International Financial Reporting Standards.**

**(Total: 25 marks)**

**36 MARGIE (DEC 10 EXAM)**  *Walk in the footsteps of a top tutor*

Margie, a public limited company, has entered into several share related transactions during the period and wishes to obtain advice on how to account for the transactions.

(a) Margie has entered into a contract with a producer to purchase 350 tonnes of wheat. The purchase price will be settled in cash at an amount equal to the value of 2,500 of Margie's shares. Margie may settle the contract at any time by paying the producer an amount equal to the current market value of 2,500 of Margie shares, less the market value of 350 tonnes of wheat. Margie has entered into the contract as part of its hedging strategy and has no intention of taking physical delivery of the wheat. Margie wishes to treat this transaction as a share based payment transaction under IFRS 2 'Share-based Payment'. **(7 marks)**

(b) Margie has acquired 100% of the share capital of Antalya in a business combination on 1 December 2009. Antalya had previously granted a share-based payment to its employees with a four-year vesting period. Its employees have rendered the required service for the award at the acquisition date but have not yet exercised their options. The fair value of the award at 1 December 2009 is $20 million and Margie is obliged to replace the share-based payment awards of Antalya with awards of its own.

Margie issues a replacement award that does not require post-combination services. The fair value of the replacement award at the acquisition date is $22 million. Margie does not know how to account for the award on the acquisition of Antalya. **(6 marks)**

(c) Margie issued shares during the financial year. Some of those shares were subscribed for by employees who were existing shareholders, and some were issued to an entity, Grief, which owned 5% of Margie's share capital. Before the shares were issued, Margie offered to buy a building from Grief and agreed that the purchase price would be settled by the issue of shares. Margie wondered whether these transactions should be accounted for under IFRS 2. **(4 marks)**

(d) Margie granted 100 options to each of its 4,000 employees at a fair value of $10 each on 1 December 2007. The options vest upon the company's share price reaching $15, provided the employee has remained in the company's service until that time. The terms and conditions of the options are that the market condition can be met in either year 3, 4 or 5 of the employee's service.

At the grant date, Margie estimated that the expected vesting period would be four years which is consistent with the assumptions used in estimating the fair value of the options granted. The company's share price reached $15 on 30 November 2010.

**(6 marks)**

**Required:**

**Discuss, with suitable computations where applicable, how the above transactions would be dealt with in the financial statements of Margie for the year ending 30 November 2010.**

**Professional marks awarded for the clarity and quality of discussion.** **(2 marks)**

**(Total: 25 marks)**

## 37 VIDENT (JUN 05 EXAM)

The directors of Vident, a public limited company, are reviewing the impact of IFRS 2 *Share-based payment* on the financial statements for the year ended 31 May 20X5 as they will be applying the reporting standard for the first time. However, the directors of Vident are unhappy about having to apply the standard and have put forward the following arguments as to why they should not recognise an expense for share-based payments:

(i) They feel that share options have no cost to their company and, therefore, there should be no expense recognised in profit or loss.

(ii) They do not feel that the expense arising from share options under IFRS 2 actually meets the definition of an expense under the *Framework* document.

(iii) The directors are worried about the dual impact of the IFRS on earnings per share, as an expense is recognised in profit or loss and the impact of share options is recognised in the diluted earnings per share calculation.

(iv) They feel that accounting for share-based payment may have an adverse effect on their company and may discourage it from introducing new share option plans.

The following share option schemes were in existence at 31 May 20X5:

| Director's name | Grant date | Options granted | Fair value of options at grant date $ | Exercise price $ | Performance conditions | Vesting date | Exercise date |
|---|---|---|---|---|---|---|---|
| J. Van Heflin | 1 June 20X3 | 20,000 | 5 | 4.50 | A | 06/20X5 | 06/20X6 |
| R. Ashworth | 1 June 20X4 | 50,000 | 6 | 6 | B | 06/20X7 | 06/20X8 |

The price of the company's shares at 31 May 20X5 is $12 per share and at 31 May 20X4 was $12.50 per share.

The performance conditions which apply to the exercise of executive share options are as follows:

**Performance Condition A**

The share options do not vest if the growth in the company's earnings per share (EPS) for the year is less than 4%. The rate of growth of EPS was 4.5% (20X3), 4.1% (20X4), 4.2% (20X5). The directors must still work for the company on the vesting date.

**Performance Condition B**

The share options do not vest until the share price has increased from its value of $12.50 at the grant date (1 June 20X4) to above $13.50. The director must still work for the company on the vesting date.

No directors have left the company since the issue of the share options and none are expected to leave before June 20X7. The shares vest and can be exercised on the first day of the due month.

The directors are uncertain about the deferred tax implications of adopting IFRS 2. Vident operates in a country where a tax allowance will not arise until the options are exercised and the tax allowance will be based on the option's intrinsic value at the exercise date.

Assume a tax rate of 30%.

**Required:**

**Draft a report to the directors of Vident setting out:**

(a) the reasons why share-based payments should be recognised in financial statements and why the directors' arguments are unacceptable; **(9 marks)**

(b) a discussion (with suitable calculations) as to how the directors' share options would be accounted for in the financial statements for the year ended 31 May 20X5, including the adjustment to opening balances; **(9 marks)**

(c) the deferred tax implications (with suitable calculations) for the company which arise from the recognition of a remuneration expense for the directors' share options. **(7 marks)**

**(Total: 25 marks)**

## 38 ASHLEE (JUN 05 EXAM)

Ashlee, a public limited company, is preparing its group financial statements for the year ended 31 March 20X5. The company applies newly issued IFRSs at the earliest opportunity. The group comprises three companies, Ashlee, the holding company, and its 100% owned subsidiaries Pilot and Gibson, both public limited companies. The group financial statements at first appeared to indicate that the group was solvent and in a good financial position. However, after the year-end, but prior to the approval of the financial statements mistakes have been found which affect the financial position of the group to the extent that loan covenant agreements have been breached.

As a result the loan creditors require Ashlee to cut its costs, reduce its operations and reorganise its activities. Therefore, redundancies are planned and the subsidiary, Pilot, is to be reorganised. The carrying value of Pilot's net assets, including allocated goodwill, was $85 million at 31 March 20X5, before taking account of reorganisation costs. The directors of Ashlee wish to include $4 million of reorganisation costs in the financial statements of Pilot for the year ended 31 March 20X5. The directors of Ashlee have prepared cash flow projections which indicate that the net present value of future net cash flows from Pilot is expected to be $84 million if the reorganisation takes place and $82 million if the reorganisation does not take place.

Ashlee had already decided prior to the year-end to sell the other subsidiary, Gibson. Gibson will be sold after the financial statements have been signed. The contract for the sale of Gibson was being negotiated at the time of the preparation of the financial statements and it is expected that Gibson will be sold in June 20X5.

The carrying amounts of Gibson and Pilot including allocated goodwill were as follows at the year-end:

|  |  | Gibson $m | Pilot $m |
|---|---|---|---|
| Goodwill |  | 30 | 5 |
| Property, plant and equipment | – cost | 120 | 55 |
|  | – valuation | 180 |  |
| Inventory |  | 100 | 20 |
| Trade receivables |  | 40 | 10 |
| Trade payables |  | (20) | (5) |
|  |  | 450 | 85 |

The fair value of the net assets of Gibson at the year-end was $415 million and the estimated costs of selling the company were $5 million.

Part of the business activity of Ashlee is to buy and sell property. The directors of Ashlee had signed a contract on 1 March 20X5, to sell two of its development properties which are carried at the lower of cost and net realisable value under IAS 2 *Inventories*. The sale was agreed at a figure of $40 million (carrying value $30 million). A receivable of $40 million and profit of $10 million were recognised in the financial statements for the year ended 31 March 20X5. The sale of the properties was completed on 1 May 20X5 when the legal title passed. The policy used in the prior year was to recognise revenue when the sale of such properties had been completed.

Additionally, Ashlee had purchased, on 1 April 20X4, 150,000 shares of a public limited company, Race, at a price of $20 per share. Ashlee had incurred transaction costs of $100,000 to acquire the shares. The company is unsure as to whether this investment should be accounted for as fair value through profit or loss, or whether it should adopt the designation of fair value through other comprehensive income in the financial statements for the year ended 31 March 20X5. The quoted price of the shares at 31 March 20X5 was $25 per share. The shares purchased represent approximately 1% of the issued share capital of Race.

There is no goodwill arising in the group financial statements other than that set out above.

**Required:**

**Discuss the implications, with suitable computations, of the above events for the group financial statements of Ashlee for the year ended 31 March 20X5.**

**(Total: 25 marks)**

**39  GREENIE (DEC 10 EXAM)**  *Walk in the footsteps of a top tutor*

(a)  Greenie, a public limited company, builds, develops and operates airports. During the financial year to 30 November 2010, a section of an airport collapsed and as a result several people were hurt. The accident resulted in the closure of the terminal and legal action against Greenie. When the financial statements for the year ended 30 November 2010 were being prepared, the investigation into the accident and the reconstruction of the section of the airport damaged were still in progress and no legal action had yet been brought in connection with the accident. The expert report that was to be presented to the civil courts in order to determine the cause of the accident and to assess the respective responsibilities of the various parties involved, was expected in 2011.

Financial damages arising related to the additional costs and operating losses relating to the unavailability of the building. The nature and extent of the damages, and the details of any compensation payments had yet to be established. The directors of Greenie felt that at present, there was no requirement to record the impact of the accident in the financial statements.

Compensation agreements had been arranged with the victims, and these claims were all covered by Greenie's insurance policy. In each case, compensation paid by the insurance company was subject to a waiver of any judicial proceedings against Greenie and its insurers. If any compensation is eventually payable to third parties, this is expected to be covered by the insurance policies.

The directors of Greenie felt that the conditions for recognising a provision or disclosing a contingent liability had not been met. Therefore, Greenie did not recognise a provision in respect of the accident nor did it disclose any related contingent liability or a note setting out the nature of the accident and potential claims in its financial statements for the year ended 30 November 2010.     **(6 marks)**

(b)  Greenie was one of three shareholders in a regional airport Manair. As at 30 November 2010, the majority shareholder held 60.1% of voting shares, the second shareholder held 20% of voting shares and Greenie held 19.9% of the voting shares. The board of directors consisted of ten members. The majority shareholder was represented by six of the board members, while Greenie and the other shareholder were represented by two members each. A shareholders' agreement stated that certain board and shareholder resolutions required either unanimous or majority decision. There is no indication that the majority shareholder and the other shareholders act together in a common way. During the financial year, Greenie had provided Manair with maintenance and technical services and had sold the entity a software licence for $5 million. Additionally, Greenie had sent a team of management experts to give business advice to the board of Manair. Greenie did not account for its investment in Manair as an associate, because of a lack of significant influence over the entity. Greenie felt that the majority owner of Manair used its influence as the parent to control and govern its subsidiary.     **(10 marks)**

(c)  Greenie has issued 1 million shares of $1 nominal value for the acquisition of franchise rights at a local airport. Similar franchise rights are sold in cash transactions on a regular basis and Greenie has been offered a similar franchise right at another airport for $2.3 million. This price is consistent with other prices given the market conditions. The share price of Greenie was $2.50 at the date of the transaction. Greenie wishes to record the transaction at the nominal value of the shares issued.

Greenie also showed irredeemable preference shares as equity instruments in its statement of financial position. The terms of issue of the instruments give the holders a contractual right to an annual fixed cash dividend and the entitlement to a participating dividend based on any dividends paid on ordinary shares. Greenie felt that the presentation of the preference shares with a liability component in compliance with IAS 32 'Financial instruments: Presentation' would be so misleading in the circumstances that it would conflict with the objective of financial statements set out in the IASB's 'Framework for the Preparation and Presentation of Financial Statements'. The reason given by Greenie for this presentation was that the shares participated in future profits and thus had the characteristics of permanent capital because of the profit participation element of the shares.                    **(7 marks)**

**Required:**

**Discuss how the above financial transactions should be dealt with in the financial statements of Greenie for the year ended 30 November 2010.**

**Professional marks awarded for the clarity and quality of discussion.**                    **(2 marks)**

**(Total: 25 marks)**

## 40    NETTE (JUN 04 EXAM)

Nette, a public limited company, manufactures mining equipment and extracts natural gas. The directors are uncertain about the role of the IASB's *Conceptual Framework for Financial Reporting 2010* (the *Framework*) in corporate reporting. Their view is that accounting is based on the transactions carried out by the company and these transactions are allocated to the company's accounting period by using the matching and prudence concepts. The argument put forward by the directors is that the *Framework* does not take into account the business and legal constraints within which companies operate. Further they have given two situations that have arisen in the current financial statements where they feel that the current accounting practice is inconsistent with the *Framework*.

### Situation 1

Nette has recently constructed a natural gas extraction facility and commenced production one year ago (1 June 20X3). There is an operating licence given to the company by the government that requires the removal of the facility at the end of its life which is estimated at 20 years. Depreciation is charged on the straight-line basis. The cost of the construction of the facility was $200 million and the net present value at 1 June 20X3 of the future costs to be incurred in order to return the extraction site to its original condition are estimated at $50 million (using a discount rate of 5% per annum). 80 per cent of these costs relate to the removal of the facility and 20% relate to the rectification of the damage caused through the extraction of the natural gas. The auditors have told the company that a provision for decommissioning has to be set up.

### Situation 2

Nette purchased a building on 1 June 20X3 for $10 million. The building qualified for a grant of $2 million which has been treated as a deferred credit in the financial statements. The tax allowances are reduced by the amount of the grant. There are additional temporary differences of $40 million in respect of deferred tax liabilities at the year-end. Also the company has sold extraction equipment which carries a five year warranty. The directors have made a provision for the warranty of $4 million at 31 May 20X4 which is deductible for tax when costs are incurred under the warranty. In addition to the warranty provision the company has unused tax losses of $70 million. The directors of the company are unsure as to whether a provision for deferred taxation is required.

(Assume that the depreciation of the building is straight line over ten years, and tax allowances of 25% on the reducing balance basis can be claimed on the building. Tax is payable at 30%.)

**Required:**

(a) Explain the importance of the *Conceptual Framework for Financial Reporting 2010* to the reporting of corporate performance and whether it takes into account the business and legal constraints placed upon companies. **(6 marks)**

(b) (i) Explain with reasons and suitable extracts/computations the accounting treatment of the above two situations in the financial statements for the year ended 31 May 20X4. **(14 marks)**

(ii) Discuss whether the treatment of the items appears consistent with the *Conceptual Framework for Financial Reporting 2010*. **(5 marks)**

**(Total: 25 marks)**

**41 ARON (JUN 09 EXAM)**  *Walk in the footsteps of a top tutor*

 *Timed question with Online tutor debrief*

The directors of Aron, a public limited company, are worried about the challenging market conditions which the company is facing. The markets are volatile and illiquid. The central government is injecting liquidity into the economy. The directors are concerned about the significant shift towards the use of fair values in financial statements. IFRS 9, together with IAS 39, requires the initial measurement of financial instruments to be at fair value. The directors are uncertain of the relevance of fair value measurements in these current market conditions.

**Required:**

(a) Briefly discuss how the fair value of financial instruments is determined, commenting on the relevance of fair value measurements for financial instruments where markets are volatile and illiquid. **(4 marks)**

(b) Further they would like advice on accounting for the following transactions within the financial statements for the year ended 31 May 2009:

(i) Aron issued one million convertible bonds on 1 June 2006. The bonds had a term of three years and were issued with a total fair value of $100 million which is also the par value. Interest is paid annually in arrears at a rate of 6% per annum and bonds, without the conversion option, attracted an interest rate of 9% per annum on 1 June 2006. The company incurred issue costs of $1 million. If the investor did not convert to shares they would have been redeemed at par. At maturity all of the bonds were converted into 25 million ordinary shares of $1 of Aron. No bonds could be converted before that date. The directors are uncertain how the bonds should have been accounted for up to the date of the conversion on 31 May 2009 and have been told that the impact of the issue costs is to increase the effective interest rate to 9.38%.

**(6 marks)**

(ii)  Aron held 3% holding of the shares in Smart, a public limited company. The investment was designated upon recognition as fair value through other comprehensive income and as at 31 May 2009 was fair valued at $5 million. The cumulative gain recognised in equity relating to this investment was $400,000. On the same day, the whole of the share capital of Smart was acquired by Given, a public limited company, and as a result, Aron received shares in Given with a fair value of $5.5 million in exchange for its holding in Smart. The company wishes to know how the exchange of shares in Smart for the shares in Given should be accounted for in its financial records.   **(4 marks)**

(iii)  The functional and presentation currency of Aron is the dollar ($). Aron has a wholly owned foreign subsidiary, Gao, whose functional currency is the zloti. Gao owns a debt instrument which is held for trading, and therefore accounted for at fair value through profit or loss. In Gao's financial statements for the year ended 31 May 2008, the debt instrument was carried at its fair value of 10 million zloti.

At 31 May 2009, the fair value of the debt instrument had increased to 12 million zloti. The exchange rates were:

|                                  | Zloti to $1 |
| -------------------------------- | ----------- |
| 31 May 2008                      | 3           |
| 31 May 2009                      | 2           |
| Average rate for year to 31 May 2009 | 2.5     |

The company wishes to know how to account for this instrument in Gao's entity financial statements and the consolidated financial statements of the group.

**(5 marks)**

(iv)  Aron granted interest free loans to its employees on 1 June 2008 of $10 million. The loans will be paid back on 31 May 2010 as a single payment by the employees. The market rate of interest for a two-year loan on both of the above dates is 6% per annum. The company is unsure how to account for the loan but wishes to classify the loans as being accounted for at amortised cost under IFRS 9 *Financial instruments.*

**(4 marks)**

**Required:**

**Discuss, with relevant computations, how the above financial instruments should be accounted for in the financial statements for the year ended 31 May 2009.**

*Note:* **The mark allocation is shown against each of the transactions above.**

*Note:* **The following discount and annuity factors may be of use**

|  | Discount factors | | | Annuity factors | | |
|---|---|---|---|---|---|---|
|  | 6% | 9% | 9.38% | 6% | 9% | 9.38% |
| 1 year | 0.9434 | 0.9174 | 0.9142 | 0.9434 | 0.9174 | 0.9174 |
| 2 years | 0.8900 | 0.8417 | 0.8358 | 1.8334 | 1.7591 | 1.7500 |
| 3 years | 0.8396 | 0.7722 | 0.7642 | 2.6730 | 2.5313 | 2.5142 |

**Professional marks will be awarded in question 2 for clarity and quality of discussion.** **(2 marks)**

**(Total: 25 marks)**

 *Calculate your allowed time, allocate the time to the separate parts*

**42 JOHAN (DEC 08 EXAM)**  *Walk in the footsteps of a top tutor*

 *Timed question with Online tutor debrief*

Johan, a public limited company, operates in the telecommunications industry. The industry is capital intensive with heavy investment in licences and network infrastructure. Competition in the sector is fierce and technological advances are a characteristic of the industry. Johan has responded to these factors by offering incentives to customers and, in an attempt to acquire and retain them, Johan purchased a telecom licence on 1 December 2006 for $120 million. The licence has a term of six years and cannot be used until the network assets and infrastructure are ready for use. The related network assets and infrastructure became ready for use on 1 December 2007. Johan could not operate in the country without the licence and is not permitted to sell the licence. Johan expects its subscriber base to grow over the period of the licence but is disappointed with its market share for the year to 30 November 2008. The licence agreement does not deal with the renewal of the licence but there is an expectation that the regulator will grant a single renewal for the same period of time as long as certain criteria regarding network build quality and service quality are met. Johan has no experience of the charge that will be made by the regulator for the renewal but other licences have been renewed at a nominal cost. The licence is currently stated at its original cost of $120 million in the statement of financial position under non-current assets.

Johan is considering extending its network and has carried out a feasibility study during the year to 30 November 2008. The design and planning department of Johan identified five possible geographical areas for the extension of its network. The internal costs of this study were $150,000 and the external costs were $100,000 during the year to 30 November 2008. Following the feasibility study, Johan chose a geographical area where it was going to install a base station for the telephone network. The location of the base station was dependent upon getting planning permission. A further independent study has been carried out by third party consultants in an attempt to provide a preferred location in the area, as there is a need for the optimal operation of the network in terms of signal quality and coverage. Johan proposes to build a base station on the recommended site on which planning permission has been obtained. The third party consultants have charged $50,000 for the study. Additionally Johan has paid $300,000 as a single payment together with $60,000 a month to the government of the region for access to the land upon which the base station will be situated. The contract with the government is for a period of 12 years and commenced on 1 November 2008. There is no right of renewal of the contract and legal title to the land remains with the government.

Johan purchases telephone handsets from a manufacturer for $200 each, and sells the handsets direct to customers for $150 if they purchase call credit (call card) in advance on what is called a prepaid phone. The costs of selling the handset are estimated at $1 per set. The customers using a prepaid phone pay $21 for each call card at the purchase date. Call cards expire six months from the date of first sale. There is an average unused call credit of $3 per card after six months and the card is activated when sold.

Johan also sells handsets to dealers for $150 and invoices the dealers for those handsets. The dealer can return the handset up to a service contract being signed by a customer. When the customer signs a service contract, the customer receives the handset free of charge. Johan allows the dealer a commission of $280 on the connection of a customer and the transaction with the dealer is settled net by a payment of $130 by Johan to the dealer being the cost of the handset to the dealer ($150) deducted from the commission ($280). The handset cannot be sold separately by the dealer and the service contract lasts for a 12 month period. Dealers do not sell prepaid phones, and Johan receives monthly revenue from the service contract.

The chief operating officer, a non-accountant, has asked for an explanation of the accounting principles and practices which should be used to account for the above events.

**Required:**

**Discuss the principles and practices which should be used in the financial year to 30 November 2008 to account for:**

(a)    the licences;                                                                                  (8 marks)

(b)    the costs incurred in extending the network;                                    (7 marks)

(c)    the purchase of handsets and the recognition of revenue from customers and dealers.                                                                              (8 marks)

**Appropriateness and quality of discussion.**                                          (2 marks)

(Total: 25 marks)

 *Calculate your allowed time, allocate the time to the separate parts*

**43  CARPART (JUN 09 EXAM)**  *Walk in the footsteps of a top tutor*

 *Timed question with Online tutor debrief*

Carpart, a public limited company, is a vehicle part manufacturer, and sells vehicles purchased from the manufacturer. Carpart has entered into supply arrangements for the supply of car seats to two local companies, Vehiclex and Autoseat.

(i)  **Vehiclex**

This contract will last for five years and Carpart will manufacture seats to a certain specification which will require the construction of machinery for the purpose. The price of each car seat has been agreed so that it includes an amount to cover the cost of constructing the machinery but there is no commitment to a minimum order of seats to guarantee the recovery of the costs of constructing the machinery. Carpart retains the ownership of the machinery and wishes to recognise part of the revenue from the contract in its current financial statements to cover the cost of the machinery which will be constructed over the next year.  **(4 marks)**

(ii)  **Autoseat**

Autoseat is purchasing car seats from Carpart. The contract is to last for three years and Carpart is to design, develop and manufacture the car seats. Carpart will construct machinery for this purpose but the machinery is so specific that it cannot be used on other contracts. Carpart maintains the machinery but the know-how has been granted royalty free to Autoseat. The price of each car seat includes a fixed price to cover the cost of the machinery. If Autoseat decides not to purchase a minimum number of seats to cover the cost of the machinery, then Autoseat has to repay Carpart for the cost of the machinery including any interest incurred.

Autoseat can purchase the machinery at any time in order to safeguard against the cessation of production by Carpart. The purchase price would be the cost of the machinery not yet recovered by Carpart. The machinery has a life of three years and the seats are only sold to Autoseat who sets the levels of production for a period. Autoseat can perform a pre-delivery inspection on each seat and can reject defective seats.  **(9 marks)**

(iii)  **Vehicle sales**

Carpart sells vehicles on a contract for their market price (approximately $20,000 each) at a mark-up of 25% on cost. The expected life of each vehicle is five years. After four years, the car is repurchased by Carpart at 20% of its original selling price. This price is expected to be significantly less than its fair value. The car must be maintained and serviced by the customer in accordance with certain guidelines and must be in good condition if Carpart is to repurchase the vehicle.

The same vehicles are also sold with an option that can be exercised by the buyer two years after sale. Under this option, the customer has the right to ask Carpart to repurchase the vehicle for 70% of its original purchase price. It is thought that the buyers will exercise the option. At the end of two years, the fair value of the vehicle is expected to be 55% of the original purchase price. If the option is not exercised, then the buyer keeps the vehicle.

Carpart also uses some of its vehicles for demonstration purposes. These vehicles are normally used for this purpose for an eighteen-month period. After this period, the vehicles are sold at a reduced price based upon their condition and mileage.

**(10 marks)**

**Professional marks will be awarded in question 3 for clarity and quality of discussion.**

**(2 marks)**

**Required:**

**Discuss how the above transactions would be accounted for under International Financial Reporting Standards in the financial statements of Carpart.**

**(Total: 25 marks)**

*Note.* **The mark allocation is shown against each of the arrangements above.**

 *Calculate your allowed time, allocate the time to the separate parts*

**44    BURLEY (DEC 09 EXAM)**  *Walk in the footsteps of a top tutor*

Burley, a public limited company, operates in the energy industry. It has entered into several arrangements with other entities as follows:

(i)     Burley and Slite, a public limited company, jointly control an oilfield. Burley has a 60% interest and Slite a 40% interest and the companies are entitled to extract oil in these proportions. An agreement was signed on 1 December 2008, which allowed for the net cash settlement of any over/under extraction by one company. The net cash settlement would be at the market price of oil at the date of settlement. Both parties have used this method of settlement before. 200,000 barrels of oil were produced up to 1 October 2009 but none were produced after this up to 30 November 2009 due to production difficulties. The oil was all sold to third parties at $100 per barrel. Burley has extracted 10,000 barrels more than the company's quota and Slite has under extracted by the same amount. The market price of oil at the year-end of 30 November 2009 was $105 per barrel. The excess oil extracted by Burley was settled on 12 December 2009 under the terms of the agreement at $95 per barrel.

Burley had purchased oil from another supplier because of the production difficulties at $98 per barrel and has oil inventory of 5,000 barrels at the year-end, purchased from this source. Slite had no inventory of oil. Neither company had oil inventory at 1 December 2008. Selling costs are $2 per barrel.

Burley wishes to know how to account for the recognition of revenue, the excess oil extracted and the oil inventory at the year-end of 30 November 2009.    **(10 marks)**

(ii)    Burley also entered into an agreement with Jorge, and Heavy, both public limited companies on 1 December 2008. Each of the companies holds one third of the equity in an entity, Wells, a public limited company, which operates offshore oilrigs. Any decisions regarding the operating and financial policies relating to Wells have to be approved by two thirds of the venturers. Burley wants to account for the interest in the entity by using proportionate consolidation, and wishes advice on the matter.

The oilrigs of Wells started operating on 1 December 1998 and are measured under the cost model. The useful life of the rigs is 40 years. The initial cost of the rigs was $240 million, which included decommissioning costs (discounted) of $20 million. At 1 December 2008, the carrying amount of the decommissioning liability has grown to $32.6 million, but the net present value of decommissioning liability has decreased to $18.5 million as a result of the increase in the risk-adjusted discount rate from 5% to 7%. Burley is unsure how to account for the oilrigs in the financial statements of Wells for the year ended 30 November 2009.

Burley owns a 10% interest in a pipeline, which is used to transport the oil from the offshore oilrig to a refinery on the land. Burley has joint control over the pipeline and has to pay its share of the maintenance costs. Burley has the right to use 10% of the capacity of the pipeline. Burley wishes to show the pipeline as an investment in its financial statements to 30 November 2009.                                     **(9 marks)**

(iii)   Burley has purchased a transferable interest in an oil exploration licence. Initial surveys of the region designated for exploration indicate that there are substantial oil deposits present but further surveys will be required in order to establish the nature and extent of the deposits. Burley also has to determine whether the extraction of the oil is commercially viable. Past experience has shown that the licence can increase substantially in value if further information as to the viability of the extraction of the oil becomes available. Burley wishes to capitalise the cost of the licence but is unsure as to whether the accounting policy is compliant with International Financial Reporting Standards                                     **(4 marks)**

**Professional marks will be awarded in question 3 for clarity and expression.**
                                     **(2 marks)**

**Required:**

**Discuss with suitable computations where necessary, how the above arrangements and events would be accounted for in the financial statements of Burley.**

                                     **(Total: 25 marks)**

## 45   SHIRES PROPERTY CONSTRUCTION

Shires Property Construction found itself in financial difficulty. The following is a trial balance at 31 December 2010 extracted from the books of the company

|  | $ |
|---|---|
| Land | 156,000 |
| Building (net) | 27,246 |
| Equipment (net) | 10,754 |
| Intangible asset – brand | 60,000 |
| Financial assets at fair value through profit or loss | 27,000 |
| Inventories | 120,247 |
| Trade receivables | 70,692 |
| Deficit on retained earnings | 39,821 |
|  | 511,760 |

|                                | $       |
|--------------------------------|---------|
| Equity shares of $1 each       | 200,000 |
| 5% Unsecured loan              | 70,000  |
| 8% Debenture loan 2013 (secured) | 80,000 |
| Interest payable on debenture  | 12,800  |
| Trade payables                 | 96,247  |
| Loans from directors           | 16,000  |
| Bank overdraft                 | 36,713  |
|                                | 511,760 |

The authorised share capital is 200,000 equity shares of $1 each.

During a meeting of shareholders and directors, it was decided to carry out a scheme of internal reconstruction. The following scheme has been agreed:

(1) Each equity share is to be redesignated as a share of $0.25.

(2) The existing $70,000 unsecured loan is to be redeemed in part by an issue of 140,000 equity shares of $0.25 each at nominal value, with the balance of the loan having an increased rate of interest of 8%.

(3) The equity shareholders are to accept a reduction in the nominal value of their shares from $1 to $0.25, and to subscribe for a new issue on the basis of 1 for 1 at a price of $0.30 per share.

(4) The debenture loan is secured against the land and buildings owned by Shires Property Construction. The debenture holders are to accept 20,000 equity shares of $0.25 each in lieu of the interest payable. It is agreed that the value of the interest liability is equivalent to the nominal value of the shares issued. The interest rate is to be increased to 9.5%. A further $9,000 of this 9.5% debenture is to be issued and taken up by the existing holders at par value.

(5) $6,000 of directors' loans is to be cancelled. The balance is to be settled by issue of 10,000 equity shares of $0.25 each.

(6) The brand and the deficit on retained earnings are to be written off.

(7) The financial assets are to be sold at their fair value of $60,000.

(8) The bank overdraft is to be repaid.

(9) $46,000 is to be paid to trade payables now and the balance at quarterly intervals.

(10) 10% of the trade receivables are to be written off.

(11) The remaining assets were professionally valued and should be included in the books and accounts as follows:

|           | $      |
|-----------|--------|
| Land      | 90,000 |
| Building  | 80,000 |
| Equipment | 10,000 |
| Inventories | 50,000 |

(12) It is expected that, due to changed conditions and new management, operating profits will be earned at the rate of $50,000 p.a. after depreciation but before interest and tax. Due to losses brought forward and tax allowances it is unlikely that any tax liability will arise until 2013.

**Required:**

(a) Prepare the statement of financial position of the Shires Property immediately after the reconstruction. **(12 marks)**

(b) Illustrate and explain how the anticipated operating profits will be divided amongst the interested parties before and after the reconstruction. (Ignore the deficit on retained earnings in determining whether any dividends are payable). **(8 marks)**

(c) Comment on the capital structure of the Shires Property subsequent to reconstruction. **(5 marks)**

**(Total: 25 marks)**

## 46 BOOMERANG

Boomerang plc was incorporated as an importer of Australian decorations and ornaments which it customises and packages before selling in the UK. The company sells its products in the luxury market and had traded profitably until four years ago when the global financial crisis began to have an impact on the business. Since that date it has suffered continuous losses which have resulted in a negative balance on retained earnings.

The company has been developing a new market for its products in concession arrangements for floor space with high-quality retailers in selected locations. The directors expect that Boomerang will return to profit in 2013. They expect profit before interest and tax to be approximately $200,000 in each of the next three years. As a result of developing this new market, it is expected that additional working capital of $500,000 will be required in 2015. As a consequence of this new strategy, Boomerang will dispose of its freehold property imminently.

However the directors are concerned that even if Boomerang achieves an annual profit before interest and tax of $200,000 it will be a number of years before a dividend could be distributed to the equity shareholders and it would be difficult to raise fresh funds from the shareholders in 2015 if there was little prospect of a dividend payment for several years.

The bank overdraft is currently unsecured and the bank has expressed concern regarding the increase in the overdraft in recent months and has requested that Boomerang takes steps to address this situation.

The directors are considering whether it would be beneficial to implement a reconstruction scheme and, in particular, whether it would be likely to receive the necessary support from the various interested parties.

The 8% debenture is currently secured by a floating charge against the inventory and receivables of Boomerang. Employees' wages and professional fees are regarded as preferential creditors. Corporate tax liabilities are not regarded as preferential creditors.

The variation of the rights of the shareholders and creditors was to be effected under legislation which requires that the scheme should be approved by a majority in number and 75% in value of each class of shareholders, by a majority in number and 75% in value of each class of creditor affected, and by the court. The directors of Boomerang have had initial discussions with their auditors to ensure the legality of this proposal.

The key elements of the proposed scheme include:

- A capital reduction scheme to reduce the existing equity shares from $1 to $0.40 per share.

- The directors will subscribe for 750,000 equity shares of $0.40 at nominal value as demonstration of commitment to the success of the scheme.

- The 4% unsecured debenture due in 2013 will be repaid.

- Disposal of the freehold property for $700,000.

- Payment of the most urgent trade payables to ensure continuing supplies amounting to approximately $200,000, plus payment of the outstanding tax liability.

- Payment of professional fees of $40,000.

- Assessment of the recoverable values of assets to recognise impairments and write-offs as appropriate.

In the event of liquidation, professional fees of $40,000 would be payable.

Assume that Boomerang is subject to an income tax rate of 25% on profit after interest for the year; ignore any other tax issues, such as utilisation of tax losses against profits.

Draft statements of financial position at 31 October 2012 before and after the proposed reconstruction scheme were as follows:

| ASSETS | Before reconstruction | After reconstruction |
|---|---|---|
| Non-current assets: | $ | $ |
| Property, plant & equipment : | | |
| Freehold property | 400,000 | nil |
| Leasehold premises | 394,000 | 370,000 |
| Plant, equipment and vehicles | 710,000 | 675,000 |
| Current assets: | | |
| Inventory | 440,000 | 400,000 |
| Receivables | 290,000 | 225,000 |
| | 2,234,000 | 1,670,000 |
| EQUITY AND LIABILITIES | $ | $ |
| Equity shares of $1 each / $0.40 each | 1,350,000 | 840,000 |
| Retained deficit | (1,346,000) | (340,000) |
| | 4,000 | 500,000 |
| Liabilities: | | |
| 4% Debentures 2013 (unsecured) | 170,000 | nil |
| 8% Debentures (secured by a floating charge) | 540,000 | 540,000 |
| Corporate tax liabilities | 190,000 | |
| Payables | 576,000 | 326,000 |
| Wages | 260,000 | 160,000 |
| Bank overdraft | 494,000 | 144,000 |
| | 2,234,000 | 1,670,000 |

**Required:**

**Draft a memorandum for the finance director of Boomerang which evaluates:**

(a)   the outcome of liquidation of Boomerang, on the basis that the values following reconstruction are a reasonable approximation to realisable values upon liquidation. Your comments should make clear the order of settlement of liabilities.

(7 marks)

(b)    the outcome of the proposed reconstruction scheme from the perspective of each of the following parties, on the assumption that any necessary legal and regulatory compliance issues have been properly dealt with, and that the forecast profit before interest and tax for the year to 31 October 2013 is reasonable:

   (i)    Holder of 10% of the equity prior to implementation of the scheme

   (ii)    8% debenture holder

   (iii)    The bank

   (iv)    Trade creditors

   Your evaluation should consider whether each of the above parties would be likely to support the reconstruction as outlined, together with any factors which may be necessary to induce or encourage them to support the scheme.        (15 marks)

As a separate issue, Boomerang is disputing a decision by the tax authorities regarding additional tax liabilities relating to earlier years, which are excluded from the statement of financial position at 31 October 2012 as currently stated. The tax authorities communicated their decision to Boomerang on 5 November and, following independent professional advice that an appeal is likely to be successful, Boomerang lodged an appeal against the decision on 28 November. As a result, Boomerang decided that the additional tax liabilities need not be included in the financial statements for the year ended 31 October 2012.

**Required:**

(c)    Evaluate how this information is likely to affect the preparation of the financial statements for the year ended 31 October 2012.        (3 marks)

(Total: 25 marks)

# CURRENT ISSUES

### 47    TRANSITION (JUN 08 EXAM)

The transition to International Financial Reporting Standards (IFRSs) involves major change for companies as IFRSs introduce significant changes in accounting practices that were often not required by national generally accepted accounting practice. It is important that the interpretation and application of IFRSs is consistent from country to country. IFRSs are partly based on rules, and partly on principles and management's judgement. Judgement is more likely to be better used when it is based on experience of IFRSs within a sound financial reporting infrastructure. It is hoped that national differences in accounting will be eliminated and financial statements will be consistent and comparable worldwide.

**Required:**

(a)    Discuss how the changes in accounting practices on transition to IFRSs and choice in the application of individual IFRSs could lead to inconsistency between the financial statements of companies.        (17 marks)

(b)    Discuss how management's judgement and the financial reporting infrastructure of a country can have a significant impact on financial statements prepared under IFRS.        (6 marks)

   Appropriateness and quality of discussion.        (2 marks)

(Total: 25 marks)

## 48    FRAMEWORK (DEC 07 EXAM)

The International Accounting Standards Board (IASB) has begun a joint project to revisit its conceptual framework for financial accounting and reporting. The goals of the project are to build on the existing frameworks and converge them into a common framework.

**Required:**

(a)    Discuss why there is a need to develop an agreed international conceptual framework and the extent to which an agreed international conceptual framework can be used to resolve practical accounting issues.                                             **(13 marks)**

(b)    Discuss the key issues which will need to be addressed in determining the basic components of an internationally agreed conceptual framework.          **(10 marks)**

Appropriateness and quality of discussion.                                             **(2 marks)**

**(Total: 25 marks)**

## 49    CORPORATE REPORTING (DEC 08 EXAM)  *Walk in the footsteps of a top tutor*

Whilst acknowledging the importance of high quality corporate reporting, the recommendations to improve it are sometimes questioned on the basis that the marketplace for capital can determine the nature and quality of corporate reporting. It could be argued that additional accounting and disclosure standards would only distort a market mechanism that already works well and would add costs to the reporting mechanism, with no apparent benefit. It could be said that accounting standards create costly, inefficient, and unnecessary regulation. It could be argued that increased disclosure reduces risks and offers a degree of protection to users. However, increased disclosure has several costs to the preparer of financial statements.

**Required:**

(a)    Explain why accounting standards are needed to help the market mechanism work effectively for the benefit of preparers and users of corporate reports.     **(9 marks)**

(b)    Discuss the relative costs to the preparer and benefits to the users of financial statements of increased disclosure of information in financial statements.

**(14 marks)**

Quality of discussion and reasoning.                                             **(2 marks)**

**(Total: 25 marks)**

## 50    WORLD ENERGY (JUN 04 EXAM)

The directors of World Energy, a public limited company, feel that their financial statements do not address a broad enough range of users' needs. The company's main business is the generation and supply of electricity and gas. They have reviewed the published financial statements and have realised that there is very little information about their corporate environmental governance and their management of the workforce (sometimes called 'Human Capital Management').

The company disclose the following social and environmental information in the financial statements:

**Corporate Environmental Governance**

(i)    the highest radiation dosage to a member of the public

(ii)   total acid gas emissions and global warming potential

(iii)  contribution to clean air through emission savings

**Human Capital Management**

(i)    its full commitment to equal opportunities

(ii)   its investment in the training of the staff

(iii)  the number of employees injured at work in the year

The company wishes to enhance its disclosures in these areas but is unsure as to what the benefits would be for the company and what constitutes current practice in these areas. The problem that the directors envisage is how to measure and report the company's performance in these areas. They are particularly concerned that their report on the management of the workforce (Human Capital Management) has no current value to the stakeholders in the company.

**Required:**

(a)    **Explain the factors that provide encouragement to companies to disclose social and environmental information in their financial statements, briefly discussing whether the content of such disclosure should be at the company's discretion.    (10 marks)**

(b)    **Describe how the current disclosure by World Energy of its 'Corporate Environmental Governance' could be extended and improved.    (7 marks)**

(c)    **Discuss the general nature of the current information disclosed by companies concerning 'Human Capital Management' and how the link between the company performance and its employees could be made more visible.    (8 marks)**

(Total: 25 marks)

## 51    GLOWBALL (PILOT 01)

The directors of Glowball, a public limited company, had discussed the study by the Institute of Environmental Management which indicated that over 35% of the world's 250 largest corporations are voluntarily releasing green reports to the public to promote corporate environmental performance and to attract customers and investors. They have heard that their main competitors are applying the 'Global Reporting Initiative'(GRI) in an effort to develop a worldwide format for corporate environmental reporting. However, the directors are unsure as to what this initiative actually means. Additionally they require advice as to the nature of any legislation or standards relating to environmental reporting as they are worried that any environmental report produced by the company may not be of sufficient quality and may detract and not enhance their image if the report does not comply with recognised standards. Glowball has a reputation for ensuring the preservation of the environment in its business activities.

Further, the directors have collected information in respect of a series of events which they consider to be important and worthy of note in the environmental report but are not sure as to how they would be incorporated in the environmental report or whether they should be included in the financial statements.

The events are as follows:

(i)     Glowball is a company that pipes gas from offshore gas installations to major consumers. The company purchased its main competitor during the year and found that there were environmental liabilities arising out of the restoration of many miles of farmland that had been affected by the laying of a pipeline. There was no legal obligation to carry out the work but the company felt that there would be a cost of around $150 million if the farmland was to be restored.

(ii)    Most of the offshore gas installations are governed by operating licences which specify limits to the substances which can be discharged to the air and water. These limits vary according to local legislation and tests are carried out by the regulatory authorities. The company has been prosecuted for infringements of an environmental law in the USA when toxic gas escaped into the atmosphere. In 20X5 the company was prosecuted five times and in 20X4 eleven times for infringement of the law. The final amount of the fine/costs to be imposed by the courts has not been determined but is expected to be around $5 million. The escape occurred over the sea and it was considered that there was little threat to human life.

(iii)   The company produced statistics that measure their improvement in the handling of emissions of gases which may have an impact on the environment. The statistics deal with:

- Measurement of the release of gases with the potential to form acid rain. The emissions have been reduced by 84% over five years due to the closure of old plants.

- Measurement of emissions of substances potentially hazardous to human health. The emissions are down by 51% on 20X1 levels.

- Measurement of emissions to water that removes dissolved oxygen and substances that may have an adverse effect on aquatic life. Accurate measurement of these emissions is not possible but the company is planning to spend $70 million on research in this area.

(iv)    The company tries to reduce the environmental impacts associated with the siting and construction of its gas installations. This is done in the way that minimises the impact on wild life and human beings. Additionally when the installations are at the end of their life, they are dismantled and are not sunk into the sea. The current provision for the decommissioning of these installations is $215 million and there are still decommissioning costs of $407 million to be provided as the company's policy is to build up the required provision over the life of the installation.

**Required:**

**Prepare a report suitable for presentation to the directors of Glowball in which you discuss the following elements:**

**(a)     current reporting requirements and guidelines relating to environmental reporting**
**(10 marks)**

**(b)     the nature of any disclosure which would be required in an environmental report and/or the financial statements for the events (i) to (iv) above.          (15 marks)**

**(The mark allocation includes four marks for the style and layout of the report.)**

**(Total: 25 marks)**

## 52   FAIR VALUE MEASUREMENT (JUN 07 EXAM)  *Walk in the footsteps of a top tutor*

Financial statements have seen an increasing move towards the use of fair values in accounting. Advocates of 'fair value accounting' believe that fair value is the most relevant measure for financial reporting while others believe that historical cost provides a more useful measure.

Issues have been raised over the reliability and measurement of fair values, and over the nature of the current level of disclosure in financial statements in this area.

**Required:**

(a)   **Discuss the problems associated with the reliability and measurement of fair values and the nature of any additional disclosures which may be required if fair value accounting is to be used exclusively in corporate reporting.** **(13 marks)**

(b)   **Discuss the view that fair value is a more relevant measure to use in corporate reporting than historical cost.** **(12 marks)**

**(Total: 25 marks)**

## 53   MANAGEMENT COMMENTARY

The International Accounting Standards Board issued IFRS Practice Statement 1 *Management Commentary* in December 2010 which provides a broad, non-binding framework for the presentation of management commentary which that relates to IFRS-prepared financial statements.

**Required:**

(a)   **Explain the purpose of the management commentary.** **(5 marks)**

(b)   **Explain the principles and framework that should be applied when preparing a management commentary.** **(10 marks)**

(c)   **Identify potential elements for inclusion within a management commentary, and explain why such items should be included in the management commentary.** **(10 marks)**

**(Total: 25 marks)**

## 54   IFRS FOR SME (JUN 06 EXAM)

International Financial Reporting Standards (IFRSs) are primarily designed for use by publicly listed companies and in many countries the majority of companies using IFRSs are listed companies. In other countries IFRSs are used as national Generally Accepted Accounting Practices (GAAP) for all companies including unlisted entities. It has been argued that the same IFRSs should be used by all entities or alternatively a different body of standards should apply to small and medium entities (SMEs).

**Required:**

(a)   **Discuss whether there is a need to develop a set of IFRSs specifically for SMEs.** **(5 marks)**

(b)   Discuss the nature of the following issues in developing IFRSs for SMEs.

   (i)    The purpose of the standards and the type of entity to who they should apply.                                                                              (5 marks)

   (ii)   How existing standards could be modified to meet the needs of SMEs.
                                                                                        (5 marks)

   (iii)  How items not dealt with by an IFRS for SMEs should be treated.      (5 marks)

   (iv)   Discuss the approach taken by the IASB in the IFRS for SME issued in July 2009.                                                                            (5 marks)

   (v)    Summarise the principle accounting issues which have been subject to either omission or simplification within the IFRS for SME.          (10 marks

                                                                                (Total: 35 marks)

(*Note:* Requirement (v) has been added to the original question to reflect the publication of IFRS for SME and inclusion in the ACCA 2011 syllabus.)


55   HOLCOMBE (JUN 10 EXAM)  *Walk in the footsteps of a top tutor*

(a)   Leasing is important to Holcombe, a public limited company as a method of financing the business. The Directors feel that it is important that they provide users of financial statements with a complete and understandable picture of the entity's leasing activities. They believe that the current accounting model is inadequate and does not meet the needs of users of financial statements.

   Holcombe has leased plant for a fixed term of six years and the useful life of the plant is 12 years. The lease is non-cancellable, and there are no rights to extend the lease term or purchase the machine at the end of the term. There are no guarantees of its value at that point. The lessor does not have the right of access to the plant until the end of the contract or unless permission is granted by Holcombe.

   Fixed lease payments are due annually over the lease term after delivery of the plant, which is maintained by Holcombe. Holcombe accounts for the lease as an operating lease but the directors are unsure as to whether the accounting treatment of an operating lease is conceptually correct.

   **Required:**

   (i)    Discuss the reasons why the current lease accounting standards may fail to meet the needs of users and could be said to be conceptually flawed;
                                                                                        (7 marks)

   (ii)   Discuss whether the plant operating lease in the financial statements of Holcombe meets the definition of an asset and liability as set out in the 'Framework for the Preparation and Presentation of Financial Statements.'
                                                                                        (7 marks)

   Professional marks will be awarded in part (a) (i) and (ii) for clarity and quality of discussion.                                                                        (2 marks)

(b) Holcombe also owns an office building with a remaining useful life of 30 years. The carrying amount of the building is $120 million and its fair value is $150 million. On 1 May 2009, Holcombe sells the building to Brook, a public limited company, for its fair value and leases it back for five years at an annual rental payable in arrears of $16 million on the last day of the financial year (30 April). This is a fair market rental. Holcombe's incremental borrowing rate is 8%.

On 1 May 2009, Holcombe has also entered into a short operating lease agreement to lease another building. The lease will last for three years and is currently $5 million per annum. However an inflation adjustment will be made at the conclusion of leasing years 1 and 2. Currently inflation is 4% per annum.

The following discount factors are relevant (8%).

|  | Single cash flow | Annuity |
|---|---|---|
| Year 1 | 0.926 | 0.926 |
| Year 2 | 0.857 | 1.783 |
| Year 3 | 0.794 | 2.577 |
| Year 4 | 0.735 | 3.312 |
| Year 5 | 0.681 | 3.993 |

**Required:**

(i) **Show the accounting entries in the year of the sale and lease back assuming that the operating lease is recognised as an asset in the statement of financial position of Holcombe;** **(6 marks)**

(ii) **State how the inflation adjustment on the short term operating lease should be dealt with in the financial statements of Holcombe.** **(3 marks)**

**(Total: 25 marks)**

56 **FINANCIAL INSTRUMENTS (DEC 09 EXAM)**  *Walk in the footsteps of a top tutor*

The definition of a financial instrument captures a wide variety of assets and liabilities including cash, evidence of an ownership interest in an entity, or a contractual right to receive, or deliver cash or another financial instrument. Preparers, auditors and users of financial statements have found the requirements for reporting financial assets and liabilities to be very complex, problematical and sometimes subjective. The result is that there is a need to develop new standards of reporting for financial instruments that are principle-based and significantly less complex than current requirements. It is important that a standard in this area should allow users to understand the economic substance of the transaction and preparers to properly apply generally accepted accounting principles.

**Required:**

(a) (i) **Discuss how the measurement of financial instruments under International Financial Reporting Standards can create confusion and complexity for preparers and users of financial statements.** **(9 marks)**

(ii) Set out the reasons why using fair value to measure all financial instruments may result in less complexity in the application of IFRS 9 *Financial Instruments* and its predecessor IAS 39 *Financial Instruments: recognition and measurement* but may lead to uncertainty in financial statements.

(9 marks)

Professional marks will be awarded in part (a) for clarity and expression

(2 marks)

(b) A company borrowed $47 million on 1 December 2008 when the market and effective interest rate was 5%. On 30 November 2009, the company borrowed an additional $45 million when the current market and effective interest rate was 7.4%. Both financial liabilities are repayable on 30 November 2013 and are single payment notes, whereby interest and capital are repaid on that date.

Required:

Discuss the accounting for the above financial liabilities under current accounting standards using amortised cost, and additionally using fair value as at 30 November 2009.

(5 marks)

(Total: 25 marks)

## 57 IFRS FOR SME APPLIED (DEC 10 EXAM)  *Walk in the footsteps of a top tutor*

(a) The principal aim when developing accounting standards for small to medium-sized enterprises (SMEs) is to provide a framework that generates relevant, reliable, and useful information which should provide a high quality and understandable set of accounting standards suitable for SMEs. There is no universally agreed definition of an SME and it is difficult for a single definition to capture all the dimensions of a small or medium-sized business. The main argument for separate SME accounting standards is the undue cost burden of reporting, which is proportionately heavier for smaller firms.

Required:

(i) Comment on the different approaches which could have been taken by the International Accounting Standards Board (IASB) in developing the 'IFRS for Small and Medium-sized Entities' (IFRS for SMEs), explaining the approach finally taken by the IASB. (6 marks)

(ii) Discuss the main differences and modifications to IFRS which the IASB made to reduce the burden of reporting for SME's, giving specific examples where possible and include in your discussion how the Board has dealt with the problem of defining an SME. (8 marks)

Professional marks will be awarded in part (a) for clarity and quality of discussion.

(2 marks)

(b) Whitebirk has met the definition of a SME in its jurisdiction and wishes to comply with the 'IFRS for Small and Medium-sized Entities'. The entity wishes to seek advice on how it will deal with the following accounting issues in its financial statements for the year ended 30 November 2010. The entity currently prepares its financial statements in accordance with full IFRS.

(i) Actuarial gains and losses arising on the defined benefit obligation are accounted for as part of the net remeasurement component for the year. The net remeasurement component is included within other comprehensive income for the year and within other components of equity on the statement of financial position.

(ii) Whitebirk purchased 90% of Close, a SME, on 1 December 2009. The purchase consideration was $5.7 million and the value of Close's identifiable assets was $6 million. The value of the non-controlling interest at 1 December 2009 was estimated at $0.7 million. Whitebirk has used the full goodwill method to account for business combinations and the estimated life of goodwill cannot be estimated with any accuracy. Whitebirk wishes to know how to account for goodwill under the IFRS for SMEs.

(iii) Whitebirk has incurred $1 million of research expenditure to develop a new product in the year to 30 November 2010. Additionally, it incurred $500,000 of development expenditure to bring another product to a stage where it is ready to be marketed and sold.

**Required:**

**Discuss how the above transactions should be dealt with in the financial statements of Whitebirk, with reference to the 'IFRS for Small and Medium-sized Entities'.** (9 marks)

(Total: 25 marks)

## UK GAAP FOCUS

### 58 KEY (DEC 09 EXAM) (UK GAAP FOCUS)

(a) Key, a public limited company, is concerned about the reduction in the general availability of credit and the sudden tightening of the conditions required to obtain a loan from banks. There has been a reduction in credit availability and a rise in interest rates. It seems as though there has ceased to be a clear relationship between interest rates and credit availability, and lenders and investors are seeking less risky investments. The directors are trying to determine the practical implications for the financial statements particularly because of large write downs of assets in the banking sector, tightening of credit conditions, and falling sales and asset prices. They are particularly concerned about the impairment of assets and the market inputs they use in impairment testing. They are afraid that they may experience significant impairment charges in the coming financial year. They are unsure as to how they should test for impairment and any considerations, which should be taken into account.

**Required:**

**Discuss the main considerations that the company should take into account when impairment testing fixed assets in the above economic climate.** (8 marks)

**Professional marks will be awarded in part (a) for clarity and expression.** (2 marks)

(b)     Additionally there are specific assets on which the company wishes to seek advice. The company holds certain fixed assets, which are in a development area and carried at cost less depreciation. These assets cost $3 million on 1 June 2008 and are depreciated on the straight-line basis over their useful life of five years. An impairment review was carried out on 31 May 2009 and the projected cash flows relating to these assets were as follows:

| Year to | 31 May 2010 | 31 May 2011 | 31 May 2012 | 31 May 2013 |
|---|---|---|---|---|
| Cash flows ($000) | 280 | 450 | 500 | 550 |

The company used a discount rate of 5%. At 30 November 2009, the directors used the same cash flow projections and noticed that the resultant value in use was above the carrying amount of the assets and wished to reverse any impairment loss calculated at 31 May 2009. The government has indicated that it may compensate the company for any loss in value of the assets up to 20% of the impairment loss.

Key holds a fixed asset, which was purchased for $10 million on 1 December 2006 with an expected useful life of 10 years. On 1 December 2008, it was revalued to $8.8 million. At 30 November 2009, the asset was reviewed for impairment as a result of current conditions and written down to its recoverable amount of $5.5 million.

Key committed itself at the beginning of the financial year to selling a subsidiary that was underperforming following the economic downturn. As a result of the economic downturn, the subsidiary was not sold by the end of the year. However, shortly after the year-end, the company accepted an offer to sell the subsidiary for $15 million. There is no binding sale agreement. The net assets and purchased goodwill of the subsidiary were $17 million and $3 million respectively at 30 November 2009 and it is assumed that the subsidiary makes neither profit nor loss to any subsequent date of disposal.

**Required:**

**Discuss with suitable computations, how to account for any potential impairment of the above assets in the financial statements for the year ended 30 November 2009.**                                        **(15 marks)**

**Note:** The following discount factors may be relevant

| | |
|---|---|
| Year 1 | 0.9524 |
| Year 2 | 0.9070 |
| Year 3 | 0.8638 |
| Year 4 | 0.8227 |

**(Total: 25 marks)**

## 59    BURLEY (DEC 09 EXAM) (UK GAAP FOCUS)

Burley, a public limited company, operates in the energy industry. It has entered into several arrangements with other entities as follows:

(i)    Burley and Slite, a public limited company, jointly control an oilfield. Burley has a 60% interest and Slite a 40% interest and the companies are entitled to extract oil in these proportions. An agreement was signed on 1 December 2008, which allowed for the net cash settlement of any over/under extraction by one company. The net cash settlement would be at the market price of oil at the date of settlement. Both parties have used this method of settlement before. 200,000 barrels of oil were produced up to 1 October 2009 but none were produced after this up to 30 November 2009 due to production difficulties. The oil was all sold to third parties at $100 per barrel. Burley has extracted 10,000 barrels more than the company's quota and Slite has under extracted by the same amount. The market price of oil at the year-end of 30 November 2009 was $105 per barrel. The excess oil extracted by Burley was settled on 12 December 2009 under the terms of the agreement at $95 per barrel.

Burley had purchased oil from another supplier because of the production difficulties at $98 per barrel and has oil stock of 5,000 barrels at the year-end, purchased from this source. Slite had no stock of oil. Neither company had oil stock at 1 December 2008. Selling costs are $2 per barrel.

Burley wishes to know how to account for the recognition of revenue, the excess oil extracted and the oil stock at the year-end.    **(10 marks)**

(ii)    Burley also entered into an agreement with Jorge, and Heavy, both public limited companies on 1 December 2008. Each of the companies holds one third of the equity in an entity, Wells, a public limited company, which operates off shore oilrigs. Any decisions regarding the operating and financial policies relating to Wells have to be approved by two thirds of the venturers. Burley wants to account for the interest in the entity by using the gross equity method, and wishes advice on the matter.

The oilrigs of Wells started operating on 1 December 1998 and are measured at cost. The useful life of the rigs is 40 years. The initial cost of the rigs was $240 million, which included decommissioning costs (discounted) of $20 million. At 1 December 2008, the carrying amount of the decommissioning liability has grown to $32.6 million, but the net present value of decommissioning liability has decreased to $18.5 million as a result of the increase in the risk-adjusted discount rate from 5% to 7%. Burley is unsure how to account for the oilrigs in the financial statements of Wells for the year ended 30 November 2009.

Burley owns a 10% interest in a pipeline, which is used to transport the oil from the offshore oilrig to a refinery on the land. Burley has joint control over the pipeline and has to pay its share of the maintenance costs. Burley has the right to use 10% of the capacity of the pipeline. Burley wishes to show the pipeline as an investment in its financial statements to 30 November 2009.    **(9 marks)**

(iii)    Burley has purchased a transferable interest in an oil exploration licence. Initial surveys of the region designated for exploration indicate that there are substantial oil deposits present but further surveys will be required in order to establish the nature and extent of the deposits. Burley also has to determine whether the extraction of the oil is commercially viable. Past experience has shown that the licence can increase substantially in value if further information as to the viability of the extraction of the oil becomes available. Burley wishes to capitalise the cost of the licence but is unsure as to whether the accounting policy is compliant with UK Financial Reporting Standards.                                          **(4 marks)**

**Required:**

**Discuss with suitable computations where necessary, how the above arrangements and events would be accounted for in the financial statements of Burley.**

**Professional marks will be awarded in question 3 for clarity and expression.**         **(2 marks)**

**(Total: 25 marks)**

## 60    CATE (JUN 10 EXAM) (UK GAAP FOCUS)

(a)    Cate is an entity in the software industry. Cate had incurred substantial losses in the financial years 31 May 2004 to 31 May 2009. In the financial year to 31 May 2010 Cate made a small profit before tax. This included significant non-operating gains. In 2009, Cate recognised a material deferred tax asset in respect of carried forward losses, which will expire during 2012. Cate again recognised the deferred tax asset in 2010 on the basis of anticipated performance in the years from 2010 to 2012, based on budgets prepared in 2010. The budgets included high growth rates in profitability. Cate argued that the budgets were realistic as there were positive indications from customers about future orders. Cate also had plans to expand sales to new markets and to sell new products whose development would be completed soon. Cate was taking measures to increase sales, implementing new programmes to improve both productivity and profitability. Deferred tax assets less deferred tax liabilities represent 25% of shareholders' equity at 31 May 2010. There are no tax planning opportunities available to Cate that would create taxable profit in the near future.
                                                                                      **(5 marks)**

(b)    At 31 May 2010 Cate held an investment in and had a significant influence over Bates, a public limited company. Cate had carried out an impairment test in respect of its investment in accordance with the procedures prescribed in FRS 11 *Impairment of fixed assets and goodwill*. Cate argued that fair value was the only measure applicable in this case as value in use was not determinable as expected cash flow estimates had not been produced. Cate stated that there were no plans to dispose of the shareholding and hence there was no binding sale agreement. Cate also stated that the quoted share price was not an appropriate measure when considering the fair value of Cate's significant influence on Bates. Therefore, Cate estimated the fair value of its interest in Bates through application of two measurement techniques; one based on earnings multiples and the other based on an option–pricing model. Neither of these methods supported the existence of an impairment loss as of 31 May 2010.                                                                     **(5 marks)**

(c)     At 1 April 2009 Cate had a direct holding of shares giving 70% of the voting rights in Date. In May 2010, Date issued new shares, which were wholly subscribed for by a new investor. After the increase in capital, Cate retained an interest of 35% of the voting rights in its former subsidiary Date. At the same time, the shareholders of Date signed an agreement providing new governance rules for Date. Based on this new agreement, Cate was no longer to be represented on Date's board or participate in its management. As a consequence Cate considered that its decision not to subscribe to the issue of new shares was equivalent to a decision to disinvest in Date. Cate argued that the decision not to invest clearly showed its new intention not to recover the investment in Date principally through continuing use of the asset and was considering selling the investment. Due to the fact that Date is a separate line of business (with separate cash flows, management and customers), Cate considered that the results of Date for the period to 31 May 2010 should be presented based on principles provided by FRS 3 *Reporting financial performance*.           **(8 marks)**

(d)     In its 2010 financial statements, Cate disclosed the existence of a voluntary fund established in order to provide a retirement benefit plan (Plan) to employees. Cate considers its contributions to the Plan to be voluntary, and has not recorded any related liability in its consolidated financial statements. Cate has a history of paying benefits to its former employees, even increasing them to keep pace with inflation since the commencement of the Plan. The main characteristics of the Plan are as follows:

(i)     the Plan is totally funded by Cate;

(ii)    the contributions for the Plan are made periodically;

(iii)   the retirement benefit is calculated based on a percentage of the final salaries of Plan participants dependent on the years of service;

(iv)    the annual contributions to the Plan are determined as a function of the fair value of the assets less the liability arising from past services.

Cate argues that it should not have to recognise the Plan because, according to the underlying contract, it can terminate its contributions to the Plan, if and when it wishes. The termination clauses of the contract establish that Cate must immediately purchase lifetime annuities from an insurance company for all the retired employees who are already receiving benefit when the termination of the contribution is communicated.                                                                                        **(5 marks)**

**Required:**

**Discuss whether the accounting treatments proposed by the company are acceptable under Financial Reporting Standards.**

**Professional marks will be awarded in this question for clarity and quality of discussion.**
**(2 marks)**

**The mark allocation is shown against each of the four parts above.**

**(Total: 25 marks)**

## 61 NORMAN (JUN 08 EXAM) (UK GAAP FOCUS)

Norman, a public limited company, has three business segments which are currently reported in its financial statements. Norman is an international hotel group which reports to management on the basis of region. The results of the regional segments for the year ended 31 May 2008 are as follows:

| Region | Revenue | | Segment profit | Segment assets | Segment liabilities |
|---|---|---|---|---|---|
| | $m | $m | $m | $m | $m |
| European | 210 | 3 | 10 | 300 | 200 |
| South East Asia | 300 | 2 | 60 | 800 | 300 |
| Other regions | 500 | 5 | 105 | 2,000 | 1,400 |

There were no significant intercompany balances in the segment assets and liabilities. The hotels are located in capital cities in the various regions, and the company sets individual performance indicators for each hotel based on its city location.

**Required:**

**Discuss the principles in SSAP 25 *Segmental reporting* for the determination of a company's reportable segments and how these principles would be applied for Norman plc using the information given above.**

**(Total: 11 marks)**

## 62 ENGINA (PILOT 01) (UK GAAP FOCUS)

Engina, a foreign company, has approached a partner in your firm to assist in obtaining a Stock Exchange listing for the company. Engina is registered in a country where transactions between related parties are considered to be normal but where such transactions are not disclosed. The directors of Engina are reluctant to disclose the nature of their related party transactions as they feel that although they are a normal feature of business in their part of the world, it could cause significant problems politically and culturally to disclose such transactions.

The partner in your firm has requested a list of all transactions with parties connected with the company and the directors of Engina have produced the following summary:

(a)    Every month, Engina sells $50,000 of goods per month to Mr Satay, the financial director. The financial director has set up a small retailing business for his son and the goods are purchased at cost price for him. The annual turnover of Engina is $300 million. Additionally Mr Satay has purchased his company car from the company for $45,000 (market value $80,000). The director, Mr Satay, owns directly 10% of the shares in the company and earns a salary of $500,000 a year, and has a personal fortune of many millions of pounds.

(b)    A hotel property had been sold to a brother of Mr Soy, the Managing Director of Engina, for $4 million (net of selling cost of $0.2 million). The market value of the property was $4.3 million but in the overseas country, property prices were falling rapidly. The carrying value of the hotel was $5 million and its value in use was $3.6 million. There was an oversupply of hotel accommodation due to government subsidies in an attempt to encourage hotel development and the tourist industry.

(c)    Mr Satay owns several companies and the structure of the group is as follows:

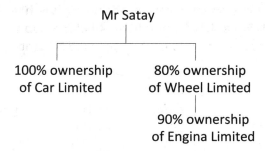

Mr Satay

100% ownership
of Car Limited

80% ownership
of Wheel Limited

90% ownership
of Engina Limited

Engina earns 60% of its profit from transactions with Car and 40% of its profit from transactions with Wheel.

**Required:**

**Write a report to the directors of Engina setting out the reasons why it is important to disclose related party transactions and the nature of any disclosure required for the above transactions under the UK regulatory system before a listing for shares and a Stock Exchange quotation can be obtained.**

**(Total: 25 marks)**

## 63    GHORSE (DEC 07 EXAM) (UK GAAP FOCUS)

Ghorse, a public limited company, operates in the fashion sector and had undertaken a group re-organisation during the current financial year to 31 October 2007. As a result the following events occurred:

The manufacturing property of the group, other than the head office, was held on an operating lease over 8 years. On re-organisation on 31 October 2007, the lease has been renegotiated and is held for 12 years at a rent of $5 million per annum paid in arrears. The fair value of the property is $35 million and its remaining economic life is 13 years. The lease relates to the buildings and not the land. The factor to be used for an annuity at 10% for 12 years is 6.8137.

**Required:**

**Discuss the accounting treatment of the above transactions and the impact that the resulting adjustment to the financial statements would have on ROCE.**

*Note:* **Your answer should include appropriate calculations where necessary and a discussion of the accounting principles involved.**

**(Total: 5 marks)**

## 64 GRANGE (DEC 09 EXAM) (UK GAAP FOCUS)

Grange, a public limited company, operates in the manufacturing sector. The draft balance sheets of the group companies are as follows at 30 November 2009:

|  | Grange $m | Park $m | Fence $m |
|---|---|---|---|
| Fixed assets: |  |  |  |
| Tangible assets | 251 | 311 | 238 |
| Investments in subsidiaries |  |  |  |
| Park | 340 |  |  |
| Fence | 134 |  |  |
| Investment in Sitin | 16 |  |  |
|  | 741 | 311 | 238 |
| Current assets | 481 | 304 | 141 |
| Creditors: amounts falling due within one year |  |  |  |
| Trade creditors | (178) | (71) | (105) |
| Provisions for liabilities | (10) | (6) | (4) |
|  | (188) | (77) | (109) |
| Net current assets | 293 | 227 | 32 |
| Total assets less current liabilities | 1,034 | 538 | 270 |
| Creditors: amounts falling due after one year | (172) | (124) | (38) |
| Net assets | 862 | 414 | 232 |
| Capital and reserves | $m | $m | $m |
| Called up share capital | 430 | 230 | 150 |
| Profit and loss reserve | 410 | 170 | 65 |
| Other reserves | 22 | 14 | 17 |
| Capital employed | 862 | 414 | 232 |

The following information is relevant to the preparation of the group financial statements:

(i) On 1 June 2008, Grange acquired 60% of the equity interests of Park, a public limited company. The purchase consideration comprised cash of $250 million. Excluding the franchise referred to below, the fair value of the identifiable net assets was $360 million. The excess of the fair value of the net assets is due to an increase in the value of non-depreciable land.

Park held a franchise right, which at 1 June 2008 had a fair value of $10 million. This had not been recognised in the financial statements of Park. The franchise agreement had a remaining term of five years to run at that date and is not renewable. Park still holds this franchise right at the year-end.

The profit and loss reserve of Park was $115 million and other reserves were $10 million at the date of acquisition.

Grange acquired a further 20% interest in Park on 30 November 2009 for a cash consideration of $90 million when the fair value of the net assets of Park was not materially different from their book value. Group policy is not to amortise goodwill but to annually impairment test. There has been no impairment of goodwill to date.

(ii) On 31 July 2008, Grange acquired a 100% of the equity interests of Fence for a cash consideration of $214 million. The identifiable net assets of Fence had a provisional fair value of $202 million, including any contingent liabilities. At the time of the business combination, Fence had a contingent liability with a fair value of $30 million. At 30 November 2009, the contingent liability met the recognition criteria of FRS12 'Provisions, contingent liabilities and contingent assets' and the revised estimate of the fair value of this liability was $25 million. The accountant of Fence is yet to account for this revised liability.

July 2008 and the valuation was not completed by 30 November 2008. The valuation was received on 30 June 2009 and the excess of the fair value over book value at the date of acquisition was estimated at $4 million. The asset had a useful economic life of 10 years at 31 July 2008.

The profit and loss reserve of Fence was $73 million and other reserves were $9 million at 31 July 2008 before any adjustment for the contingent liability.

On 30 November 2009, Grange disposed of 25% of its equity interest in Fence for a consideration of $80 million. The disposal proceeds had been credited to the cost of the investment in the balance sheet.

(iii) On 30 June 2008, Grange had acquired a 100% interest in Sitin, a public limited company for a cash consideration of $39 million. Sitin's identifiable net assets were fair valued at $32 million.

On 30 November 2009, Grange disposed of 60% of the equity of Sitin when its identifiable net assets were $36 million. The sale proceeds were $23 million. Grange could still exert significant influence after the disposal of the interest. The only accounting entry made in Grange's financial statements was to increase cash and reduce the cost of the investment in Sitin.

(iv) Grange acquired a plot of land on 1 December 2008 in an area where the land is expected to rise significantly in value if plans for regeneration go ahead in the area. The land is currently held at cost of $6 million in fixed assets until Grange decides what should be done with the land. The market value of the land at 30 November 2009 was $8 million but as at 15 December 2009, this had reduced to $7 million as there was some uncertainty surrounding the viability of the regeneration plan.

(v) Grange anticipates that it will be fined $1 million by the local regulator for environmental pollution. It also anticipates that it will have to pay compensation to local residents of $6 million although this is only the best estimate of that liability. In addition, the regulator has requested that certain changes be made to the manufacturing process in order to make the process more environmentally friendly. This is anticipated to cost the company $4 million.

(vi) Grange has a property located in a foreign country, which was acquired at a cost of 8 million dinars on 30 November 2008 when the exchange rate was $1 = 2 dinars. At 30 November 2009, the property was revalued to 12 million dinars. The exchange rate at 30 November 2009 was $1 = 1.5 dinars. The property was being carried at its value as at 30 November 2008. The company policy is to revalue property whenever material differences exist between book and fair value. Depreciation on the property can be assumed to be immaterial.

(vii) Grange has prepared a plan for reorganising the parent company's own operations. The board of directors has discussed the plan but further work has to be carried out before they can approve it. However, Grange has made a public announcement as regards the reorganisation and wishes to make a reorganisation provision at 30 November 2009 of $30 million. The plan will generate cost savings. The directors have calculated the value in use of the net assets of the parent company as being $870 million if the reorganisation takes place and $830 million if the reorganisation does not take place. Grange is concerned that the parent company's fixed assets have lost value during the period because of a decline in property prices in the region and feel that any impairment charge would relate to these assets. There is no reserve within other reserves relating to prior revaluation of these fixed assets.

(viii) Grange uses accounting policies which maximise its return on capital employed. The directors of Grange feel that they are acting ethically in using this approach as they feel that as long as they follow 'professional rules', then there is no problem. They have adopted a similar philosophy in the way they conduct their business affairs. The finance director had recently received information that one of their key customers, Brook, a public limited company, was having serious liquidity problems. This information was received from a close friend who was employed by Brook. However, he also learned that Brook had approached a rival company, Field, a public limited company, for credit and knew that if Field granted Brook credit then there was a high probability that the outstanding balance owed by Brook to Grange would be paid. Field had approached the director for an informal credit reference for Brook who until recently had always paid promptly. The director was intending to give Brook a good reference because of its recent prompt payment history as the director felt that there was no obligation or rule which required him to mention the company's liquidity problems. (There is no change required to the financial statements as a result of the above information.)

**Required:**

(a) **Calculate the gain or loss arising on the disposal of the equity interest in Sitin.**

(6 marks)

(b) **Prepare a consolidated balance sheet of the Grange Group at 30 November 2009 in accordance with UK Financial Reporting Standards.** (35 marks)

(Total: 41 marks)

## 65 ASHANTI (JUN 10 EXAM) (UK GAAP FOCUS)

The following financial statements relate to Ashanti, a public limited company.

**Ashanti Group: Profit and Loss Account and Statement of Total Recognised Gains and Losses for the year ended 30 April 2010.**

|  | Ashanti $m | Bochem $m | Ceram $m |
|---|---|---|---|
| Turnover | 810 | 235 | 142 |
| Cost of sales | (686) | (137) | (84) |
| | | | |
| Gross profit | 124 | 98 | 58 |
| Distribution costs | (30) | (21) | (26) |
| Administration expenses | (55) | (29) | (12) |
| Other operating income | 31 | 17 | 12 |
| | | | |
| Operating profit before interest | 70 | 65 | 32 |
| Net interest costs | (8) | (6) | (8) |
| | | | |
| Profit on ordinary activities before tax | 62 | 59 | 24 |
| Taxation | (21) | (23) | (10) |
| | | | |
| Profit on ordinary activities after taxation | 41 | 36 | 14 |
| | | | |
| Statement of Total Recognised Gains and Losses | | | |
| Profit for financial year | 41 | 36 | 14 |
| Gains (net) on fixed assets revaluation | 12 | 6 | – |
| Actuarial losses on defined benefit plan | (14) | – | – |
| | | | |
| Total Recognised Gains and Losses for year | 39 | 42 | 14 |

The following information is relevant to the preparation of the group financial statements:

1   On 1 May 2008, Ashanti acquired 70% of the equity interests of Bochem, a public limited company. The purchase consideration comprised cash of $150 million and the fair value of the identifiable net assets was $160 million at that date. The share capital and retained earnings of Bochem were $55 million and $85 million respectively and other reserves were $10 million at the date of acquisition. The excess of the fair value of the identifiable net assets at acquisition is due to an increase in the value of plant, which is depreciated on the straight-line method and has a five year remaining life at the date of acquisition. Ashanti disposed of a 10% equity interest to the non-controlling interest (i.e. minority interest) of Bochem on 30 April 2010 for a cash consideration of $34 million. The carrying value of the net assets of Bochem at 30 April 2010 was $210 million before any adjustments on consolidation. Goodwill has been impairment tested annually and as at 30 April 2009 had reduced in value by 15% and at 30 April 2010 had lost a further 5% of its original value before the sale of the equity interest to the MI.

2   Bochem acquired 80% of the equity interests of Ceram, a public limited company, on 1 May 2008. The purchase consideration was cash of $136 million. Ceram's identifiable net assets were fair valued at $115 million. On 1 November 2009,

Bochem disposed of 50% of the equity of Ceram for a consideration of $90 million. Ceram's identifiable net assets were $160 million at the date of disposal. After the disposal, Bochem can still exert significant influence. Goodwill had been impairment tested and no impairment had occurred. Ceram's profits are deemed to accrue evenly over the year.

3    Ashanti has sold stock to both Bochem and Ceram in October 2009. The sale price of the stock was $10 million and $5 million respectively. Ashanti sells goods at a gross profit margin of 20% to group companies and third parties. At the year-end, half of the stock sold to Bochem remained unsold but the entire stock sold to Ceram had been sold to third parties.

4    On 1 May 2007, Ashanti purchased a $20 million five-year bond with annual interest of 8%, which is also the effective rate, payable on 30 April. The bond is classified as fair value through profit or loss. At 30 April 2010, the carrying value of the bond was $20 million and interest has just been received as normal, but there are reports that the issuer of the bond is in financial difficulty. The market rate of interest is now 10% and Ashanti estimates that the only amounts which will be received in settlement of the bond will be as follows: $1.6 million on 30 April 2011, $1.4 million on 30 April 2012 and $16.5 million on 30 April 2013. The only accounting entries made in the financial statements for the above bond since 30 April 2009 were to correctly account for the interest received.

5    Ashanti sold $5 million of goods to a customer who recently made an announcement that it is restructuring its debts with its suppliers including Ashanti. It is probable that Ashanti will not recover the amounts outstanding. The goods were sold after the announcement was made although the order was placed prior to the announcement. Ashanti wishes to make an additional provision of $8 million against the total debtor balance at the year end, of which $5 million relates to this sale.

6    Ashanti owned a piece of plant and machinery, which cost $12 million and was purchased on 1 May 2008. It is being depreciated over 10 years on the straight-line basis with zero residual value. On 30 April 2009, it was revalued to $13 million and on 30 April 2010, the plant and machinery was again revalued to $8 million. However, an impairment review indicated that the recoverable amount of the asset was $9 million. The whole of the revaluation loss had been posted to the statement of total recognised gains and losses and depreciation has been charged for the year. It is Ashanti's company policy not to make transfers for excess depreciation following revaluation and there is no obvious consumption of economic benefits regarding the plant and machinery.

7    Ashanti anticipates that it will be fined $40,000 by the local regulator for a mis-selling offence. The company has not paid the fine at the year end nor has it accounted for it. It also anticipates that there will be an additional obligation to pay $170,000 to its customers for the mis-selling. The regulator has requested that the company make future changes to its system of selling and this is expected to cost $150,000 of which $30,000 relates to re-training.

8    Ignore any taxation effects of the above adjustments and the disclosure requirements of FRS 3 *Reporting Financial Performance*.

**Required:**

**Prepare a Consolidated Profit and Loss Account and Statement of Total Recognised Gains and Losses for the year ended 30 April 2010 for the Ashanti Group.**

**(35 marks)**

## 66 MARRGRETT (DEC 08 EXAM) (UK GAAP FOCUS)

Marrgrett, a public limited company, is currently planning to acquire and sell interests in other entities and has asked for advice on the impact of FRS 2 'Accounting for Subsidiary Undertakings', FRS 7 'Fair values in Acquisition Accounting', FRS 10 'Goodwill and Intangible assets' and any other relevant standards on these plans.

The company is considering purchasing additional shares in an associate, Josey, a public limited company. The holding will increase from 30% stake to 70% stake by offering the shareholders of Josey, cash and shares in Marrgrett. Marrgrett anticipates that it will pay £5 million in transaction costs to lawyers and bankers including the costs of raising capital for the acquisition. Josey had previously been the subject of a management buyout. In order that the current management shareholders may remain in the business, Marrgrett is going to offer them share options in Josey subject to them remaining in employment for two years after the acquisition. Additionally, Marrgrett will offer the same shareholders shares in the holding company which are contingent upon a certain level of profitability being achieved by Josey. Each shareholder will receive shares of the holding company up to a value of £50,000, if Josey achieves a pre-determined rate of return on capital employed for the next two years.

Josey has several marketing-related intangible assets that are used primarily in marketing or promotion of its products. These include trade names and internet domain names. These are not currently recognised in Josey's financial statements. Josey operates in a country where depreciation is calculated in accordance with local tax law rather than by reference to the estimated useful life of the fixed assets. Because of its plans to change the overall structure of the business, Marrgrett wishes to recognise a re-organisation provision at the date of the business combination and has assigned provisional values to some of the assets of Josey.

To finance the acquisition of Josey, Marrgrett intends to dispose of a partial interest in two subsidiaries. Marrgrett will retain control of the first subsidiary but will sell the apparent controlling interest in the second subsidiary, Wells, a public limited company. Marrgrett decided to dispose of Wells, partially to its management. The group will retain 45% of the ordinary shares, management will have 35% of the ordinary shares and other shareholders will hold 20%. All shareholders will hold share options which are convertible into ordinary shares. The options are held in the same proportion as the ordinary shares. Management's options are only convertible if certain profit targets are met. The remainder are convertible after three years.

**Required:**

**Discuss the principles and nature of the accounting treatment of the above plans under Financial Reporting Standards.**

**Note: this requirement includes 2 professional marks for the quality of the discussion.**

**(25 marks)**

# Section 2

# ANSWERS TO PRACTICE QUESTIONS

## SECTION A-TYPE QUESTIONS

## GROUP FINANCIAL STATEMENTS

1      GLOVE (JUN 07 EXAM)  *Walk in the footsteps of a top tutor*

**Key answer tips**

As with many of the group accounting questions, the difficulty in part (a) lies in the accounting issues included rather than the consolidation process itself. The best way to approach these questions is to deal with the issues individually and then note down the adjustments you need to make in the consolidated accounts. In this case there are financial instruments and a part exchanged asset. Be careful not to spend too much time on these adjustments as you still have to do the consolidation. If you are getting bogged down, leave them and move on. Part (b) is difficult to score well on, but part (c) should be straightforward if you have done your homework.

(a)     **Statement of financial position of Glove Group at 31 May 20X7**

|  | $m |
|---|---|
| Assets |  |
| Non-current assets: |  |
| Property, plant and equipment (W8) | 320.00 |
| Trade name (W7) | 4.00 |
| Goodwill (W3) | 10.16 |
| Financial assets at fair value | 10.00 |
|  | 344.16 |
| Current assets | 114.00 |
|  | 458.16 |
| Total assets | 458.16 |

|  | $m |
|---|---|
| Ordinary shares | 150.00 |
| Other components of equity (W5) | 32.35 |
| Retained earnings (W5) | 150.96 |
| Non controlling interest (W4) | 28.92 |
| Total equity | 362.23 |
| Non-current liabilities (W6) | 48.93 |
| Current liabilities | 47.00 |
| Total equity and liabilities | 458.16 |

**Workings**

*Before you start the consolidation, sort out the accounting issues.*

**ISSUE 1 – THE CONVERTIBLE BOND**

The bond has to be split into a liability and an equity component under IAS 39 *Financial instruments: recognition and measurement.*

|  |  | $m | Discount factor 8% $m | NPV of cash flow $m |
|---|---|---|---|---|
| 31 May 20X7 | Interest | 1.8 | 1/1.08 | 1.67 |
| 31 May 20X8 | Interest | 1.8 | 1/1.082 | 1.54 |
| 31 May 20X9 | Interest and capital | 31.8 | 1/1.083 | 25.24 |
| | Total liability element | | | 28.45 |
| | Total equity element (balance) | | | 1.55 |
| | | | | 30.00 |

**Balance of liability element at 31 May 20X7**

|  | $m |
|---|---|
| Balance at 1 June 20X6 | 28.45 |
| Interest 8% | 2.28 |
| Cash paid | (1.80) |
| Balance at 31 May 20X7 | 28.93 |

Equity will be credited with $1.55 million and this amount will not be remeasured. The liability will be accounted for at amortised cost as the company does not wish to measure it at fair value through profit or loss. Thus the following entries will now occur:

|  |  | $m |
|---|---|---|
| Dr | Non-current liabilities | 1.55 |
| Cr | Equity | 1.55 |
| Dr | Retained earnings (group) (2.28–1.8) | 0.48 |
| Cr | Non-current liabilities | 0.48 |

### ISSUE 2 – THE PLANT EXCHANGE

**Plant exchange**

The exchange has commercial substance since the land generated no immediate economic benefits as it was not being used but the plant will be. The cost of the plant will be measured at the fair value of the asset given up. Therefore, the plant will be valued at $7 million. The gain will be recognised in profit or loss at $3 million ($7 million – $4 million).

The following entries will occur:

|  |  | $m |
|---|---|---|
| Dr | Plant | 3 |
| Cr | Retained earnings (group) | 3 |

*Only once you have looked at the accounting issues should you start the consolidation. Please note this is an old syllabus question. The P2 questions to date are averaging 6 accounting issues to deal with as well as the consolidation.*

*Now you are ready to start the consolidation.*

**(W1) Shareholding (Direct Method)**

|  | Body | Fit |
|---|---|---|
| Glove | 80% | (80% of 70%) 56% |
| Non controlling interest | 20% | 44% |

**(W2) Net assets**

|  | Body | | Fit | |
|---|---|---|---|---|
|  | Acq'n date | Rep date | Acq'n date | Rep date |
|  | $m | $m | $m | $m |
| Ordinary shares | 40 | 40 | 20 | 20 |
| Other comp of equity | 4 | 5 | 8 | 8 |
| Retained earnings | 10 | 25 | 6 | 10 |
| **Book values** | 54 | 70 | 34 | 38 |
| Revaluation – land (60 – 54) | 6 | 6 |  |  |
| Revaluation – land (39 – 34) |  |  | 5 | 5 |
| (given 60 & 39 in Qn) | 60 | 76 | 39 | 43 |
| Trade name (W7) | 5 | 4 |  |  |
| **Fair value** | 65 | 80 | 39 | 43 |

**(W3)  Goodwill**

*Remember goodwill is based on the fair values of the net assets at acquisition.*

|  | Body $m | Fit $m |
|---|---|---|
| Purchase consideration | 60.00 | 30.00 |
| Less: indirect holding adjustment |  | (6.00) |
|  | 60.00 | 24.00 |
| FV of NCI at acquisition: |  |  |
| Body: 20% × 65 (W2) | 13.00 |  |
| Fit: 44% × 39 (W2) |  | 17.16 |
|  | 73.00 | 41.16 |
| FV of NA at acquisition (W2) | (65.00) | (39.00) |
| Goodwill to SOFP | 8.00 | 2.16 |

**(W4)  Non-controlling interest**

*Remember NCI is calculated on a proportionate basis to match the goodwill accounting policy for each subsidiary.*

|  | $m |
|---|---|
| Body: FV of NCI at acquisition (20% × 65)(W2) | 13.00 |
| (20% × (80 − 65))(W2) | 3.00 |
| Fit: FV of NCI at acquisition (44% × 39)(W2) | 17.16 |
| (44% × (43 − 39))(W2) | 1.76 |
| Less: indirect holding adjustment | (6.00) |
|  | 29.92 |

**(W5)  Reserves**

*Do 'other reserves' first, if there are any in the question. Exclude these when you do your retained earnings calculation.*

| | Other components $m | Retained earnings $m |
|---|---|---|
| Glove | 30.80 | 135.00 |
| Post acquisition: | | |
| Body (4 – 5 × 80%) (((65-4) – (80-5)) × 80%) | 0.80 | 11.20 |
| Fit (39 – 43 × 56%) | | 2.24 |
| Plant exchange (ISSUE 2) | | 3.00 |
| Bond (ISSUE 1) | 1.55 | (0.48) |
| | 32.35 | 150.96 |

**(W6) Non-current liabilities**

| | $m |
|---|---|
| Glove | 45.00 |
| Body | 2.00 |
| Fit | 3.00 |
| | 50.00 |
| Bond (ISSUE 1) re equity element | (1.55) |
| Bond (ISSUE 1) re finance charge and liability | 0.48 |
| | 48.93 |

**(W7) Trade name**

An internally generated intangible asset is not normally recognised under IAS 38 *Intangible assets* but where it forms part of the business acquired, IFRS 3 *Business combinations* requires separate recognition of that intangible if fair value can be measured reliably even if it involves the use of experts. Thus, under IFRS 3 and IAS 38 Glove should recognise an intangible asset at 1 June 20X5 of $5 million. This will effectively reduce the value placed on goodwill. The trade name will be amortised over ten years. Thus, the accounting entry for this will be:

| | | $m |
|---|---|---|
| Dr | Retained earnings (group) | 0.8 |
| | Non controlling interest | 0.2 |
| Cr | Trade name (2/10 × $5m) | 1 |

*Note the net asset working is deals with the retained earnings and NCI part.*

You need to remember to bring the trade name on the consolidated statement of financial position. It is now an acquired asset ($5m – $1m) = $4m.

(W8) **Property, plant and equipment**

|  | $m |
|---|---|
| Glove | 260 |
| Body | 20 |
| Fit | 26 |
| Plant exchange | 3 |
| Revaluation (6 + 5) | 11 |
|  | ——— |
|  | 320 |
|  | ——— |

(b) **Reverse acquisitions**

A reverse acquisition usually involves the smaller listed company (Glove) issuing a large number of shares to the acquiring company (Shine) so that the acquiring company's shareholders end up controlling the listed company.

This is a way of obtaining a stock exchange listing as a private company may arrange to have itself 'acquired' by a smaller public company as a means of obtaining a listing. Although the public company that issues shares (Glove) is regarded as the legal parent and the private company (Shine) is regarded as the legal subsidiary, the private company that initiated and arranged the combination is deemed to be the acquirer if it is determined to have obtained control over the financial and operating policies of the public company, rather than vice versa.

Therefore, for financial reporting purposes in a reverse acquisition, the legal parent is the acquiree and the legal subsidiary is the acquirer. The carrying amounts of the assets and liabilities of the legal subsidiary (Shine) do not change as a result of the acquisition; it is the assets and liabilities of the legal parent (Glove) which are remeasured at fair value. The consideration is deemed to be the fair value of the equity shares in the legal subsidiary (Shine) issued to the owners of the legal parent (Glove).

IFRS 3 *Business combinations* provides some guidance on reverse acquisitions.

(c) **Management commentary**

**Purpose of the Management Commentary (MC)**

The IFRS Practice Statement (PS) *Management Commentary* was published in December 2010 and provides a broad, non-binding framework for the presentation of management commentary that relates to financial statements that have been prepared in accordance with International Financial Reporting Standards (IFRSs)

It is a narrative report that provides a context within which to interpret the financial position, financial performance and cash flows of an entity. Management are able to explain its objectives and its strategies for achieving those objectives. Users routinely use the type of information provided in management commentary to help them evaluate an entity's prospects and its general risks, as well as the success of management's strategies for achieving its stated objectives. For many entities, management commentary is already an important element of their communication with the capital markets, supplementing as well as complementing the financial statements.

This PS helps management to provide useful commentary to financial statements prepared in accordance with IFRS information. The users are identified as existing and potential members, together with lenders and creditors.

### Framework for presentation of management commentary

The following principles should be applied when a management commentary is prepared:

(a)   to provide management's view of the entity's performance, position and progress; and

(b)   to supplement and complement information presented in the financial statements.

Consequently, the MC should include information which is both forward-looking and adheres to the qualitative characteristics of information as described in the 2010 Conceptual Framework for Financial Reporting.

The management commentary should provide information to help users of the financial reports to assess the performance of the entity and the actions of its management relative to stated strategies and plans for progress. That type of commentary will help users of the financial reports to understand, risk exposures and strategies of the entity, relevant non-financial factors and other issues not otherwise included within the financial statements.

Management commentary should provide management's perspective of the entity's performance, position and progress. Management commentary should derive from the information that is important to management in managing the business.

### Elements of management commentary

Although the particular focus of management commentary will depend on the facts and circumstances of the entity, management commentary should include information that is essential to an understanding of:

(a)   the nature of the business;

(b)   management's objectives and its strategies for meeting those objectives;

(c)   the entity's most significant resources, risks and relationships;

(d)   the results of operations and prospects; and

(e)   the critical performance measures and indicators that management uses to evaluate the entity's performance against stated objectives.

It can be adopted by entities, where applicable, any time from the date of issue in December 2010.

| ACCA marking scheme | | |
|---|---|---|
| | | *Marks* |
| (a) | Goodwill and NCI | 7 |
| | Reserves | 8 |
| | Non-current liabilities | 4 |
| | Convertible bond | 5 |
| | Plant | 3 |
| | Trade name | 3 |
| | | —— |
| | | 30 |
| | | |
| (b) | Reverse acquisitions | 6 |
| (c) | Management commentary | 14 |
| | | —— |
| Total | | 50 |
| | | —— |

## 2 ANDASH (DEC 06 EXAM)

**Key answer tips**

Group statements of cash flow are relatively straight forward to deal with. This one has a number of complications, with the purchase of associate, disposal of subsidiary and share based payment transactions. Deal with the individual items and put the answer into the cash flow. Always deal with the easy adjustments first. You should find parts (b) and (c) provide easy marks because these topics are central to the syllabus.

(a) **Andash Group statement of cash flows for year-ended 31 October 20X6**

| | $m | $m |
|---|---|---|
| Cash flows from operating activities | | |
| Profit before taxation (w(i)) | | 323 |
| Adjustments for profit on sale of subsidiary | (8) | |
| Depreciation | 260 | |
| Impairment of goodwill (w(iv)) | 78 | |
| Associate's profit (w(iii)) | (1) | |
| Finance costs | 148 | 477 |
| | | 800 |
| Increase in trade rec'ables (2,400 – 1,500 + 4 (w(v))) | (904) | |
| Increase in inventories (2,650 – 2,300 + 8 (w(v))) | (358) | |
| Increase in trade payables (4,700 – 2,800 + 6 (w(v))) | 1,906 | 644 |
| Cash generated from operations | | 1,444 |
| Interest paid (40 + 148 – 70) | | (118) |
| Income taxes paid (w(vi)) | | (523) |
| Net cash from operating activities | | 803 |
| Cash flows from investing activities | | |
| Purchase of associate (w(iii)) | (10) | |
| Purchase of property, plant and equipment (w(ii)) | (1,320) | |
| Sale of subsidiary (32 – 5 (w(v))) | 27 | (1,303) |
| | | (500) |
| Cash flows from financing activities: | | |
| Proceeds of issue of share capital (w(vii)) | 10 | |
| Dividend paid to non-controlling interests | (20) | |
| Proceeds from long term borrowings | 400 | |
| Dividends paid | (50) | 340 |
| Net decrease in cash and equivalents | | (160) |
| Cash and equivalents at 1 November 20X5 | | 300 |
| Cash and equivalents at 31 October 20X6 | | 140 |

*Workings*

|  |  | $m |
|---|---|---|
| (i) | Profit before tax per draft | 400 |
|  | Associate's profit (iii) | 1 |
|  | Impairment of goodwill (iv) | (78) |
|  | Profit before tax as amended | 323 |

(ii) **Property, plant and equipment**

IFRS 2 *Share-based payment* says that the fair value of the goods and services received should be used as the value of the share options issued. Therefore, the plant should be valued at $9 million and the share options at the same amount. There is no need to adjust depreciation because of the date of purchase, but other reserves will fall by $1 million.

|  | $m |
|---|---|
| Property, plant and equipment – balance 31 October 20X5 | 4,110 |
| Purchases – non-cash ⎤ above | 9 |
| Over valuation         ⎦ | 1 |
| Depreciation | (260) |
| Sale of subsidiary | (10) |
| Purchases in period (balancing figure) | 1,320 |
| Property, plant and equipment per SOFP | 5,170 |

(iii) **Associate – Joma**

The investment in the associate should be measured using the equity method.

|  | $m | $m |
|---|---|---|
| Cost of investment |  |  |
| FV of shares issued |  | 50 |
| **Cash paid** |  | 10 |
|  |  | 60 |
| Share of post-acquisition reserves (25% × ($32 – $20)m) | 3 |  |
| Inter company profit eliminated (25% × ($16 – $8)m) | (2) | 1 |
|  |  | 61 |

(iv) **Impairment of Goodwill-Broiler**

|  | Goodwill $m | Net assets $m | Total $m |
|---|---|---|---|
| Carrying amount | 90 | 240 | 330 |
| Unrecognised NCI (90 × 40/60) | 60 | – | 60 |
|  | 150 | 240 | 390 |
| Recoverable amount |  |  | 260 |
| Impairment loss |  |  | (130) |

Goodwill will be reduced by 60% of 130, i.e. **$78 million**. Profit or loss will be charged with this amount.

(v)  **Sale of subsidiary**

The sale of the subsidiary should be taken into account in the statement of cash flows as follows:

|  | Dr $m | Cr $m |
|---|---|---|
| Plant, property and equipment | | 10 |
| Inventory | | 8 |
| Trade receivables | | 4 |
| Cash and cash equivalents | | 5 |
| Trade payables | 6 | |
| Current tax payable | 7 | |
| Cash proceeds | 32 | |
| Goodwill disposed of | | 10 |
| Profit on sale | | 8 |
| | ___ | ___ |
| | 45 | 45 |
| | ___ | ___ |

(vi)  **Income taxes paid**

| | $m |
|---|---|
| Current  and deferred tax 31/10/X5 (770 + 300) | 1,070 |
| Statement of comprehensive income charge | 160 |
| Cash paid (balancing figure) | (523) |
| Sale of subsidiary | (7) |
| | ____ |
| Current and deferred tax 31/10/X6 (300 + 400) | 700 |
| | ____ |

(vii)  **Shares issued**

Cash flow from the issue of shares is $(60 − 50) i.e. $10 million (from the statement of changes in equity). The shares issued for the purchase of Joma are taken out of the issue proceeds set out in the statement of changes in equity.

(b)  In many cases, the business focus is solely on profitability, with interpretation of financial information focusing on traditional ratios such as gross margin, net margin, return on capital employed. However, a business cannot survive without cash and cash flows cannot be ignored when assessing the performance of an entity.

Statements of cash flows enable users of the financial statements to assess the liquidity, solvency and financial adaptability of a business. A statement of cash flows provides information that is not available from the statement of financial position and the statement of comprehensive income.

A statement of cash flows is believed to provide useful information to users of the financial statements for the following reasons:

- Unlike profits, cash flows are not affected by an entity's choice of accounting policies or by the exercise of judgement. Cash flows can be verified objectively and therefore they allow little scope for 'creative accounting'.

- Cash flow information is thought to have predictive value. It may assist users of financial statements in making judgements on the amount, timing and degree of certainty of future cash flows.

- It gives an indication of the relationship between profitability and cash generating ability, and thus of the quality of the profit earned. The reconciliation of operating profit to the net cash flow generated by operating activities is particularly useful in this context and highlights movements in working capital.

- Cash flow may be more easily understood than profit, particularly by users who are unfamiliar with the technical aspects of financial reporting.

- The statement of cash flows provides information that may be useful in interpreting the statement of comprehensive income and statement of financial position. For example, it shows cash flow from capital transactions as well as from revenue transactions. It may highlight a company's financial adaptability (for example, its ability to generate future profits and cash flows by selling non-current assets or by issuing shares).

However, statements of cash flows are based on historical information and therefore do not provide complete information for assessing future cash flows. Neither cash flow nor profit provide a complete picture of a company's performance when looked at in isolation.

**Measuring cash flow performance**

There are a number of different ways cash flow performance can be assessed.

**Cash generation from operations**

Cash from operations should be compared to the profit from operations (cash from operations / profit from operations). If the ratio is greater than 1 it means that all profits have been converted into cash, which is a good performance.

Overtrading may be indicated by:

- high profits and low cash generation
- large increases in inventory, receivables and payables.

*Dividend and interest payments*

These should be compared to cash generated from trading operations to see whether the normal operations can sustain such payments. In most years they should.

*Capital expenditure and financial investment*

The nature and scale of a company's investment in non-current assets is clearly shown in the cash flow. This may be a cause of a net cash outflow in the period, but this should pay benefits in the future with increased profits.

*Cash flow*

The statement clearly shows the end result in cash terms of the company's activities in the year. However, the importance of this figure alone must not be overstated. A decrease in cash in the year may be for very sound reasons (e.g. there was surplus cash last year) or may be mainly the result of timing (e.g. a new loan was raised just after the end of the accounting period).

*Free cash flow*

Free cash flow represents the cash that an entity has left after paying out the cash to maintain its asset base. It is calculated as:

*Free cash flow = Net profit + depreciation /amortisation – change in working capital – capital expenditure*

*(Or FCF = operating cash flow – capital expenditure.)*

This is the amount of cash left over after paying expenses and operating investments. It is the cash available to be used in investing in new projects or repaid to shareholders. A negative free cash flow is not necessarily a bad thing, as an entity may be investing to provide increased cash inflows in the future.

(c)   Window dressing is the act of showing a better position in the financial statements than actually exists. It is a form of creative accounting and while the financial statements may have been prepared in accordance with accounting standards, there is bias in the way the figures are presented. If the intention is to deceive stakeholders, then the practice of window dressing is unethical.

**Aims of window dressing**

The aim of window dressing is to improve the financial statements and show them in a more favourable light than they should be. It can be used to hide liquidity problems or to make the financial statements look better to present to lenders of finance. It can also be used to make the accounts look better to encourage investors.

**Methods of window dressing**

There are a number of ways to window dress the financial statements.

- **Sale and leaseback** – sell an asset before the year-end and lease it back. This increases cash but does involve a commitment to pay rentals. The entity may sell the assets before the year-end and lease it back post year-end.

- **Short term borrowing** just before year-end shows a better ability to repay debts although it does increase liabilities.

- **Receipt of receivables** – asking customers to pay their debts early so the cash is received before the end of the reporting period. Discounts are usually offered to customers so they will agree to this. This makes the cash position look better and it does improve liquidity but it usually reduces profits.

- **Bringing sales forward** – asking customers to take sales early so they can be recognised before the year-end. This increases revenue and profits but not cash. Unfortunately it brings problems for following financial year as the sales cannot be recognised again, so effectively the company is taking next year's sales into the current year.

- **Changing depreciation policies** – if an entity decides to extend the useful life of non-current assets this will reduce the statement of comprehensive income depreciation charge and increase the non-current assets in the statement of financial position.

- **Recognising intangible assets** – if this can be done it improves asset values although if amortised this expense will be recognised in profit or loss. If the intangible is not amortised it will give higher asset values that are not necessarily true.

- **Changing valuation policies** such as inventory and provisions. Any change in valuation methods will affect profit. This is especially the case for inventory.

It is often argued that cash flows and balances cannot be manipulated because cash flow is a matter of fact. It is not subject to estimates and it can only be treated in one way. However, there is still some scope for manipulation of cash flows.

Cash balances are measured at a point in time. This means that it is possible to arrange receipts and payments of cash so that the cash balance is some particular amount. A business may make a special effort to collect debts just before the year-end; likewise, it may also delay paying creditors until just after the year-end.

A business may also structure transactions so that the cash balance is favourably affected. For example, if assets are acquired under leasing agreements cash outflows are spread over several accounting periods rather than one accounting period.

**Ethical issues**

Arranging transactions to window dress the financial statements and make them look better than actually is the case is not an ethical way of preparing financial statements.

In preparing financial statements, the preparer must ensure that the information is prepared honestly and fairly and that it can be relied upon by the users of those financial statements. If the financial statements are altered so that they do not present fairly the financial position and performance of the entity then they may be misleading to users.

| ACCA marking scheme | | |
|---|---|---|
| | | *Marks* |
| (a) | Cash flows from operating activities | 2 |
| | Adjustments | 4 |
| | Cash generated from operations | 3 |
| | Interest | 2 |
| | Tax | 2 |
| | Associate | 3 |
| | Plant, property and equipment | 2 |
| | Sale of subsidiary | 3 |
| | Non controlling interest | 2 |
| | Long term borrowings | 1 |
| | Dividend paid | 1 |
| | Goodwill | 3 |
| | | ─── |
| | | 28 |
| | | ─── |
| (b) | Cash flow discussion | 10 |
| (c) | Window dressing discussion | 12 |
| | | ─── |
| Total | | 50 |
| | | ─── |

**3    EJOY (JUN 06 EXAM)**  *Walk in the footsteps of a top tutor*

**Key answer tips**

The difficulties in part (a) arise from the accounting issues included rather than the consolidation process itself. The style of the group accounting questions has changed to include accounting issues as well as the consolidation. The best way to approach these questions is to deal with the issues individually and then note down the adjustments you need to make in the consolidated accounts. In this case there is a joint venture, a dividend paid by the subsidiary in the year of acquisition, impairment of a financial asset and a financial instrument. Be careful not to spend too much time on these adjustments as you still have to do the consolidation. If you are getting bogged down, leave them and move on. Parts (b) and (c) are book knowledge, but you will have to think carefully through the mini-scenario in part (d).

(a)    **Ejoy Group – Consolidated statement of profit or loss for year-ended 31 May 20X6**

|  | Ejoy $m | Zbay $m | Group $m |
|---|---|---|---|
| Revenue | 2,500.0 | 1,500.0 | 4,000.0 |
| Cost of sales | (1,800.0) | (1,200.0) | |
| Impairment loss (W3) | (26.3) | | (3,026.3) |
| Gross profit | 673.7 | 300.0 | 973.7 |
| Other income | 70 | 10.0 | |
| Joint venture adj (W4) | (3) | | |
| Dividend from Tbay (Issue 1) | (24) | | 53.0 |
| Distribution costs | (130) | (120.0) | (250.0) |
| Administrative expenses | (100) | (90.0) | (190.0) |
| Finance costs | (50) | (40.0) | |
| Impaired financial asset (Issue 2) | | (42.2) | (132.2) |
| Financial asset – FV hedge (Issue 3) | (1.7) | | |
| Swap contract – FV hedge (Issue 4) | 1.7 | | |
| Interest on financial asset (Issue 2) | | 1.1 | |
| Swap interest received (Issue 4) | 0.5 | | 1.6 |
| Profit before tax | | | 456.1 |
| Income tax expense | (200.0) | (26.0) | (226.0) |
| Profit for period from continuing operations | 237.2 | (7.1) | 230.1 |

Discontinued operations:

| | |
|---|---:|
| Loss for the period from discontinued operations (Issue 1) | (11.0) |
| Profit for the period | 219.1 |

Attributable to:

| | |
|---|---:|
| Owners of the parent (bal fig) | 214.5 |
| Non-controlling interest (W5) | 4.6 |
| | 243.1 |

***Workings***

**ISSUE 1 – TBAY**

*When you have a held-for-sale subsidiary (Tbay), you need an impairment test with recoverable amount based upon fair value less costs to sell as there is a commitment to sell.*

Impairment test re Tbay – the carrying value must be calculated – both net assets and goodwill at the date of the impairment test.

Note that the group share of the dividend received from Tbay by Ejoy is eliminated from the group statement of comprehensive income.

**Net assets at 31 May 20X6**

| | $m | $m |
|---|---:|---:|
| Net assets at 1 December 20X5 (Per Qn) | | 310 |
| 1 December 20X5 – 31 May 20X6 | | |
| Profit 30 × 6/12 | 15 | |
| Less distribution at Dec X5 | (40) | (25) |
| Net assets at 31 May 20X6 | | 285 |

| **Goodwill** | $m |
|---|---:|
| Purchase consideration | 216 |
| NCI at date of acquisition (40% × 310) | 124 |
| | 340 |
| FV of net asset at acquisition (per Qn) | (310) |
| Proportionate goodwill | 30 |

**Impairment test:**

|  |  |
|---|---|
| Carrying value of net interest in subsidiary: | $m |
| Share of net assets (285 × 60%) | 171 |
| Unimpaired proportionate goodwill | 30 |
|  | 201 |
| Fair value less costs to sell | (175) |
| ((300 × 60%) = 180 less selling costs (5)) |  |
| Impairment loss on discontinued activity | 26 |

Tbay – then needs to be separately presented in the statement of profit or loss.

*E.g. Statement of profit or loss*

Revenue

Profit for the period from continuing operations     x

Profit for the period from discontinued operations

(30 × 6/12) = 15 – 26 (impairment loss)    (11)

*Remember you are being method marked...get your thoughts down on paper.*

**ISSUE 2 – Zbay's financial asset**

The question at point (iv) tells us Zbay has a financial asset and the borrower is in financial difficulty.

*An impairment test is necessary on this asset.*

Impairment Test – 1 June 20X5

|  | $m |
|---|---|
| Carrying Value | 60.0 |
| Recoverable Amount (20m × 1/1.06$^2$) | 17.8 |
| Impairment loss | (42.2) |

Again this must be expensed via profit or loss.

Don't forget you will then need to reflect the impact on finance income. This asset has been correctly designated to be measured at amortised cost.

**Amortised cost table**

| Date | Bal b/wd | Finance Income 6% | Cash received | Bal c/fwd |
|---|---|---|---|---|
| 1 June 20X5 | 17.8 | 1.1 | nil | 18.9 |

### ISSUE 3 – Ejoy's purchase of a financial asset

Initial recognition

Dr Financial asset – $50m

Cr Cash – $50m

IFRS 9 requires that financial assets are measured at fair value as follows:

|  | $m |
|---|---|
| Cost | $50.0 |
| Fair value at reporting date | $48.3 |
| Loss on equity instrument | (1.7) |

*Accounting for an equity instrument intended to be held on a continuing basis would normally be that it is designated to be measured at fair value through other comprehensive income. However because Ejoy has followed a hedging strategy and taken out an interest rate swap to protect the asset we have a designated FAIR VALUE HEDGE. The loss should therefore be taken to profit or loss and matched against any gain on the swap contract.*

### ISSUE 4 – Ejoy's interest rate swap

As Ejoy has experienced a loss on the financial asset of $1.7m there will be a matching gain on $1.7 million on the swap.

In their statement on financial position (not required) Ejoy would show a derivative asset of $1.7m

Dr Derivative asset 1.7m

Cr Profit or loss – gain on derivative (swap) 1.7m

Interest received of $0.5m on the swap contract will be accounted for in income as normal.

*Only once you have dealt with the accounting issues should you move to the consolidation workings.*

### *Workings*

### (W1)  Group Structure

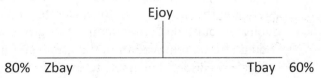

Tbay is acquired with a view to resale – you are told it meets the criteria for being a disposal group and therefore IFRS 5 applies. It is therefore excluded from line-by-line consolidation and is, instead, included as a one-line entry after arriving at profit for the year on continuing operations.

Immediately after acquisition Tbay paid a dividend of $40m. 60% of this (40m × 60% = 24m) will have been received by Ejoy who has treated it as other income. IAS 27 requires that dividends received in the year of acquisition are taken to profit or loss in the individual financial statements of the recipient. They are then eliminated like any other transaction or balance between group members.

**(W2) Goodwill – proportionate basis (Zbay)**

|  | Zhay $m |
|---|---|
| Cost of investment | 520 |
| NCI at acquisition (20% × 600) | 120 |
|  | 640 |
| FV of NA at acquisition (given in Qn) | (600) |
| Proportionate goodwill | 40 |

**(W3) Impairment test at reporting date – Zbay**

|  |  | $m |
|---|---|---|
| Carrying value of net interest in Zbay: |  |  |
| Net assets at acquisition | 600.0 |  |
| Profit for year to 31 May 20X5 | 20.0 |  |
| Draft profit for year to 31 May 20X6 | 34.0 |  |
| Adjust re impaired loan asset (Issue 2) | (42.2) |  |
| Adjust re loan asset income (Issue 2) | 1.1 |  |
| Take group share (80%) | 612.9 | 490.3 |
| Proportionate goodwill (W2) |  | 40.0 |
|  |  | 530.3 |
| Recoverable amount (630 × 80%) |  | 504.0 |
| Impairment loss to profit or loss |  | 26.3 |

**(W4) Joint venture**

> *IFRS 11 Joint arrangements specify the accounting requirements for joint ventures.*

When the joint arrangement is such that the joint venture parties have an interest in the net assets of the separate joint venture entity, then it should be equity accounted. Consequently, the group share of any unrealised profits should also be removed from the group statement of comprehensive income. The gain on disposal of assets to the joint venture is $6 million; 50% of the gain on the disposal should be eliminated as this is the proportion of the interest the group retains. Therefore, **$3 million** will be eliminated from other income.

(W5)  **Non-controlling interest**

|  | $m |
|---|---|
| Zbay 20% × ($7.1m) per Por L schedule | (1.4) |
| Tbay 40% × $30m × 6/12 | 6.0 |
|  | 4.6 |

(b)  IAS 24 *Related party disclosures* states that a party is related to an entity if:

- the party, directly or indirectly, controls, is controlled by or is under common control with the entity (e.g. parent/subsidiary or subsidiaries of the same group)

- one party has an interest in another entity that gives it significant influence over the entity (e.g. an associate) or has joint control over the entity (e.g. joint venturers are related parties)

In addition members of key management and close family members of related parties are also themselves related parties.

(c)  In the absence of related party disclosures, users of financial statements would assume that an entity has acted independently and in its own best interests. Most importantly, this assumes that all transactions have been entered into willingly and at arm's length (i.e. on normal commercial terms at fair value). Where related party relationships and transactions exist, this assumption may not be justified. These relationships and transactions lead to the danger that financial statements may have been distorted or manipulated, both favourably and unfavourably. The most obvious example of this type of transaction would be the sale of goods or rendering of services from one party to another on non-commercial terms (this may relate to the price charged or the credit terms given). Other examples of disclosable transactions are agency, licensing and leasing arrangements, transfer of research and development and the provision of finance, guarantees and collateral. Collectively this would mean there is hardly an area of financial reporting that could not be affected by related party transactions.

It is a common misapprehension that related party transactions need only be disclosed if they are not at arm's length. This is not the case. For example, a parent may instruct all members of its group to buy certain products or services (on commercial terms) from one of its subsidiaries. In the absence of the related party relationships, these transactions may not have occurred. If the parent were to sell the subsidiary, it would be important for the prospective buyer to be aware that the related party transactions would probably not occur in the future. Indeed even where there are no related party transactions, the disclosure of the related party relationship is still important as a subsidiary may obtain custom, receive favourable credit ratings, and benefit from a superior management team simply by being a part of a well respected group.

(d)  The subsidiaries of X are related parties to each other and to X itself as they are under common control.

One of the important aspects of related party relationships is that one of the parties may have its interests subordinated to those of another party, i.e. it may not be able to act in its own best interest. This appears to be the case in this situation. B (or at least one of its directors) believes that the price it is charging A is less than it could have achieved by selling the goods to non-connected parties. In effect these sales have not been made at an arm's length fair value. The obvious implication of this is that the transactions have moved profits from B to A. If the director's figures are accurate B would have made a profit on these transactions of $6 million (20 – 14) rather than the $1 million it has actually made. The transactions will also affect reported revenue and cost of sales and working capital in the individual financial statements of A and B. Some might argue that as the profit remains within the group, there is no real overall effect as, in the consolidated financial statements, intra-group transactions are eliminated. This is not entirely true. The implications of these related party sales are serious:

- B has a non controlling interest of 45% and they have been deprived of their share of the $5 million transferred profit. This could be construed as oppression of the minority and is probably illegal.

- There is a similar effect on the profit share that the directors of B might be entitled to under the group profit sharing scheme as B's profits are effectively $5 million lower than they should be.

- Shareholders, independent analysts or even the (independent) managers of B would find it difficult to appraise the true performance of B. The related party transaction gives the impression that B is under-performing.

- This may lead to the minority selling their shares for a low price (because of poor returns) or calls for the company's closure or some form of rationalisation which may not be necessary.

- The tax authorities may wish to investigate the transactions under transfer pricing rules. The profit may have been moved to A's financial statements to avoid paying tax in B's tax jurisdiction which may have high levels of taxation.

- In the same way as B's results appear poorer due to the effect of the related party transactions, A's results would look better. This may have been done deliberately. X may intend to dispose of A in the near future and thus its more favourable results may allow X to obtain a higher sale price for A.

| ACCA marking scheme | | Marks |
|---|---|---|
| (a) | Goodwill | 9 |
| | Joint venture | 2 |
| | Financial assets | 7 |
| | Dividend | 2 |
| | Statement of comprehensive income | 6 |
| | Tbay | 6 |
| | Non-controlling interest | 3 |
| | | 35 |
| (b) – (d) | Discussion (4+3+6) | 13 |
| Professional marks for quality and clarity of discussion | | 2 |
| Total: | | 50 |

**4     LATERAL (DEC 05 EXAM)**

**Key answer tips**

The key to part (b) is to recognise that the remaining holding in Plank is that of an associate. Therefore, at the year-end, Plank is not consolidated. You also need to recognise that Think has treated the asset held for sale incorrectly. Otherwise, the calculations are relatively straightforward. It is difficult to score well on parts (c) and (d), because you need to make a separate point for each mark.

(a)     **Profit/loss on sale of shares in Plank**

Where there has been a disposal and control has been lost IFRS 3 *Business combinations* (revised in 2008) requires that the group should derecognise all traces of the subsidiary from its accounts (the net assets, the goodwill, and the non-controlling interest) and the reintroduce the remaining interest at its fair value. Any gain or loss arising is taken to income as an exceptional item.

|  |  | $m |
|---|---|---|
| Proceeds |  | 180 |
| FV of residual holding (given) |  | 366 |
|  |  | 546 |
| CV of subsidiary in group FS: |  |  |
| NA at disposal date:(W1) | 848 |  |
| Unimpaired goodwill (W2) | 50 |  |
|  | 898 |  |
| Less: NCI at disposal date (W3) | (349) | (549) |
| Loss  to the group to be reported in  income |  | (3) |

(b)     **Lateral Group – Statement of financial position as at 31 October 20X5**

| Non-current assets: | $m | $m |
|---|---|---|
| Property, plant and equipment (W4) | 1,098 |  |
| Investment in associate (Part (a)) | 366 |  |
| Financial assets at amortised cost (W5) | 33 |  |
| Goodwill (Think only) (W2) | 44 | 1,541 |
| Current assets |  |  |
| Inventories | 385 |  |
| Trade receivables | 250 |  |
| Cash and equivalents | 70 | 705 |
| Total assets |  | 2,246 |

| Equity and liabilities | $m |
|---|---|
| Share capital | 400 |
| Retained earnings (W6) | 956 |
| Non controlling interest (Think only) (W3) | 110 |
| | |
| Total equity | 1,466 |
| Non-current liabilities | 310 |
| Current liabilities | 470 |
| | |
| | 2,246 |

### Workings

#### (W1) Net assets

| | Think | | Plank | |
|---|---|---|---|---|
| | at acq'n | at rep date | at acq'n | at rep date |
| | $m | $m | $m | $m |
| OSC | 250 | 250 | 500 | 500 |
| Reserves | 150 | 280 | 210 | 290 |
| FVA – bal fig | Nil | Nil | 90 | 90 |
| Depreciation | Nil | Nil | Nil | (32)* |
| | | | | |
| | 400 | 530 | 800 | 848 |
| Less URPS (W4) | | (5) | | |
| Less dep'n adj (20% × 10) (W4) | | (2) | | |
| | | | | |
| | 400 | 523 | 800 | 848 |

\* Reducing balance depreciation {(20% × 90 = 18) + (20% × (90 − 18) = 14)} = 32

#### (W2) Goodwill

| | Think | Plank |
|---|---|---|
| | $m | $m |
| Cost of investment per question | 380 | 340 |
| Plus correction re proceeds** | | 180 |
| | | |
| Correct cost of investment | | 520 |
| Fair value of NCI | 90 | 330 |
| | | |
| | 470 | 850 |
| Less  FV of NA at acquisition (W1) | (400) | (800) |
| | | |
| Full goodwill at acquisition | 70 | 50 |
| Less goodwill impaired | (26) | |
| | | |
| Unimpaired goodwill | 44 | 50 |

\*\* The proceeds are added back because they were deducted in error and so the 340 does not represent the original fair value of the consideration.

| Impairment review – Think | $m |
|---|---|
| Net Assets | 523 |
| Goodwill | 70 |
| | 593 |
| Recoverable amount | (567) |
| Impairment loss | 26 |
| 80% to RE (W6) | 21 |
| 20% to NCI (W3) | 5 |

(W3) **Non controlling interest:**

| Think | $m |
|---|---|
| FV of NCI at acquisition | 90 |
| 20% (523 – 400) | 25 |
| Less goodwill impairment loss | (5) |
| To SOFP | 110 |

| Plank | $m |
|---|---|
| FV of NCI at acquisition | 330 |
| 40% (848 – 800) | 19 |
| To disposal calculation (Part (a)) | 349 |

(W4) **Property, plant and equipment**

The plant and equipment will be shown as held for sale in the individual financial statements of Think but in the group accounts this will not be the case as it is an inter-company sale. The items disclosed as held for sale are incorrectly valued at the fair value less costs to sell. (IFRS 5 says that held for sale items should be valued at the lower of their carrying value and fair value less costs to sell, i.e. $10m (and not $15m so there is a purp of $5m and the company has valued the item incorrectly in any event). The plant should be included with the remainder of the group plant and equipment and depreciated (20% × $10m =$2m)

| | Think $m | Lateral $m | Total $m |
|---|---|---|---|
| Property, plant and equipment 31/10/X5 | 390 | 700 | 1,090 |
| Held for sale asset (15–5 profit) | 10 | | |
| Dep'n on held for sale asset @ 20% | (2) | | 8 |
| | 398 | 700 | 1,098 |

(W5) **Financial asset measured at amortised cost**

|  | Amortised cost b/fwd | Interest 10% | Interest rec'd | Amortised cost c/fwd |
|---|---|---|---|---|
|  | $m | $m | $m | $m |
| 1 November 20X3 | 30 | 3.00 | (1.76) | 31.24 |
| 1 November 20X4 | 31.24 | 3.12 | (1.76) | 32.60 |
|  |  | ——— | ——— |  |
|  |  | 6.12 | 3.52 |  |
|  |  | ——— | ——— |  |

Effectively the instrument had not been accounted for under IFRS 9. Only the cash received has been accounted for. Therefore, retained earnings should be credited with $2.6 million ($6.12m − $3.52m) and the debt instrument shown at $32.6 million (rounded to be an adjustment of $3m).

(W6) **Retained earnings**

| Group retained profits | $m |
|---|---|
| Parent company | 850 |
| Plus the gain on the financial asset at amortised cost (33 30) | 3 |
| Plus the gain to the parent company on the sale of the investment not yet recorded (proceeds 180 less cost of investment sold (100/300 × 520) | 7 |
| Less goodwill impaired (W2) | (21) |
| Plus the group % of the post acquisition profits of Think – as represented by the change in net assets 80% (523 – 400) | 98 |
| Plus the group % of the post acquisition profits of Lateral – as represented by the change in net assets 40% (848 – 800) | 19 |
|  | ——— |
|  | 956 |
|  | ——— |

Alternative retained earnings working (for info)

| Group retained profits | $m |
|---|---|
| Parent company | 850 |
| Plus the gain on the financial asset (33 – 30) | 3 |
| Plus the group % of the post acquisition profits of Think – as represented by the change in net assets 80% (523 – 400) | 98 |
| Loss on share disposal (part (a)) | (3) |
| Plank (60% × 48) | 29 |
| Less goodwill impaired | (21) |
|  | ——— |
|  | 956 |
|  | ——— |

KAPLAN PUBLISHING

(c) The *Framework* defines an asset as:

'a resource controlled by the entity as a result of past events and from which future economic benefits are expected to flow to the entity.'

Goodwill is an intangible asset and as such has no physical presence. Goodwill is acquired on the acquisition of another entity. It is measured as the difference between the fair value of the cost of investment and the fair value of net assets acquired.

With reference to the definition of an asset above, goodwill is controlled by the purchased entity. While it is not an asset that is used in the day to day business of an entity, a specific price has been paid for it and on acquisition of the entity to which the goodwill relates, the investor obtains access to the goodwill inherent in that business.

In terms of past events and future benefits, goodwill occurs from the past operation of the business and the specific circumstances that relate to that goodwill. It can occur from the development of an internal brand, from good relations with suppliers and customers and any other factor that gives the business a value in excess of the book value of its assets.

It is expected that the acquiring business will gain future economic benefits as a result of acquiring the assets of the entity and its goodwill as those assets are now under its control, and the factors that generated the goodwill in the first place are likely to continue. Note that in some cases this does not happen and the goodwill is written down as impaired in the financial statements of the acquiring entity.

As can be seen above, goodwill meets the definition of an asset in the Framework.

(d) The main reason for the proposed amendments to the *Framework* is the convergence project the IASB is undertaking with the FASB. The two Boards are aiming to converge accounting standards and an integral part of that is the conceptual framework on which the standards are based.

The Framework has an important role in financial reporting and is the source of reference in dealing with an accounting issue where no standard exists. In US GAAP, the conceptual framework is less important.

Currently the aim is to develop a conceptual framework on sound principles that can be used as the basis for developing accounting standards. The revised conceptual framework will update and refine the existing concepts to reflect changes in markets, business practices and the economic environment over the period since the concepts were originally developed.

The Conceptual Framework for Financial Reporting 2010 was approved by the IASB and FASB and issued in September 2010. It contains two approved chapters of the proposed common framework as follows:

- Chapter 1 – the objective of general purpose financial reporting
- Chapter 3 – qualitative characteristics of useful information

There is no significant change to the underlying purpose and objectives of the Framework as established in the 1989 document. The objectives are described as:

- providing information useful in making investment and credit decisions
- providing information useful in assessing cash flow prospects
- providing information about an entity's resources, claims to those resources and changes in resources and claims.

The users of financial statements are expected to have a reasonable knowledge of business and economic activities and be able to read a financial report. They are expected to review and analyse the information with reasonable diligence.

The two fundamental qualitative characteristics of financial information stated as:

- relevance, and
- faithful representation.

**Relevant information** helps users to evaluate the potential effects of past, present, or future transactions or other events on future cash flows (predictive value) or to confirm or correct their previous evaluations (confirmatory value). Timeliness is another aspect of relevance as information loses its usefulness if not provided in a reasonable timescale.

To be useful in making decisions, information must be a **faithful representation** of the resources and obligations, transactions and events that it purports to represent.

Additionally, there are four enhancing characteristics which enhance the usefulness of information as follows:

**Comparability**, including consistency, enhances the usefulness of financial reporting information. It enables users to identify similarities and differences between two sets of financial information.

**Verifiability** provides assurance to users regarding its credibility and reliability.

**Understandability** is the quality of information that enables users to comprehend its meaning. It is enhanced when information is classified, characterised, and presented clearly and concisely.

The constraints on financial reporting are:

- materiality
- benefits and costs.

Information is material if its omission or misstatement could influence the resource allocation decisions that users make on the basis of an entity's financial report.

The benefits of financial reporting information should justify the costs of providing and using it.

| ACCA marking scheme | | |
|---|---|---|
| | | *Marks* |
| (a) | Gain/loss on sale of shares | 4 |
| (b) | Plant and equipment | 4 |
| | Associate | 4 |
| | Investment | 4 |
| | Goodwill | 7 |
| | Sundry NCA | 2 |
| | Retained earnings | 5 |
| | Non controlling Interest | 2 |
| | | 32 |
| (c) | Goodwill | 6 |
| (d) | Conceptual framework | 12 |
| Total | | 50 |

**5    BRAVADO (JUN 09 EXAM)**  *Walk in the footsteps of a top tutor*

**Key answer tips**

As with many of the group accounting questions, much of the difficulty in part (a) lies in the accounting issues included rather than the preparation of the statement of financial position itself. In particular the question refers to "draft financial statements" which is normally an indication that there are accounting errors within the statements as currently presented. The best way to approach a this type of question is to have a sound knowledge and understanding of the standard workings and layout for the answer, and then to deal with the individual *issues* identified in the question, completing the statement as you deal with each issue. This question includes the following issues: step acquisition and contingent consideration (both IFRS 3 revised) accounting for an associate, financial assets, foreign currency and directors' loans. Ensure that you do not spend too much time on these issues to the exclusion of completing the statement of financial position itself. Start your workings with those issues you find quickest and easiest to deal with. Parts (b) and (c) of the question, which include the professional marks, should be a good source of marks for a well-prepared student as they include ethical and other issues associated with misstatements in the accounts.

(a)    **Bravado – Consolidated Statement of Financial Position at 31 May 2009**

| Assets: | $m | $m |
|---|---|---|
| Non-current assets: | | |
| Property, plant and equipment (W8) | 708.00 | |
| Goodwill (W3) | 25.00 | |
| Investment in associate (W6) | 22.50 | |
| Financial assets at FV through OCI (Issue 1) | 44.60 | 800.10 |
| | | |
| Current assets: | | |
| Inventories (Issue 2) | 245.00 | |
| Trade receivables W11 | 168.00 | |
| Loans to directors (Issue 3) | 1.00 | |
| Cash and cash equivalents (102 + 100 + 8 – 1) (Issue 3) | 209.00 | 623.00 |
| | | |
| Total assets | | 1,423.10 |

| Equity and liabilities | $m | $m |
|---|---|---|
| Equity attributable to owners of parent | | |
| Share capital | 520.00 | |
| Retained earnings (W5) | 272.22 | |
| Other components of equity (W5) | (6.40) | 785.82 |
| | | |
| Non-controlling interest (W4) | | 148.88 |
| | | |
| Total equity of the group | | 934.70 |
| Non-current liabilities | | |
| Long-term borrowings | 140.00 | |
| Deferred tax (W9) | 39.40 | 179.40 |
| | | |
| Current liabilities | | |
| Trade and other payables (W7) | 217.00 | |
| Current tax payable | 92.00 | 309.00 |
| | | |
| Total equity and liabilities | | 1,423.10 |

**Workings**

*ISSUE 1 – THE FINANCIAL ASSET AT FVTOCI*

The foreign equity instrument has been designated to be measured at fair value through other comprehensive income, with any movement in fair value taken to equity.

**Investment a/c – FV through OCI**

| 1 June 2007 | 49.5 | | |
|---|---|---|---|
| (11m × 4.5) | | | |
| *Gain to equity* | *1.5* | Bal c/fwd  31 May 2008 | 51.0 |
| | | (10m × 5.1) | |
| | 51.0 | | 51.0 |
| | | | |
| Bal b/fwd | 51.0 | *Loss to equity* | 17.4 |
| | | Bal c/fwd 31 May 2009 | 33.6 |
| | | (7m × 4.8) | |
| | 51.0 | | 51.0 |

| Summary of financial assets at FVTOCI | $m |
|---|---|
| Bravado – as above | 33.6 |
| Message | 6.0 |
| Mixted | 5.0 |
| | ____ |
| TO SOFP | 44.6 |
| | ____ |

*ISSUE 2 – WRITE DOWN OF INVENTORY*

The inventory must be carried at the lower of cost and NRV under IAS 2 Inventory.

| **Cost** | $m |
|---|---|
| 200,000 units × $1,500 | 300 |
| 100,000 units × $1,000 | 100 |
| | ____ |
| TO SOFP | 400 |
| | ____ |

| **Net realisable value per unit** | |
|---|---|
| Selling price | 1,450 |
| Less selling costs | (10) |
| | ____ |
| TO SOFP | 1,440 |
| Less Conversion costs | (500) |
| | ____ |
| | 940 |
| | ____ |

| NRV | $m |
|---|---|
| 200,000 units × $1,440 | 288 |
| 100,000 units × $940 | 94 |
| | ____ |
| | 382 |
| | ____ |

| Inventory write down required | $m |
|---|---|
| Cost | 400 |
| NRV | 382 |
| | ____ |
| | 18 |
| | ____ |

| Summary of inventory | $m |
|---|---|
| Bravado (135 – 18) | 117 |
| Message | 55 |
| Mixted | 73 |
| | ——— |
| To consolidated SOFP | 245 |
| | ——— |

*ISSUE 3 – THE LOAN TO DIRECTORS*

Showing the loan as cash and cash equivalents is misleading. It should be reclassified as loan to director within current assets.

| | $m |
|---|---|
| Dr Current assets- loans to directors | 1 |
| Cr Cash | 1 |

**Consolidation workings**

*Deal with the accounting issues so that you can complete the statement of financial position as you proceed through the question.*

(W1) **Shareholdings of subsidiaries**

*This requires knowledge of IFRS 3 Revised as there is a step acquisition. The initial shareholding is remeasured to fair value at the date control is acquired. Any gain or loss on remeasurement is taken to profit or loss.*

| | Message | Mixted |
|---|---|---|
| Glove | 80% | 70% (6+64) |
| Non controlling interest | 20% | 30% |
| | | $m |
| Dr Cost of investment | | 5 |
| Cr Profit | | 5 |

(W2)  **Net assets**

*Ensure that you include any fair value adjustments at both the date of acquisition and also assess their impact at the reporting date.*

| MESSAGE | Acq date | Rep date | Post-acq'n |
|---|---|---|---|
| | $m | $m | $m |
| Ordinary shares | 220 | 220 | |
| Retained earnings | 136 | 150 | |
| Other equity | 4 | 4 | |
| | 360 | 374 | |
| FV adj – land (400 – 360) | 40 | 40 | |
| Fair value (given in question) | 400 | 414 | 14 |

| MIXTED | Acq'n date | Rep date | Post-acq'n |
|---|---|---|---|
| | $m | $m | $m |
| Ordinary shares | 100 | 100 | |
| Retained earnings | 55 | 80 | |
| Other equity | 7 | 7 | |
| Book values | 162 | 187 | |
| FV adj - PPE(173 – 162 | 14 | 14 | |
| Less: Dep'n (14 x 1/7) | | (2) | |
| Fair value (170 + 6) | 176 | 199 | |
| Deferred tax liability* | (3) | (3) | |
| Add: deferred tax (2 x 30%) | | 0.6 | 2.4 |
| | 173 | 196.6 | 23.6 |

| *Deferred tax | |
|---|---|
| Carrying Value | 176 |
| Tax Base | 166 |
| Temporary diff (10 x 30%) | 3 |

(W3) **Goodwill**

*Calculated using the preferred basis per IFRS 3 revised and per ACCA-approved answers to previous examination papers. The calculations required goodwill to be calculated on a fair value basis per IFRS 3 Revised, with the calculation for Mixted resulting in negative goodwill.*

| **MESSAGE** | $m |
|---|---|
| Purchase consideration | 300 |
| Fair value of NCI | 86 |
| | 386 |
| FV of NA at acquisition (W2) | 400 |
| FV goodwill (all relates to parent in bargain purchase) | 14 |

| **MIXTED** | $m |
|---|---|
| Purchase consideration | 133 |
| (128 + 5 re initial purchase remeasured | |
| Contingent consideration | 12 |
| FV of NCI at acquisition | 53 |
| | 198 |
| FV of NA at acquisition (W2) | 173 |
| FV goodwill to SOFP | 25 |

Total goodwill for the consolidated statement of financial position is $25m.

(W4) **Non-controlling interest**

*Non-controlling interest is measured on a fair value basis to be consistent with the goodwill accounting policy.*

| | $m |
|---|---|
| **MESSAGE** | |
| FV of NCI at acquisition | 86.00 |
| 20% (414 − 400)(W2) | 2.80 |
| | 88.80 |
| **MIXTED** | |
| FV of NCI at acquisition | 53.00 |
| 30% (196.6 − 173)(W2) | 7.08 |
| To SOFP | 148.88 |

(W5a) **Other components of equity**

*Keep the working for retained earnings and other components of equity separate. Return to your earlier workings to identify any elements which have been identified or calculated which now need to be included within either retained earnings or other reserves.*

|  | $m |
|---|---|
| Bravado | 12.0 |
| Investment in Assoc (W6) | (1.0) |
| Financial asset – impaired | (17.4) |
|  | (6.4) |

(W5b) **Retained earnings**

|  | $m |
|---|---|
| Bravado | 240.00 |
| Less: Inventory write-down (Issue 2) | (18.00) |
| Add: remeasurement of initial holding to FV | 5.00 |
|  | 227.00 |
| Message (414 − 400) = 14 × 80% | 11.20 |
| Mixted (196.6 − 173) = 23.6 × 70%) | 16.52 |
| Share of associate profit (W6) | 2.50 |
| Gain on reclassification of Clarity (W6) | 1.00 |
| Gain on bargain purchase (W3) | 14.00 |
| Total to group SOFP | 272.22 |

*Associates are equity-accounted in the group financial statements. The gain of 1 recorded within other equity should now be deemed realised once the shareholding has been increased to 25%. An adjustment is required to reclassify this gain as follows:*

|  | $m |
|---|---|
| Dr Other components of equity (9–8) | 1 |
| Cr Retained earnings | 1 |

### (W6) Share of associate – Clarity

|  | $m |
|---|---|
| Cost (9 + 11) | 20.0 |
| Share of post acq'n profit (25% × 10) | 2.5 |
| Total to SOFP | 22.5 |

### (W7) Current liabilities – trade payables

*Remember to include the contingent consideration as a current liability.*

|  | $m |
|---|---|
| Bravado | 115 |
| Message | 30 |
| Mixted | 60 |
| Contingent consideration | 12 |
| Total to SOFP | 217 |

### (W8) Property, plant and equipment

*Remember to include the impact of the fair value adjustments at the reporting date.*

|  | $m |
|---|---|
| Bravado | 265 |
| Message | 230 |
| Mixted | 161 |
| FVA adj – land (W2) | 40 |
| FVA adj – PPE (W2) | 14 |
| FVA adj – PPE dep'n (W2) | (2) |
| Total to SOFP | 708 |

### (W9) Deferred Tax

*Remember to include the impact of deferred tax identified at the date of acquisition.*

| | $m |
|---|---|
| Bravado | 25 |
| Message | 9 |
| Mixted | 3 |
| Arising on acquisition | 3 |
| Movement to year-end (W2) | (0.6) |
| | |
| Total to SOFP | 39.4 |

(b)     **Goodwill calculated on a proportionate basis**

*Part (b) requires goodwill to be calculated on a proportionate basis – i.e. the alternative basis to that adopted by Bravado and to comment on the outcome.*

| | Message | Mixted |
|---|---|---|
| | $m | $m |
| Consideration | 300 | 145.0 |
| FV of NCI at acqu'n (20% × 400) | 80 | |
| FV of NCI at acqu'n (30% × 173) | | 51.9 |
| | | |
| | 380 | 196.9 |
| FV of NA at acquisition (W2) | (400) | (173.0) |
| | | |
| Gain on bargain purchase | (20) | 23.9 |

In the case of Mixted, the proportionate method of calculating goodwill results in a smaller value for total assets on the group statement of financial position. Consequently, any write off for impairment of goodwill may have a smaller effect upon the group financial statements. Additionally in the case of Message, it results in a higher gain on the bargain purchase which increases the reported income.

*Part (c) of the question requires comment on the ethical and other responsibilities of directors where there may be a misclassification or misstatement within the accounts. Any comments should be applied to the specific situation identified within the question.*

(c)     Showing a loan as cash and cash equivalents is misleading. The Framework says that financial statements should have certain characteristics:

(a)     understandability

(b)     relevance

(c)     reliability

(d)     comparability

These concepts would preclude the showing of directors' loans in cash. Such information needs separate disclosure as it is relevant to users as it shows the nature of the practices carried out by the company. Reliability requires information to be free from bias and faithfully represent transactions. Comparability is not possible if transactions are not correctly classified. Directors are responsible for the statutory financial statements and if they believe that they are not complying with IFRS, they should take all steps to ensure that the error or irregularity is rectified. Every director will be deemed to have knowledge of the content of the financial statements. In some countries loans to directors are illegal and directors can be personally liable. Directors have a responsibility to act honestly and ethically and not be motivated by personal interest and gain. If the ethical conduct of the directors is questionable then other areas of the financial statements may need scrutiny. A loan of this nature could create a conflict of interest as the directors' personal interests may interfere or conflict with those of the company's. The accurate and full recording of business activities is essential to fulfil the financial and legal obligations of a director as is the efficient use of corporate assets. The loan to a director conflicts with the latter

| | ACCA marking scheme | Marks |
|---|---|---|
| (a) | Message | 5 |
| | Mixted | 6 |
| | Clarity | 4 |
| | Financial asset at FVTOCI | 3 |
| | Retained earnings | 3 |
| | Post acquisition reserves | 2 |
| | Other components of equity | 2 |
| | Current liabilities | 1 |
| | NCI | 2 |
| | Inventories | 2 |
| | PPE | 2 |
| | Financial asset at FVTOCI | 1 |
| | Deferred tax | 1 |
| | Trade receivables | 1 |
| | | 35 |
| (b) | Message | 3 |
| | Mixted | 3 |
| | Explanation | 2 |
| (c) | Subjective | 7 |
| Total | | 50 |

**Examiner's comments**

This question required the preparation of a consolidated statement of financial position using the full goodwill method, a calculation and explanation of the impact on the calculation of goodwill if the non-controlling interest was calculated on a proportionate basis and a discussion of the ethics of showing a loan to a director as cash and cash equivalents. The main body of the question required candidates to deal with the calculation of goodwill in a simple situation, the calculation of goodwill where there was a prior holding in the subsidiary, an investment in an associate, a foreign currency transaction, deferred tax and impairment of inventory. Generally speaking the basic calculation of goodwill under the full goodwill method was well done by candidates. However the calculation of goodwill in a more complex situation where there was a prior holding, contingent consideration and deferred taxation was less well done. Candidates often calculated the change in the fair value of the available for sale financial instrument correctly although many used the wrong basis for the exchange rates. The main problem with this element of the question was the double entry for the transaction. Part of the change in fair value should have been charged to profit or loss and part to other components of equity. Many candidates did not deal with the transaction in this way. Many candidates did not complete the retained earnings calculation and often there was doubt over where the gain on bargain purchase should be recorded. (Group retained profits) The calculation of the impairment of inventories was dealt with quite well by candidates, as was the increase in the value of PPE and land. Often the increase in the depreciation charge as a result of the revaluation of PPE was not calculated correctly, nor was the deferred taxation effect. The main problem for candidates in calculating the NCI was the determination of the correct figure for post acquisition reserves especially as many candidates did not treat the depreciation charge and deferred taxation correctly. In part b of the question, a surprising number of candidates could not calculate goodwill using the proportionate basis. Candidates often calculated goodwill correctly in the simple case but as soon as any complexity was introduced the calculations were inaccurate. Many candidates left out part c completely. This was a little disturbing as part c dealt with the ethics of showing loans to directors as cash. Those candidates who answered the question dealt with the issues quite well.

**6    WARRBURT (DEC 08 EXAM)**  *Walk in the footsteps of a top tutor*

**Key answer tips**

As with many of the group accounting questions, much of the difficulty in part (a) lies in the accounting issues included rather than the preparation of the cash flow statement itself. In particular the question refers to "draft financial statements" which is normally an indication that there are accounting errors within the statements as currently presented. The best way to approach a cash flow question is to have a sound knowledge and understanding of the standard presentation for the statement, and then to deal with the individual issues identified in the question, completing the statement as you deal with each issue. This question includes the following issues: financial assets, retirement benefits, non-current asset additions including foreign currency, purchase of an interest in an associate and payments for taxation and dividends. Ensure that you do not spend too much time on these issues to the exclusion of completing the cash flow statement itself. Start your workings with those issues you find quickest and easiest to deal with. Parts (b) and (c) of the question, which include the professional marks, should be a good source of marks for a well-prepared student.

(a)  **Warrburt Group Statement of cash flows for year ended 30 November 2008**

| | $m | $m | |
|---|---:|---:|---:|
| Net loss before tax | | (21) | |
| Adjustments to operating activities | | | |
| Gain on disposal of financial assets at FVTOCI (W1) | (7) | | |
| Gain on assets destroyed (3 – 1) (W3) | (2) | | |
| Other investment income (31 – 7 – 2)(W1) | (22) | | |
| Retirement benefit expense (W2) | 10 | | |
| Depreciation | 36 | | |
| Profit on sale of PPE (63 – 56) | (7) | | |
| Exchange loss (W8) | 2 | | |
| Associates profit (working (W4) | (8) | | |
| Impairment of goodwill and intangible assets | 32 | | |
| Finance costs | 9 | 43 | |
| | —— | | |
| Decrease in trade receivables (92 – 163) | 71 | | |
| Decrease in inventories (135 – 198) | 63 | | |
| Decrease in trade payables (115 – 21 – 180) | (86) | 48 | 70 |
| | —— | —— | |
| Cash paid to retirement benefit scheme (W2) | | (10) | |
| Finance costs paid (W6) | | (8) | |
| Income taxes paid (W5) | | (39) | (57) |
| | | —— | |
| Cash flows from investing activities: | | | |
| Sale of financial assets at FVTOCI (W1) | | 45 | |
| Purchase of PPE (W8) | | (57) | |
| Proceeds from sale of PPE | | 63 | |
| Dividend received from associate (W4) | | 2 | |
| Purchase of associate (W4) | | (96) | |
| Other investment income | | 22 | (21) |
| | | —— | |
| Cash flows from financial activities: | | | |
| Proceeds of issue of share capital (595 – 650) | | 55 | |
| Repayment of long term borrowings (64 – 20) | | (44) | |
| Non-controlling interest dividend (W7) | | (5) | |
| Dividends paid per SOCIE | | (9) | (3) |
| | | —— | —— |
| Net decrease in cash and cash equivalents | | | (11) |
| Cash and cash equivalents at beginning of period | | | 323 |
| | | | —— |
| Cash and cash equivalents at end of period | | | 312 |
| | | | —— |

*Workings*

*Deal with the accounting issues so that you can complete the statement of cash flows as you proceed through the question.*

**ISSUE – FINANCIAL ASSETS at FVTOCI**

**(W1)  Financial assets at FVTOCI**

The sale proceeds of the financial assets were $45 million thus creating a profit on disposal of $7 million. However, there is also realisation of a gain on earlier revaluations in equity and this has correctly been transferred to retained earnings.

The other income per the statement of comprehensive income must be broken down to its various elements to ensure that they are correctly accounted for within the statement of cash flows as follows:

|  | $m |
|---|---|
| Sale proceeds | 45 |
| Carrying value | (38) |
| | ─── |
| Profit on disposal of financial assets | 7 |
| Gain on destroyed assets (3 – 1) (W3) | 2 |
| Other investment income | 22 |
| | ─── |
| Other income per SOCI | 31 |
| | ─── |

---

*This requires knowledge of accounting for defined benefit obligations, so that the cash flow impact can be identified.*

---

**ISSUE – THE DEFINED BENEFIT RETIREMENT LIABILITY**

**(W2)**  The benefits paid to beneficiaries of the retirement benefit scheme are paid out of the scheme's assets and not the company's. Hence there is no cash flow effect for the benefits paid and nor is there a cash flow impact for the expense charged.  There will be a cash flow for contributions paid into the scheme.

---

*This requires knowledge of accounting for non-current assets, so that the cash flow impact can be identified.*

---

**ISSUE – THE LOSS ON DESTROYED ASSETS AND REPLACEMENT BY INSURANCE COMPANY**

**(W3)**  The loss on the disposal of the destroyed assets of $1 million and the fair value of the new plant at $3 million provided by the insurance company, giving a gain of $2 million, should not be recognised in the statement of cash flows; the machines were obtained directly by the insurance company and not by Warrburt.

*This requires knowledge of accounting for associates so that the cash flow impact can be identified.*

### ISSUE – THE ASSOCIATE

(W4)  **Associate**

|  | $m |
|---|---|
| Investment in associate – cash paid in year | 96 |
| Add: Share of profit after tax for period $24m × 25% | 8 |
| Less: Share of tax ($8m × 25%) included within tax charge | (2) |
| Less: Dividend received $8m × 25% | (2) |
|  | ––– |
| Balance c'fwd per SOFP | 100 |
|  | ––– |

Work backwards from the year-end balance to identify the cash paid. Therefore, cash paid for the investment is $96 million, and cash received from the dividend is $2 million. The share of the profit of the associate before tax is $8 million and tax thereon will therefore be $2 million, which has been wrongly included in the group tax charge.

*This requires knowledge of accounting for income tax of the group, excluding that of the associate.*

### ISSUE – INCOME TAX

(W5)  **Taxation**

|  | $m |
|---|---|
| Opening tax balances (26 + 42) | 68 |
| Charge for the year per IS | 31 |
| Deferred tax re financial asset at FVTOCI revaluation gain | 3 |
| Deferred tax on property revaluation gains | 2 |
| Tax on associate profit (working (iv)) | (2) |
| Less: closing tax balances (28 + 35) | (63) |
|  | ––– |
| Cash paid | 39 |
|  | ––– |

The tax charge on the financial asset ($3m) and the revaluation gain ($2m) is adjusted on the tax charge for the year.

In the statement of comprehensive income for the year, Warrburt has accounted for the associate's share of profit before tax in arriving at the group loss before tax. The share of associate's tax is therefore within the group income tax charge and must be removed.

**(W6)   Short term provisions**

|  | $m |
|---|---|
| Opening balance | 4 |
| Finance costs per Group IS | 9 |
| Closing balance | (5) |
|  | ——— |
| Cash paid | 8 |
|  | ——— |

**(W7)   Non controlling Interest**

|  | $m |
|---|---|
| Opening balance | 53 |
| NCI share of total comprehensive income | 22 |
| Closing balance | (70) |
|  | ——— |
| Cash paid | 5 |
|  | ——— |

*This requires knowledge of accounting for foreign currency transactions, together with identifying cash flows associated with additions to property, plant and equipments.*

**(W8)   Additions of PPE and foreign exchange losses on amount payable**

The purchase of imported plant and equipment will be recorded at 380 million dinars ÷ 5, i.e. $76 million. However, this has not been paid for in full by the year-end, so only the cash outflow during the year should be recognised in the statement of cash flows. At 31 October 2008, the cash outflow will be recorded at 280 million dinars ÷ 4.9, i.e. $57 million giving a loss on exchange of $1 million (57 – 280/5). At the year end the monetary liability will be recorded at 100 million dinars ÷ 4.8, i.e. $21 million giving a loss on exchange of $1 million (21 – (100/5). The total loss will be eliminated from cash generated from operations ($2 million), the cash flow will be $57 million and the decrease in trade payables will be $86 million.

| **Property plant & equipment** | $m |
|---|---|
| Opening PPE  balance b'fwd | 360 |
| Net gain on property revaluation | 2 |
| Deferred tax on property revaluation (see tax working) | 2 |
| Gain on assets destroyed and replaced (tfr to other income) | 2 |
| NCA purchased in foreign currency* | 76 |
| Less: depreciation | (36) |
| Less: disposals | (56) |
|  | ——— |
| Closing PPE bal c'fwd | 350 |
|  | ——— |

***Note:*** The addition was purchased in foreign currency – use the rate ruling on the date of the transaction, 30 June 2008, to record both the cost of the asset and the liability for the amount payable.

| Trade payables | $m |
|---|---|
| Opening balance b'fwd | 180 |
| NCA purchased in foreign currency* | 76 |
| Payment made in foreign currency | (57) |
| Exchange loss on payment in foreign currency | 1 |
| Exchange loss on outstanding payable in foreign currency | 1 |
| Movement – decrease in payables for the year | (86) |
| | ___ |
| Closing balance c'fwd | 115 |
| | ___ |

| Summary of accounting for foreign asset: | Dinar m | Rate | $m |
|---|---|---|---|
| 30 June 2008 – purchase and liability recorded | 380 | 5.0 | 76 |
| 31 Oct 2008 – payment | (280) | 4.9 | (57) |
| 31 Oct 2008 - exchange loss on payment (280/5.0) – (280/4.9) – within admin expenses | | | 1 |
| 30 Nov 2008 - exchange loss on year-end payable (100/5) – (100/4.8) – within admin expenses | | | 1 |
| | ___ | | ___ |
| 30 Nov 2008 – balance c'wd within trade payables | 100 | | 21 |
| | ___ | | ___ |

---

*The remaining narrative parts of the question should not be under-estimated. They require specific and detailed points to achieve a good mark, rather than general, vague or imprecise comments not applied to the information provided.*

---

(b)   Financial statement ratios can provide useful measures of liquidity but an analysis of the information in the cash flow statement, particularly cash flow generated from operations, can provide specific insights into the liquidity of Warrburt. It is important to look at the generation of cash and its efficient usage. An entity must generate cash from trading activity in order to avoid the constant raising of funds from non-trading sources. The 'quality of the profits' is a measure of an entity's ability to do this. The statement of cash flow shows that the company has generated cash in the period despite sustaining a significant loss ($92m cash flow but $21m loss). The problem is the fact that the entity will not be able to sustain this level of cash generation if losses continue.

An important measure of cash flow is the comparison of the cash from operating activity to current liabilities. In the case of Warrburt, this is $70m as compared to $155m. Thus the cash flow has not covered the current liabilities.

Operating cash flow ($70 million) determines the extent to which Warrburt has generated sufficient funds to repay loans, maintain operating capability, pay dividends and make new investments without external financing. Operating cash flow appears to be healthy, partially through the release of cash from working capital. This cash flow has been used to pay contributions to the pension scheme, pay finance costs and income taxes. These uses of cash generated would be normal for any entity. However, the release of working capital has also financed in part the investing activities of the entity which includes the purchase of an associate and property, plant and equipment. The investing activities show a net cash outflow of $21 million after accounting for investment income which has been financed partly out of working capital and partly out of cash generated from operations which include changes in working capital. It seems also that the issue of share capital has been utilised to repay the long term borrowings and pay dividends. Also a significant amount of cash has been raised through selling the financial assets at FVTOCI. This may not continue in the future as it will depend on the liquidity of the market. This action seems to indicate that the long term borrowings have effectively been 'capitalised'. The main issue raised by the cash flow statement is the use of working capital to partially finance investing activities. However, the working capital ratio and liquidity ratios are still quite healthy but these ratios will deteriorate if the trend continues.

(c) Companies can give the impression that they are generating more cash than they are, by manipulating cash flow. The way in which acquisitions, loans and, as in this case, the sale of assets, is shown in the statement of cash flows, can change the nature of operating cash flow and hence the impression given by the financial statements. The classification of cash flows can give useful information to users and operating cash flow is a key figure. The role of ethics in the training and professional lives of accountants is extremely important. Decision-makers expect the financial statements to be true and fair and fairly represent the underlying transactions.

There is a fine line between deliberate misrepresentation and acceptable presentation of information. Pressures on management can result in the misrepresentation of information. Financial statements must comply with International Financial Reporting Standards (IFRS), the Framework and local legislation. Transparency, and full and accurate disclosure is important if the financial statements are not to be misleading. Accountants must possess a high degree of professional integrity and the profession's reputation depends upon it. Ethics describe a set of moral principles taken as a reference point. These principles are outside the technical and practical application of accounting and require judgement in their application. Professional accountancy bodies set out ethical guidelines within which their members operate covering standards of behaviour, and acceptable practice. These regulations are supported by a number of codes, for example, on corporate governance which assist accountants in making ethical decisions. The accountant in Warrburt has a responsibility not to mask the true nature of the statement of cash flow. Showing the sale of assets as an operating cash flow would be misleading if the nature of the transaction was masked. Users of financial statements would not expect its inclusion in this heading and could be misled. The potential misrepresentation is unacceptable. The accountant should try and persuade the directors to follow acceptable accounting principles and comply with accounting standards. There are implications for the truth and fairness of the financial statements and the accountant should consider his position if the directors insist on the adjustments by pointing the inaccuracies out to the auditors.

| ACCA marking scheme | | |
|---|---|---|
| | | *Marks* |
| (a) | Net loss before tax | 1 |
| | Financial instruments | 4 |
| | Retirement benefit | 3 |
| | Property, plant and equipment | 6 |
| | Insurance proceeds | 2 |
| | Associate | 4 |
| | Goodwill and intangibles | 1 |
| | Finance costs | 2 |
| | Taxation | 4 |
| | Working capital | 4 |
| | Proceeds of share issue | 1 |
| | Repayment of borrowings | 1 |
| | Dividends | 1 |
| | Non-controlling interest | 1 |
| | | —— |
| | | 35 |
| (b) | Discussion, including professional marks | 10 |
| (c) | Discussion, including professional marks | 5 |
| | | —— |
| Total | | 50 |
| | | —— |

**Examiner's comments**

This question required candidates to produce a statement of cash flows which involved adjusting for disposal of financial assets, dealing with the cash consequences of a retirement benefit liability, adjusting for the purchase of a subsidiary and the purchase of property, plant and equipment (PPE) from overseas as well as the normal adjustments required to produce a statement of cash flows. Candidates generally performed well on part (a) of the question producing good answers, which were rewarded with good marks on this part. The main issues, which caused problems, were the new IAS 1 format of the financial statements, which many candidates were not familiar with and the treatment of the benefits paid by the trustees of the defined benefit scheme, which had no cash flow effect. The calculation of the exchange loss on the PPE was problematical for some candidates from the viewpoint of how to treat it in the statement of cash flows. Also the calculation of trade payables often failed to take into account the creditor for the purchase of plant.

Part (b) of the question required a discussion of the key issues which the cash flow highlighted. Candidates were required to use the information in their answers to part a of the question in order to determine the cash flow problems which the company had such as the use of working capital to finance the investing activities of the company. Many candidates did not use the information in the first part of the question in answering this part but gave general advantages and disadvantages of statements of cash flows. This did attract some credit but in questions such as this one, candidates answered part (b) before part (a) and then failed to gain marks for as they failed to relate their answers to part (a).

Part (c) of the question required candidates to discuss the ethical responsibilities of an accountant when the directors have made suggestions of unethical practices. Candidates needed to discuss the nature of technical good practice and integrity and what is acceptable practice in terms of deliberate misrepresentation and presentation. This part of the question was quite well answered. However, candidates should develop a greater understanding of ethical principles rather than simple the ability to reiterate the ethical codes.

**7     MEMO (JUN 04 EXAM)**

**Key answer tips**

Part (a) is a normal straightforward consolidation – there are a few adjustments to be dealt with but nothing too complicated, except perhaps accounting for the group exchange difference, which surprisingly does not appear to attract many examination marks.  It is a good question to test your understanding of the requirement of IAS 21 that goodwill arising should be treated as a foreign currency asset and retranslated at the end of each reporting period.  Otherwise the consolidation proceeds as normal.

Part (b) of the question is mainly discussion of presentation and functional currency.

(a)     **Memo Group – Consolidated statement of financial position as at 30 April 20X4**

|  | $m |
|---|---|
| Goodwill (W3) | 11.1 |
| Property, plant and equipment (297 + (146/2.1)) | 366.5 |
| Current Assets (355 + (102/2.1) – 0.6 (W8)) | 403.0 |
|  | ——— |
|  | 780.6 |
|  | ——— |

|  | $m |
|---|---|
| Equity shares of $1 | 60.0 |
| Share premium account | 50.0 |
| Retained earnings (W5) | 364.3 |
| Foreign exchange reserve (W7) | 8.8 |
|  | ——— |
|  | 483.1 |
| Non controlling interest (W4) | 19.8 |
|  | ——— |
| Total equity of the group | 502.9 |
| Non-current liabilities (30 + ((41 – 2 (W9))/2.1) – 5 (inter-co)) | 43.6 |
| Current liabilities (205 + ((60 + 1.2 (W8))/2.1)) | 234.1 |
|  | ——— |
|  | 780.6 |
|  | ——— |

**Consolidated statement of profit or loss and other comprehensive income for the year ended 30 April 20X4**

| | $m |
|---|---|
| Revenue (200 + (142/2.0) – 6 (W8)) | 265.0 |
| Cost of sales (120 + ((96 + 2.6 (W3))/2.0) – 6 + 0.6 (W8)) | (163.9) |
| | ───── |
| Gross profit | 101.1 |
| Distribution and administrative expenses (30 + (20/2)) | (40.0) |
| Interest payable (2/2) | (1.0) |
| Interest receivable | 4.0 |
| Net exchange gains on transactions (W8/W9) ((2.0 – 1.2)/2.0) | 0.4 |
| | ───── |
| Profit before taxation | 64.5 |
| Tax (20 +(9/2.0)) | (24.5) |
| | ───── |
| Profit for the year | 40.0 |
| Other comprehensive income – items that may be reclassified to profit or loss in future periods: | |
| Exchange difference on translation of foreign subsidiary (W7) | 11.7 |
| | ───── |
| Total comprehensive income for the year | 51.7 |
| | ───── |

| Profit attributable to: | $m |
|---|---|
| Owners of the parent – bal fig | 38.3 |
| Non-controlling interest (W10) | 1.7 |
| | ───── |
| Profit for the year | 40.0 |
| | ───── |

| Total comprehensive income attributable to: | $m |
|---|---|
| Owners of the parent (bal fig) | 47.1 |
| Non-controlling interest (W10) | 4.6 |
| | ───── |
| Total comprehensive income for the year | 51.7 |
| | ───── |

*Workings*

(W1) **Group structure**

Memo

75%

Random

**(W2)  Net assets and summarised translation**

|  | At acq'n | At rep date |  |  |
|---|---|---|---|---|
|  | Cr(m) | Cr(m) | Rate | $m |
| Equity capital | 146 | 146 |  |  |
| Share premium | 20 | 20 |  |  |
| Pre-acquisition retained earnings | 80 | 80 |  |  |
|  |  | 132.0 | 2.5 | 52.8 |
| Post-acq'n earnings (95 – 80) |  | 15.0 ) |  |  |
| Ex loss on settled liability (W8) |  | (1.2) ) | **Bal fig** | **17.6** |
| Ex gain on restated foreign loan |  | 2.0 ) |  |  |
|  | 132 | 147.8 | 2.1 | 62.9 |

The net assets are translated at the exchange rate ruling at that date. The net assets at the reporting date are translated at the rate applicable at that date. Post-acquisition reserves of the subsidiary in $ are the balancing figure.

**(W3)  Goodwill in functional currency and retranslation schedule**

|  | Cr(m) | Rate | $m |
|---|---|---|---|
| Cost of acquisition | 120.0 |  |  |
| FV of NCI at acquisition | 38.0 |  |  |
|  | 158.0 |  |  |
| Less: FV net assets acquired (W2) | (132.0) |  |  |
| Full goodwill at acquisition | 26.0 |  |  |
| Impairment in year – 10% | (2.6) | 2.0 | 1.3 |
| Unimpaired at reporting date | 23.4 | 2.1 | 11.1 |

As the full goodwill method has been used, the impairment is allocated between the group and NCI based upon their respective shareholdings:

Group (75% × 1.3) = $1.0m (W5)

NCI (25% × 1.3) = $0.3 (W4)

Gain or loss on retranslation of goodwill:

|  | Cr(m) | Rate | $m |
|---|---|---|---|
| At acquisition | 26.0 | 2.5 acq'n rate | 10.4 |
| Impaired in year 10% | (2.6) | 2.0 ave | (1.3) |
| **Exchange gain on retranslation** |  | **Bal fig** | **2.0** |
| At rep date | 23.4 | 2.1 cl rate | 11.1 |

As the full goodwill method has been used, the exchange gain on retranslation is allocated between the group and NCI based upon their respective shareholdings:

Group (75% × $2.0m) = $1.5m (W5)

NCI (25% × $2.0m) = $0.5m (W4)

### (W4) Non-controlling Interest

|  | Cr(m) | Rate | $m |
|---|---|---|---|
| FV of NCI at acquisition | 38.0 | 2.5 | 15.2 |
| 25% × (147.8 – 132) (W2) | 4.0 | 2.0 | 2.0 |
| NCI share of goodwill impairment (W3) |  |  | (0.3) |
| NCI % of goodwill retranslation gain (W3) |  |  | 0.5 |
| NCI % of net assets retranslation gain (W6) |  |  | 2.4 |
|  |  |  | ———— |
|  |  |  | 19.8 |
|  |  |  | ———— |

### (W5) Group retained earnings

|  | $m |
|---|---|
| Memo | 360.0 |
| (75% × 147.8 – 132) (W2) (i.e. average rate) | 5.9 |
| Unrealised profit on inventory (W8) | (0.6) |
| Group share of goodwill impairment (W3) | (1.0) |
|  | ———— |
|  | 364.3 |
|  | ———— |

### (W6) Gain or loss on retranslation of net assets

|  | Cr(m) | Rate | $m |
|---|---|---|---|
| At acquisition | 132.0 | 2.5 acq'n rate | 52.8 |
| Profit for year | 15.8 | 2.0 ave | 7.9 |
| **Exchange gain on retranslation** |  | **Bal fig** | **9.7** |
|  | ———— |  | ———— |
| At rep date | 147.8 | 2.1 cl rate | 70.4 |
|  | ———— |  | ———— |

The exchange gain on retranslation of net assets is allocated between the group and NCI based upon their respective shareholdings:

Group (75% × $9.7m) = $7.3m (W7)

NCI (25% × $9.7m) = $2.4m (W4)

(W7) **Summary of exchange gains on retranslation**

|  | Total | Group | NCI |
|---|---|---|---|
|  | $m | $m | $m |
| Goodwill (W3) | 2.0 | 1.5 | 0.5 |
| Net assets (W6) | 9.7 | 7.3 | 2.4 |
| At rep date | 11.7 | 8.8 | 2.9 |

The total exchange gains on retranslation for the year of $11.7m are accounted for s n item of other comprehensive income for the year. The group share of the gains is included as an item of other components of equity – it is effectively an unrealised amount. The NCI share of the gains on retranslation for the year is included in the NCI balance at the reporting date.

(W8) **Intercompany purchases from Memo**

|  | $m |
|---|---|
| Profit made by Memo $6 million × 20% | 1.2 |
| Profit remaining in inventory at year-end (½) | 0.6 |

|  | CRm |
|---|---|
| Purchase from Memo in crowns ($6 million × 2) | 12.0 |
| *Less* payment made ($6 million × 2.2) | (13.2) |
| Exchange loss to profit or loss of Random | (1.2) |

The exchange loss will be translated at the average rate (2 CR to $1) into dollars, i.e. $0.6 million. The fact that group cash flows have been affected by foreign currency fluctuations would mean that this loss will be reported in the group profit or loss.

The adjusting journal is:

| DR | Profit or loss – exchange loss | CR 1.2m ($0.6m) |
|---|---|---|
| CR | Current liabilities | CR 1.2m ($0.6m) |

This is adjusted in Random's accounts in Crowns (W2).

(W9) **Intercompany loan**

There is no exchange difference in the financial statements of Memo as the loan is denominated in dollars. However, there is an exchange gain arising in the financial statements of Random.

|  | CRm |
|---|---|
| Loan at 1 May 20X3 $5 million at 2.5 | 12.5 |
| Loan at 30 April 20X4 $5 million at 2.1 | 10.5 |
| Exchange gain to Random profit or loss | 2.0 |

This will be translated into dollars at 30 April 20X4 and will appear in the consolidated profit or loss (2 million crowns ÷ 2, i.e. $1 million). The reason is that the loan was taken out in the currency of the holding company and the subsidiary was exposed to the foreign currency risk.

**(W10) Allocation of profit for the year and total comprehensive income**

|  | Cr(m) | Rate | $m |
|---|---|---|---|
| Profit aft tax | 15.8 | | |
| Goodwill impaired | (2.6) | | |
| **NCI % of profit for year – 25%** | **13.2** | **2.0** | **1.7** |
| NCI % of exchange gains on retranslation (W7) | | | 2.9 |
| **NCI share of total comp income** | | | **4.6** |

(b) The **functional currency** is the currency of the primary economic environment where the entity operates. In most cases this will be the local currency.

The functional currency is the currency an entity will use in its day to day transactions. IAS 21 specifically states that an entity should consider the following factors in determining its functional currency:

- the currency that mainly influences sales prices for goods and services
- the currency of the country whose competitive forces and regulations mainly determine the sales price of goods and services
- the currency that mainly influences labour, material and other costs of providing goods and services
- the currency in which funding from issuing debt and equity is generated
- the currency in which receipts from operating activities are usually retained.

The first three points are seen to be the primary factors in determining functional currency.

The **presentation currency** is the currency in which the entity presents its financial statements. This can be different from the functional currency, particularly if the entity in question is a foreign owned subsidiary. It may have to present its financial statements in the currency of its parent, even though that is different from its own functional currency.

| ACCA marking scheme | | Marks |
|---|---|---|
| (a) | Consolidated statement of financial position | |
| | Translation of sub statement of financial position | 6 |
| | Goodwill | 4 |
| | Non controlling interest | 2 |
| | Post acquisition reserves | 1 |
| | Group statement of financial position | 5 |
| | Consolidated statement of comprehensive income | 5 |
| | Unrealised profit | 4 |
| | Loan | 3 |
| | | 30 |
| (b) | Definition of functional currency | 5 |
| | Definition of presentation currency | 3 |
| Total (adjusted) | | 38 |

**8    BETH (DEC 07 EXAM)**  *Online question assistance*

**Key answer tips**

This past examination question has been revised to include accounting for a step acquisition (introduced by IFRS 3 Revised). It also includes several accounting adjustments for non-current assets, unrealised profits and foreign currency, share-based payments and factoring. You should deal with the accounting adjustments first, so that they can then be incorporated into the completed group statement of financial position.

Part (b) of the question deals with the benefits of producing an environmental report, together with associated ethical and social issues.

(a)    **Beth Group**

**Consolidated statement of financial position at 30 November 2007**

|  | $m |
|---|---|
| **Assets** | |
| **Non-current assets** | |
| Property, plant and equipment (1,900 + 12 – 2) | 1,910 |
| Intangible assets | 300 |
| Goodwill | 40 |
| Investment in associate | 183 |
| | ——— |
| | 2,433 |

|  | $m |
|---|---|
| **Current assets** | |
| inventories | 900 |
| Trade receivables (600 + 60 – 1 + 50) | 709 |
| Cash and cash equivalents | 540 |
| | ——— |
| | 2,149 |
| | ——— |
| **Total assets** | 4,582 |
| | ——— |

|  | $m |
|---|---|
| Equity capital of $1 | 1,500 |
| Other reserves (300 + 9) | 309 |
| Retained earnings | 463 |
| Non-controlling interest (W4) | 72 |
| | ——— |
| Total equity of the group | 2,344 |
| Non-current liabilities (700 + 11 + 2) | 713 |
| Current liabilities (1,380 + 100 + 45) | 1,525 |
| | ——— |
| **Total equity and liabilities** | 4,582 |
| | ——— |

Where the acquirer already has an investment in the company and a further investment means that control is acquired then this is a step acquisition (piecemeal acquisition). In these circumstances the previously held investment is remeasured at fair value and the change in value reported in profit or loss. The original investment in Lose of $40m now has a fair value of the investment of $70m giving a gain of $30m.

*Workings*

(W1) **Net Assets**

|  | Lose At acq'n $m | Lose At rep date $m | Gain At acq'n $m | Gain At rep date $m |
|---|---|---|---|---|
| Ordinary shares | 100 | 100 | 200 | 200 |
| Retained profits | 150 | 200 | 260 | 300 |
| Fair value adj | Nil | Nil | Nil | Nil |
| Total | 250 | 300 | 460 | 500 |

| Corrections | | |
|---|---|---|
| Reverse the write off of improvement expenditure as it should be capitalised (W10) |  | 10 |
| Decommissioning costs – both NCA and liability (W10) |  | 2 |
|  |  | (2) |
| Less: additional depreciation on the improvements (W10) |  | (2) |
|  | 250 | 308 |

(W2) **Goodwill**

|  | Lose $m |
|---|---|
| Cost of Investment (70 as revalued plus 160) | 230 |
| Fair value of NCI at acquisition | 60 |
|  | 290 |
| Less FV of NV at acquisition (W2) | (250) |
| Full goodwill at acquisition | 40 |

### (W3) **Group retained earnings**

|  | $m |
|---|---|
| Retained earnings – Beth | 400 |
| Gain on revaluation of initial investment in Lose (70 – 40) | 30 |
| Less Impairment loss on associate goodwill (W5) | (6) |
| Less the group % of the associate's URPS prov'n 30% × (28 – 18) | (3) |
| Loss on monetary item – foreign currency (W6) | (1) |
| Factor – reversal of entry (W7) | 5 |
| Share options (W8) | (9) |
| Provision (W9) | (11) |
| Group % of the post acquisition profits: | |
| Lose 80% × (308 – 250) | 46 |
| Gain 30% × (500 – 460) | 12 |
| Retained earnings at 30 November 2007 | 463 |

### (W4) **Non-controlling interest in Lose**

|  | $m |
|---|---|
| FV of NCI at acquisition | 60 |
| 20% × (308 – 250)(W1) | 12 |
|  | 72 |

### (W5) **Intercompany profit and the associate 'Gain'**

IAS 28 requires profits and losses resulting from transactions between the investor and an associate to be recognised in the investor's financial statements only to the extent of the unrelated investor's interests in the associate. Effectively part of Beth's profit on the sale is eliminated to the extent of the company's shareholding in Gain.

|  | $m |
|---|---|
| Inventory: selling price | 28 |
| Cost | (18) |
| Profit | 10 |

Profit eliminated $10 million × 30%, i.e. $3 million

Dr   Profit or loss/ retained earnings $3 million

Cr   Investment in associate $3 million

Associate

|                          |              | $m   |
|--------------------------|--------------|------|
| Cost of investment       |              | 180  |
| 30% × (500 − 460)(W1)    |              | 12   |
|                          |              | ———  |
|                          |              | 192  |
|                          |              |      |
| Less the purp            |              | (3)  |
|                          |              | ———  |
| Carrying value           |              | 189  |
| Recoverable amount       | (30% × 610)  | 183  |
|                          |              | ———  |
| Impairment loss          |              | 6    |

(W6) **Deposit paid**

If the payment to the supplier is a deposit and is refundable, then the amount is deemed to be a monetary amount which should be retranslated at the year end.

Deposit paid 50% × 12 million euros ÷ 0.75 = $8 million

At 30 November 2007, the deposit would be retranslated at 6 million euros ÷ 0.85, i.e. $7 million. Therefore, there will be an exchange loss of $(8 − 7) million, i.e. $1 million.

Dr    Retained earnings $1 million

Cr    Trade receivables $1 million

(W7) **Factored trade receivables**

IFRS 9 requires derecognition of a financial asset if the contractual rights to the cash flows have expired or the financial asset has been transferred and so have the risks and rewards of ownership of the asset. In the case of the sale of the trade receivables, the first criterion above has been met, but the second has not necessarily been met. Although the trade receivables are high quality debts, there is still a risk of default particularly as they are long dated, and that risk still lies with Beth. Therefore, the trade receivables should continue to be recognised at amortised cost and the monies received shown as a current liability. The reversing entries should be:

|                             | $m  |
|-----------------------------|-----|
| Dr    Trade receivables     | 50  |
| Cr    Current liabilities   | 45  |
|        Retained earnings    | 5   |

(W8) **Share options**

200 options × (10,000 − 1,100) × 1/2 × $10 = $8.9 million

Dr    Retained earnings $9 million (rounded)

Cr    Equity $9 million

At the grant date, the fair value of the award is determined, but then at each reporting date until vesting, a best estimate of the cumulative charge to profit or loss is made, taking into account:

(i)     the grant date fair value of the award ($10 per option)

(ii)    the current best estimate of the number of awards that will vest (89%)

(iii)   the expired portion of the vesting period (1 year)

(W9)  **Environmental provision**

An enterprise must recognise a provision if, and only if:

(i)     a present obligation (legal or constructive) has arisen as a result of a past event (the obligating event)

(ii)    payment is probable ('more likely than not'), and

(iii)   the amount can be estimated reliably

In this case, a provision should be made to include the costs of contamination in the countries where the law is to be enacted or has been enacted as there will be a legal obligation in those countries. Moral obligations to rectify environmental damage do not justify making a provision. Therefore, a provision of $(7 + 4) million, i.e. $11 million, should be made.

Dr     Retained earnings $11 million

Cr     Non-current liabilities $11 million

(W10) **Operating Lease**

Lose should capitalise the leasehold improvements of $10 million and depreciate them over the term of the lease in accordance with IAS 16 *Property, plant and equipment*. Because the improvements have occurred, an obligation arises out of the past event, and a provision of $2 million should be made for the conversion of the building back to its original condition.

Thus the following entries should be made in Lose's financial statements:

|  |  | $m |
|---|---|---|
| Dr | Property, plant and equipment | 10 |
| Cr | Profit or loss | 10 |
| Dr | Property, plant and equipment | 2 |
| Cr | Provision for 'decommissioning' | 2 |

Depreciation on the capitalised amounts should be charged over the term of the lease as depreciation is charged in full on property, plant and equipment in the year of acquisition. Thus depreciation will be accounted for as follows:

|  |  | $m |
|---|---|---|
| Dr | Profit or loss ($10m + $2m) ÷ 6 years | 2 |
| Cr | Property, plant and equipment | 2 |

(b) An environmental report allows an organisation to communicate with different stakeholders. The benefits of an environmental report include:

(i) evaluating environmental performance can highlight inefficiencies in operations and help to improve management systems. Beth could identify opportunities to reduce resource use, waste and operating costs.

(ii) communicating the efforts being made to improve social and environmental performance can foster community support for a business and can also contribute towards its reputation as a good corporate citizen. At present Beth has a poor reputation in this regard.

(iii) reporting efforts to improve the organisation's environmental, social and economic performance can lead to increased consumer confidence in its products and services.

(iv) commitment to reporting on current impacts and identifying ways to improve environmental performance can improve relationships with regulators, and could reduce the potential threat of litigation which is hanging over Beth.

(v) investors, financial analysts and brokers increasingly ask about the sustainability aspects of operations. A high quality report shows the measures the organisation is taking to reduce risks, and will make Beth more attractive to investors.

(vi) disclosing the organisation's environmental, social and economic best practices can give a competitive market edge. Currently Beth's corporate image is poor and this has partly contributed to its poor stock market performance.

(vii) the international trend towards improved corporate sustainability is growing and access to international markets will require increasing transparency, and this will help Beth's corporate image.

(viii) large organisations are increasingly requiring material and service suppliers and contractors to submit performance information to satisfy the expectations of their own shareholders. Disclosing such information can make the company a more attractive supplier than their competitors, and increase Beth's market share.

It is important to ensure that the policies are robust and effective and not just compliance based.

(c) Corporate social responsibility (CSR) is concerned with business ethics and the company's accountability to its stakeholders, and about the way it meets its wider obligations. CSR emphasises the need for companies to adopt a coherent approach to a range of stakeholders including investors, employees, suppliers, and customers. Beth has paid little regard to the promotion of socially and ethically responsible policies. For example, the decision to not pay the SME creditors on the grounds that they could not afford to sue the company is ethically unacceptable. Additionally, Beth pays little regard to local customs and cultures in its business dealings.

The stagnation being suffered by Beth could perhaps be reversed if it adopted more environmentally friendly policies. The corporate image is suffering because of its attitude to the environment. Environmentally friendly policies could be cost effective if they help to increase market share and reduce the amount of litigation costs it has to suffer. The communication of these policies would be through the environmental report, and it is critical that stakeholders feel that the company is being transparent in its disclosures.

Evidence of corporate misbehaviour (Enron, World.com) has stimulated interest in the behaviour of companies. There has been pressure for companies to show more awareness and concern, not only for the environment but for the rights and interests of the people they do business with. Governments have made it clear that directors must consider the short-term and long-term consequences of their actions, and take into account their relationships with employees and the impact of the business on the community and the environment. The behaviour of Beth will have had an adverse effect on their corporate image.

CSR requires the directors to address strategic issues about the aims, purposes, and operational methods of the organisation, and some redefinition of the business model that assumes that profit motive and shareholder interests define the core purpose of the company. The profits of Beth will suffer if employees are not valued and there is poor customer support.

Arrangements should be put in place to ensure that the business is conducted in a responsible manner. The board should look at broad social and environmental issues affecting the company and set policy and targets, monitoring performance and improvements.

| **ACCA marking scheme** | | Marks |
|---|---|---|
| (a) | Goodwill – Lose | 5 |
| | Non-controlling interest | 1 |
| | Group reserves | 2 |
| | Associate and impairment | 5 |
| | Intercompany profit | 2 |
| | Foreign currency | 4 |
| | Receivables factoring | 4 |
| | Share options | 4 |
| | Provision | 3 |
| | Operating lease | 3 |
| | Other statement of financial position items | 2 |
| | | 35 |
| (b) | Benefits of environmental report | 8 |
| (c) | Discussion of ethical and social responsibilities | 5 |
| | Professional marks | 2 |
| Total | | 50 |

**Examiner's comments**

This question required candidates to prepare a consolidated statement of financial position, to describe the advantages to the company in question of an environmental report and to discuss the ethical and social responsibilities of the company, discussing whether a change in the company's attitude in this regard could improve business performance .The preparation of the group statement of financial position involved dealing with:

(i)     a step by step acquisition,

(ii)    an associate company,

(iii)   eliminating inter group profit,

(iv)   with foreign currency transactions,

(v)    factored trade receivables

(vi)   share options

(vii)  environmental provisions

(viii) operating leases

Thus there was a significant amount of detail in the question. The above elements could nearly all be dealt with in isolation from the group accounting aspects of the question so that candidates could score quite well even if the step acquisition was poorly answered. Candidates generally answered the step acquisition quite well. However the effect of the above on the group reserves was poorly answered. Many candidates did not correctly deal with the elimination of inter group profit between the associate and the holding company generally taking out the whole of the profit rather than 30% thereof. Several candidates did not consider the impairment of the associate. Many candidates did not realise that if a payment to the supplier is a deposit and is refundable, then the amount is deemed to be a monetary amount which should be retranslated at the year end. Similarly, the factored trade receivables should not have been derecognised and therefore should remain on the statement of financial position. This point was not recognised by many candidates. The calculation of the share options was generally well done but the calculation of the non-controlling interest was surprisingly poorly done considering that there was relatively little adjustment required to the subsidiary's closing reserves. Candidates often had differing views as to the nature of the environmental provision and markers were instructed to give credit for a well argued case. This is a good example of a case where a brief discussion of the issues would have been useful. Many candidates did not realise that leasehold improvements should be capitalised and depreciated and that a provision for the conversion of the building back to its original state was required.

Parts b/c required the use of the information in the question to discuss the advantages to the company of an environmental report and to discuss the ethical and social responsibilities of the company. The question was quite well answered although many candidates did not spend long enough on this part of the question, only writing a few lines. The main problem with the answers to this part was that many candidates did not consider the ethical issues involved. Two professional marks were awarded for the quality of the appraisal and analysis of the position of the company in respect of its environmental and social policy. This would mean not simply regurgitating the facts of the case but having the ability to conceptualise the facts and produce key conclusions from those facts.

## 9    ROD (DEC 07 EXAM)

**Key answer tips**

It is particularly important to establish the group structure as you are dealing with a D-shaped group. Rod has direct and indirect holdings in Line giving Rod control over Line.

Also, Rod has set up a defined benefit pension scheme. This is perhaps unrealistic when most defined benefit schemes are being closed to new members, but it is in the syllabus. The marks for the pension are straightforward, provided you know how pensions are dealt with.

(a)    **The accounting treatment of the defined benefit pension scheme**

The following will be recognised in profit or loss:

|  | $m |
|---|---|
| Service cost component (110 + 10) | 120 |
| Net interest component (11 − 10) | 1 |
|  | ——— |
|  | 121 |
|  | ——— |

| Relevant to the statement of financial position are: | $m |
|---|---|
| Scheme assets | |
| Cash contributed | 100 |
| Interest return @ 10% | 10 |
| Remeasurement gain (bal.fig) | 6 |
|  | ——— |
| Fair value of plan assets | 116 |
|  | ——— |
| Scheme liabilities | |
| Past service cost | 110 |
| Interest cost @10% | 11 |
| Current service cost | 10 |
|  | ——— |
| Present value of obligation | 131 |
|  | ——— |

Net pension liability of ($131m − $116m) **$15 million**.

IAS 19 requires that remeasurement (i.e. actuarial) gains and losses, together with return on assets other than included in the interest return) are recognised in other comprehensive income. The interest charge and interest return are based upon the discount rate for the pension obligation to determine a net interest cost to recognise in profit or loss for the year, and are a reflection of the time value of money on what is essentially a long-term liability.

The charge to profit or loss is (120 + 11 − 10) $121m. Past service costs are recognised in full immediately there is an obligation: i.e. following the announcement. The remeasurement gain on the pension scheme assets is taken to other comprehensive income. The pension liability in the statement of financial position will be reported as $15 million.

(b)     **Rod**

**Consolidated statement of financial position as at 30 November 20X2**

| Non-current assets | $m |
|---|---|
| Property, plant and equipment (W4) | 1,930 |
| Intangible assets (W3) | 132 |
| | 2,062 |
| Current assets: | |
| Inventory (300 + 135 + 65 – 20 (development costs)) | 480 |
| Trade receivables (240 + 105 + 49 – 100 (pension cash)) | 294 |
| Cash at bank and in hand (90 + 50 + 80) | 220 |
| Total assets | 3,056 |

| Equity and liabilities | $m |
|---|---|
| Equity capital | 1,500 |
| Share premium account | 300 |
| Retained earnings (W6) | 570 |
| Other equity components equity  (part (a)) | 6 |
| Non controlling interest (W5) | 265 |
| Total equity | 2,641 |
| Non-current liabilities (135 + 25 + 20) | 180 |
| Pension liability (Part (a)) | 15 |
| Current liabilities (100 + 70 + 50) | 220 |
| Total equity and liabilities | 3,056 |

*Workings*

(W1)  **Group structure**

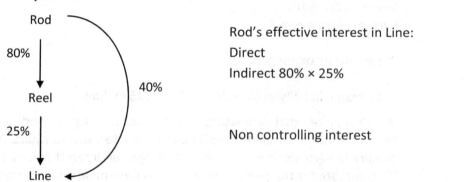

| | |
|---|---|
| Rod's effective interest in Line: | |
| Direct | 40% |
| Indirect 80% × 25% | 20% |
| | 60% |
| Non controlling interest | 40% |

(W2) **Net assets in Reel**

|  | Acq date $m | Rep date $m |
|---|---|---|
| Equity capital | 500 | 500 |
| Share premium | 100 | 100 |
| Retained earnings | 100 | 200 |
| Fair value adjustment (710 – 700) | 10 | – |
| Development costs written off (note 1) | – | (20) |
| Trade discount less dep'n (6 – 1) (note 2) | – | (5) |
|  | 710 | 775 |

**Note 1**

The development costs have been reinstated having already been written off. The development costs do not meet the criteria in IAS 38 for capitalisation and amortisation and, although the standard does not specifically preclude this practice, the costs cannot be treated as inventory as they have been previously written off as incurred. IAS 38 is quite strict as regards the costs which can be classified as development costs partly because the standard relates to all intangible assets and such assets have to show that they will generate probable future economic benefits in excess of the costs. All of the costs will be written off post acquisition reserves as they were reinstated after acquisition.

**Note 2**

IAS 16 *Property, plant and equipment* states that any trade discounts and rebates should be deducted from the cost of an asset and not recognised in profit or loss. Hence this practice is reversed with the resultant decrease in the depreciation charge and net profit.

**Net assets in Line**

|  | Acq date $m | Rep date $m |
|---|---|---|
| Equity capital | 200 | 200 |
| Share premium | 50 | 50 |
| Retained earnings | 50 | 60 |
| Excess depreciation (W4) | – | 14 |
|  | 300 | 324 |

(W3) **Goodwill**

| Reel |  | $m |
|---|---|---|
| Cost of investment | 640 |  |
| FV of NCI at acquisition (20% × 710) (W2) | 142 |  |
|  |  | 782 |
| FV of NA at acquisition (W2) |  | (710) |
| Goodwill |  | 72 |

| Line | $m | $m |
|---|---|---|
| Cost of investment – direct | 160 | |
| – indirect (80% × 100) | 80 | |
| | | 240 |
| FV of NCI at acquisition (40% × 300 (W2)) | | 120 |
| | | 360 |
| FV of NA at acquisition (W2)) | | (300) |
| Goodwill | | 60 |

**Note:** As goodwill is calculated on a proportionate basis for both subsidiary entities, the FV of NCI at the date of acquisition is based upon the NCI share of the net assets at acquisition, rather than being subject to separate measurement.

Total goodwill to statement of financial position: $72m + $60m = $132m

(W4)  **Property, plant and equipment**

| Line | Per FS | | Original cost |
|---|---|---|---|
| | $m | $m | $m |
| Original cost | 300 | | |
| Depreciation – 20X1 (six years) | (50) | | |
| Carrying value 30 Nov 20X1 | 250 | | 250 |
| Revaluation reserve (bal. fig) | 70 | | |
| Carrying value after revaluation | 320 | | |
| Depreciation for year (5 years) | (64) | | (50) |
| Carrying value 30 Nov 20X2 | 256 | | 200 |
| Revaluation reserve is eliminated | | 70 | |
| Retained earnings are increased by the | | | |
| excess depreciation charged (64 – 50) above | | (14) | |
| Reduction in value of PPE | | 56 | |

**Group property, plant and equipment**

|  |  | $m |
|---|---:|---:|
| Rod | 1,230 | |
| Reel | 505 | |
| Line | 256 | 1,991 |
| Less: adjustment to historical cost | | (56) |
| trade discount net of depreciation (W2) | | (5) |
| | | 1,930 |

**(W5) Non controlling interest**

| | $m |
|---|---:|
| **Reel** – FV of NCI at acquisition (20% × 710) (W2) | 142 |
| Share of post-acq'n retained earnings (20% × (775 – 710)) (W2) | 13 |
| | 155 |
| **Line** – FV of NCI at acquisition (40% × 300) (W2) | 120 |
| Share of post-acq'n retained earnings (40% × (324 – 300)) (W2) | 10 |
| Less: NCI share of cost of investment by Reel in Line (20% × 100) | (20) |
| | 265 |

**(W6) Consolidated retained earnings**

| | $m |
|---|---:|
| Rod | 625 |
| Reel 80% × (775 – 710) (W2) | 52 |
| Line 60% × (324 – 300) (W2) | 14 |
| | 691 |
| Pension Scheme charge to profit or loss (part a) | (121) |
| | 570 |

| ACCA marking scheme (adjusted) | | Marks |
|---|---|---:|
| (a) | Defined benefit pension scheme | 6 |
| (b) | Shareholdings | 2 |
| | Equity – Line | 6 |
| | Property, plant and equipment – Line | 4 |
| | Equity – Reel | 8 |
| | Fair value adjustment | 2 |
| | Group PPE | 2 |
| | Group retained earnings | 3 |
| | Receivables | 1 |
| | Inventories | 1 |
| Total | | 35 |

**10   ASHANTI (JUN 10 EXAM)**  *Walk in the footsteps of a top tutor*

### Key answer tips

As with many of the group accounting questions, the difficulty in the consolidation lies in the accounting issues included rather than the consolidation process itself. The best way to approach these questions is to deal with the issues individually and then note down the adjustments you need to make in the consolidated accounts. In this case there is unrealised profit in inventory, impairment of a financial asset and also property, plant and equipment, a holiday pay accrual and impairment of goodwill. There are share transactions; one resulting in a loss of control, which will require calculation of a gain or loss on disposal, and also an equity transfer where there has been no loss of control. It is a good idea to leave the impairment test until after other workings as you are likely to have to identify a new carrying value for the entity subject to the impairment test; you can only do this after having dealt with the accounting issues. Be careful not to spend too much time on these adjustments as you still have to do the consolidation. If you are getting bogged down, leave them and move on. Parts (b) and (c) focus upon reclassification of financial assets, together with the ethical implications of earnings management.

(a)   **Consolidated statement of profit or loss and other comprehensive income**

|  | Ashanti $m | Bochem $m | 6/12 of year Ceram $m | Adjusts. $m | Group SOCI $m |
|---|---|---|---|---|---|
| Revenue | 810.0 | 235.0 | 71 | (15) | 1,096.00 |
| Restructuring customer (Issue 2) | (5.0) | | | | |
| Cost of sales | (686.0) | (137.0) | (42) | 15 | |
| URPS re Bochem (Issue 1) | (1.0) | | | | |
| FVA dep'n (W2) | | (2.0) | | | |
| Holiday pay accrual (Issue 4) | (0.21) | | | | |
| PP&E impaired (Issue 3) | (1.6) | | | | |
| Goodwill impaired (W3) | | (2.2) | | | (857.01) |
| | | | | | |
| Gross profit | | | | | 238.99 |
| Distribution costs | (30.0) | (21.0) | (13) | | (64.00) |
| Admin expenses | (55.0) | (29.0) | (6) | | (90.00) |
| Impaired receivable (Issue 2) | (3.0) | | | | (3.00) |
| Fin asset - FVTPorL (Issue 5) | (5.0) | | | | (5.00) |
| Gain on disposal of subsidiary (W4) | | 3.8 | | | 3.80 |
| Share of associate profit (W6) | | 2.1 | | | 2.10 |
| Other income | 31.0 | 17.0 | 6 | | 54.00 |
| Finance costs | (8.0) | (6.0) | (4) | | (18.00) |
| | | | | | |
| Profit before tax | | | | | 118.89 |
| Tax | (21.0) | (23) | (5) | | (49.00) |
| | | | | | |
| Profit for the year | | 37.7 | 7 | | 69.89 |

Other comprehensive income for the year which will not be reclassified to profit or loss in future periods net of tax:

| | | | |
|---|---|---|---|
| Remeasurement losses on defined benefit plan | (14.0) | | (14.00) |
| Net gains on PPE revaluations | 12.0 | 6 | |
| Adjustment re PPE revaluation (Issue 3) | 1.6 | | 19.60 |
| Total comprehensive income for the year | 43.7 | | 75.49 |

| | | | |
|---|---|---|---|
| Profit for the year attributable to: | | | |
| Re B: (37.7 × 30%) | 11.31 | | |
| Re C: (7.0 × 44%) | | 3.08 | 14.39 |
| Owners of the parent | | | 55.50 |
| | | | 69.89 |

| | | | |
|---|---|---|---|
| Total comprehensive income for the year attributable to: | | | |
| Re B: (43.7 × 30%) | 13.11 | | |
| Re C: (7.0 × 44%) | | 3.08 | 16.19 |
| Owners of the parent | | | 59.30 |
| | | | 75.49 |

### Workings

### ISSUE 1 – UNREALISED PROFIT IN INVENTORY

Ashanti has sold goods at a profit to both Bochem and Ceram; group revenue and cost of sales will need to be adjusted by a total of $15 million. However, the unrealised profit in inventory applies only to half of the goods sold to Bochem during the year. The unrealised profit, based upon sales margin (i.e. percentage of selling price) in the accounts of the seller, Ashanti, is as follows:

| | %age | $000 |
|---|---|---|
| Cost | 80 | |
| Profit | 20 | 1,000 |
| Transfer price | 100 | 5,000 |

### ISSUE 2 – CUSTOMER UNDERGOING RECONSTRUCTION

The issue here is how the revenue and costs should be can be accounted for at the time the sale is made. When the goods are sold, Ashanti is already aware that the customer is in financial difficulties. The costs can be taken to cost of sales as the risks and rewards associated with those goods has been transferred to the customer. However, revenue should only be recorded where it is probable that there will be an inflow of economic benefits which can be reliably measured. Based upon the available information, this would not appear to be the case; the revenue should not be included in the financial statements to 30 April 2010, and should only be accounted for when received. Therefore, reduce revenue by $5 million and also remove this sum from the allowance to be made against total receivables.

### ISSUE 3 – THE PROPERTY IMPAIRMENT

The best way to approach this is to prepare a working which identifies the accounting treatment based upon historical cost and also based upon revalued amounts. This will help to identify the amount of any fall in value (i.e. impairment) which can be set against revaluation reserve within equity and how much is charged against income. If the PP&E is revalued, the annual depreciation charge is recalculated based upon the revised valuation and the remaining estimated useful life of the PP&E. Remember to account for the transfer of excess depreciation from revaluation reserve to retained earnings.

| | | Cost basis $000 | Revaluation basis $000 | Reval'n Res $000 |
|---|---|---|---|---|
| 01.05.08 | Purchase | 12,000 | 12,000 | |
| Depreciation | (1/10) (1/10) | (1,200) | (1,200) | |
| Revaluation | | | 2,200 | 2,200 |
| | | _____ | _____ | _____ |
| CV at 30.04.09 | | 10,800 | 13,000 | 2,200 |
| Depreciation | (1/10) (1/9) | (1,200) | (1,440) | (240) |
| Revaluation | | | (3,560) | |
| | | _____ | _____ | _____ |
| CV at 30.04.10 | | 9,600 | 8,000 | 1,960 |
| | | _____ | _____ | _____ |

Of the downward revaluation totalling $3.560 million, $1.960 million can be set against revaluation reserve for that asset, and the balance of $1.6 million is charged to profit or loss in the year.

### ISSUE 4 – HOLIDAY PAY ACCRUAL

At the reporting date, Ashanti should make an accrual for unused holiday entitlement as there is an entitlement which can be claimed by employees, creating an obligation to Ashanti. It is measured based upon probable amount of the claim as follows:

| | | | $000 | $m |
|---|---|---|---|---|
| $\dfrac{900 \times 3 \times 95\%}{900 \times 255} \times 19,000$ | | $\dfrac{2,565}{229,500} \times 19,000$ | 212,353 | 0.21 |

### ISSUE 5 – FINANCIAL ASSET – FVTPorL

As the bond is classified as fair value through profit or loss, fair value at the reporting date can be determined by discounting the expected future cash flows using the current market rate of interest. Any change in fair value is taken to profit or loss for the year.

| Date | Cashflow ($000) | 10% discount factor | $000 |
|------|-----------------|---------------------|------|
| 30.04.11 | 1,600 | 0.909 | 1,454 |
| 30.04.12 | 1,400 | 0.826 | 1,156 |
| 30.04.13 | 16,500 | 0.751 | 12,391 |
| | | | 15,001 |
| Fall in FV to PorL | | | 4,999 |
| Carrying value | | | 20,000 |

**Consolidation workings**

*Include dates of share purchases and disposals for each member of the group. Ensure that you can identify the right information at each key date for each subsidiary.*

**(W1) Group structure**

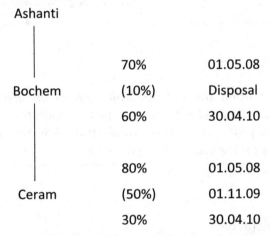

Ashanti

| | | |
|---|---|---|
| Bochem | 70% | 01.05.08 |
| | (10%) | Disposal |
| | 60% | 30.04.10 |
| Ceram | 80% | 01.05.08 |
| | (50%) | 01.11.09 |
| | 30% | 30.04.10 |

The share disposal by Ashanti in respect of Bochem does not change control of that company by Ashanti. This is accounted for as a transaction between equity holders. The calculation of the NCI share of profit in Bochem must be time-apportioned based upon the NCI percentage for each part of the year. The share disposal by Bochem in respect of Ceram results in a loss of control by the group; a gain or loss on disposal must be accounted for at 1 November 2010. There must also be recognition and accounting of the results of Ceram as an associate from the date of loss of control to the reporting date – i.e. the last six months of the year.

*This requires knowledge of accounting for fair value adjustments, including accounting for depreciation on a fair value adjustment. Remember that a depreciation charge for one year on the fair value adjustment must be included in the group statement of comprehensive income. If there is a purchase or disposal of shares during the year, a summary of net assets will also be required at that date.*

(W2) **Net Assets**

| Bochem | Acquisition date $m | Reporting date $m |
|---|---|---|
| Equity shares | 55 | ) |
| Retained earnings | 85 | ) 210 |
| Other equity components | 10 | ) |
| FVA – plant (bal fig) | 10 | 10 |
| Dep'n on FVA (2/5) | | (4) |
| | 160 | 216 |

**Note:** Remember to include one year depreciation charge on the fair value adjustment in the group statement of comprehensive income – $2 million.

| Ceram | Acquisition date $m | Reporting date $m |
|---|---|---|
| Given in question | 115 | 160 |

*Goodwill is calculated using the full goodwill method per IFRS 3 revised for all members of the group. Deal with the Impairments separately so that you clearly identify impairment in year – this needs to be included in the group statement of comprehensive income for the year to 30 April 2010.*

(W3) **Goodwill**

| Bochem | $m |
|---|---|
| Purchase consideration | 150.0 |
| Fair value of NCI at acquisition | 54.0 |
| | 204.0 |
| Fair value of net assets at acquisition (W2) | (160.0) |
| Full goodwill at acquisition | 44.0 |
| Impairment in earlier year (15%) | (6.6) |
| Impairment in year (5%) to group SOCI | (2.2) |
| Unimpaired goodwill to group SOFP | 35.2 |

*Goodwill is calculated using the full goodwill method per IFRS 3 revised for all members of the group. Remember that, in respect of Ceram, Ashanti exercises control via its' controlling interest in Bochem; therefore, use only the group share of the cost of acquisition, together with the fair value of the NCI in Ceram to calculate goodwill.*

| **Ceram** | **$m** |
|---|---|
| Effective cost to group 70% × $136m | 95.2 |
| Fair value of NCI at acquisition | 26.0 |
| | 121.2 |
| Fair value of net assets at acquisition (W2) | (115.0) |
| Unimpaired goodwill to group SOFP | 6.2 |

*There is a loss of control in Ceram during the year as Bochem disposes of a 50% interest in the share capital of that company. A gain or loss on disposal attributable to Bochem must be calculated for inclusion in the group financial statements. Ensure that this is included in the correct column of your working paper for the group SOCI.*

(W4)  **Gain or loss on disposal of controlling interest in Ceram**

| **Bochem disposal of controlling interest** | | **$m** |
|---|---|---|
| Fair value of consideration received | | 90.0 |
| Fair value of residual holding at disposal date | | 45.0 |
| | | 135.0 |
| CV of Ceram at disposal date: | | |
| Net assets (W2) | 160.0 | |
| Unimpaired goodwill (W3) | 6.2 | |
| | 166.2 | |
| CV of NCI at disposal date | (35.0) | 131.2 |
| Gain on disposal to Bochem | | 3.8 |

*There is no loss of control by Ashanti in Bochem as a result of the share disposal. Consequently there is no gain or loss to the group arising on this transaction; instead, it is regarded as a transaction between equity holders, which will result in an increase or decrease in equity.*

**(W5)** **Disposal of shares by Ashanti in Bochem without loss of control**

| Bochem | | $m |
|---|---|---|
| Proceeds of share disposal | | 34.0 |
| CV of Bochem at transaction date: | | |
| Net assets (W2) | 216.0 | |
| Unimpaired goodwill (W3) | 35.2 | |
| | ——— | |
| Change in NCI (10% × 251.2) | 251.2 | 25.1 |
| | | ——— |
| Increase in equity | | 8.9 |

**(W6)** **Income from associate**

| | $m |
|---|---|
| 6/12 × 30% × $14m | 2.1 |

---

*This part of the question requires you to state and explain when reclassification of financial instruments may be possible. You should begin by identifying circumstances when this may be required, and then go on to explain how any reclassification is accounted for.*

---

(b)   Classification of financial instruments is determined upon initial recognition. In some cases, there may only be one classification possible, as in the case of financial assets held for trading which must be accounted as fair value through profit or loss. Other financial assets, for example loans and receivables, may be accounted for either as fair value through profit or loss, or may be designated to be measured at amortised cost, provided they meet eligibility criteria.

In the case of financial assets, IFRS 9 requires a reassessment of whether any initial designation of classification remains appropriate when an entity changes its business model. IFRS 9 states that such reclassifications are expected to be 'very infrequent'. Whether the business model has changed is a decision made by the senior management of the entity, and may be a consequence of factors either internal to the entity, or from the external business environment. Such changes in business model would be demonstrable to external parties; i.e. a clear shift in strategy. One example of a change in business model would be if an entity closed down part of its business.

Examples which would not be regarded as changes in business model include:

*   The temporary disappearance of a particular market for financial assets.

*   The transfer of financial assets between parts of the entity with different business models.

*   A change of intention in respect of particular financial assets, even where there have been significant changes in market conditions.

Where reclassification is required, then all affected financial assets are reclassified from the first day of the next reporting period (the reclassification date), with no restatement of prior periods required. There should be disclosure of objectives and policies for managing risks from financial instruments, which would presumably include any changes to the business model during that period, even though reclassification does not take place until the beginning of the next accounting period.

A financial asset may be reclassified from amortised cost to fair value. If this happens, it is measured at fair value at the date of reclassification date, with any gain or loss on reclassification taken to profit or loss. If there is reclassification from fair value to amortised cost, then fair value at the reclassification date becomes the new carrying value.

Allowing reclassification, even in limited circumstances, may allow an entity to manage its reported profit or loss by avoiding future fair value gains or losses on the reclassified assets.

*This part of the question deals with one possible consequence of reclassification of financial assets, management of earnings, and requires you to discuss the nature of management of earnings, and whether such a process is ethically acceptable.*

(c)   'Earnings management' has been defined in various ways. It can be described as the purposeful intervention in the external financial reporting process with the intent of obtaining some private gain. Alternatively it can be the use of judgment in financial reporting and in structuring transactions to alter financial reports to either mislead stakeholders about the underlying economic performance of the company, or to influence contractual outcomes that depend on reported accounting judgments.

Incentives lie at the heart of earnings management. Managers should make accounting judgments and decisions solely with the intention of fairly reporting operating performance. However, there are often economic incentives for managers to engage in earnings management, because the value of the firm and the wealth of its managers or owners are normally linked to reported earnings. Contractual incentives to manage earnings arise when contracts between a company and other parties rely upon financial statements to determine financial exchanges between them. By managing the results of operations, managers can alter the amount and timing of those exchanges. Contractual situations could stimulate earnings management. These would include debt covenants, management compensation agreements, job security, and trade union negotiations. Market incentives to manage earnings arise when managers perceive a connection between reported earnings and the company's market value. Regulatory incentives to manage earnings arise when reported earnings are thought to influence the actions of regulators or government officials. By managing the results of operations, managers may influence the actions of regulators or government officials, thereby minimising political scrutiny and the effects of regulation.

One way in which directors can manage earnings is by manipulation of accruals with no direct cash flow consequences. Examples of accrual manipulation include under-provisioning for irrecoverable debt expenses, delaying of asset write-offs and opportunistic selection of accounting methods. Accrual manipulation is a convenient form of earnings management because it has no direct cash flow implications and can be done after the year-end when managers are better informed about earnings. However, managers also have incentives to manipulate real activities during the year with the specific objective of meeting certain earnings targets. Real activity manipulation affects both cash flows and earnings.

Where management does not try to manipulate earnings, there is a positive effect on earnings quality. The earnings data is more reliable because management is not influencing or manipulating earnings by changing accounting methods, or deferring expenses or accelerating revenues to bring about desired short-term earnings results. The absence of earnings management does not, however, guarantee high earnings quality. Some information or events that may affect future earnings may not be disclosed in the financial statements. Thus, the concept of earnings management is related to the concept of earnings quality. One major objective of the IASB Framework is to assist investors and creditors in making investing and lending decisions. The Framework refers not only to the reliability of financial statements, but also to the relevance and predictive value of information presented in financial statements.

Entities have a social and ethical responsibility not to mislead stakeholders. Ethics can and should be part of a corporate strategy, but a company's first priority often is its survival and optimising its profits in a sustainable way. Management of earnings may therefore appear to have a degree of legitimacy in this regard but there is an obvious conflict. An ethical position that leads to substantial and long-term disadvantages in the market place will not be acceptable to an entity.

It is reasonable and realistic not to rely exclusively on personal morality. A suitable economic, ethical and legal framework attempts to ensure that the behaviour of directors conforms to moral standards. Stakeholders depend on the moral integrity of the entity's directors. Stakeholders rely upon core values such as trustworthiness, truthfulness, honesty, and independence although these cannot be established exclusively by regulation and professional codes of ethics. Thus there is a moral dilemma for directors in terms of managing earnings for the benefit of the entity, which might directly benefit stakeholders and themselves whilst at the same time possibly misleading the same stakeholders.

| ACCA marking scheme | | |
|---|---|---|
| | | *Marks* |
| (a) | Consolidated SOCI | 5 |
| | Bochem | 8 |
| | Ceram | 6 |
| | Inventory | 2 |
| | Bond | 4 |
| | PPE | 3 |
| | Impairment of customer | 2 |
| | Employee benefits | 2 |
| | NCI | 3 |
| | | 35 |
| (b) | Amendments to IAS 32 & 39 | 4 |
| | Management of earnings | 3 |
| (c) | Description of man't of earnings | 3 |
| | Moral/ethical considerations | 3 |
| | Professional marks | 2 |
| Total | | 50 |

**Examiner's comments**

The question required candidates to prepare a consolidated statement of comprehensive income, describe the amendments to the rules regarding reclassification of financial assets, and discuss how these rules could lead to 'management of earnings'. Further candidates were asked to discuss the nature of and incentives for 'management of earnings' and whether such a process could be deemed to be ethically acceptable. Candidates generally performed well in this question. Candidates were required to calculate goodwill on the purchase of a subsidiary in order to determine the impairment of goodwill to be charged in profit or loss. Candidates seemed to have a good knowledge of the calculation of goodwill under the full goodwill method. The question also dealt with the sale of an equity interest in a subsidiary which resulted in a positive movement in equity which was dealt by a movement on equity and not through other comprehensive income. Finally as regards the group accounting, candidates had to deal with the sale of a controlling interest which resulted in the retention of an associate interest. Generally candidates performed well this part of the question. The question also required candidates to deal with the accounting for a financial asset. Candidates made a reasonable attempt at this element of the question. Other elements of the question included dealing with revenue recognition, revaluation gains/losses on property, plant and equipment, calculating non controlling interest and accruing holiday pay for the entity. In a question such as this, it is very easy to make a mistake in calculation. Thus it is always important to show workings in a clear concise manner so that marks can be allocated for the principles and method used by the candidate.

## 11 RIBBY, HALL AND ZIAN (JUN 08 EXAM)  *Online question assistance*

**Key answer tips**

There are several technical issues to deal with in this question. There is a foreign subsidiary entity which requires that the goodwill calculation to be made in foreign currency, and then retranslated at the reporting date. There is also a loan from one subsidiary to the foreign subsidiary on which exchange differences need to be accounted for correctly. Other technical issues to deal with prior to completing the consolidation include employee benefits, share-based payments and intra-group trading.

The final part of the question deals with ethical and professional issues relating to the accounting profession.

(a)   The functional currency is the currency of the primary economic environment in which the entity operates (IAS 21). The primary economic environment in which an entity operates is normally the one in which it primarily generates and expends cash. An entity's management considers the following factors in determining its functional currency (IAS 21):

(i)   the currency that dominates the determination of the sales prices; and

(ii)   the currency that most influences operating costs

The currency that dominates the determination of sales prices will normally be the currency in which the sales prices for goods and services are denominated and settled. It will also normally be the currency of the country whose competitive forces and regulations have the greatest impact on sales prices. In this case it would appear that currency is the dinar as Zian sells its products locally and the prices are determined by local competition. However, the currency that most influences operating costs is in fact the dollar, as Zian imports goods which are paid for in dollars although all selling and operating expenses are paid in dinars. The emphasis is, however, on the currency of the economy that determines the pricing of transactions, as opposed to the currency in which transactions are denominated.

Factors other than the dominant currency for sales prices and operating costs are also considered when identifying the functional currency. The currency in which an entity's finances are denominated is also considered. Zian has partly financed its operations by raising a $4 million loan from Hall but it is not dependent upon group companies for finance. The focus is on the currency in which funds from financing activities are generated and the currency in which receipts from operating activities are retained.

Additional factors include consideration of the autonomy of a foreign operation from the reporting entity and the level of transactions between the two. Zian operates with a considerable degree of autonomy both financially and in terms of its management. Consideration is given to whether the foreign operation generates sufficient functional cash flows to meet its cash needs which in this case Zian does as it does not depend on the group for finance.

It would be said that the above indicators give a mixed view but the functional currency that most faithfully represents the economic effects of the underlying transactions, events, and conditions is the dinar, as it most affects sales prices and is most relevant to the financing of an entity. The degree of autonomy and independence provides additional supporting evidence in determining the entity's functional currency.

(b) **Consolidated Statement of Financial Position of Ribby Group at 31 May 2008**

| Assets | $m |
|---|---|
| Non-current assets | |
| Goodwill (W3) | 16.8 |
| Property, plant and equipment (W8) | 414.7 |
| Financial assets at fair value (W13) | 23.3 |
| | 454.8 |
| Current assets (W14) | 51.0 |
| Total assets | 505.8 |

| Equity and liabilities | $m |
|---|---|
| Equity shares | 60.0 |
| Other components of equity (W6) | 31.8 |
| Retained earnings (W5) | 121.7 |
| Total shareholders' equity | 213.5 |
| Non-controlling interests (W4) | 59.6 |
| Total equity | 273.1 |
| Non-current liabilities (W15) | 89.7 |
| Current liabilities (W16) | 143.0 |
| | 505.8 |

**Workings**

**(W1) Group structure**

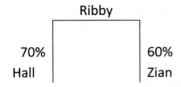

**(W2a) Net assets – Hall**

|  | Acq'n date $m | Rep date $m |
|---|---|---|
| Share capital | 40 | 40 |
| Retained earnings | 60 | 80 |
| Other Equity | 10 | 10 |
| FVA – Land | 10 | 10 |
| Prov'n for URP (W12) |  | (4) |
|  | 120 | 136 |

**(W2b) Net assets and summary translation schedule – Zian**

|  | Acq'n date Dinar(m) | Rep date Dinar(m) | Rate | $m |
|---|---|---|---|---|
| Equity capital | 209 | 209 |  |  |
| Pre-acq'n retained earnings | 220 | 220 |  |  |
| FVA – Land | 66 | 66 |  |  |
|  |  | 495 | 11 | 45.0 |
| Post acq'n RE (299 – 220) |  | 79 | Bal fig | 2.2 |
| Loan – FX loss (W7) |  | (8) |  |  |
|  | 495 | 566 | 12 | 47.2 |

**(W3a) Goodwill – Hall**

|  | $m |
|---|---|
| Cost of investment | 98 |
| FV of NCI at acquisition (30% of $120m) (W2a) | 36 |
|  | 134 |
| Less: FV of net assets at acquisition (W2a) | (120) |
| Goodwill | 14 |

**(W3b) Goodwill and retranslation schedule – Zian**

| | Dinar (m) |
|---|---|
| – calculated in functional currency, then translated | |
| Cost of investment | 330 |
| FV of NCI at acquisition (40% × 495m dinar (W2b)) | 198 |
| | ———— |
| | 528 |
| FV of net assets at acquisition (W2b) | (495) |
| | ———— |
| Goodwill at acquisition – no impairment | 33 |

Translated at closing rate @ 12 = $2.8m

The exchange gain or loss on retranslation of goodwill at the reporting date must also be identified as follows:

| | Dinar(m) | Rate | $m |
|---|---|---|---|
| Goodwill at acquisition | 33 | 11 | 3.0 |
| **FX gain (loss) on retranslation (W5)** | | **Bal fig** | **(0.2)** |
| | ———— | | ———— |
| Goodwill at reporting date | 33 | 12 | 2.8 |
| | ———— | | ———— |

As goodwill was calculated using the proportionate basis, all of the exchange gain or loss on retranslation is allocated to the parent in (W5).

**(W4) Non-controlling Interest**

| | $m |
|---|---|
| Hall: FV at recognition (30% × $120m) (W2a) | 36.0 |
| (30% ×($136m − $120m)) (W2a)) | 4.8 |
| Zian: (40% × $47.2m) (W2b) | 18.8 |
| | ———— |
| | 59.6 |
| | ———— |

**(W5) Group reserves**

| | $m |
|---|---|
| Ribby | 120.0 |
| Hall: (70% × (136 − 120) (W2a) | 11.2 |
| Zian (60% × 2.2) (W2b) | 1.3 |
| Ribby – building impaired (W8) | (0.8) |
| Ribby – penalty re early loan repayment (W9) | (1.0) |
| Ribby – cash bonus (W10) | (3.0) |
| Ribby – share options (W10) | (1.8) |
| Ribby – past service cost – pension costs (W11) | (4.0) |
| Exchange loss on retranslation of goodwill (W3b) | (0.2) |
| | ———— |
| | 121.7 |
| | ———— |

**(W6) Other components of equity**

|  | $m |
|---|---|
| Ribby | 30.0 |
| Ribby – equity re share options (W10) | 1.8 |
|  | 31.8 |

**(W7) Zian – Exchange loss on loan from Hall**

Loans between subsidiaries cannot be treated as part of the holding company's net investment in a foreign subsidiary (IAS 21). Zian will recognise an exchange difference on the loan from Hall in profit or loss and the exchange difference will flow through to the consolidated statement of profit or loss and will not be reclassified as a separate component of equity.

|  | Dinar (m) |
|---|---|
| Loan at 1 June 2007 $4m at 10 dinars | 40 |
| Loan at 31 May 2008 $4m at 12 dinars | 48 |
| Exchange loss | 8 |

The loan of $4 million should be eliminated on consolidation from both financial assets (W13) and non-current liabilities (W15).

**(W8) Tangible assets** (including building impaired)

|  | $m | $m |
|---|---|---|
| Ribby | 250.0 |  |
| Hall (120 + 10(FVA) (W2a)) | 130.0 |  |
| Zian ((360 + 66(FVA) (W2b))/12) | 35.5 |  |
|  |  | 415.5 |
| Building – impairment loss |  |  |
| 1 June 2007 cost 40m dinar @ 10 | 4.0 |  |
| Depreciation (20 years) | (0.2) |  |
|  | 3.8 |  |
| 31 May 2008 36m dinar @12 | 3.0 | (0.8) |
|  |  | 414.7 |

**(W9) Early repayment of loan**

As Ribby entered into an agreement to repay the debt early plus a penalty, it should adjust the carrying value of the financial liability to reflect actual and revised estimated cash flows (IFRS 9). Therefore, the carrying amount of the loan liability should be increased by $1 million and be transferred to current liabilities.

## (W10) Cash bonus and share options to employees of Ribby

A liability of $3 million should be accrued for the bonus to be paid in cash to the employees of Ribby. The management should also recognise an expense of (12/18 × 90% × $3 million) $1.8 million, with a corresponding increase in equity. The terms of the share options have not been fixed and, therefore, the grant date becomes 30 November 2008 as this is the date that the terms and conditions will be fixed. However, IFRS 2 requires the entity to recognise the services when received and, therefore, adjustment is required to the financial statements. Once the terms are fixed, the fair value can be calculated and any adjustments made.

|  | $m |
| --- | --- |
| DR Expense – in retained earnings (W5) | 4.8 |
| CR Equity (W6) | 1.8 |
| CR Current liabilities (W16) | 3.0 |

## (W11) Defined benefit plan – past service cost

A past service cost of $4 million should be recognised immediately as, following revision of IAS 19 in 2011, past services costs are recognised as part of the current service cost component, irrespective of whether or not the associated benefits have vested. Thus the following entries will be required to account for the past service costs.

|  | $m |
| --- | --- |
| DR Retained earnings (W5) | 4.0 |
| CR Non-current liabilities (defined benefit obligation) (W15) | 4.0 |

## (W12) Accounting for sale of inventory (see part (c))

The transaction should not be shown as a sale. Inventory should be reinstated at $2 million instead of $6 million and a decrease in retained earnings of $4 million should occur in the accounting records of Hall.

| CR Inventory (W14) | $4m |
| --- | --- |
| DR Retained earnings of Hall (W2a) | $4m |

The cash position should be reversed also by increasing Ribby's cash balance by $6m (W14) and also increasing Hall's overdraft by $6m (W16).

## (W13) Financial assets at fair value

|  | $m |
| --- | --- |
| Ribby | 10.0 |
| Hall | 5.0 |
| Zian (148m dinar @ 12) | 12.3 |
| Elimination of loan from Hall to Zian (W15) | (4.0) |
|  | 23.3 |

**(W14) Current assets**

|  | $m |
|---|---|
| Ribby | 22.0 |
| Hall | 17.0 |
| Zian (120m dinar @ 12) | 10.0 |
| Inventory adjustment (W12) | (4.0) |
| Cash reinstated re window dressing transaction (W12) | 6.0 |
|  | 51.0 |

**(W15) Non-current liabilities**

|  |  | $m |
|---|---|---|
| Ribby | 90.0 |  |
| Hall | 5.0 |  |
| Zian (48 + 8 (W7) m dinar @ 12) | 4.7 |  |
|  |  | 99.7 |
| Increase carrying amount of loan liability (W9) |  | 1.0 |
| Eliminate of loan from Hall to Zian (W13) |  | (4.0) |
| Past service cost (W11) |  | 4.0 |
| Loan & penalty reclassified to current liabs (W9)(W16) |  | (11.0) |
|  |  | 89.7 |

**(W16) Current liabilities**

|  | $m |
|---|---|
| Ribby | 110.0 |
| Hall | 7.0 |
| Zian (72m dinar @ 12) | 6.0 |
| Cash bonus to Ribby employees (W10) | 3.0 |
| Cash reinstated re window dressing transaction (W12) | 6.0 |
| Loan & penalty reclassified from N-C liabs (W9)(W15) | 11.0 |
|  | 143.0 |

(c) **Accounting and ethical implications of sale of inventory**

Manipulation of financial statements often does not involve breaking laws but the purpose of financial statements is to present a fair representation of the company's position, and if the financial statements are misrepresented on purpose then this could be deemed unethical. The financial statements in this case are being manipulated to show a certain outcome so that Hall may be shown to be in a better financial position if the company is sold. The retained earnings of Hall will be increased by $4 million, and the cash received would improve liquidity. Additionally this type of transaction was going to be carried out again in the interim accounts if Hall was not sold. Accountants have the responsibility to issue financial statements that do not mislead the public as the public assumes that such professionals are acting in an ethical capacity, thus giving the financial statements credibility.

A profession is distinguished by having a:

(i)     specialised body of knowledge

(ii)    commitment to the social good

(iii)   ability to regulate itself

(iv)    high social status

Accountants should seek to promote or preserve the public interest. If the idea of a profession is to have any significance, then it must make a bargain with society in which they promise conscientiously to serve the public interest. In return, society allocates certain privileges. These might include one or more of the following:

- the right to engage in self-regulation
- the exclusive right to perform particular functions
- special status

There is more to being an accountant than is captured by the definition of the professional. It can be argued that accountants should have the presentation of truth, in a fair and accurate manner, as a goal.

| ACCA marking scheme (adjusted) | | | |
|---|---|---|---|
| | | | Marks |
| (a) | Consideration of factors | | 6 |
| | Conclusion | | 2 |
| | | | —— |
| | | | 8 |
| | | | —— |
| (b) | Translation of Zian | | 6 |
| | Loan | | 2 |
| | Goodwill: Zian | | 4 |
| | Non-controlling interest | | 4 |
| | Building | | 3 |
| | Early repayment of loan | | 1 |
| | Pension | | 2 |
| | Inventory | | 1 |
| | Bonus 3 | | |
| | Goodwill: Hall | | 2 |
| | Retained earnings | Hall | 2 |
| | | Zian | 1 |
| | | Ribby | 3 |
| | Other reserves | | 1 |
| | | | —— |
| | | | 35 |
| | | | —— |
| (c) | Accounting | | 2 |
| | Ethical discussion | | 3 |
| | Quality of discussion | | 2 |
| | | | —— |
| | | | 7 |
| | | | —— |
| | Total | | 50 |
| | | | —— |

**Examiner's comments**

This question required candidates to determine the functional currency of an overseas subsidiary, and prepare a consolidated statement of financial position for a simple group structure involving an overseas subsidiary and several adjustments for foreign currency loans, employee compensation, past service pension costs, intercompany profit elimination, and early repayment of long term loans. The final part required candidates to discuss the manipulation of financial statements and the nature of accountants responsibilities the profession and to society. The first part of the question was answered well by many candidates but at the same time many candidates discussed the method used to translate the financial statements of an overseas subsidiary, which was not answering the question set. The answer to this part of the question required candidates to use the information in the scenario and if candidates did use the information then they achieved a higher mark than those that simply quoted the accounting standard.

Part b of the question was quite well answered. Candidates seemed to generally understand the method used to translate the financial statements of an overseas subsidiary. Some candidates used incorrect exchange rates to translate the statement of financial position of the subsidiary but most candidates managed to compute goodwill correctly, which was encouraging. The adjustments to the financial statements were mainly to the holding company/group account, which meant that candidates could calculate any adjustment without worrying about the effect on the non controlling interest (minority interest). Thus many candidates scored well when discussing the adjustments. Although the question does not ask for a discussion of the adjustments, it is good practice for candidates to write a brief explanation of the accounting practice used in answering the particular part of the question. Many candidates dealt with the past service cost, the early repayment of the loan and the accounting for the sale of the inventory very well. However the bonus payable to the employees was not dealt with quite as well with candidates not time apportioning half of the bonus and expensing the other half.

Part c of the question was not well answered and many candidates did not attempt it. It required a discussion of the role of a profession and its responsibility to society. It was a little worrying that many candidates did not know the distinguishing features of a profession or the demands that society places on the profession.

## 12   JOCATT GROUP (DEC 10 EXAM)  *Walk in the footsteps of a top tutor*

**Key answer tips**

As with many of the group accounting questions, much of the difficulty in part (a) lies in the accounting issues included rather than the preparation of the cash flow statement itself. In particular the question refers to "draft financial statements" which is normally an indication that there are accounting errors within the statements as currently presented. The best way to approach a cash flow question is to have a sound knowledge and understanding of the standard format for the statement, and then to deal with the individual issues identified in the question, completing the statement as you deal with each issue. You should expect to deal with a change in group structure in an ACCA P2 statement of cash flows examination question; in this particular case, there is acquisition of a subsidiary during the year. In addition, this question includes the following accounting issues: financial assets, defined benefit scheme, investment property, property, plant and equipment, purchase of an interest in an associate during the year, together with payments for taxation and dividends. Ensure that you do not spend too much time on these issues to the exclusion of completing the cash flow statement itself. Start your workings with those issues you find quickest and easiest to deal with. The two elements of part (b) of the question, which include the professional marks, should be a good source of marks for a well-prepared student.

(a)    **Jocatt Group: Statement of Cash flows for the year ended 30 November 2010**

|  | $m | $m |
|---|---|---|
| Cash flows from operating activities: | | |
| Profit before tax | | 45 |
| Adjustments to operating activities: | | |
| Retirement benefit current and past service cost (working (vii)) | 16 | |
| Depreciation on PPE | 27 | |
| Loss on replacement of investment property component part (working (viii)) | 0.5 | |
| Amortisation of intangible assets (working (ix)) | 17 | |
| Profit on sale of land (working (vi)) | (9) | |
| Profit on investment property (working (viii)) | (1.5) | |
| Associates profit | (6) | |
| Impairment of goodwill (working (i)) | 31.5 | |
| Gain on remeasurement of initial holding in Tigret (working (i)) | (1) | |
| Finance costs (inc net interest component on defined benefit plan) | 8 | |
| Cash paid to retirement benefit scheme (working (vii)) | (7) | |
| Decrease in trade receivables (113 – 62 + 5) | 56 | |
| Decrease in inventories (128 – 105) | 23 | |
| Increase in trade payables (144 – 55) | 89 | 243.5 |
| | | |
| Cash generated from operations | | 288.5 |
| Finance costs paid (exc net int comp on defined benefit plan) | | (6) |
| Income taxes paid (working (iv)) | | (16.5) |
| | | |
| Cash flow from operating activities | | 266 |
| Cash flows from investing activities: | | |
| Purchase of associate (working (iii)) | (48) | |
| Purchase of PPE (working (vi)) | (98) | |
| Purchase of subsidiary (15 – 7) (working (ii)) | (8) | |
| Additions-investment property (working (viii)) | (1) | |
| Proceeds from sale of land (working (vi)) | 15 | |
| Intangible assets (working (ix)) | (12) | |
| Purchases of fin assets at FV through OCI (working (x)) | (5) | (157) |

Cash flows from financing activities:

| | | |
|---|---|---|
| Repayment of long-term borrowings (71 – 67) | (4) | |
| Rights issue NCI (working (v)) | 2 | |
| Non-controlling interest dividend (working (v)) | (13) | |
| Dividends paid by Jocatt (per SOCIE) | (5) | (20) |
| | | |
| Net increase in cash and cash equivalents | | 89 |
| Cash and cash equivalents at beginning of period | | 143 |
| | | |
| Cash and cash equivalents at end of period | | 232 |

**Workings**

*Reconcile the opening and closing cash and cash equivalents balances to identify the net increase or decrease in the year. You can then complete the final three lines of the statement. If there is a change in group structure, it is usually a good idea to deal with the impact of that; it should help you to identify items that need to be accounted for when dealing with other workings required to answer the question.*

(i) **Goodwill on acquisition of Tigret 1 December 2009**

| | $m |
|---|---|
| Cash paid | 15 |
| Shares issued | 15 |
| Fair value of initial equity interest held prior to acquisition | 5 |
| (initial cost of $4m plus $1m remeasurement gain to PorL ) | |
| | |
| Fair value of consideration paid to acquire control | 35 |
| Fair value of non-controlling interest | 20 |
| | |
| | 55 |
| Identifiable net assets | (45) |
| Deferred tax (45 – 40) × 30% | 1.5 |
| | |
| Full goodwill on acquisition | 11.5 |

*Having calculated goodwill in acquisition of the new subsidiary, you can now reconcile the movement in the carrying value of goodwill between the two reporting dates; there is likely to be impairment of goodwill during the year – this should be accounted for as an adjustment to profit in the statement of cash flows.*

| Goodwill reconciliation | $m |
|---|---|
| Opening balance at 1 December 2009 | 68 |
| On acquisition of Tigret | 11.5 |
| Impairment in year to Porl – bal fig | (31.5) |
| Closing balance at 30 November 2010 | 48.0 |

*The final element of accounting for the acquisition of a subsidiary during the year is to account for the net cash impact of the acquisition – this typically will result in a cash outflow to be classified as an investing activity.*

(ii) **Net cash impact of acquisition of subsidiary in year:**

| | $m |
|---|---|
| Cash outflow as part of consideration paid to acquire control | (15) |
| Cash balance acquired | 7 |
| Net cash outflow arising from acquisition of subsidiary | (8) |

*Similarly, there has been an investment in an associate during the year. There is likely to be a cash outflow to pay for the purchase of the shares – this should be classified as an investing activity in the statement of cash flows. Remember to adjust for the share of profit or loss after tax as this is not a cash flow and to include any dividends received during the year from the associate (if appropriate) as an investing activity cash inflow.*

(iii) **Associate**

| | $m |
|---|---|
| Opening balance at 1 December 2009 | Nil |
| Cost of investment in associate (cash outflow) | 48 |
| Share of assoc profit after tax for period | 6 |
| Dividend received (cash inflow) | nil |
| Closing balance at 30 November 2010 | 54 |

*Reconcile the opening and closing balances for both the income tax liability and the deferred tax provision in a single working, ensuring that you include any charge for the year included in profit or loss. You should also ensure that you correctly deal with any tax-related balances on a subsidiary acquired or disposed of during the year.*

(iv)    **Taxation**

|  | $m | $m |
|---|---|---|
| Opening tax balances at 1 December 2009: | | |
| Deferred tax | 41 | |
| Current tax | 30 | |
|  | —— | 71 |
| Deferred tax on acquisition (working (i)) | | 1.5 |
| Charge for year per profit or loss | 11 | |
| Deferred tax on fin assets at FVTOCI remeasurement gains | 1 | |
|  | —— | 12 |
| Less closing tax balances at 30 November 2010: | | |
| Deferred tax | 35 | |
| Current tax | 33 | |
|  | —— | (68) |
| Cash paid | | 16.5 |

The tax charge on the gain on financial assets at fair value through other comprehensive income ($1m) is adjusted in the tax charge for the year.

*When reconciling the movement in non-controlling interest (NCI) between the two reporting dates, ensure that you recognise any new NCI on acquisition of a subsidiary with less than 100% ownership of shares, and derecognise any NCI where there has been a disposal of a subsidiary during the year.*

(v)    **Non-controlling interest**

|  | $m |
|---|---|
| Opening balance at 1 December 2009 | 36 |
| On acquisition (working (i)) | 20 |
| NCI share of total comp. income for year | 10 |
| Dividend paid (per SOCIE) | (13) |
| Rights issue (5 × 40%) | 2 |
| Closing balance at 30 November 2010 | 55 |

The receipt from the rights issue is a cash inflow into the group. Therefore the dividend paid will be $13 million and the cash received from the rights issues will be $2 million; both should be disclosed separately and classified within financing activities.

*The reconciliation of PPE should include recognition of PPE which is now controlled by the group on acquisition of the subsidiary. Note that the carrying value of PPE disposed of is removed and any gain or loss on disposal accounted for as an adjustment within operating activities. The cash disposal proceeds received are classified as a cash inflow within investing activities.*

(vi) **PPE**

|  | $m |
|---|---|
| Opening balance at 1 December 2009 | 254 |
| Revaluation loss (per SOCIE) | (7) |
| Plant in exchange transaction | 4 |
| Sale of land | (10) |
| Depreciation | (27) |
| On acquisition of Tigret | 15 |
| Current year cash additions | 98 |
| | ——— |
| Closing balance at 30 November 2010 | 327 |

The profit on the sale of the land is $9 million, comprising cash received $15m plus plant at valuation $4 million less carrying value $10 million.

*The movement on the defined benefit plan during the year comprises the current and past service cost for the year (i.e. service cost component) and the net interest component, together with the movement on net remeasurement component. Remember that the movement on the net remeasurement component is taken to other comprehensive income for the year - it is therefore not an item that should be adjusted for within operating activities. Normally the cash contributions paid are identified as a reconciling item – they would normally be disclosed as a cash outflow within operating activities.*

(vii) **Defined benefit scheme**

|  |  | $m |
|---|---|---|
| Opening balance at 1 December 2009 |  | 22 |
| Current and past service cost for the year (10 + 6) | 16 |  |
| Net interest component | 2 |  |
| | ——— | |
| |  | 18 |
| Net remeasurement component gain for year |  | (8) |
| Contributions paid bal fig |  | (7) |
| | | ——— |
| Closing balance at 30 November 2010 |  | 25 |

(viii)   **Investment property**

|  | $m |
|---|---|
| Opening balance at 1 December 2009 | 6 |
| Acquisition | 1 |
| Disposal | (0.5) |
| Gain | 1.5 |
| Closing balance at 30 November 2010 | 8 |

(ix)   **Intangible assets**

|  | $m |
|---|---|
| Opening balance at 1 December 2009 | 72 |
| Acquisitions (8 + 4) | 12 |
| Tigret | 18 |
| Amortisation | (17) |
| Closing balance at 30 November 2010 | 85 |

(x)   **Financial assets at FV through OCI**

|  | $m |
|---|---|
| Opening balance at 1 December 2009 | 90 |
| Acquisitions (cash) | 5 |
| Tigret now accounted for as a subsidiary | (4) |
| Total gain ($2m per SOCIE plus $1m tax) | 3 |
| Closing balance at 30 November 2010 | 94 |

(xi)   **Share capital**

|  |  |
|---|---|
| Opening balance at 1 December 2009 | 275 |
| Tigret acq'n - part consideration in shares at NV | 15 |
| Closing balance at 30 November 2010 | 290 |

(b)   (i)   The vast majority of companies use the indirect method for the preparation of statements of cash flow. Most companies justify this on the grounds that the direct method is too costly. The direct method presents separate categories of cash inflows and outflows whereas the indirect method is essentially a reconciliation of the net income reported in the statement of financial position with the cash flow from operations. The adjustments include non-cash items in the statement of comprehensive income plus operating cash flows that were not included in profit or loss. The direct method shows net cash from operations made up from individual operating cash flows. Users often prefer the direct method because it shows the major categories of cash flows. The complicated adjustments required by the indirect method are difficult to understand and provide entities with more leeway for manipulation of cash flows. The adjustments made to reconcile net profit before tax to cash from operations are confusing to users. In many cases these cannot be reconciled to observed changes in the statement of financial position. Thus users will only be able to understand the size of the difference between net profit before tax and cash from operations. The direct method allows for reporting operating cash flows by understandable categories as they can see the amount of cash collected from customers, cash paid to suppliers, cash paid to employees and cash paid for other operating expenses. Users can gain a better understanding of the major trends in cash flows and can compare these cash flows with those of the entity's competitors.

*You should focus upon trying to make specific comments to answer the question requirement. What are the potential problems for users of statements of cash flows?*

An issue for users is the abuse of the classifications of specific cash flows. Misclassification can occur amongst the sections of the statement. Cash outflows that should have been reported in the operating section may be classified as investing cash outflows with the result that companies enhance operating cash flows. The complexity of the adjustments to net profit before tax can lead to manipulation of cash flow reporting. Information about cash flows should help users to understand the operations of the entity, evaluate its financing activities, assess its liquidity or solvency or interpret earnings information.

*You should make specific comments for each problem that may be faced by users of financial statements*

A problem for users is the fact that entities can choose the method used and there is not enough guidance on the classification of cash flows in the operating, investing and financing sections of the indirect method used in IAS 7.

(ii)

*You should try to apply each of the fundamental ethical principles to the situation in the question. Try to avoid making general or vague comments, or referring to issues which are not relevant to the circumstances outlined in the question. Marks will be awarded for specific application and explanation of ethical issues associated with the situation in the question.*

The directors wish to manipulate the statement of cash flows in order to enhance their income. As stated above, the indirect method lends itself more easily to the manipulation of cash flows because of the complexity of the adjustments to net profit before tax and the directors are trying to make use of the lack of accounting knowledge of many users of accounts who are not sophisticated in their knowledge of cash flow accounting.

Corporate reporting involves the development and disclosure of information, which the entity knows is going to be used. The information has to be truthful and neutral. The nature of the responsibility of the directors requires a high level of ethical behaviour. Shareholders, potential shareholders, and other users of the financial statements rely heavily on the financial statements of a company as they can use this information to make an informed decision about investment. They rely on the directors to present a true and fair view of the company. Unethical behaviour is difficult to control or define. The directors must consider how to best apply accounting standards even when faced with issues that could cause them to lose income. The directors should not pursue self-interest or fail to maintain objectivity and independence, and must act with appropriate professional judgement. Therefore the proceeds of the loan should be reported as cash flows from financial activities.

| ACCA marking scheme | | | |
|---|---|---|---|
| | | | *Marks* |
| (a) | | Net profit before tax | 1 |
| | | Retirement benefit expense | 2 |
| | | Depreciation on PPE | 1 |
| | | Depreciation on investment property | 1 |
| | | Amortisation of intangible assets | 1 |
| | | Profit on sale of land | 1 |
| | | Profit on investment property | 1 |
| | | Associates profit | 1 |
| | | Impairment of goodwill | 4 |
| | | Fin assets at FV through OCI | 1 |
| | | Finance costs | 1 |
| | | Decrease in trade receivables | 1 |
| | | Decrease in inventories | 1 |
| | | Increase in trade payables | 1 |
| | | Cash paid to defined benefit scheme | 1 |
| | | Finance costs paid | 1 |
| | | Income taxes paid | 2 |
| | | Purchase of associate | 1 |
| | | Purchase of PPE | 2 |
| | | Purchase of subsidiary | 1 |
| | | Additions – investment property | 1 |
| | | Proceeds from sale of land | 1 |
| | | Intangible assets | 1 |
| | | Purchases of fin assets at FVTOCI | 1 |
| | | Repayment of long-term borrowings | 1 |
| | | Rights issue NCI | 1 |
| | | Non-controlling interest dividend | 1 |
| | | Dividends paid | 1 |
| | | Net increase in cash and cash equivalents | 1 |
| | | | 35 |
| (b) | (i) | Subjective | 6 |
| | (ii) | Subjective | 7 |
| | | Professional | 2 |
| Total | | | 50 |

**Examiner's comments**

This question required candidates to prepare a consolidated statement of cash flows for a group using the indirect method. The question required candidates to calculate goodwill on the acquisition of an entity where the group already held an investment in the entity. The goodwill needed to be calculated in order to ascertain the impairment of goodwill which was an adjustment to the operating activities of the group. Candidates performed well on this part of the question but often failed to take account of the deferred taxation adjustment. The question also required candidates to deal with the acquisition of the subsidiary in preparing the cash flow statement and to calculate the cash flows relating to the associate, PPE, non-controlling interest, deferred taxation, a defined benefit scheme, investment property, intangible assets and available-for-sale investments (now removed by IFRS 9). This part of the question was well answered. There were some elements of a cash flow question which are relatively easy to answer and candidates generally obtained the marks in these areas.

The main areas where candidates found difficulties were:

(1)     Ensuring that the purchase of the subsidiary was dealt with in calculating cash flows across the range of assets and liabilities.

(2)     The treatment of the past service costs relating to the defined benefit scheme

(3)     The calculation of the cash flows on taxation, although many candidates made a good attempt at this calculation.

Part b of the question required candidates to comment on the directors' view that the indirect method of preparing statements of cash flows is more useful and informative to users than the direct method and to discuss the reasons why the directors may wish to report the loan proceeds as an operating cash flow rather than a financing cash flow commenting on whether there are any ethical implications of adopting this treatment. The first part of this element of the question was often poorly answered. In fact often it was not attempted. Currently there is a debate over whether the direct method should be used in preference to the indirect method and thus candidates should be aware of the advantages and disadvantages of the methods. It shows that candidates are not reading widely enough and are focusing on a narrow range of topical issues. The ethical part of the question was quite well answered although many candidates did not read the question fully enough as it stated that the directors were to receive extra income if the operating cash flow exceeded a predetermined target for the year. Part of the answer to the question was therefore contained in the scenario. This further exemplifies the points raised in the introduction to this report (refer to ACCA web site for general introduction to the Examiner's Report).

**13  GRANGE (DEC 09 EXAM)**  *Walk in the footsteps of a top tutor*

**Key answer tips**

As with many of the group accounting questions, the difficulty in part (b) lies in the accounting issues included rather than the consolidation process itself. The best way to approach these questions is to deal with the issues individually and then note down the adjustments you need to make in the consolidated accounts. In this case there is revaluation and reclassification of non-current assets and determining whether a provision for environmental damage is required. There are also equity transfers between the group and non-controlling interest shareholders for two of the subsidiaries. Be careful not to spend too much time on these adjustments as you still have to do the consolidation. If you are getting bogged down, leave them and move on. Part (a) is a self-contained calculation of the gain or loss following loss of control of a subsidiary company. Part (c) should also be a source of marks with some thought before answering the question.

(a)  **Disposal of equity interest in Sitin**

*The disposal of shares results in a loss of control in Sitin; this requires a calculation of the gain or loss on disposal to be included in the group financial statements per IFRS 3 revised.*

The gain recognised in profit or loss would be as follows:

| Disposal on 30 November 2009 | | $m |
|---|---:|---:|
| Fair value of consideration received | | 23 |
| Fair value of residual interest: Associate to recognise on SOFP | | 13 |
| Less: net assets derecognised | (35) | |
| Less: goodwill derecognised ($39M – $32m) | (7) | (42) |
| | | ——— |
| Loss on disposal | | (6) |
| | | ——— |

*Notes:*

- Grange group entitled to their share of post-acquisition retained earnings up to disposal date: i.e. 100% ($35m – $32) = $3m.

- Need to recognise an associate based upon the fair value of the residual holding at 30 November 2009 which enabled Grange to exercise significant influence from that date.

(b) **Grange plc**

**Consolidated Statement of Financial Position at 30 November 2009**

|  | $m |
|---|---|
| Assets: | |
| Non-current assets: | |
| Intangible assets: goodwill (W3) | 38.00 |
| Intangible assets: franchise (W2) | 7.00 |
| Property, plant and equipment (W8) | 784.47 |
| Investment property – land (Issue 1) | 8.00 |
| Investment in associate (Part (a)) | 13.00 |
| | 850.47 |
| Current assets: ($475+ $304 + $141) | 920.00 |
| Total assets | 1770.47 |

|  | $m |
|---|---|
| Equity and liabilities | |
| Equity share capital | 430.00 |
| Retained earnings (W5) | 401.67 |
| Other components of equity (W5) | 56.98 |
| | 888.65 |
| Non-controlling interest (W4) | 141.82 |
| | 1,030.47 |
| Total equity of the group | 1,030.47 |
| Non-current liabilities: ($172 + $124 + $38) | 334.00 |
| Current liabilities | |
| Trade and other payables ($178 = $71 + $105) | 354.00 |
| Provisions (W9) | 52.00 |
| Total equity and liabilities | 1,770.47 |

*Workings*

*ISSUE 1 – THE PLOT OF LAND*

The plot of land is not being used for operational purposes, and Grange has not yet decided what to do with this asset. IAS 40 *Investment property* requires that such land should be classified as an investment property, rather than property, plant and equipment per IAS 16. It will therefore be measured at fair value, with changes in fair value taken to profit or loss. The subsequent fall in value is a non-adjusting event per IAS 10.

| Plot of land | $m |
|---|---|
| Initial recognition at cost within PPE (to be removed) | 6.0 |
| Increase in fair value to profit or loss | 2.0 |
| To group SOFP as investment property | 8.0 |

*ISSUE 2 – THE ENVIRONMENTAL ISSUES*

The anticipated fines of $1 million, together with the expected payments to local residents of $6 million are unavoidable obligations arising from past events and must be recognised in the financial statements. The request from the regulator to make changes to the manufacturing process does not amount to an unavoidable obligation arising from past event, and therefore should not be recognised.

*ISSUE 3 – THE FOREIGN PROPERTY*

Application of IAS 16 *Property, plant and equipment*, requires that if assets are revalued, any increase in carrying value is taken to revaluation reserve within equity. As this is a foreign property, the exchange rate at the reporting date is used to translate the year-end valuation of 12 million dinars.

|  | Dinar / Exchange rate | $m |
|---|---|---|
| Cost at acquisition | 8,000,000 / 2 | 4 |
| Increase in carrying value |  | 4 |
|  |  | ___ |
| Fair value at reporting date | 12,000,000 / 1.5 | 8 |
|  |  | ___ |

*ISSUE 4 – RESTUCTURING PROVISION & POSSIBLE IMPAIRMENT OF GRANGE*

There is not yet a detailed formal plan, together with communication to those likely to be affected by any restructuring. Consequently, there is no legal or constructive obligation to recognise and no provision can be made at the reporting date.

Leave the impairment review until last as it will be affected by any accounting adjustments required in respect of Grange. The question does provide some information regarding value in use and how any impairment should be allocated. See W7 within answer.

*Consolidation workings*

*Include any accounting adjustments relating to subsidiaries in the net assets working, so that their impact upon the group reserves and non-controlling interest can be easily dealt with.*

(W1) **Group structure**

Grange

| Park | 60% | Fence | 100% | Sitin | 100% |
|---|---|---|---|---|---|
| Purchase | 20% | Disposal | (25%) | Disposal | (60%) |
| Subsidiary | 80% | Subsidiary | 75% | Associate | 40% |

The share transactions during the year in respect of Park and Fence do not change control of those companies by Grange. They are therefore accounted for as transactions between equity holders. The disposal transaction in relation to Sitin results in a loss of control by Grange; a gain or loss on disposal must be accounted for, together with recognition of a subsidiary.

*This requires knowledge of accounting for fair value adjustments – in particular, criteria for recognition of the franchise as an intangible asset. You should also assess their impact at the reporting date, together with any other accounting adjustments required at the reporting date.*

(W2) **Net Assets**

| Park | Acquisition date | Reporting date | Post-acq'n |
|---|---|---|---|
| | $m | $m | $m |
| Equity shares | 230 | 230 | |
| Retained earnings | 115 | 170 | |
| Other equity components | 10 | 14 | 4 |
| FVA – land (bal fig) | 5 | 5 | |
| Per question | 360 | | |
| FVA – franchise | 10 | 10 | |
| Franchise amortisation | | (3) | |
| | 370 | 426 | 56 |

*This requires knowledge of accounting for fair value adjustments. You should also assess the impact of the revised estimate of the contingent liability, together with depreciation on the fair value adjustment for 16 months to the reporting date.*

| Fence | Acquisition date | Reporting date | Post-acq'n |
|---|---|---|---|
| | $m | $m | $m |
| Equity shares | 150 | 150 | |
| Retained earnings | 73 | 65 | |
| Other equity components | 9 | 17 | 8 |
| Contingent liability | (30) | (25) | |
| Per question | 202 | | |
| FVA – plant | 4 | 4 | |
| Plant dep'n (16/120 months) | | (0.53) | |
| | 206 | 210.47 | 4.47 |

*Goodwill is calculated using the full goodwill method per IFRS 3 revised for all members of the group.*

(W3) **Goodwill**

| | Park $m | Fence $m |
|---|---|---|
| Purchase consideration | 250 | 214 |
| Fair value of NCI at acquisition | 150 | n/a |
| | 400 | 214 |
| Fair value of net assets at acquisition (W2) | (370) | (206) |
| Full goodwill to SOFP | 30 | 8 |

*Non-controlling interest is measured on a fair value basis to be consistent with the goodwill accounting policy. Note also that there is a transfer between equity holders which must be accounted for.*

(W4) **Non-controlling interest**

| **Park** | | $m |
|---|---|---|
| FV of NCI at acquisition | | 150.0 |
| NCI % of post-acq'n mvt in net assets (W2) | 40% × (426 – 370) | 22.4 |
| Equity transfer on share purchase by group (W6) | | (85.2) |
| | | 87.2 |

| **Fence** | $m |
|---|---|
| Equity transfer on sale of shares by group (W6) | 54.62 |
| | 54.62 |

*Keep the working for retained earnings and other components of equity separate. Return to your earlier workings to identify any elements which have been calculated earlier which now need to be included within either retained earnings or other components of equity.*

**(W5)  Reserves –**

| Other components of equity | $m |
|---|---|
| Grange | 22.0 |
| Park 60% × (14 – 10) (W2) | 2.4 |
| Fence 100% × (17 – 9) (W2) | 8.0 |
| Equity movement re share transactions with NCI: | |
| Park (W6) | (4.8) |
| Fence (W6) | 25.38 |
| Revaluation of foreign property (Issue 3) | 4.0 |
| | 56.98 |

| Retained earnings | $m |
|---|---|
| Grange | 410.0 |
| Park 60% × (56 – 4) (W2) | 31.2 |
| Fence 100% × (4.47 – 8.0) (W2) | (3.53) |
| Sitin 100% × (35 – 32)  (part (a)) | 3.0 |
| Sitin – loss on disposal (part (a)) | (6.0) |
| Provision for environmental claims (Issue 2) | (7.0) |
| Investment property – land revalued (issue 1) | 2.0 |
| Impairment (Issue 4) (W7) | (28.0) |
| | 401.67 |

*When dealing with transactions between equity holders, you need to identify the carrying value of the entity or NCI as applicable to determine the change in carrying value in exchange for the cash received or paid.*

**(W6)  Transactions between equity holders**

| Park | Group buy additional 20% | | $m |
|---|---|---|---|
| | Cash paid | | (90.0) |
| | Decrease in NCI | 20% × 426 (W2) | 85.2 |
| | Net decrease in equity | | (4.8) |

*There is an alternative calculation for a decrease in NCI as follows:*

|  |  | $m |
|---|---|---|
| FV of NCI at acquisition |  | 150.0 |
| NCI share of change in net assets | 40% × 56 (W2) | 22.4 |
|  |  | 172.4 |
| Change in NCI | 20/40 | (86.2) |
|  |  | 86.2 |

If this alternative basis is adopted, the decrease in equity will be $1 million greater, with a consequent increase of $1 million in the NCI balance at the reporting date.

| Fence | Group sell 25% |  | $m |
|---|---|---|---|
|  | Cash received |  | 80.00 |
|  | Increase in NCI | 25% × (210.47 (W2) + 8.0 (W3)) | (54.62) |
|  | Increase in equity |  | 25.38 |

*In performing the impairment review, identify any accounting adjustments relating to Grange so that the correct carrying value of the entity, as a cash generating unit, is used.*

**(W7)  Impairment review – Grange**

|  |  | $m |
|---|---|---|
| Carrying value per draft FS |  | 862.0 |
| Revaluation of foreign property (Issue 3) |  | 4.0 |
| Provision for environmental claims (Issue 2) |  | (7.0) |
| Investment property revaluation (Issue 1) |  | 2.0 |
| Sitin – restatement of CV to FV of residual holding | ($13m – $16m) | (3.0) |
|  |  | 858.0 |
| Value in use before restructuring |  | 830.0 |
| Impairment – against property, plant and equipment |  | 28.0 |

**(W8) Property plant and equipment**

|  |  | $m |
|---|---|---|
| Grange |  | 257 |
| Park |  | 311 |
| Fence |  | 238 |
| FVA – Park – land (W2) |  | 5 |
| FVA – Fence – plant less dep'n (W2) | (4.0 – 0.53) | 3.47 |
| Revaluation of foreign property (Issue 3) |  | 4 |
| Investment property reclassified – land (Issue 1) |  | (6) |
| Impairment of Grange PPE (W7) |  | (28) |
|  |  | 784.47 |

**(W9) Provisions for liabilities**

|  | $m |
|---|---|
| Grange | 10 |
| Park | 6 |
| Fence | 4 |
| Contingent liability re Fence (W2) | 25 |
| Environmental provision (Issue 2) | 7 |
|  | 52 |

(c) Rules are a very important element of ethics. Usually this means focusing upon the rules contained in the accounting profession's code of professional conduct and references to legislation and corporate codes of conduct. They are an efficient means by which the accounting profession can communicate its expectations as to what behaviour is expected.

A view that equates ethical behaviour with compliance to professional rules could create a narrow perception of what ethical behaviour constitutes. Compliance with rules is not necessarily the same as ethical behaviour. Ethics and rules can be different. Ethical principles and values are used to judge the appropriateness of any rule.

Accountants should have the ability to conclude that a particular rule is inappropriate, unfair, or possibly unethical in any given circumstance. Rules are the starting point for any ethical question and rules are objective measures of ethical standards. In fact, rules are the value judgments as to what is right for accountants and reflect the profession's view about what constitutes good behaviour. Accountants who view ethical issues within this rigid framework are likely to suffer a moral crisis when encountering problems for which there is no readily apparent rule.

An overemphasis on ethical codes of behaviour tends to reinforce a perception of ethics as being punitive and does not promote the positive aspects of ethics that are designed to promote the reputation of an accounting firm and its clients, as well as standards within the profession. The resolution of ethical problems depends on the application of commonly shared ethical principles with appropriate skill and judgment. Ethical behaviour is based on universal principles and reasoned public debate and is difficult to capture in 'rules'.

Accountants have to make accounting policy choices on a regular basis. Stakeholders rely on the information reported by accountants to make informed decisions about the entity at hand. All decisions require judgment, and judgment depends on personal values with the decision needing to be made on some basis such as following rules, obeying authority, caring for others, justice, or whether the choice is right. These values and several others compete as the criterion for making a choice. Such personal values incorporate ethical values that dictate whether any accounting value chosen is a good or poor surrogate for economic value. To maintain the faith of the public, accountants must be highly ethical in their work. The focus on independence (conflict of interest) and associated compliance requirements may absorb considerable resources and conceptual space in relation to ethics in practice. This response is driven by a strong commitment within the firms to meet their statutory and regulatory obligations. The primary focus on independence may have narrowed some firms' appreciation of what constitutes broader ethical performance. As a result it may be that the increasing codification and compliance focus on one or two key aspects of ethical behaviour may be in fact eroding or preventing a more holistic approach to enabling ethics in practice.

If the director tells Field about the liquidity problems of Brook, then a confidence has been betrayed but there is a question of honesty if the true situation is not divulged. Another issue is whether the financial director has a duty to several stakeholders including the shareholders and employees of Grange, as if the information is disclosed about the poor liquidity position of Brook, then the amounts owing to Grange may not be paid. However, there is or may be a duty to disclose all the information to Field but if the information is deemed to be insider information then it should not be disclosed.

The finance director's reputation and career may suffer if Brook goes into liquidation especially as he will be responsible for the amounts owing by Brook. Another issue is whether the friend of the director has the right to expect him to keep the information private and if the shareholders of Grange stand to lose as a result of not divulging the information there may be an expectation that such information should be disclosed. Finally, should Field expect any credit information to be accurate or simply be a note of Brook's credit history? Thus it can be seen that the ethical and moral dilemmas facing the director of Grange are not simply a matter of following rules but are a complex mix of issues concerning trust, duty of care, insider information, confidentiality and morality.

| ACCA marking scheme | | |
|---|---|---|
| | | *Marks* |
| (a) | Fair value of consideration | 1 |
| | Fair value of residual interest | 1 |
| | Net assets | 2 |
| | Goodwill | 2 |
| | | ___ |
| | | 6 |
| | | ___ |
| (b) | Property plant & equipment | 6 |
| | Investment property | 2 |
| | Goodwill | 3 |
| | Retained earnings | 8 |
| | Other components of equity | 5 |
| | Non-controlling interest | 2 |
| | Non-current liabilities/trade and other payables | 1 |
| | Provisions for liabilities | 3 |
| | Intangible assets | 2 |
| | Current assets | 1 |
| | Investment in associate | 2 |
| | | ___ |
| | | 35 |
| | | ___ |
| (c) | Subjective up to | 7 |
| | Professional marks | 2 |
| | | ___ |
| Total | | 50 |
| | | ___ |

**Examiner's comments**

This required candidates to calculate a gain or loss on the disposal of an equity interest in a subsidiary, to prepare a consolidated statement of financial position and to discuss the relationship of ethical behaviour to professional rules. Candidates generally performed well in this question. The calculation of the loss arising on the disposal of the equity interest was extremely well answered with many candidates scoring full marks on this part of the question. The second part of the question additionally dealt with an acquisition of a further interest in a subsidiary and the disposal of a partial interest in a subsidiary as well as the treatment of contingent liabilities on consolidation, investment property, provisions for environmental claims, restructuring provisions and impairment. The breadth of topic areas was quite large. The main issues that candidates had were the calculations of the negative and positive movements in equity arising from the sale and purchase of equity holdings. Additionally the calculation of post acquisition reserves was quite complex and candidates did not always score well in this regard. However although candidates found it difficult to calculate post acquisition reserves, markers gave credit for the method and workings shown. The treatment of the non-consolidation adjustments (investment property, provisions for environmental claims, restructuring provisions etc) was generally well answered although a major failing often involved the non-recognition of the restructuring provision, as a constructive obligation did not exist. Part c of the question required candidates to discuss the relationship between ethical behaviour and professional rules. The question required candidates to comment on the ethical behaviour of a director where the director possessed confidential information. Candidates performed well on this part of the question but it must be emphasised that it is important to refer to the information in the question when writing the answer.

## 14 TREE

**Key answer tips**

This is a good question for testing knowledge dealing with the more advanced aspects of IFRS 3 and other practical aspects of dealing with a group statement of profit or loss and other comprehensive income. In particular, as a basis for dealing with those issues, you should begin by establishing the group structure, together with any changes in shareholding following acquisition. This should then enable you to deal with the consequences of selling shares in a subsidiary; in one situation control is lost, whilst in the other situation, control is retained. There are also other accounting issues to deal with as would be expected in an ACCA P2 question which should be tackled individually before including them in your finished statement.

(a) **Tree Group – Statement of profit or loss and other comprehensive income for the year ended 31 December 20X7**

|  | Tree $m | Branch $m | Leaf $m 6 mths | Adjust $m | SOCI $m |
|---|---|---|---|---|---|
| Revenue | 4,000 | 3,200 | 1,250 | (200) | 8,250.0 |
| Cost of sales | (3,000) | (2,800) | (1,180) | 200 |  |
| URP (W1) |  | 5 |  |  | (6,779.0) |
| Dep'n re FVA (W2) |  | (4) |  |  |  |
|  |  |  |  |  |  |
| Gross profit |  |  |  |  | 1,471.0 |
| Distribution costs | (240) | (80) | (26) |  | (346.0) |
| Admin expenses | (200) | (72) | (34) |  | (306.0) |
|  |  |  |  |  |  |
| Operating profit |  |  |  |  | 819.0 |
| Leaf – loss on disposal (W8) |  |  |  |  | (37.2) |
| Share of associate loss (W6) |  |  |  |  | (6.4) |
| Finance costs | (20) | (8) | (20) |  | (48.0) |
| Investment income (W3) | 100 |  |  | (48) | 52.0 |
|  |  |  |  |  |  |
| Profit before tax |  |  |  |  | 779.4 |
| Income tax | (180) | (72) | (6) |  | (258.0) |
|  |  |  |  |  |  |
| Profit for year |  | 169 | (16) |  | 521.4 |
| Other comp income: |  |  |  |  |  |
| Item that may be reclassified in future periods: |  |  |  |  |  |
| Cash flow hedge (W10) | 2 |  |  |  | 2.0 |
| Items that will not be reclassified in future periods: |  |  |  |  |  |
| Fin asset at FVTOCI (W9) | 19 |  |  |  | 19.0 |
| Net remeasurement component on defined benefit plan (W11) | (2) |  |  |  | (2.0) |
|  |  |  |  |  |  |
| Total comprehensive income |  | 169 | (16) |  | 540.4 |

**Profit for the year attributable to:**

| | | | |
|---|---|---|---|
| Non-controlling interests: | | | |
| Branch 6/12 × 25% × 169 | 21.1 | ) | |
| Branch 6/12 × 40% × 169 | 33.8 | ) | 51.7 |
| Leaf 20% × (16) | (3.2) | ) | |
| Group profit (bal fig) | | | 469.7 |
| | | | 521.4 |

**Total comp income attributable to:**

| | |
|---|---|
| Non-controlling interests as above: | 51.7 |
| Group profit (bal fig) | 488.7 |
| | 540.4 |

**Group structure:**

Tree

| | | | | |
|---|---|---|---|---|
| Branch | 75% | | Leaf | 80% Subsidiary 6 mths |
| | Disposal | | (15%) | (40%) Disposal |
| | Subsidiary for year | | 60% | 40% Associate 6 mths |
| Transfer between equity holders | | | Calculate gain/loss on disposal | |

*Workings*

(W1) **Adjustments for inter company trading**

The total intra-group trading must be removed from sales and cost of sales (purchases) – i.e. $200m

In addition the unrealised profit must be removed; this is based on the inventory held at the SOFP dates. The inter-company profit in the opening inventory of Tree was $40m × 25%, i.e. $10m, and in the closing inventory was $20m × 25%, i.e. $5m. These amounts are adjusted in cost of sales; the net effect is to reduce cost of sales by $5m.

(W2) **Depreciation adjustment due to fair valuation adjustment of Branch assets**

| | |
|---|---|
| Year ended 31 December 20X6 $20m × 6/12 × 20% = | $2m |
| Year ended 31 December 20X7 $20m × 20% = | $4m – i.e. current year |
| Cumulative depreciation adjustment re FVA | $6m |

(W3) **Investment income**

Intra-group dividend is cancelled on consolidation. Note (v) in the question states that Branch paid a dividend of $80m in April. At this date Tree had a 60% interest in Branch. Therefore, Tree's share of the dividend was $48m. This is removed from the investment income of Tree on consolidation. Remaining investment income for group statement of comprehensive income is therefore: $100m – $48m = $52m

(W4)  **Net assets**

| Branch | Acq'n date | | Disposal date |
|---|---|---|---|
| | $m | | $m |
| Share capital | 800 | | 800 |
| Retained earnings | 400 | b/fwd | 500 |
| | | 6/12 of year | 84 |
| FVA P&E (W2) | 20 | less dep'n per (W2) | 14 |
| FVA Land | 180 | | 180 |
| | _____ | | _____ |
| | 1,400 | | 1,578 |
| | _____ | | _____ |

| Leaf | Acq'n date | | Disposal date |
|---|---|---|---|
| | $m | | $m |
| Share capital | 600 | | 600 |
| Retained earnings | 200 | b/fwd | 200 |
| | | 6/12 of year | (16) |
| FVA Land | 100 | | 100 |
| | _____ | | _____ |
| | 900 | | 884 |
| | _____ | | _____ |

(W5)  **Goodwill – full goodwill method**

| | Branch | Leaf |
|---|---|---|
| | $m | $m |
| Cost of investment | 1,250 | 820 |
| Fair value of the NCI | 400 | 200 |
| Net assets at acquisition (W4) | (1,400) | |
| Net assets at acquisition (W4) | | (900) |
| | _____ | _____ |
| Full goodwill on acquisition | 250 | 120 |
| | _____ | _____ |

(W6)  Share of associate's loss after tax: 6/12 × (32) = (16) × 40% = (6.4) and no impairment loss.

(W7)  Impairment test for Leaf – only the group share of the loss for the last period should be included within the impairment review as follows:

| | $m | |
|---|---|---|
| Fair value of shareholding assessed as | 370.0 | |
| Less: group share of loss (W6) | (6.4) | |
| | _____ | |
| | 363.6 | |
| Recoverable amount – greater of | | |
| Value in use – 920 x 40% | 368 | |
| FV less costs to sell – 860 × 40% | 344 | Not impaired |

**(W8)   Leaf gain or loss on disposal**

|  |  |  | $m |
|---|---|---|---|
| Proceeds |  |  | 400.0 |
| FV of remaining equity interest |  |  | 370.0 |
|  |  |  | 770.0 |
| C V of subsidiary at disposal date: |  |  |  |
| Net assets (W4) |  | 884.0 |  |
| Unimpaired goodwill (W5) |  | 1200.0 |  |
| Less: NCI at disposal date: |  |  |  |
| FV of NCI at acquisition | 200.0 |  |  |
| Share of post acq'n loss (20% × 16) | (3.2) | (196.8) | (807.2) |
| Loss on disposal for group SOCI |  |  | (37.2) |

**(W9)   Financial assets at fair value through other comprehensive income**

Initial recognition is at fair value of $21m; it is correct to capitalise the $1m transaction costs. The investment should be valued at fair value as at the reporting date with any increase or decrease in fair value during the year taken to other comprehensive income.

$40m – 21m = Gain of $19m to include within other comprehensive income.

**(W10) Cash flow hedge**

As Tree has a forward contract this needs to be valued at fair value and included on the SOFP. The forward contract would appear to be advantageous in comparison with the situation at the reporting date. Tree has a derivative asset for the SOFP of 2m (32m –34m). As this is a designated and documented as a cash flow hedging instrument the gain is taken to equity and reported in other comprehensive income.

**(W11) Defined benefit pension plan**

|  | $m |
|---|---|
| Net obligation b/fwd | 50.0 |
| Net interest component @ 5% | 2.5 |
| Current service cost | 5.0 |
| Past service costs – recognised in full | 3.0 |
| Cash contribution into the plan | (4.0) |
| Net remeasurement component loss for the year (bal fig) | 2.0 |
| Net obligation c/fwd | 58.5 |

Past service costs, announced on 31 December 20X7, are recognised in full even though they do not vest for a further two years. This additional obligation does not incur a finance cost as the announcement was made at the reporting date. The net remeasurement component loss for the year is taken to other comprehensive income.

(b)     The disposal of shares in Branch is not relevant for calculation of a gain or loss on disposal for inclusion in the group statement of comprehensive income. Tree still retains a controlling interest in Branch; it is a subsidiary throughout the year – only the calculation of NCI will be time-apportioned as part of the results reported for the year. Instead, in accordance with IFRS 3 Revised, the transaction is regarded as one between shareholder groups.

In principle, this will result in a difference which will be a transfer to or from equity in exchange for a change in NCI as follows:

|  | $m |
|---|---|
| Cash received on disposal of shares | 280.0 |
| increase in NCI share of NA and goodwill at disposal date: | |
| 15% × (1,578 (W4) + 250 (W5)) | 274.2 |
| | ——— |
| Increase in equity | 5.8 |
| | ——— |

# SECTION B-TYPE QUESTIONS

## REPORTING STANDARDS

### 15   FINANCIAL PERFORMANCE AND OCI (JUN 05 EXAM)

**Key answer tips**

This question tests the current issues topic of financial performance and the reasons for the proposed changes to the current rules. It is the sort of question that is very difficult to answer without the requisite knowledge. It is an important area so try and note some of the Examiner's key points from the answer.

(a)     The main reasons why the two boards have decided to co-operate in a joint project regarding the presentation of other comprehensive income (OCI) are as follows:

(i)     There are many different formats and classifications used for financial statements and different time periods used for comparative data in different countries.

(ii)    There are no common definitions as regards the key elements of financial performance and no agreement on the standard definitions of the key ratios which would then determine the nature of the information that financial statements should provide. There has been an increase in the reporting of alternative and often inconsistent financial performance measures that has led to confusion and often has misled users.

(iii)     There has been an increase in the use of pro forma reporting which would tend to suggest that the existing totals and sub totals in financial statements are not being used or relied upon as much as in the past.

(iv)     There are benefits in separating transactions and events that are recorded at historical cost from those recorded at fair value. Also, the differentiation between trading and holding gains gives useful information. This 'mixed attribute' model is causing concern over the effects on reported performance.

(v)      There is often insufficient disaggregation of data which prevents effective financial analysis of performance.

(vi)     There has been an inconsistency in the use of 'recycling' in financial statements of different jurisdictions which has led to issues of reporting gains and losses twice.

(vii)    Information is inconsistently classified within and outside totals and subtotals.

(b)     The amendments to IAS 1 do not specify which items should be presented as part of other comprehensive income (OCI), or require that any new or additional items are presented in this way. This will be determined by the requirements of individual reporting standards which specify that particular items must be accounted for in this way. One example is IFRS 9 *Financial instruments*, which permits changes in fair value of some financial asset equity instruments to be taken to OCI in the year, provided appropriate designation has been made upon initial recognition. This may change as existing reporting standards are either revised or withdrawn and replaced by new reporting standards which may require reporting of items in OCI, rather than profit or loss for the year.

Instead, the amendments focus upon how items of OCI should be presented in the annual financial statements. One issue considered was whether there should be one combined statement of total comprehensive income for the year, or whether separate statements should be permitted for profit or loss for the year, and items of OCI. The arguments in favour of having a single statement of total comprehensive income include:

•    a lack of consistency and comparability in reported information where a choice of presentation method is permitted.

•    many recently issued new or revised reporting standards have narrowed down or eliminated choice of accounting treatment together with associated presentation and disclosures in order to reduce complexity in financial reporting. One example of this is recently revised IAS 19 *Employee benefits*, which now requires remeasurement gains and losses to be accounted for as part of other comprehensive income. Previously, there were three permitted accounting treatments for such gains and losses. Having one specified accounting treatment would follow the lead given by those recently issued or revised reporting standards to reduce complexity in financial reporting.

•    It would confirm the importance of items of OCI in reporting overall financial performance and position of an entity. If two separate statements were permitted, it would be possible for items of OCI to be de-emphasised or relegated in importance in comparison with other elements of reporting financial performance and position.

The amendments have retained the right of entities to choose whether or not to report items of OCI as part of a single statement of total performance, or to have separate statements for profit or loss and OCI respectively. However, to ensure that items of OCI are not de-emphasised in any way, when separate statements are prepared:

- the statement of OCI must immediately follow the statement of profit or loss, and ensure that there is no confusion between which items have been classified to profit or loss and which items have been classified to OCI.

- the statement of OCI must be given equal prominence with the statement of profit or loss for the year.

- A second issue considered was whether to present items of OCI net of tax, or to show them before related tax, with one tax adjustment for all items of reported OCI. Arguably, presentation of amounts of OCI before their tax effects could be useful and relevant information to users of financial statements. This is a continuation of the existing requirements, which ensure that entities disclose the tax effects of all items of comprehensive income, but permits some flexibility in how it is reported.

A third issue considered was whether items of OCI should be classified or grouped together based upon specified criteria. This could be useful if the criteria applied was regarded as logical, appropriate and reportable by those who by those who applied any such criteria, and also by those who used that information.

This has the danger of being regarded as arbitrary classification or grouping of information, which may undermine consistency and comparability of financial reporting information. However, if done on a basis which is generally regarded as being relevant to users of financial statements, such grouping or classification of information could be helpful.

The amendments to IAS 1 require that items of OCI are grouped together, based upon whether or not they may be recycled to profit or loss in a subsequent accounting period. Based upon this classification, items which may be recycled to profit or loss in a subsequent accounting period include:

- Foreign exchange gains and losses arising on translation of financial statements of a foreign operation per IAS 21. This will normally arise upon disposal of a foreign subsidiary, with the net cumulative foreign exchange gain or loss being included as part of the reported profit or loss on disposal.

- Cash flow hedging arrangements per IAS 39.

Items which will not be subject to recycling to profit or loss in a subsequent accounting period include:

- Revaluation of property, plant and equipment per IAS 16 and revaluation of intangible assets per IAS 38

- Remeasurement gains and losses arising on defined benefit pension plans per IAS 19

- Financial assets measured at fair value through other comprehensive income per IFRS 9.

(c)   Recycling is an issue for both the current performance statements and the single statement of comprehensive income. Recycling occurs where an item of financial performance is reported in more than one accounting period because the nature of the item has in some way changed. It raises the question as to whether gains and losses originally reported in one section of the statement should be reported in another section at a later date. An example would be gains/losses on the retranslation of the net investment in an overseas subsidiary. These gains could be reported annually on the retranslation of the subsidiary and then again when the subsidiary was sold.

The main arguments for recycling to take place are as follows:

* when unrealised items become realised they should be shown again
* when uncertain measurements become certain they should be reported again
* all items should be shown in operating or financing activities at some point in time as all items of performance are ultimately part of operating or financing activities of an entity.

There is no conceptual justification for recycling. Once an item has been recognised in a statement of financial performance it should not be recognised again in a future period in a different part of that statement. Once an item is recognised in the statement there is an assumption that it can be reliably measured and therefore it should be recognised in the appropriate section of the statement with no reason to show it again.

Gains and losses should not be based on the notion of realisation. Realisation may have been a critical event historically but given the current financial exposures of many entities, such a principle has limited value. A realised gain reflects the same economic gain as an unrealised gain. Items should be classified in the performance statement on the basis of characteristics which are more useful than realisation. The effect of realisation is explained better in the statement of cash flows. Realisation means different things in different countries. In Europe and Asia it refers to the amount of distributable profits but in the USA it refers to capital maintenance. The amount of distributable profits is not an accounting but a legal issue, and therefore realisation should not be the overriding determinant of the reporting of gains and losses.

Changes in the financial reporting requirements relating to financial assets as introduced by IFRS 9 eliminated the 'available-for-sale' classification of financial assets as defined by IAS 39. Accounting for such financial assets required recycling of amounts previously taken to other comprehensive income, typically upon disposal. This equivalent category of financial assets based upon IFRS 9 is financial assets measured at fair value through other comprehensive income, which does not require recycling of any amounts previously taken to other comprehensive income in previous accounting periods.

An alternative view could be that an unrealised gain is more subjective than a realised gain. In many countries, realised gains are recognised for distribution purposes because of their certainty because this gives more economic stability to the payment of dividends.

| ACCA marking scheme | | Marks |
|---|---|---|
| (a) | Reasons for convergence | 8 |
| (b) | Amendments to IAS 1 comments | 10 |
| (c) | Recycling discussion | 7 |
| Total | | 25 |

## 16 INVESTMENTS IN OTHER ENTITIES

**Key answer tips**

This question tests current knowledge of new and revised reporting standards that were issued in 2011. A good approach to answering this question is to explain why the new and revised reporting standards have been introduced, before proceeding on to make specific comments about each reporting standard in turn.

The issue of the new and revised reporting standards relating to interests in other entities forms part of the response by the accounting profession to the global financial crisis. In particular, the previous reporting standards were not sufficiently extensive to provide unambiguous guidance on accounting requirements in all commercial situations where one entity may have an interest in another. This had the consequence that a range of accounting treatments had developed over time when dealing with interests in other entities.

As a separate, but related, issue the new and revised reporting standards represents a move towards increased convergence between IFRS and US GAAP in accounting for interests in other entities.

Note that the five new and revised reporting standards were issued as a 'pack of five' and should be adopted on an 'all-or-none' basis by entities. The one exception to this requirement is that IFRS 12 can be adopted early as an individual reporting standard as this relates to disclosure requirements only. The five new or revised reporting standards are effective for accounting periods commencing on or after 1 January 2013, with earlier adoption permitted.

Each of the new and revised reporting standards will now be considered in turn:

**IFRS 10 *Consolidated financial statements***

IFRS 10 replaces most, but not all, of IAS 27. There is now a single basis of control to determine whether consolidation of entities is required. This definition should be subject to continuous assessment, and should be considered at least at each reporting date to determine that control continues to be exercised. In developing the new standard, it is hoped that areas of divergent practice which had developed will be removed, such as:

- Having control with less than a majority of voting rights
- Accounting for special purpose entities
- Determining whether there is a principal or agent relationship
- Consideration of protective rights, which only become effective upon specified circumstances arising.

IFRS 10 identifies that control consists of three components:

1   Power over the investee; this is normally exercised through the majority of voting rights, but could also arise through other contractual arrangements.

2   Exposure or rights to variable returns (positive and/or negative) from involvement; and

3   The ability to use power over the investee to affect the amount of investor returns. The ability to use power over an investee to affect returns is regarded as a crucial determinant in deciding whether or not control is exercised.

IFRS 10 identifies that there is normally a correlation between exposure or rights to variable returns and the exercise of power, although this may not be conclusive in itself to identify a control relationship.

Power relates only to substantive, rather than protective rights. The former arises where there is practical ability to exercise rights of control at the time when relevant decisions are made. This would comprise right which are currently exercisable, rather than potential voting rights, which may arise from exercise of share options at some later date. The latter may arise where control may only be exercised only upon pre-determined circumstances arising at some later date. Examples of the latter situation could be the rights of lenders to restrict the permitted activities of a borrower that could significantly change the credit risk attached to those borrowings, or the rights of a lender to seize assets in the event of non-compliance with loan repayment conditions.

IFRS 10 also considers whether a portion of an entity (referred to as a "silo") can be considered as a separate entity for the purposes of consolidation. This may lead to the situation of consolidation of only that part of a separate entity over which control is exercised. For this to be the case, the definition of control as previously outlined must apply to distinguishable or ring-fenced assets and liabilities.

Additionally, IFRS 10 considers whether it is possible to exercise control without holding a majority of the voting shares, and in the absence of any additional factors, such as contractual arrangements to control the composition of the board of directors. If the three components of control are present then, even without the majority of voting shares, one entity may control another and therefore account for it as a subsidiary in group accounts. This could arise, for example, where one entity holds 48% of the voting shares in another entity, with the remaining shareholdings spread between considerable numbers of other shareholders. If the other shareholders are unconnected with each other and have expressed no particular voting preferences in the past, it may be that control can be exercised by the majority shareholder, even though they do not own or control most of the voting shares.

Note that IFRS 10 does not change the basic mechanics of how a consolidation is performed – it clarifies when control is exercised and therefore when consolidation is required.

### IFRS 11 *Joint arrangements*

IFRS 11 supersedes IAS 31 *Interests in joint ventures*. It now requires the equity method of accounting for those arrangements which can be identified as a joint venture and removes the alternative method of proportionate method of consolidation permitted by IAS 31.

Key definitions are as follows:

- **Joint arrangements** are defined as arrangements where two or more parties have joint control, and that this will only apply if the relevant activities require unanimous consent of those who collectively control the arrangement. They may take the form of either joint operations or joint ventures. The key distinction between the two forms is based upon the parties' rights and obligations under the joint arrangement.

- **Joint operations** are defined as joint arrangements whereby the parties that have joint control have rights to the assets and obligations for the liabilities. Normally, there will not be a separate entity established to conduct joint operations. IFRS 11 requires that joint operators each recognise their share of assets, liabilities, revenues and expenses of the joint operation. This may consist of maintaining a joint operation account to record transactions undertaken on behalf of the joint operation, together with balances due to or from other parties to the joint operation.

- **Joint ventures** are defined as joint arrangements whereby the parties have joint control of the arrangement and have rights to the net assets of the arrangement. This will normally be established in the form of a separate entity to conduct the joint venture activities. The equity method of accounting must be used in this situation in accordance with IAS 28 (revised).

The disclosure requirements applicable to accounting for joint arrangements are specified in IFRS 12 *Disclosure of interests in other entities*.

**IFRS 12 *Disclosure of interests in other entities***

IFRS 12 applies to entities that have an interest in subsidiaries, joint arrangements and associates – i.e. where there is control, joint control or significant influence. IFRS 9 (or IAS 39 if IFRS 9 not yet adopted) details the accounting requirements where control, joint control or significance does not apply and require that any equity interest in another entity is measured at fair value.

IFRS 12 Is designed to provide relevant information to users of financial statements. As such it requires disclosure of details relating to the composition of the group, details of non-controlling interests within the group, identification and evaluation of risks associated with any interests held in other entities which give rise to control, joint control or significant influence. In principle, there are more detailed and extensive disclosures required by IFRS 12 which has collated, and extended, the disclosure requirements previously contained in several reporting standards.

**IAS 27 *Separate financial statements* (Revised)**

IAS 27 (revised) applies when an entity has interests in subsidiaries, joint ventures or associates and either elects to, or is required to, prepare separate non-consolidated financial statements.

If the financial statements are not consolidated, they must therefore present interests in other entities at cost or in accordance with IFRS 9 *Financial instruments (*or IAS 39 if IFRS 9 not yet adopted). To the extent that IAS 27 used to apply to consolidated financial statements, those requirements have either been deleted or transferred to IFRS 10 or IFRS 12 respectively.

**IAS 28 *Investments in associates and joint ventures* (Revised)**

IAS 28 (revised) specifies the accounting treatment for associates, together with the requirements of equity accounting. It will therefore continue to apply to situations where significant influence is exercised over an associate, and where there is a joint arrangement in the form of a joint venture as defined in IFRS 11 *Joint arrangements*. Note that IFRS 9 does not apply to interests in an associate and/or joint venture where the equity method is to be applied.

An interest in an associate or joint venture should be accounted for in the separate financial statements of an entity in accordance with accordance with IAS 27 (Revised)

| ACCA marking scheme | |
|---|---|
| | *Marks* |
| Context/reasons etc | 4 |
| IFRS 10 | 7 |
| IFRS 11 | 4 |
| IFRS 12 | 4 |
| IAS 27 (revised) | 3 |
| IAS 28 (revised) | 3 |
| | — |
| Total | 25 |
| | — |

## 17    FAIR VALUE MEASUREMENT (IFRS 13)

**Key answer tips**

This question deals solely with the requirements if IFRS 13. You therefore need to attempt each part of the question requirement in a logical order, ensuring that you allocate your time to the marks available so that you attempt all part of the question.

(a)    **Reasons for the issue of IFRS 13**

IFRS 13 *Fair value measurement* was issued by the International Accounting Standards Board (IASB) in May 2011 and is effective for accounting periods commencing on or after 1 January 2013, with earlier adoption permitted. It represents completion of a joint project between the IASB and the equivalent body in the US, the Financial Accounting Standards Board (FASB) to converge the definition of what constitutes a fair value measurement, and how it is defined and determined by entities who apply the new reporting standard.

One key point to remember that IFRS 13 does not add to the situations or circumstances when fair value measurement is required by current reporting standards. Equally, it is also important to remember that IFRS 13 does not apply in all situations, for example it does not apply in the following situations:

(i)     When a different measurement is required by a reporting standard, even though it may have some similarities with fair value. For example, measurements such as net realisable value, replacement cost and value in use may be required in different situations when preparing financial statements. However, they are not fair value measurements and are not covered by the requirements of IFRS 13.

(ii)    The requirements of IFRS 13 do not apply to the transactions covered by IFRS 2 *Share-based payment* and IAS 17 *Leases*, where the specific requirements of those standards should be applied where relevant.

There are several reasons for the issue of IFRS 13 as follows:

(i)     To overcome inconsistency in the way that fair value measurements required by a reporting standard are determined for inclusion in the financial statements of an entity.

(ii)    To overcome increasing complexity in how fair value measurements are currently determined by individual entities in different situations. There is currently guidance in several reporting standards, on a piecemeal basis, to help determine fair value measurements when required, which is not necessarily consistent of comprehensive for preparers of financial statements to apply.

(iii)   To form part of the response of the accountancy profession to the global financial crisis.

(iv) To increase and converge the supporting disclosure requirements to provide information that is relevant to users of financial statements, so that they understand the basis upon which a fair value measurement has been determined and applied with a set of financial statements.

(v) To increase the extent of convergence between IFRS GAAP and US GAAP as there is now a common definition for fair value measurement, together with a structure or framework for how it is to be determined when required by either IFRS GAAP or US GAAP.

Note that, even though the definition of what constitutes a fair value measurement, together with supporting disclosures, in accordance with IFRS 13 may be converged with the equivalent US GAAP requirement, the situations when it may be required by either GAAP have still to be converged. This means that there may still be differences between IFRS GAAP and US GAAP when a fair value measurement is required by one GAAP in a given situation, but not required by the other, and vice versa.

(b) **How fair value is determined by IFRS 13:**

The definition included with IFRS 13 is as follows:

"...the price that would be received to sell an asset or paid to transfer a liability in an orderly transaction between market participants at the measurement date" (Para 9).

In effect, this is an exit price that would be received upon disposal of an asset, or upon transfer of a liability, at the specific date required. Note that transfer of a liability is not the same as settlement of a liability at a specific date as, for example, early settlement of a liability may result in incurring early redemption penalty charges, or even an early settlement rebate may be applicable in certain circumstances.

Fair value is therefore focuses upon the assumptions of the marketplace and is not entity-specific. It takes into account any assumptions about risk as the exit price is measured using the same assumptions and taking into account the same characteristics of the asset or liability as considered by relevant by market participants. Such characteristics would normally include the condition and location of the asset, together with any restrictions on its sale or use.

If elements of the above definition are considered in more detail; "orderly transaction" refers to the situation that the circumstances of the potential sale of an asset or transfer of a liability would not be undertaken in a distress or emergency situation. Therefore, the best possible price should be capable of being attained through the operation of a normal market mechanism which requires the interaction of buyers and sellers. The consequence of this approach is that an entity's view of what may or may not be fair value is not relevant – it is determined by the market mechanism.

A further implication of a transaction being regarded as orderly is that there is sufficient exposure of the asset or the liability to the relevant market. This will involve any related marketing activity usually associated with a particular asset or liability to enable a reliable fair value measurement to be made at the required date, normally, but not always, the reporting date of an entity.

It can be appreciated that if the market for an asset or liability is active, then a certain level of business activity is likely to lead to a reliable indicator of fair value. If there is a low level of business activity, there is a risk that any prices agreed may not be a reliable indicator of fair value. However, if it can be demonstrated that there has been sufficient time for competitive forces to apply, and that appropriate marketing activity has been undertaken, even when there are few transactions taking place, they may still be regarded as orderly and therefore reliable.

IFRS 13 also considers what it refers to as the unit of account; this is the individual asset or liability or group of assets or liabilities, required to be measured to fair value by a particular reporting standard. However, the measurement to fair value should only take into account the characteristics of the asset or liability to be measured; it should not take into account the characteristics of the transaction itself. For example, if a bulk quantity of an asset was to be valued based upon its' disposal value, the transaction value achieved may be affected by the number of units or quantity of the asset that is to be measured. Any value achieved may be affected by whether either a premium or discount to the normal unit price is applicable to a particular transaction, purely due to the quantity of an asset to be sold. However, such a premium or discount is a characteristic of the transaction, not of the asset or liability to be measured, and therefore should be ignored when measuring fair value.

**Which market?**

IFRS 13 assumes that any fair value measurement for an asset or liability is based upon the value as determined by the principal market for that asset or liability or, in the absence of a principal market, in the most advantageous market for that asset or liability. In this situation, the principal market is regarded as the one with the greatest volume and level of activity for that asset or liability that can be accessed by the entity. The most advantageous market is the one that maximises the amount that would be received for the asset or paid to extinguish the liability after transport and transaction costs. In many cases, the principal market and the most advantageous market will be the same, but this may not always be the case.

Note that, where there is no principal market, and the most advantageous market is used to determine fair value, transactions costs are taken into account to determine which is the most advantageous market, even though they are then omitted when determining fair value of the asset or liability. This can be illustrated as follows:

An asset is sold in two different active markets at different prices, and an entity is able to access both markets at the measurement date as follows:

|                   | Market 1 | Market 2 |
|-------------------|----------|----------|
|                   | $        | $        |
| Price             | 31       | 29       |
| Transactions cost | (5)      | (2)      |
| Transport cost    | (3)      | (3)      |
|                   | 23       | 24       |

If Market 1 is the principal market for the asset (i.e. the market with the greatest volume and level of activity for the asset to be measured), the fair value of the asset would be measured using the price that would be received in that market, after taking into account transport costs, to arrive at a fair value of ($31 − $3) $28. Transactions costs are ignored as they are a characteristic of the transaction, not of the asset to be measured.

In neither market is the principal market, the fair value of the asset would be measured using the price in the most advantageous market. This is defined as the market that maximises the net amount that would be received in a sale, after taking both transactions costs and transport costs – i.e. the net amount that would be received in each of the respective markets. In this situation, Market 2 maximises the net amount that would be received at $24. Consequently, fair value is measured at the price in that market, $29, less transport costs of $3 to arrive at a fair value measurement of $26. Notice in this situation, transactions costs are taken into account to determine which is the most advantageous market but, having determined this, they are then excluded from the determination of the fair value measurement.

IFRS 13 sets out a valuation approach that refers to a broad range of techniques. These techniques are threefold: the market, income and cost approaches. When measuring fair value, the entity is required to maximise the use of observable inputs and minimise the use of unobservable inputs. To this end, the standard introduces a fair value hierarchy, which prioritises the inputs into the fair value measurement process.

IFRS 13 requires that fair value is measured on a consistent basis, using as much objective data or information as possible, and thus minimising the extent to which unsupported or subjective assessment is made as part of the fair value measurement process. Consequently, IFRS 13 identifies a three-tier fair value hierarchy based upon the nature of the inputs used to determine a fair value measurement. In applying the hierarchy, entities are required to maximise as far a possible the use of higher level inputs as identified below.

|  | **Asset or Liability to be measured** | **Example** |
| --- | --- | --- |
| **Level 1** | Equity shares in a listed entity | Unadjusted quoted prices in an active market for an identical asset or liability i.e. identical shares |
| **Level 2** | Equity shares in an unlisted entity | Quoted price for a similar asset in an active market, adjusted to reflect that the shares to be measured are not listed. |
| **Level 3** | Cash generating unit | Profit or cash flow information using own data. |

Level 1 inputs (the highest level) are unadjusted quoted prices for identical assets or liabilities in an active market at the measurement date.

An active market is regarded as one in which transactions take place with sufficient frequency and volume for reliable pricing information to be provided. This may still be possible where there is a low volume of transactions, provided that there has been sufficient time for reasonable marketing and other market-related activity to take place and where it is clear that any such transactions are not based upon distress transactions.

Level 2 inputs are inputs other than quoted prices in level 1 that are observable for that specific asset or liability. They could be, for example, quoted prices for a similar asset or liability in an active market; they would need to be adjusted to reflect what should be an active market for an identical asset, perhaps by use of additional research data.

The nature and extent of the inputs used in a particular fair value measurement, together with their relative significance, will determine whether they are regarded as having been determined by mainly level 2 or level 3 inputs.

Level 3 inputs are unobservable inputs, the use of which should be minimised as far as possible. Where observable inputs are not available, level 3 unobservable inputs should be developed to reflect the assumptions that market participants would use when determining an appropriate price for an asset or liability.

An asset or liability is then regarded as having been measured using the highest level of inputs that were significant to its valuation.

(c) **Explain the nature of disclosures required by the new reporting standard**

The reporting standard together with the supporting guidance notes, include more extensive disclosure requirements in contrast with previous requirements. Consequently, this is likely to result in additional time and cost being incurred by entities as they achieve compliance with the requirements of IFRS 13 for the first time, and thereafter in subsequent years.

The nature of the disclosures include:

- Methods and inputs used in the process to determine a fair value measurement, together with any changes in valuation techniques which have been applied from one reporting date to the next;

- Information relating to the hierarchy level which is applicable to a particular fair value measurement included within the financial statements;

- Any transfers between level one and level two of the valuation hierarchy;

- For the lowest category within the hierarchy, level three, requirements include details of assumptions used to help determine fair value measurement, a reconciliation of opening and closing balances and additional information regarding unobservable inputs.

This standard is relatively straightforward in terms of the principles it seeks to apply – i.e. to provide a consistent and transparent basis for the determination of a fair value measurement when it is required. However, many entities in formalising their approach to fair value measurement may need to undertake additional work to demonstrate compliance with IFRS 13.

| ACCA marking scheme | | |
|---|---|---:|
| | | *Marks* |
| (a) | Introduction of IFRS 13 | 5 |
| (b) | How fair value is measured | 15 |
| (c) | Disclosures explained | 5 |
| | | —— |
| Total | | 25 |
| | | —— |

**18    ROCKBY (JUN 04 EXAM)**

**Key answer tips**

Make sure that you have a good understanding of IFRS 5 before you choose to attempt this question. IFRS 5 is triggered when an asset qualifies as being held for sale or has been disposed of. These two sets of conditions are not exactly the same.

(a)    Under IFRS 5 *Non-current assets held for sale and discontinued operations*, a non-current asset or disposal group (in this case Bye – as it is a cash generating unit) should be classified as held for sale if its carrying amounts will be recovered principally through a sale transaction rather than through continuing use. The criteria which have to be met are:

(i)     a commitment to a plan

(ii)    the asset is available for immediate sale

(iii)   actively trying to find a buyer

(iv)    sale is highly probable

(v)     asset is being actively marketed

(vi)    unlikely to be significant changes to the plan.

These criteria seem to have been met in this case. Before classification of the item as held for sale an impairment review will need to be undertaken irrespective of any indication or otherwise of impairment. Any loss will be recognised in profit or loss. The figure of $4.5 million will be used as fair value less costs to sell. The net assets and goodwill will be written down to $4.5 million with the write off going against goodwill in the first instance.

IFRS 5 requires items held for sale to be reported at the lower of carrying value and fair value less costs to sell. IFRS 5 requires extensive disclosure on the face of the statement of comprehensive income and in the notes regarding the subsidiary. In the statement of financial position, it should be presented separately from other assets and liabilities. The assets and liabilities should not be offset. There are additional disclosures to be made concerning the facts and circumstances leading to the disposal and the segment in which the subsidiary is presented under IFRS 8 *Operating segments.*

(b)    **Non-current assets**

(i)     To qualify as a held for sale asset, the sale must be highly probable and generally must be completed within one year. In the case of the operating lease assets, they will not qualify as held for sale assets at 31 March 20X4 as the company has not made a decision as to whether they should be sold or leased. They should, therefore, be shown as non-current assets and depreciated. Held for sale assets are not depreciated. The carrying value of the assets will be $10 million. Held for sale assets are valued at the lower of carrying value and fair value less selling costs under IFRS 5. The assets are not impaired because the value in use is above the carrying value.

The plant would not be classed as a held for sale asset at 31 March 20X4 even though the plant was sold at auction prior to the date that the financial statements were signed. The held for sale criteria were not met at the end of the reporting period and IFRS 5 prohibits the classification of non-current assets as held for sale if the criteria are met after the end of the reporting period and before the financial statements are signed. The company should disclose relevant information in notes to the financial statements for the year-ended 31 March 20X4.

(ii)   Under IFRS 5, a non-current asset qualifies as held for sale if it is available for immediate sale in its present condition subject to the usual selling terms. The company should have the intent and the ability to sell the asset in its present condition. At 31 March 20X3, although the company ultimately wishes to sell the property, it would be unlikely to achieve this until the subsidence was dealt with. Additionally the company's view was that the property should be sold when the renovations were completed which would have been at 1 June 20X3. Also as at 31 March 20X3, the company had not attempted to find a buyer for the property. Hence the property could not be classed as held for sale at that date.

As at 31 March 20X4, the property had not been sold although it had been on the market for over nine months. The market conditions had deteriorated significantly and yet the company did not wish to reduce the price. It seems as though the price asked for the property is in excess of its fair value especially as a bid of $8.3 million was received shortly after the year-end (20 April 20X4). The property has been vacated and, therefore, is available for sale but the price does not seem reasonable in relation to its current fair value ($10 million price as opposed to $8.3 million bid and ultimate sale of $7.5 million). Therefore, it would appear that at 31 March 20X4, the intent to sell the asset might be questionable. The property fails the test set out in IFRS 5 as regards the reasonableness of price and, therefore, should not be classed as held for sale.

*Memorandum note:* If the land and buildings had been classified as held for sale then the property would be impaired if at either date the carrying value was greater than the fair value less costs to sell.

| 31 March 20X3: | Carrying value | $5m |
| | Renovations | $2.3 |
| | | ——— |
| | Carrying value | $7.3 |
| | | ——— |
| | Fair value (say) | $10 |
| | | ——— |
| 31 March 20X4: | Carrying value | $7 |
| | Fair value (20/04/04) (bid) | $8.3 |
| | | ——— |
| | Selling price (net of costs) 1/06/04 | $7.5 |
| | | ——— |

Thus the land and buildings would not have been impaired at either date.

| ACCA marking scheme | | | |
|---|---|---|---|
| | | | *Marks* |
| (a) | | Discussion    IFRS 5 | 5 |
| | | Impairment    IFRS 5 | 3 |
| (b) | (i) | Operating lease | 4 |
| | (ii) | Plant | 3 |
| | (iii) | Property | 5 |
| | | | ___ |
| Total | | | 20 |
| | | | ___ |

## 19    CATE (JUN 10 EXAM)  *Walk in the footsteps of a top tutor*

**Key answer tips**

This multi-topic question has a mark allocation against each topic to help you allocate your time. Normally, each element of the multi-topic question is independent of each other, and can therefore be attempted in any order. You should apply good exam technique and attempt each part in the order which you find easiest to deal with. Remember to clearly identify which order you attempted each part of the question so that the examiner can clearly follow what you have done.

*A good starting point is to state and explain the criteria for recognition of a deferred tax asset. Develop your answer to apply this information to the scenario. You should then be able to identify and explain whether this complies with IAS 12. If it does not, you should state this clearly, and explain the appropriate accounting treatment in the circumstances.*

(a)    A deferred tax asset should be recognised for deductible temporary differences, unused tax losses and unused tax credits to the extent that it is probable that taxable profit will be available against which the deductible temporary differences can be utilised. The recognition of deferred tax assets on losses carried forward does not seem to be in accordance with IAS 12 *Income taxes*. Cate is not able to provide convincing evidence that sufficient taxable profits will be generated against which the unused tax losses can be offset. According to IAS 12 the existence of unused tax losses is strong evidence that future taxable profit may not be available against which to offset the losses. Therefore when an entity has a history of recent losses, the entity recognises deferred tax assets arising from unused tax losses only to the extent that the entity has sufficient taxable temporary differences or there is convincing other evidence that sufficient taxable profit will be available. As Cate has a history of recent losses and as it does not have sufficient taxable temporary differences, Cate needs to provide convincing other evidence that sufficient taxable profit would be available against which the unused tax losses could be offset. The unused tax losses in question did not result from identifiable causes, which were unlikely to recur (IAS 12) as the losses are due to ordinary business activities. Additionally there are no tax planning opportunities available to Cate that would create taxable profit in the period in which the unused tax losses could be offset (IAS 12).

Thus at 31 May 2010 it is unlikely that the entity would generate taxable profits before the unused tax losses expired. The improved performance in 2010 would not be indicative of future good performance as Cate would have suffered a net loss before tax had it not been for the non-operating gains.

Cate's anticipation of improved future trading could not alone be regarded as meeting the requirement for strong evidence of future profits. When assessing the use of carry-forward tax losses, weight should be given to revenues from existing orders or confirmed contracts rather than those that are merely expected from improved trading. Estimates of future taxable profits can rarely be objectively verified. Thus the recognition of deferred tax assets on losses carried forward is not in accordance with IAS 12 as Cate is not able to provide convincing evidence that sufficient taxable profits would be generated against which the unused tax losses could be offset.

*A good starting point is to set out the definition of recoverable amount as used in an impairment test. It should then be applied as far as practicable to the situation in the question. As with part (a), if the accounting treatment does not comply with a reporting standard, this should be identified and explained.*

(b)  **Investment**

Cate's position for an investment where the investor has significant influence and its method of calculating fair value can be challenged.

An asset's recoverable amount represents its greatest value to the business in terms of its cash flows that it can generate i.e. the higher of fair value less costs to sell (which is what the asset can be sold for less direct selling expenses) and value in use (the cash flows that are expected to be generated from its continued use including those from its ultimate disposal). The asset's recoverable amount is compared with its carrying value to indicate any impairment. Both net selling price (NSP) and value in use can be difficult to determine. However it is not always necessary to calculate both measures, as if the NSP or value in use is greater than the carrying amount, there is no need to estimate the other amount.

It should be possible in this case to calculate a figure for the recoverable amount. Cate's view that market price cannot reflect the fair value of significant holdings of equity such as an investment in an associate is incorrect as IAS 36 prescribes the method of conducting the impairment test in such circumstances by stating that if there is no binding sale agreement but an asset is traded in an active market, fair value less costs to sell is the asset's market price less the costs of disposal. Further, the appropriate market price is usually the current bid price.

Additionally the compliance with IAS 28, Investments in associates is in doubt in terms of the non-applicability of value in use when considering impairment. IAS 28 explains that in determining the value in use of the investments, an entity estimates:

(i) its share of the present value of the estimated future cash flows expected to be generated by the associate, including the cash flows from the operations of the associate and the proceeds on the ultimate disposal of the investment; or

(ii) the present value of the estimated future cash flows expected to arise from dividends to be received from the investment and from its ultimate disposal.

Estimates of future cash flows should be produced. These cash flows are then discounted to present value hence giving value in use.

It seems as though Cate wishes to avoid an impairment charge on the investment.

*This part of the question deals mainly with IFRS 5; you should state and apply the criteria for a disposal group to be regarded as 'held for sale'.*

(c) **Disposal group 'held for sale'**

IAS 27 *Consolidated and separate financial statements* first moved IFRS to the use of the economic entity model when considering group accounting. This concept has been retained in IFRS 10 *Consolidated financial statements* which supersedes IAS 27 for all matters dealing with consolidated accounts. The economic entity approach treats all providers of equity capital as shareholders of the entity, even when they are not shareholders in the parent company. IFRS 5 has been amended such that if there is an intention to dispose of a controlling interest in a subsidiary which meets the definition of 'held for sale', then the net assets are classified as 'held for sale', irrespective of whether the parent was expected to retain an interest after the disposal. A partial disposal of an interest in a subsidiary in which the parent company loses control but retains an interest as an associate or trade investment creates the recognition of a gain or loss on the entire interest. A gain or loss is recognised on the part that has been disposed of and a further holding gain or loss is recognised on the interest retained, being the difference between the fair value of the interest and the book value of the interest. The gains are recognised in the statement of comprehensive income. Any prior gains or loss recognised in other components of equity would now become realised in the statement of comprehensive income.

In this case, Cate should stop consolidating Date on a line-by-line basis from the date that control was lost. Further investigation is required into whether the holding is treated as an associate or trade investment. IAS 28 *Investments in associates and joint ventures* defines significant influence as the power to participate in financial and operating decision-making, but not control or joint control as defined by Appendix A of IFRS 10. The agreement that Cate is no longer represented on the board or able to participate in management would suggest loss of significant influence despite the 35% of voting rights retained. The retained interest would be recognised at fair value.

An entity classifies a disposal group as held for sale if its carrying amount will be recovered mainly through selling the asset rather than through usage and intends to dispose of it in a single transaction.

The conditions for a non-current asset or disposal group to be classified as held for sale are as follows:

(i)   The assets must be available for immediate sale in their present condition and its sale must be highly probable.

(ii)  The asset must be currently marketed actively at a price that is reasonable in relational to its current fair value.

(iii) The sale should be completed or expected to be so, within a year from the date of the classification.

(iv)  The actions required to complete the planned sale will have been made and it is unlikely that the plan will be significantly changed or withdrawn.

(v)   Management is committed to a plan to sell.

Cate has not met all of the conditions of IFRS 5 but it could be argued that the best presentation in the financial statements was that set out in IFRS 5 for the following reasons.

The issue of dilution is not addressed by IFRS and the decision not to subscribe to the issue of new shares of Date is clearly a change in the strategy of Cate. Further, by deciding not to subscribe to the issue of new shares of Date, Cate agreed to the dilution and the loss of control which could be argued is similar to a decision to sell shares while retaining a continuing interest in the entity. Also Date represents a separate line of business, which is a determining factor in IFRS 5, and information disclosed on IFRS 5 principles highlights the impact of Date on Cate's financial statements. Finally, the agreement between Date's shareholders confirms that Cate has lost control over its former subsidiary.

Therefore, in the absence of a specific Standard or Interpretation applying to this situation, IAS 8 *Accounting policies*, changes in accounting estimates and errors states that management should use its judgment and refer to other IFRS and the Framework.

Thus considering the requirements of IFRS 10 and the above discussion, it could be concluded that the presentation based on IFRS 5 principles selected by the issuer was consistent with the accounting treatment required by IFRS 10 when a parent company loses control of a subsidiary.

---

*This part of the question deals mainly with determining whether or not an obligation exists in relation to a post-retirement benefit plan, and, if there is, what form that obligation takes, and how it should be accounted for.*

---

(d)   **Defined benefit plan**

The Plan is not a defined contribution plan because Cate has a legal or constructive obligation to pay further contributions if the fund does not have sufficient assets to pay all employee benefits relating to employee service in the current and prior periods (IAS 19). All other post-employment benefit plans that do not qualify as a defined contribution plan are, by definition therefore defined benefit plans. Defined benefit plans may be unfunded, or they may be wholly or partly funded. Also IAS 19 indicates that Cate's plan is a defined benefit plan as IAS 19 provides examples where an entity's obligation is not limited to the amount that it agrees to contribute to the fund. These examples include: (a) a plan benefit formula that is not linked solely to the amount of contributions (which is the case in this instance); and (b) those informal practices that give rise to a constructive obligation. According to the terms of the Plan, if Cate opts to terminate, Cate is responsible for discharging the liability created by the plan. IAS 19 says that an entity should account not only for its legal obligation under the formal terms of a defined benefit plan, but also for any constructive obligation that arises from the enterprise's informal practices.

Informal practices give rise to a constructive obligation where the enterprise has no realistic alternative but to pay employee benefits. Even if the Plan were not considered to be a defined benefit plan under IAS 19, Cate would have a constructive obligation to provide the benefit, having a history of paying benefits. The practice has created a valid expectation on the part of employees that the amounts will be paid in the future. Therefore Cate should account for the Plan as a defined benefit plan in accordance with IAS 19. Cate has to recognise, at a minimum, its net present liability for the benefits to be paid under the Plan.

| ACCA marking scheme | | |
|---|---|---|
| | | *Marks* |
| (a) | Deferred tax | 5 |
| (b) | Investment in associates | 5 |
| (c) | IFRS 5 discussion and conclusion | 8 |
| (d) | IAS 19 discussion and conclusion | 5 |
| Professional marks | | 2 |
| | | — |
| Total | | 25 |
| | | — |

**Examiner's comments**

The question dealt with real world scenarios taken from corporate financial statements. It is important that the exam paper reflects actual issues in financial statements and that candidates can apply their knowledge to these scenarios. The first scenario dealt with deferred tax assets and their recognition in the financial statements. This part of the question was well answered. Part b dealt with impairment of assets where an entity wished to use a method not in accordance with the standard. It required candidates to apply their knowledge to the situation and not just repeat the rules in the standard. This part of the question was well answered.

Part c looked at a situation where a company had a direct holding of shares which were not subscribed for by the holding company with the result that the interest was reduced to that of an associate. The question required candidates to determine whether the results should be presented based on the principles provided by IFRS 5 *Non-current assets held for sale and discontinued operations*. Candidates performed quite well on this part. The key to success is to set out the principles in the standard and then to apply each one to the case in point.

The final part dealt with the existence of a voluntary fund established in order to provide a post-retirement benefit plan to employees. The entity considered its contributions to the plan to be voluntary, and had not recorded any related liability in its consolidated financial statements. The entity had a history of paying benefits to its former employees, and there were several other pieces of information in the question. Candidates had to apply their knowledge of defined benefit schemes to the scenario. It did not require an in-depth knowledge of the accounting standard but an ability to apply the principles. The question was answered satisfactorily by candidates.

## 20    MACALJOY (DEC 07 EXAM)     *Online question assistance*

**Report to the Directors of Macaljoy plc**

**Terms of reference**

This report sets out the differences between a defined contribution and defined benefit plan, and the accounting treatment of the company's pension plans. It also discusses the principles involved in accounting for warranty claims, and the accounting treatment of those claims.

(a)    **Pension plans – IAS 19**

A defined contribution plan is a pension plan whereby an employer pays fixed contributions into a separate fund and has no legal or constructive obligation to pay further contributions (IAS 19). Payments or benefits provided to employees may be a simple distribution of total fund assets, or a third party (an insurance company) may, for example, agree to provide an agreed level of payments or benefits. Any actuarial (i.e. remeasurement) and investment risks of defined contribution plans are assumed by the employee or the third party. The employer is not required to make up any shortfall in assets and all plans that are not defined contribution plans are deemed to be defined benefit plans. Actuarial risk is the risk that the assumptions and estimations made when accounting for the defined benefit plan differ from what subsequently occurs in practice.

Defined benefit, therefore, is the residual category whereby, if an employer cannot demonstrate that all actuarial and investment risk has been shifted to another party and its obligations limited to contributions made during the period, then the plan is a defined benefit plan. Any benefit formula that is not solely based on the amount of contributions, or that includes a guarantee from the entity or a specified return, means that elements of risk remain with the employer and must be accounted for as a defined benefit plan. An employer may create a defined benefit obligation where no legal obligation exists if it has a practice of guaranteeing the benefits. An employer's obligation under a defined benefit plan is to provide the agreed amount of benefits to current and former employees. The differentiating factor between defined benefit and defined contribution schemes is in determining where the risks lie.

In a defined benefit scheme it is the employer that underwrites the vast majority of costs so that if investment returns are poor or costs increase the employer needs to either make adjustments to the scheme or to increase levels of contribution. Alternatively, if investment returns are good, then contribution levels could be reduced. In a defined contribution scheme the contributions are paid at a fixed level and, therefore, it is the scheme member who is shouldering these risks. If they fail to take action by increasing contribution rates when investment returns are poor or costs increase, then their retirement benefits will be lower than they had planned for.

For defined contribution plans, the cost to be recognised in the period is the contribution payable in exchange for service rendered by employees during the period. The accounting for a defined contribution plan is straightforward because the employer's obligation for each period is determined by the amount to be contributed for that period. Often, contributions are based on a formula that uses employee compensation in the period as its base. No actuarial or remeasurement assumptions are required to measure the obligation or the expense, and there are no remeasurement gains or losses to account for.

The employer should account for the contribution payable at the end of each period based on employee services rendered during that period, reduced by any payments made during the period. If the employer has made payments in excess of those required, the excess is a prepaid expense to the extent that the excess will lead to a reduction in future contributions or a cash refund.

For defined benefit plans, the amount recognised in the statement of financial position should be the present value of the defined benefit obligation (that is, the present value of expected future payments required to settle the obligation resulting from employee service in the current and prior periods), and reduced by the fair value of plan assets at the statement of financial position date. If the balance is an asset, the amount recognised may be limited under IAS 19 by application of the asset ceiling test.

In the case of Macaljoy, the 1990 plan is a defined benefit plan as the employer has the investment risk as the company is guaranteeing a pension based on the service lives of the employees in the scheme. The employer's liability is not limited to the amount of the contributions. There is a risk that if the investment returns fall short the employer will have to make good the shortfall in the scheme. The 2006 plan, however, is a defined contribution scheme because the employer's liability is limited to the contributions paid.

A curtailment occurs when there is a significant reduction in the number of employees covered by the plan. This gives rise to past service costs which are recognised at the earlier of:

- when the related restructuring costs are recognised, or
- when the related termination benefits are recognised, or
- when the curtailment occurs.

Curtailments, by definition, have a material impact on the entity's financial statements. The fact that no new employees are to be admitted to the 1990 plan does not constitute a curtailment because future service qualifies for pension rights for those in the scheme prior to 31 October 2006.

The accounting for the two plans is as follows. The company does not recognise any assets or liabilities for the defined contribution scheme but charges the contributions payable for the period ($10 million) to operating profit. The contributions paid by the employees will be part of the wages and salaries cost and when paid will reduce cash. The accounting for the defined benefit plan results in a liability of $15 million as at 31 October 2007, a charge in profit or loss of $20.5m for both the net interest component ($$0.5m) and the service cost component ($20m), and a net charge of $$1.5m in other comprehensive income for the remeasurement component (see Appendix 1).

(b)     **Provisions – IAS 37**

An entity must recognise a provision under IAS 37 if, and only if:

(i)     a present obligation (legal or constructive) has arisen as a result of a past event (the obligating event)

(ii)    it is probable ('more likely than not'), that an outflow of resources embodying economic benefits will be required to settle the obligation

(iii)   the amount can be estimated reliably.

An obligating event is an event that creates a legal or constructive obligation and, therefore, results in an enterprise having no realistic alternative but to settle the obligation. A constructive obligation arises if past practice creates a valid expectation on the part of a third party. If it is more likely than not that no present obligation exists, the enterprise should disclose a contingent liability, unless the possibility of an outflow of resources is remote.

The amount recognised as a provision should be the best estimate of the expenditure required to settle the present obligation at the statement of financial position date, that is, the amount that an enterprise would rationally pay to settle the obligation at the statement of financial position date or to transfer it to a third party. This means provisions for large populations of events such as warranties, are measured at a probability weighted expected value. In reaching its best estimate, the entity should take into account the risks and uncertainties that surround the underlying events.

Expected cash outflows should be discounted to their present values, where the effect of the time value of money is material using a risk adjusted rate (it should not reflect risks for which future cash flows have been adjusted). If some or all of the expenditure required to settle a provision is expected to be reimbursed by another party, the reimbursement should be recognised as a separate asset when, and only when, it is virtually certain that reimbursement will be received if the entity settles the obligation. The amount recognised should not exceed the amount of the provision. In measuring a provision future events should be considered. The provision for the warranty claim will be determined by using the expected value method.

The past event which causes the obligation is the initial sale of the product with the warranty given at that time. It would be appropriate for the company to make a provision for the Year 1 warranty of $280,000 and Year 2 warranty of $350,000, which represents the best estimate of the obligation (see Appendix 2). Only if the insurance company have validated the counter claim will Macaljoy be able to recognise the asset and income. Recovery has to be virtually certain. If it is virtually certain, then Macaljoy may be able to recognise the asset. Generally contingent assets are never recognised, but disclosed where an inflow of economic benefits is probable.

The company could discount the provision if it was considered that the time value of money was material. The majority of provisions will reverse in the short term (within two years) and, therefore, the effects of discounting are likely to be immaterial. In this case, using the risk adjusted rate (IAS 37), the provision would be reduced to $269,000 in Year 1 and $323,000 in Year 2. The company will have to determine whether this is material.

**Appendix 1 – Statement of financial position at 31 October 2007:**

|  | $m |
|---|---|
| Net defined benefit obligation | 15.0 |

**Statement of comprehensive income – year ended 31 October 2007:**

|  | $m |
|---|---|
| Profit or loss: |  |
| Net interest component | 0.5 |
| Service cost component | 20.0 |
|  | 20.5 |
| Other comprehensive income: |  |
| Net remeasurement component | 1.5 |
| Total comprehensive income charge for the year | 22.0 |

The accounting for the defined benefit plan is as follows:

|  | Plan assets – FV | Plan obligation – PV | Net obligation |
|---|---|---|---|
|  | $m | $m | $m |
| Balance b/fwd | (190.0) | 200 | 10.0 |
| Interest @5% | (9.5) | 10 | 0.5 |
| Service cost |  | 20 | 20.0 |
| Benefits paid | (19.0) | (19) | – |
| Contributions into plan | 17.0 |  | (17.0) |
| Remeasurement component (bal fig) | 27.5 | 29 | 1.5 |
| Balance c/fwd | 225.0 | 240 | 15.0 |

**Appendix 2 – Warranty**

**Year 1 warranty**

|  | Expected value | Discounted expected value (4%) |
|---|---|---|
|  | $000 | $000 |
| 80% × Nil | 0 |  |
| 15% × 7,000 × $100 | 105 |  |
| 5% × 7,000 × $500 | 175 |  |
|  | 280 | 269 |

**Year 2 extended warranty**

| | Expected value | Discounted expected value (4%) |
|---|---|---|
| | $000 | $000 |
| 70% × Nil | 0 | |
| 20% × 5,000 × $100 | 100 | |
| 10% × 5,000 × $500 | 250 | |
| | 350 | 323 |

| ACCA marking scheme | | |
|---|---|---|
| | | *Marks* |
| (a) | Pensions | |
| | (i) Explanation | 7 |
| | (ii) Calculation | 7 |
| | | 14 |
| (b) | Provisions | |
| | (i) Explanation | 6 |
| | (ii) Calculation | 3 |
| | Structure of report | 2 |
| Total | | 25 |

**Examiner's comments**

This question required candidates to discuss the differences between a defined benefit and defined contribution scheme, to show the accounting entries for such schemes and to discuss the principles and accounting for warranty claims. The question examined the fundamental principles behind certain employee benefits and provisioning. It was surprising that several candidates confused the two types of scheme. Also at this level, it is important that candidates have an in depth knowledge of the differences between the two schemes rather than just a general view of the differences. The question was quite well answered and candidates often produced good quality answers. Professional marks were awarded for the structure of the report and consideration of certain factors, that is:

(i)     the intended purpose of the document

(ii)    its intended users and their needs

(iii)   the appropriate type of document

(iv)    logical and appropriate structure/format

(v)     nature of background information and technical language

(vi)    detail required

(vii)   clear, concise and precise presentation

## 21 FINANCIAL INSTRUMENTS

**Key answer tips**

Don't be put off by the title to this question. It's an exercise dealing with the basics of IFRS 9 dealing with financial assets and IAS 39 dealing with financial liabilities. You should try to make a good attempt at it, even if you hope the topic does not come up in your exam!

(a) **Definitions:**

IAS 32 provides the basic definitions to enable classification as a financial asset, financial liability or equity. The definition has been retained in relation to financial assets following the publication of IFRS 9 in November 2009.

A financial instrument is defined as any contract that gives rise to a financial asset of one entity and a financial liability or equity instrument of another entity. An entity's asset is a financial asset if it is cash, an equity instrument of another entity, a contractual right to receive cash or to exchange financial assets/liabilities on terms potentially favourable to the entity or a contract which may be settled in the entity's own equity instruments. Examples are trade receivables and investments in equity or loans.

An entity's liability is a financial liability if it is a contractual right to deliver cash or to exchange financial assets/liabilities on terms potentially unfavourable to the entity or a contract which may be settled in the entity's own equity instruments. Examples are trade payables and loans. An equity instrument is a contract in respect of the residual interest in the assets of another entity once all that entity's liabilities have been deducted.

A derivative is a financial instrument that derives its value in response to the changes in the price of some underlying item, e.g. shares, foreign exchange rates, interest rates. Derivatives require no initial investment or the investment is small. They are settled at a future date and transform the risk profile of the entity. Examples of derivatives include options, swaps, forward contracts and futures.

**Recognition:**

The basic recognition criteria for financial assets and financial liabilities are contained within IFRS 9 for financial assets and IAS 39 for financial liabilities respectively. When IFRS 9 was published in November 2009, it dealt only with recognition and measurement of financial assets. In due course, the scope of IFRS 9 will be extended to include recognition and measurement of financial liabilities, impairment and hedging arrangements.

An entity should recognise a financial asset or a financial liability on its statement of financial position when the entity becomes a party to the contractual provisions of the instrument, rather than when the contract is settled.

An entity should derecognise a financial asset when either of the following has occurred:

- The asset has been sold so that the risks and rewards of ownership have passed away.
- The contractual rights to the cash flow of the financial asset have expired.

An entity should derecognise a financial liability when the liability has been extinguished.

The four categories of financial asset previously recognised by IAS 39, together with their accounting treatment, no longer apply. Arguably, the provisions of IFRS 9 will simplify the categorisation and accounting treatment of financial assets for many, but not necessarily all, entities.

Upon initial recognition of a financial asset, it is measured at fair value. This is likely to be purchase consideration paid, and will normally exclude transactions costs. Subsequent measurement will then depend upon the nature of the financial instrument as follows:

**Equity instruments:**

Equity instruments are normally measured at **fair value through profit or loss**. This designation will include any financial assets held for trading purposes and will also include equity derivatives. Unlike IAS 39, there is no longer a general exception for unquoted equity investments to be measured at cost. Instead, IFRS 9 provides guidance when cost may, or may not be, a reliable indicator of fair value.

This is now likely to include convertible debt as such financial assets will fail the contractual cash flow characteristics test to be measured at amortised cost (see below).

It is also possible to designate **equity instruments at fair value through other comprehensive income**. Such a designation is irrevocable and must take place upon initial recognition of the financial asset. Initial recognition will also include directly attributable transactions costs. This designation cannot include equity instruments held for trading, nor can it include equity derivatives. It is expected to include long-term strategic investments held on a continuing basis; i.e. not those acquired with the primary intention of taking advantage in changes in fair value.

Where financial assets are designated as fair value through other comprehensive income, any changes in fair value will be reflected as part of other comprehensive income. This accounting treatment will therefore deal with the effect of any impairment through other comprehensive income. There is no requirement to make transfers between equity and profit or loss to account for impairment losses; there is no recycling of any gains or losses recognised in earlier periods. Note that dividend income received on such financial assets will continue to be recognised in profit or loss for the year, unless it represents a recovery of part of the investment.

**Debt instruments:**

As with equity instruments, IFRS 9 specifies that the normal accounting treatment for debt instruments is that they are measured at fair value though profit or loss. However, it is possible to measure debt instruments at amortised cost provided the following two tests are passed.

*   The business model test which considers the underlying purpose for holding the financial asset. If the purpose is to collect in contractual cash flows, normally up to maturity date, this would suggest that the test has been passed. If the purpose is to dispose of such financial assets in response to changes in fair value, this would suggest that the business model test has been failed.

- The contractual cash flow characteristics test considers the nature of the cash flows and other returns on a debt instrument. The cash flows must be solely returns of principal and interest if the debt instrument is to be measured at amortised cost. If this is not the case, for example convertible debt includes the right to opt for conversion of the debt into equity shares at a later date, the test is failed.

Therefore, debt instruments may be measured at fair value through profit or loss if they fail either or both of the two test noted above. It is still possible to measure a debt instrument at fair value though profit or loss even if both tests have been passed if, by doing so, an accounting mismatch that could arise from measuring assets and liabilities on different bases is reduced or removed. The recognition and measurement criteria of IFRS 9 may therefore result in debt instruments which are traded on an active market (i.e. with a reliable fair value) being measured at amortised cost.

Financial liabilities are sow also dealt with by IFRS 9, which was amended in October 2010. In effect, the two classifications from IAS 39 have been transferred into IFRS 9. They are ether financial liabilities at fair value through profit or loss, or financial liabilities measured at amortised cost.

Where financial assets or liabilities are measured at amortised cost, the consequence is that a constant rate of return or constant rate of finance cost is recognised in profit or loss each year.

Note that IFRS 9 retains the option, initially included within IAS 39, for entities to continue to measure some financial liabilities at fair value through profit or loss, rather than amortised cost. This is referred to as the fair value option and would apply where such an accounting treatment either eliminates or substantially reduces an accounting mismatch.

**Impairment of financial assets:**

The recognition and measurement criteria within IFRS 9 simplify the accounting for impairment of financial assets. Those financial assets measured at fair value, either through profit or loss, or through other comprehensive income, recognise any impairment during the accounting period within changes to fair value. In the case of financial assets at fair value through profit or loss, there is no recycling or recognition in profit or loss of any amounts taken to other comprehensive income.

For financial assets measured at amortised cost, IAS 39 requires that there must be an assessment as to whether or not there is objective evidence that a financial asset is impaired. If there is evidence that this may be the case, an impairment review must be performed.

Derivative financial assets and financial liabilities, unless they are part of a formalised and documented hedging arrangement, must be accounted for as fair value through profit or loss. This is still currently deal with by IAS 39.

Any formalised and documented hedging arrangements are also still dealt with by IAS 39. The net impact of any fair value hedge should be taken to profit or loss for the year and should be monitored to ensure that it is still an effective hedging arrangement. The impact of any cash flow hedge arrangement should be taken to other comprehensive income for the year, and would normally result in recognition of a financial asset or financial liability at each reporting date whilst the cash flow hedge arrangement was in operation.

(b)  (i)  In all circumstances, the financial liability is initially recorded at the fair value of the consideration received, i.e. the cash received. It is then accounted for using amortised cost. This means the liability varies for two reasons, first an increase by the finance cost which should be charged to profit or loss at a constant actuarial rate (DR finance charge, CR liability) and second a reduction by the actual cash paid (DR liability, CR cash).

| Instrument 1 | Balance b'fwd $ | Effective rate 10% $ | Cash return $ | Bal c'fwd $ |
|---|---|---|---|---|
| Year 1 | 100,000 | 10,000 | (nil) | 110,000 |
| Year 2 | 110,000 | 11,000 | (121,000) | nil |

| Instrument 2 | Balance b'fwd $ | Effective rate 10% $ | Cash return $ | Bal c'fwd $ |
|---|---|---|---|---|
| Year 1 | 82,645 | 8265 | | 90,910 |
| Year 2 | 90,910 | 9090 | (100,000) | nil |

| Instrument 3 | Balance b'fwd $ | Effective rate 10% $ | Cash return $ | Bal c'fwd $ |
|---|---|---|---|---|
| Year 1 | 95,000 | 9,500 | (2,000) | 102,500 |
| Year 2 | 102,500 | 10,250 | (112,750) | nil |

(ii)  This transaction is a cash flow hedge and is currently regulated by the provisions of IAS 39 until IFRS 9 is extended to include hedging arrangements. Because the forward rate agreement has no fair value at its inception, the need to account for the derivative first arises at the end of the reporting period when it has a value and the change in value has to be recorded. Because it has been designated a cash flow hedge, the change in value is recognised in other comprehensive income to be carried forward at 31 July to match against the future cash flow. The value of this contract is in showing a loss of $20,000 at the end of the reporting period because Thompson is locked into buying €400,000 for $200,000 when everyone else can buy for $180,000, hence Thompson is $20,000 worse off because it hedged the position.

To recognise the loss in equity:

DR Other comprehensive income          $20,000

CR Liability – derivative                    $20,000

Note that if this transaction had not been designated a hedging instrument then the loss would be recognised immediately in profit or loss. Please note therefore the same derivative entered into by two different entities can be accounted for by them in two different ways depending on whether it is designated a hedge or not.

In the following January the forward contract will be settled and closed, and the balance of the reserve capitalised as Thompson is buying a non-current asset. Thompson has known all along that the cost of the asset was being fixed at $200,000.

DR Liability – derivative          $20,000
CR Cash                          $20,000
DR Plant                         $200,000
CR Cash                          $180,000
CR Reserves                      $20,000

(iii) MacDonald has an equity instrument which IFRS 9 requires to be measured at fair value. As it is held for trading purposes, it cannot be designated as fair value through other comprehensive income; it must be through profit or loss. Initial recognition is at the consideration paid of $25 million, excluding any transactions costs.

| | |
|---|---|
| DR Asset | $25m |
| CR Cash | $25m |

At the end of the reporting period, the asset must be remeasured to fair value following the measurement rules in IFRS 9. The gain is recorded in income.

| | |
|---|---|
| DR Asset | $50m |
| CR Profit or loss | $50m |

On disposal the asset is derecognised and a gain on disposal reported in income.

| | |
|---|---|
| DR Cash | $200m |
| CR Asset | $75m |
| CR Profit or loss | $125m |

## 22 AMBUSH (DEC 05 EXAM)

**Key answer tips**

This question requires extensive knowledge of the requirements of IAS 39 and IFRS 9 with only 4 marks allocated to numerical aspects. Therefore, to attempt this question you must be confident in your knowledge and understanding of accounting for financial instruments.

**Report to the Directors of Ambush, a listed entity**

(a) The following report sets out the principal aspects of IAS 39 and IFRS 9 in relation to financial assets and liabilities.

### Classification of financial assets and their measurement

Financial assets are initially measured at fair value which will normally be the fair value of the consideration paid. Transaction costs are included in the initial carrying value of the instrument unless it is carried at fair value through profit or loss when these costs are recognised in profit or loss.

Financial assets are classified into categories as follows:

- Financial instruments at fair value through profit or loss; this may include either equity instruments, or debt instruments which fail to be designated to be measured at amortised cost. It will include any financial assets held for trading purposes and derivates. Any increase or decrease in fair value is taken to profit or loss. Unrealised holding gains are therefore recognised by applying this accounting treatment. As such, this accounting treatment automatically incorporates accounting for any impairment losses.

- Equity instruments at fair value through other comprehensive income. This category is designated upon initial recognition and is irrevocable. The consequence is that any changes in fair value, including the impact of any holding gains and losses, together with impairment, is recognised in other comprehensive income. Only interest income and dividend income is recognised in profit or loss.

- Financial assets measured at amortised cost, based upon a constant interest rate over the life of the asset. This will comprise debt instruments where the financial asset has complied with two requirements or tests, and the entity has chosen to designate the financial assets to be measured at amortised cost. If either of the requirements has not been complied with, or the entity does not make the designation, such financial assets will be measured at fair value through profit or loss.

The two tests are as follows:

- The business model test – the financial asset is held primarily to collect the contractual cashflows associated with the financial asset, and

- The contractual cash flows characteristics test – the cashflows consist solely of collection of interest and principal based upon the amount outstanding. Note that convertible debt would not pass the two tests above as it also contains the right or the option to convert the debt into shares at some later date.

IFRS 9 requires that investments in unquoted equity instruments are measured at fair value. The new standard then provides guidance when cost may, or may not, be a reliable approximation to fair value. This is a change from IAS 39 where cost was permitted as a default basis of measurement for unquoted equity investments.

Therefore, the introduction of IFRS 9 has gone some way to simplification and standardisation of recognition, measurement and accounting for impairment of financial assets.

### Classification of financial liabilities and their measurement

Financial liabilities are initially measured at fair value in accordance with IFRS 9, which will normally be the fair value of the consideration received. Transaction costs are included in the initial carrying value of the instrument unless it is carried at fair value through profit or loss when these costs are recognised in profit or loss.

Financial liabilities have two categories: those at fair value through profit or loss, and other liabilities which are measured at amortised cost based upon a constant interest rate over the life of the liability. As with financial assets, those liabilities designated as fair value through profit or loss will include financial liabilities held for trading purposes, together with any derivatives.

### Fair value option

Subject to the restrictions referred to above, the standard permits entities to designate irrevocably on initial recognition a financial asset or liability as one to be measured at fair value with gains and losses recognised in profit or loss.

The fair value option was generally introduced to reduce profit or loss volatility as it can be used to measure an economically matched position in the same way (at fair value). Additionally it can be used in place of the normal requirement to separate embedded derivatives as the entire contract is measured at fair value with changes reported in profit or loss, thus removing the possibility of an accounting mismatch.

Although the fair value option can be of use, it can be used in an inappropriate manner thus defeating its original purpose. For example, entities might apply the option to instruments whose fair value is difficult to estimate so as to smooth profit or loss as valuation of these instruments might be subjective.

Also, if an entity applied the option to financial liabilities, it might result in recognising gains or losses for changes in its own credit worthiness.

The introduction of IFRS 9 has re-emphasised the importance of fair value as the primary basis for measurement of financial assets and financial liabilities. It is regarded as being relevant information to users of financial information and, in many cases, can be reliably measured for inclusion in the financial statements.

(b) (i) For financial assets measured at amortised cost, IFRS 9 requires an entity to assess at the end of each reporting period whether there is any objective evidence that financial assets are impaired and whether the impairment impacts on future cash flows. Objective evidence that financial assets are impaired includes the significant financial difficulty of the issuer and whether it becomes probable that the borrower will enter bankruptcy or other financial reorganisation.

If any objective evidence of impairment exists, the entity recognises any associated impairment loss in profit or loss. Only losses that have been incurred from past events can be reported as impairment losses. Therefore, losses expected from future events, no matter how likely, cannot be recognised.

A loss is incurred only if both of the following two conditions are met:

1 There is objective evidence of impairment as a result of one or more events that occurred after the initial recognition of the asset (a 'loss event').

2 The loss event has an impact on the estimated future cash flows of the financial asset or group of financial assets that can be reliably estimated.

For financial assets measured at amortised cost, impaired assets are measured at the present value of the estimated future cash flows discounted using the original effective interest rate of the financial assets. Any difference between the carrying amount and the new value of the impaired asset is an impairment loss, which is taken to profit or loss.

For investments in unquoted equity instruments which are measured at cost as a reliable approximation to fair value, impaired assets are measured at the present value of the estimated future cash flows discounted using the current market rate of return for a similar financial asset. Any difference between the previous carrying amount and the new measurement of the impaired asset is recognised as an impairment loss in profit or loss.

(ii) The loan to Bromwich complies with both the business model test and the contractual cash flows characteristics test. It is therefore appropriate for this financial asst to be designated at amortised cost.

There is objective evidence of impairment because of the financial difficulties and reorganisation of Bromwich. The impairment loss on the loan will be calculated by discounting the estimated future cash flows. The future cash flows will be $100,000 on 30 November 20X7. This will be discounted at an effective interest rate of 8% for two years to give a present value of $85,733.

The loan will, therefore, be impaired by ($200,000 – $85,733) i.e. $114,267.

(**Note:** IFRS 9, and previously IAS 39, requires accrual of interest on impaired loans at the original effective interest rate. In the year to 30 November 20X6 interest of 8% of $85,733, i.e. $6,859 would be accrued.)

| | | ACCA marking scheme | |
|---|---|---|---:|
| | | | *Marks* |
| (a) | (i) | Layout | 2 |
| | | Classification of assets | 2 |
| | | Sub category | 1 |
| | | Classification of liabilities | 1 |
| | | Reclassifications | 1 |
| | | Tainted | 1 |
| | | Subsequent measurement | 3 |
| | | Accounting – amortised cost/fair value | 4 |
| | | | —— |
| | | Available | 15 |
| | | **Maximum** | **10** |
| | (ii) | Nature | 1 |
| | | Initial introduction | 2 |
| | | Inappropriate use: smoothing | 1 |
| | | volatility | 1 |
| | | liabilities | 1 |
| | | | —— |
| | | Available | 6 |
| | | **Maximum** | **5** |
| (b) | (i) | Objective evidence | 1 |
| | | Impairment loss – profit/loss | 1 |
| | | Two conditions | 2 |
| | | All financial assets | 2 |
| | | Measurement + unquoted equity investments | 3 |
| | | | —— |
| | | Available | 9 |
| | | **Maximum** | **6** |
| | (ii) | Calculation and impairment explanation | |
| | | **Available/Maximum** | **4** |
| | | | —— |
| | Total available | | 34 |
| | | | —— |
| | **Maximum** | | **25** |

## 23 ARTWRIGHT (DEC 04 EXAM)

### Key answer tips

This question requires a detailed knowledge of IAS 39 and IFRS 9 and should be avoided unless you have this knowledge. This is a complex standard and it is frequently examined, so make sure you review this question carefully.

(a) All derivatives have to be initially recognised at fair value, i.e. at the consideration given or received. As financial instruments, all derivatives are initially recognised when the company becomes a party to the contract. All derivatives have to be recognised in the statement of financial position by measuring them at fair value.

**Derivative A**: Artwright has entered into this derivative for speculative purposes. IFRS 9 requires that all derivatives held as a financial asset which is not part of a hedging arrangement are accounted for at fair value through profit or loss. In other words Artwright is seeking to make a gain on this transaction (though of course it could make a loss as well). It has no existing exposure to the risk of fluctuating oil prices so it cannot be regarded as hedging a risk. This transaction increases the risk profile of the company. It can be argued that it is a simple gamble. In such circumstances the derivative is classified as fair value through profit or loss. The loss of $20 million that has been incurred has to be immediately recognised profit or loss.

**Derivative B**: Artwright appears to have entered into the derivative so that it will act like an insurance policy against changes in the fair value of the asset. As such this is an example of hedging. In fact the asset concerned has risen in value – and with the derivative acting as a hedging instrument would be expected to behave, creates the opposite effect, i.e. the derivative creates a loss.

IAS 39 currently deals with hedge accounting requirements until such time as the provisions of IFRS 9 are extended to include this issue. This type of hedging is known as a fair value hedge as the risk being hedged is the change in value of a recognised asset or liability. As with all hedging the effect is to reduce the overall risk profile of the company. Assuming that the preconditions of hedge accounting are properly met then the standard applies the principle of substance over form. IAS 39 requires that both the gain and loss are immediately offset against each other in profit or loss. The loss on the derivative is $10 million.

**Derivative C** – Artwright appears to have entered into the derivative again as a type of hedge, i.e. to minimise the overall risk profile of the company. In other words (as has happened) if the price of the raw material that the company knows that it will have buy in the future rises it will be covered / compensated by the gain that will occur in respect of the derivative that has been entered into. This type of hedge arrangement is a cash flow hedge as the risk being hedged is a prospective cash flow. As with the fair value hedge, accounting requirements are specified in IAS 39 until the provisions of IFRS 9 are extended to include this issue. In such circumstances it is not possible to have an immediate offset / pairing of a gain and a loss as the future cash outflow has yet to occur. The gain on the derivative acting as a cash flow hedging instrument is therefore recognised in other comprehensive income and taken to other components of equity where, in effect, it is held pending at some future date the actual cash flow. At that later date it can then be reclassified (recycled) out of other comprehensive income and offset in profit or loss against the cash flow.

(b)    **Impairment of receivables**

The financial asset is impaired if its carrying amount is greater than the present value of the expected future cash flows discounted at the financial instrument's original effective interest rate.

Normally, receivables would be expected to be designated to be measured at amortised cost, provided that both the business model test and contractual cash flow characteristics test is complied with per IFRS 9.

In the case of Artwright, the following impairment will occur:

| | Due dates | |
|---|---|---|
| | *31/5/X5* | *30/11/X5* |
| | *$000* | *$000* |
| Total contractual cash flows | 1,050 | 1,100 |
| Total expected cash flows | 1,000 | 1,040 |
| Difference = loss | 50 | 60 |
| Discount factors at 10% for 6 months/1 year | 0.953 | 0.909 |
| Impairment | 47.65 | 54.54 |

Therefore, the total impairment of the loans outstanding at 30 November 20X4 is $102,190 ($47,650 + $54,540).

**Conversion of receivable to a loan**

The financial difficulties of the customer are an indication of an impaired asset. The question arises as to whether a borrower's financial difficulties will cause the recognition of an impairment loss. Whether the loan is impaired will depend on the terms of the restructured loan. The loss due to impairment will be the difference between the asset's carrying amount and the expected future cash flows under the new loan agreement. The discount rate used will be the effective interest rate (10%). The present value of the future principal and interest payments will in this case be equal to the carrying amount of (200,000 − 100,000 + 16,500) $116,500 and no impairment will be recognised.

(c) **Derecognition of a financial asset – factoring of receivables**

The question arises as to whether the sale of the receivables should result in them being derecognised in the statement of financial position. Artwright has in effect transferred control of a financial asset and in doing so has created a new financial liability. The provision of the limited guarantee creates the new liability which should be recognised at fair value. Because Artwright has transferred the control over the receivables and the bank has the contractual right to receive cash payments from the trade receivables and Artwright, then the transaction should be derecognised and treated as a sale.

The sale would be recorded as follows:

| | *DR* | *CR* |
|---|---|---|
| | *$000* | *$000* |
| Cash received | 440 | |
| Loss on disposal – profit or loss | 72 | |
| Receivables (sold) | | 500 |
| Liabilities (fair value of guarantee) | | 12 |
| | 512 | 512 |

| | ACCA marking scheme | |
|---|---|---|
| | | *Marks* |
| (a) | Discussion A | 4 |
| | Discussion B | 4 |
| | Discussion C | 4 |
| (b) | Impairment of receivables | 2 |
| | Calculation | 4 |
| | Conversion of receivable to loan | 4 |
| (c) | Derecognition    – discussion | 3 |
| | – calculation | 3 |
| | | ___ |
| Available | | 28 |
| | | ___ |
| **Maximum** | | **25** |
| | | ___ |

## 24    PANEL (DEC 05 EXAM)

**Key answer tips**

This question requires you to be able to understand how various accounting treatments affect the deferred tax provision and to be able to apply that understanding.

(a)    (i)    IAS 12 *Income taxes* adopts a statement of financial position approach to accounting for deferred taxation. The IAS adopts a full provision approach to accounting for deferred taxation. It is assumed that the recovery of all assets and the settlement of all liabilities have tax consequences and that these consequences can be estimated reliably and are unavoidable. IFRSs recognition criteria are generally different from those embodied in tax law, and thus temporary differences will arise which represent the difference between the carrying amount of an asset and liability and its basis for taxation purposes (tax base). The principle is that a company will settle its liabilities and recover its assets over time and at that point the tax consequences will crystallise.

Thus a change in an accounting standard will often affect the carrying value of an asset or liability which in turn will affect the amount of the temporary difference between the carrying value and the tax base. This in turn will affect the amount of the deferred taxation provision which is the tax rate multiplied by the amount of the temporary differences (assuming a net liability for deferred tax).

(ii)    A company has to apply IAS 12 to the temporary differences between the carrying amount of the assets and liabilities in its opening IFRS statement of financial position (1 November 20X3) and their tax bases (IFRS 1 *First time adoption of IFRS*). The deferred tax provision will be calculated using tax rates that have been enacted or substantially enacted by the end of the reporting period. The carrying values of the assets and liabilities at the date of the opening statement of financial position will be determined by reference to IFRS 1 and will use the applicable IFRSs in the first IFRS financial statements. Any adjustments required to the deferred tax balance will be recognised directly in retained earnings.

Subsequent statements of financial position (at 31 October 20X4 and 31 October 20X5) will be drawn up using the IFRSs used in the financial statements to 31 October 20X5. The deferred tax provision will be adjusted as at 31 October 20X4 and then as at 31 October 20X5 to reflect the temporary differences arising at those dates.

(b)    (i)    The tax deduction is based on the option's intrinsic value which is the difference between the market price and exercise price of the share option. It is likely that a deferred tax asset will arise which represents the difference between the tax base of the employee's service received to date and the carrying amount which will effectively normally be zero.

The recognition of the deferred tax asset should be dealt with on the following basis:

(a)    if the estimated or actual tax deduction is less than or equal to the cumulative recognised expense then the associated tax benefits are recognised in the profit or loss

(b)    if the estimated or actual tax deduction exceeds the cumulative recognised compensation expense then the excess tax benefits are recognised in other comprehensive income and held in a separate component of equity.

As regards the tax effects of the share options in the year to 31 October 20X4, the tax deduction is nil, so less than the cumulative recognised expense of $20 million (40 ÷ 2) So the tax benefit will be recognised in profit or loss.

The tax benefit is 30% × $16 million ÷ 2 = $2.4 million, which will be recognised within the deferred tax provision.

At 31 October 20X5, the options have been exercised. Tax receivable will be 30% × $46 million, i.e. $13.8 million. The deferred tax asset of $2.4 million is no longer recognised as the tax benefit has crystallised at the date when the options were exercised.

For a tax benefit to be recognised in the year to 31 October 20X4, the provisions of IAS 12 should be complied with as regards whether the deferred tax asset should be recognised.

(ii)    Plant acquired under a finance lease will be recorded as property, plant and equipment and a corresponding liability for the obligation to pay future rentals. Rents payable are apportioned between the finance charge and a reduction of the outstanding obligation. A temporary difference will arise between the value of the plant for accounting purposes and its tax base. The tax base is the equivalent of the outstanding obligation as the annual rental payments qualify for tax relief.

|  | Value in FS $m |  | Tax base $m | Temporary difference $m |
|---|---|---|---|---|
| PV of minimum payments | 12 | Liability | 12 |  |
| Depreciation (1/5) | (2.4) | Repaid | (3) |  |
| Receivables (sold) |  | Interest (8% × 12) | (0.96) |  |
|  | 9.6 |  | 9.96 | 0.36 |

A deferred tax asset of $0.36m at 30% i.e. $108,000 will arise.

(iii) The subsidiary, Pins, has made a profit of $2 million on the transaction with Panel. These goods are held in inventory at the year-end and a consolidation adjustment of an equivalent amount will be made against profit and inventory. Pins will have provided for the tax on this profit as part of its current tax liability. This tax will need to be eliminated at the group level and this will be done by recognising a deferred tax asset of $2 million × 30%, i.e. $600,000. Thus any consolidation adjustments that have the effect of deferring or accelerating tax when viewed from a group perspective will be accounted for as part of the deferred tax provision. Group profit will be different to the sum of the profits of the individual group companies. Tax is normally payable on the profits of the individual companies. Thus there is a need to account for this temporary difference. IAS 12 does not specifically address the issue of which tax rate should be used calculate the deferred tax provision. IAS 12 does generally say that regard should be had to the expected recovery or settlement of the tax. This would be generally consistent with using the rate applicable to the transferee company (Panel) rather than the transferor (Pins).

(iv) The recognition of the impairment loss by Nails reduces the carrying value of the property, plant and equipment of the company and hence the taxable temporary difference. The deferred tax liability will, therefore, be reduced accordingly. No deferred tax would have been recognised on the goodwill in accordance with IAS 12 and, therefore, the impairment loss relating to the goodwill does not cause an adjustment to the deferred tax position.

| | Goodwill $m | PP & E $m | Tax base $m |
|---|---|---|---|
| Balance at 31 October 20X5 | 1 | 6 | |
| Impairment loss | (1) | (0.8) | |
| | – | 5.2 | 4 |

The deferred tax liability before the impairment loss is (6 – 4) at 30%, i.e. $0.6 million. After the impairment loss it is (5.2 – 4) at 30%, i.e. $0.36 million, thus reducing the liability by $0.24 million.

| ACCA marking scheme | | | |
|---|---|---|---|
| | | | *Marks* |
| (a) | (i) | Discussion | 5 |
| | (ii) | IFRS 1 | 4 |
| (b) | (i) | Share options | 4 |
| | (ii) | Leased asset | 4 |
| | (iii) | Unrealised profit | 4 |
| | (iv) | Impairment loss | 4 |
| Total | | | 25 |

## 25 SELTEC (JUN 10 EXAM)  *Walk in the footsteps of a top tutor*

**Key answer tips**

This two-part question is set in a scenario of an entity operating in the edible oils sector. Part (a) deals with derivatives and hedge accounting for 14 marks. The use and application of definitions will help in a technically demanding area of the syllabus. Part (b) deals with accounting for brands and the purchase of two companies for 9 marks. You should apply your knowledge of IAS 38 *Intangible assets* and IFRS 3 (revised) *Business combinations* to deal with each issue separately to gain as many marks as possible. There are also 2 professional marks available for clarity and quality of discussion within your answer, so ensure that you use appropriate presentation and professional language in your answer.

*Begin with stating the criteria for recognition and measurement criteria in relation to derivative financial instruments.*

(a)  IFRS 9 *Financial instruments* introduced in November 2009, and revised in October 2010, currently only applies to financial assets and financial liabilities. In due course, it will be updated to deal with derivatives, at which point the relevant requirements of IAS 39 will be withdrawn. IAS 39 *Financial instruments: recognition and measurement* states that a derivative is a financial instrument:

(i)  whose value changes in response to the change in an underlying variable such as an interest rate, commodity or security price, or index; such as the price of edible oil,

(ii)  that requires no initial investment, or one that is smaller than would be required for a contract with similar response to changes in market factors; in the case of the future purchase of oil, the initial investment is nil, and

(iii)  that is settled at a future date.

However, when a contract's purpose is to take physical delivery in the normal course of business, then normally the contract is not considered to be a derivative contract, unless the entity has a practice of settling the contracts on a net basis. In this case the contracts will be considered to be derivative contracts and should be accounted for at fair value through profit and loss.

Even though the entity sometimes takes physical delivery, the entity has a practice of settling similar contracts on a net basis and taking delivery, only to sell shortly afterwards. Hedge accounting techniques may be used if the conditions in IAS 39 are met.

IAS 39 permits hedge accounting under certain circumstances provided that the hedging relationship is: formally designated and documented, including the entity's risk management objective and strategy for undertaking the hedge, identification of the hedging instrument, the hedged item, the nature of the risk being hedged, and how the entity will assess the hedging instrument's effectiveness; and expected to be highly effective in achieving offsetting changes in fair value or cash flows attributable to the hedged risk as designated and documented, and the effectiveness can be reliably measured.

Seltec would use cash flow or fair value hedge accounting. A fair value hedge is a hedge of the exposure to changes in fair value of a recognised asset or liability or a previously unrecognised firm commitment to buy or sell an asset at a fixed price or an identified portion of such an asset, liability or firm commitment, that is attributable to a particular risk and could affect profit or loss. The gain or loss from the change in fair value of the hedging instrument is recognised immediately in profit or loss. At the same time the carrying amount of the hedged item is adjusted for the corresponding gain or loss with respect to the hedged risk, which is also recognised immediately in net profit or loss.

A cash flow hedge is a hedge of the exposure to variability in cash flows that

(i)     is attributable to a particular risk associated with a recognised asset or liability (such as all or some future interest payments on variable rate debt) or a highly probable forecast transaction, and

(ii)    could affect profit or loss [IAS 39]. The portion of the gain or loss on the hedging instrument that is determined to be an effective hedge is recognised in OCI and reclassified to profit or loss when the hedged cash transaction affects profit or loss [IAS 39].

IAS 39 is restrictive because of the difficulty of isolating and measuring the cash flows attributable to the specific risks for the non-financial items. Assuming all of the documentation criteria are met, Seltec can use hedge accounting but may favour a fair value hedge in order to reduce earnings volatility. All price changes of the edible oil will be taken into account including its type and geographical location and compared with changes in the value of the future. If the contracts have different price elements, then ineffectiveness will occur. Hedge accounting can be applied as long as the ineffectiveness is not outside the range 80%–125%.

IAS 39 defines an embedded derivative as a component of a hybrid instrument that also includes a non-derivative host contract, with the effect that some of the cash flows of the instrument vary in a way similar to a stand-alone derivative. As derivatives must be accounted for at fair value in the statement of financial position with changes recognised through profit or loss, so must some embedded derivatives.

IAS 39 requires that an embedded derivative should be separated from its host contract and accounted for as a derivative when:

(i)     the economic risks and characteristics of the embedded derivative are not closely related to those of the host contract;

(ii)    a separate instrument with the same terms as the embedded derivative would meet the definition of a derivative; and

(iii)   the entire instrument is not measured at fair value with changes in fair value recognised in profit or loss.

If an embedded derivative is separated, the host contract is accounted for under the appropriate standard. A foreign currency denominated contract contains an embedded derivative unless it meets one of the following criteria:

(i)     the foreign currency denominated in the contract is that of either party to the contract,

(ii)   the currency of the contract is that in which the related good or service is routinely denominated in commercial transactions,

(iii)  the currency is that commonly used in such contracts in the market in which the transaction takes place.

In this case the pound sterling is not the functional currency of either party, oil is not routinely denominated in sterling but dollars as most of Seltec's trade as regards the oil appears to be in dollars and the currency is not that normally used in business transactions in the environment in which Seltec carries out its business. Additionally, the economic risks are not closely related as currency fluctuations and changes in the price of oil have different risks. The host contract is not measured at fair value but would meet the definition of a derivative if it were a separate instrument with the same terms. The currency derivative should therefore be accounted for at fair value through profit or loss.

---

*Begin by stating the definition of an intangible asset, together with factors to be considered in determining whether recognition is appropriate, which can then be applied to the circumstances in the scenario.*

---

(b)   Intangible assets are classified as having an:

(i)    Indefinite life: No foreseeable limit to the period over which the asset is expected to generate net cash inflows for the entity; or a

(ii)   Definite life: A limited period of benefit to the entity.

Factors that should be considered are:

(i)    The entity's commitment to support the brand

(ii)   The extent to which the brand has long-term potential that is not underpinned by short-term fashion or trends. That is, the brand has had a period of proven success

(iii)  The extent to which the products carrying the brand are resistant to changes in the operating environment. These products should be resistant to changes in legal, technological and competitive environments.

The brand of oil, which has been in existence for many years, is likely to have an indefinite life as it has already proven its longevity having been successful for many years. However the oil named after a famous film star is likely to decline in popularity as the popularity of the film star declines. It is a new product and its longevity has not been proven and therefore it is likely to have a finite life. An intangible asset with an indefinite useful life should not be amortised. Its useful life should be reviewed each reporting period to determine whether events and circumstances continue to support an indefinite useful life assessment for that asset. If they do not, the change in the useful life assessment from indefinite to finite should be accounted for as a change in an accounting estimate. The asset should also be assessed for impairment in accordance with IAS 36.

The cost less residual value of an intangible asset with a finite useful life should be amortised on a systematic basis over that life. The amortisation method should reflect the pattern of benefits but if the pattern cannot be determined reliably, it should be amortised by the straight-line method.

A business combination is a transaction or event in which an acquirer obtains control of one or more businesses. A business is defined as an integrated set of activities and assets that is capable of being conducted and managed for the purpose of providing a return directly to investors or other owners, members or participants in the form of dividends, lower costs or other economic benefits to investors or owners. The two entities do not meet the definition of a business in IFRS 3 (Revised) *Business combinations* as they do not have any processes such as real estate management which are applied to the retail space that they own. The entities do not generate any outputs such as rental income. Therefore the acquisition should be treated as a purchase of assets.

| ACCA marking scheme | |
|---|---|
| | *Marks* |
| Hedge accounting | 5 |
| Futures | 5 |
| Embedded derivative | 4 |
| Brands | 5 |
| Business combinations | 4 |
| Professional marks | 2 |
| | ——— |
| Total | 25 |
| | ——— |

**Examiner's comments**

The question was a case study type question based around a company in the edible oil industry. The company processed and sold edible oils and used several financial instruments to spread the risk of fluctuation in the price of edible oils. Additionally, the company was unclear as to how the purchase of the brands and certain entities should be accounted for. It involved knowledge of derivatives, hedging and embedded derivatives at a fundamental level. Candidates did not have to apply their knowledge to any degree but simply had to recognise the nature of various financial instruments involved and discuss their accounting treatment. This knowledge is essential knowledge and will be examined in future diets. Candidates' answers were satisfactory in the main but few candidates recognised the embedded derivative. The accounting for the brands was quite well answered with many students gaining high marks. The final part required candidates to apply IFRS 3 *Business combinations* to a scenario. The answers were often quite poor with the main weakness being the application of the knowledge and the understanding of the nature of the purchase of the entities.

## 26    SAVAGE (DEC 05 EXAM)

**Key answer tips**

This question has virtually all the numerical elements of pension accounting that you are likely to come across. You must learn which figures appear where in the financial statements.

(a)    **Amounts recognised in the statement of financial position**

|  | at 31 October 20X5 $m | at 31 October 20X4 $m |
|---|---|---|
| Present value of the obligation | 3,375 | 3,000 |
| Fair value of plan assets (3,170 – 8) | 3,162 | 2,900 |
| Liability recognised in SOFP | 213 | 100 |

**Expense recognised in profit or loss for year-ended 31 October 20X5**

|  | $m |
|---|---|
| Net interest component | 14 |
| Service cost component | 165 |
| Expense in profit or loss | 179 |

**Amount recognised in other comprehensive income**

|  | $m |
|---|---|
| Net remeasurement component: |  |
| Loss on obligation (working) | 64 |
| Gain on plan assets (working) | (85) |
| Net remeasurement component gain | (21) |

*Workings and comments:*

|  | Plan assets – FV $m | Plan obligation – PV $m | Net obligation $m |
|---|---|---|---|
| Balance b/fwd | (2,900) | 3,000 | 100 |
| Interest @6% | (174)) | 188 | 14 |
| Current service cost |  | 40 | 40 |
| Past service cost |  | 125 | 125 |
| Benefits paid | 42 | (42) | --- |
| Contributions into plan | (45) |  | (45) |
| Remeasurement component (bal fig) | (85) | 64 | (21) |
| Balance c/fwd | (3,162) | 3,375 | 213 |

The company will recognise $125 million past service costs immediately as the benefits vest on 1 November 20X4. The interest cost should be based on the discount rate and the present value of the scheme liabilities at the beginning of the year but should reflect changes in scheme liabilities during the period. Hence the past service costs have been included in scheme liabilities for this purpose. The finance cost on the plan obligation has therefore been calculated based upon the balance brought forward of $3,000m plus the past service costs recognised at the start of the year amounting to $165m.

The interest on the plan assets represents the change in the value of those assets due to the passage of time by application of the discount rate. As the contributions and benefits were assumed to be paid at the end of the period, no adjustment is required to the opening balance.

The contributions that have not been paid will not count as an asset of the fund at the reporting date. The fair value of the plan assets is therefore $3,162m (3,170 – 8) i.e. net of contributions not paid.

Revised IAS 19 now requires that actuarial gains and losses (i.e. remeasurement gains and losses) are recognised in other comprehensive income for the year.

(b)     The contributions payable by Savage to the trustees will not count as an asset for the purposes of the valuation of the fund. IAS 19 states that plan assets should not include unpaid contributions due from the reporting entity to the fund.

The introduction of changes to a defined benefit plan, such as enhanced future benefits payable in respect of past service provided by employees is normally referred to as past service costs. The company will therefore recognise $125m at 1 Nov 20X4. A company should recognise past service costs in full at the earliest of three dates:

* when the related restructuring costs are recognised, or
* when the related termination benefits are recognised, or
* when the curtailment occurs.

Following revision of IAS 19, it is no longer necessary to spread past service costs over any vesting period which employees are still required to work to earn the enhanced benefits.

| ACCA marking scheme | | |
|---|---|---|
| | | *Marks* |
| (a) | Statement of financial position | 3 |
| | Changes in present value/assets | 12 |
| | Profit or loss | 5 |
| | Other comprehensive income | 3 |
| | Movement in net liability | 3 |
| | | ——— |
| | Available | 26 |
| | Maximum | 21 |
| (b) | Explanation | |
| | Past service costs | 2 |
| | Contributions | 2 |
| | | ——— |
| Available | | 30 |
| **Maximum** | | **25** |

## 27 EGIN (JUN 06 EXAM)

**Key answer tips**

This question covers related party transactions so a good knowledge of the standard is required. Part (a) of the question covers IAS 24 in detail – and there are a lot of easy marks to be gained here. Part (b) is not too difficult and could be attempted first.

(a) (i) **Importance and criteria determining a related party relationship**

Related party transactions form part of the normal business process. Companies operate their businesses through complex group structures and acquire interests in other entities for commercial or investment purposes. Control or significant influence is exercised by companies in a wide range of situations. These relationships affect the financial position and results of a company and can lead to transactions that would not normally be undertaken. Similarly those transactions may be priced at a level which is unacceptable to unrelated parties.

It is possible that even where no transactions occur between related parties, the operating results and financial position can be affected. Decisions by a subsidiary company can be heavily influenced by the holding company even though there may be no intercompany transactions. Transactions can be agreed upon terms substantially different from those with unrelated parties. For example the leasing of equipment between group companies may be at a nominal rental.

The assumption in financial statements is that transactions are carried out on an arm's length basis and that the entity has independent discretionary power over its transactions. If these assumptions are not true, then disclosure of this fact should be made. Even if transactions are at arm's length, disclosure of related party transactions is useful information as future transactions may be affected. The *Framework* says that information contained in financial statements must be neutral, that is free from bias. Additionally the document says that information must represent faithfully the transactions it purports to represent. Without the disclosure of related party information, it is unlikely that these qualitative characteristics can be achieved.

IAS 24 *Related party disclosures* defines a related party (paragraph 9). The definition includes the following:

A party is related to an entity if:

(a) (i) the party controls, is controlled by, or is under common control with, the entity or

(ii) has an interest in the entity that gives it significant influence over the entity or

(iii) has joint control over the entity

(b) the party is an associate or joint venture

(c) the party is a member of the key management personnel of the entity or its parent

(d)    the party is a close family member of anyone referred to in (a) or (c) above

(e)    the party is controlled or significantly influenced by an individual in (c) or (d) above

(f)    a post-employment benefit plan for the benefit of some or all of the employees of the entity or any of its other related parties.

Control is the power to govern the financial and operating policies of an entity so as to obtain benefits from its activities. The power does not need to be used for control to exist. Entities subject to common control from the same source are related parties because of the potential effect on transactions between them. Common control will exist where both entities are subject to control from management boards having a controlling nucleus of directors in common. Significant influence is the power to participate in the financial and operating policy decisions of the entity without controlling those policies. Significant influence can occur by share ownership, statute or agreement.

(ii)    **Egin Group**

**Group structure:**

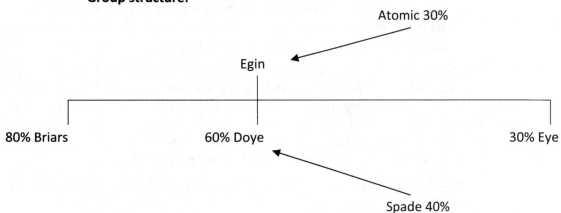

Briars, Doye and Eye are all related parties of Egin because Briars and Doye are controlled by and are under the common control of Egin and Egin has significant influence over Eye. Additionally because there is a controlling nucleus of directors in common (i.e. the directors of Egin are also the directors of Briars and Doye), Briars and Doye are also related parties. Briars and Doye are not necessarily deemed to be related parties of Eye. There is only one director in common so any influence will probably be exerted by the four other directors. It will be necessary to determine whether the director is deemed to be a key member of management of the companies or can control or significantly influence policies in their dealings. Additionally, relationships between parents and subsidiaries should be disclosed even if there have not been any transactions between them (IAS 24 paragraph 12). Thus there should be disclosure of the relationship between Tang and Egin during the period even though Tang has now been sold.

The company, Blue, is a related party of Briars as the director controls Blue and is a member of the key management personnel of Briars. If the director is considered to be a related party of Egin, i.e. because the director acts as a consultant to the group, then this information should be disclosed in the group financial statements.

(iii) **Spade and the Group**

Spade, being an investor in Doye, is a related party of that company and disclosure of the sale of plant and equipment will have to be made. The fact that Egin and Spade have an investment in the same company, Doye, does not itself make them related parties. The Egin group and Spade will only be related parties if there is the necessary control or influence. For example if Spade persuaded Egin to sell plant and equipment at significantly below its retail value then Egin would have subordinated its interests in agreeing to the transaction.

(iv) **Atomic and the Group**

Atomic is a related party to Egin and to Briars and Doye as Atomic has significant influence over Egin which controls Briars and Doye. The same does not necessarily apply to Eye. It would have to be proven that Atomic could significantly influence Eye because of its holding in Egin. It may be difficult to exercise such influence in an associate (Eye) of an associated company (Egin).

Management should describe the basis of the pricing between related parties which is the normal list selling price. However, related party transactions are between parties where one party has control or significant influence and by definition are not at arm's length. Therefore, the transactions between related parties should not be described as arm's length.

(b) IAS 21 *The effects of changes in foreign exchange rates* requires goodwill arising on the acquisition of a foreign operation and fair value adjustments to acquired assets and liabilities to be treated as belonging to the foreign operation. They should be expressed in the functional currency of the foreign operation and translated at the closing rate at the end of each reporting period. Effectively goodwill is treated as a foreign currency asset which is retranslated at the closing rate.

In this case the goodwill arising on the acquisition of Briars would be treated as follows:

|  | Euros m | Rate | $m |
|---|---|---|---|
| Cost of acquisition | 50 | | |
| FV NCI (20% × 45) | 9 | | |
|  | 59 | | |
| Less: FV of net assets at acquisition | (45) | | |
| Goodwill at 1 June 20X5 | 14 | 2.0 | 7.0 |
| Impairment | (3) | 2.5 | (1.2) |
| Exchange loss (difference) | | | (1.4) |
| Goodwill at 31 May 20X6 | 11 | 2.5 | 4.4 |

At 31 May 20X6, the goodwill will be retranslated at 2.5 euros to the dollar to give a figure of $4.4 million. Therefore this will be the figure for goodwill in the statement of financial position and an exchange loss of $1.4 million recorded in other comprehensive income (translation reserve). The impairment of goodwill will be expensed in profit or loss to the value of $1.2 million. (The closing rate has been used to translate the impairment; however, there may be an argument for using the average rate.)

The loan to Briars will effectively be classed as a financial liability measured at amortised cost. It is the default category for financial liabilities that do not meet the definition of financial liabilities at fair value through profit or loss. For most entities, most financial liabilities will fall into this category. When a financial liability is recognised initially in the statement of financial position, the liability is measured at fair value. IFRS 13 defines fair value as the amount for which a liability can be transferred, between knowledgeable, willing parties in an arm's length transaction. In other words, fair value is an actual or estimated transaction price on the reporting date for a transaction taking place between unrelated parties that have adequate information about the asset or liability being measured.

Since fair value is a market transaction price, on initial recognition fair value will often be equal to the amount of consideration paid or received for the financial asset or financial liability, excluding any associated transactions costs. Accordingly, IFRS 13 identifies that that the best evidence of the fair value of any asset or liability is the transaction price, although entities should take steps to ensure that the price paid to acquire an asset, or transfer a liability does meet with the requirements of IFRS 13 in terms of the hierarchy of inputs used to determine fair value. However for longer-term receivables or payables that do not pay interest or pay a below-market interest, they should instead be measured initially at the present value of the cash flows to be received or paid.

Thus in Briars financial statements the following entries will be made:

| Date | $000 | Euros 000 | Exchange rate |
|---|---|---|---|
| | | *Loan amount* | |
| 01/06/05 ($10m/$1.06^2$) | 8,900 | 17,800 | $1 = 2 euros |
| 31/05/06 ($8,900,000 × 1.06) | 9,434 | 23,585 | $1 = 2.5 euros |
| | | 5,785 | |

The increase in the loan amount will represent interest of 17,800,000 × 0.06, i.e. 1,068,000 euros and an exchange loss of (5,785 – 1,068) i.e. 4,717,000 euros. These amounts will be recognised in profit or loss in the individual accounts of Briars. (An alternative calculation could be $8.9 million × 0.06 = $534,000 translated at average rate (2.3) = 1,228,000 euros, giving an exchange loss of 4,557,000 euros.)

| ACCA marking scheme | | | | Marks |
|---|---|---|---|---|
| (a) | (i) | Reasons and explanation | | 5 |
| | (ii) | Egin | | 5 |
| | | Spade | | 3 |
| | | Atomic | | 3 |
| (b) | | Goodwill | | 5 |
| | | Loan | | 5 |
| Available | | | | 26 |
| **Maximum** | | | | **25** |

## 28    ENGINA (PILOT 01)

**Key answer tips**

Don't forget to write your answer in a report format – it is worth four easy marks. Some of your answer needs to be the reasons why there is disclosure of related parties – as well as discussion of the scenario. The background information is fairly easy to earn marks providing you know it.

Brice and Partners<br>Brice Lane<br>Bridlington<br>(Date)

The Directors
Engina and Co.
Orange Lane
Edmond

Dear Sirs

**Related Party Transactions**

We are writing to explain the reasons why it is important to disclose Related Party Transactions while at the same time explaining the nature of the disclosure required under current International Financial Reporting Standards. We appreciate the cultural and political sensitivity of the disclosure of such transactions in your country and the fact that such opinions will not change in the short term.

However, a key factor in your thoughts about the disclosure of related party transactions is the fact that in addition to the requirements of the accounting standard (IAS 24 *Related party disclosures*), local Stock Exchanges often impose additional disclosures on companies which require a listing. Further guidance is often found in local income tax statutes, companies legislation and public reporting requirements. We hope that the following general discussion and specific comments on the transactions undertaken in your company will assist your understanding of quite a complex and sensitive area.

Related party relationships are part of the normal business process. Entities operate the separate parts of their business through subsidiaries and associates, and acquire interests in other enterprises for investment or commercial reasons. Thus control or significant influence can be exercised over the investee by the investing company. These relationships can have a significant effect on the financial position and operating results of the company and lead to transactions which would not normally be undertaken. For example, a company may sell a large proportion of its production to its parent company because it cannot and could not find a market elsewhere. Additionally the transactions may be effected at prices which would not be acceptable to unrelated parties.

Even if there are no transactions between the related parties, it is still possible for the operating results and financial position of an enterprise to be affected by the relationship. A recently acquired subsidiary can be forced to finish a relationship with a company in order to benefit group companies. Transactions may be entered into on terms different from those applicable to an unrelated party. For example, a holding company may lease equipment to a subsidiary on terms unrelated to market rates for equivalent leases.

In the absence of contrary information, it is assumed that the financial statements of an entity reflect transactions carried out on an arm's length basis and that the entity has independent discretionary power over its actions and pursues its activities independently. If these assumptions are not justified because of related party transactions, then disclosure of this fact should be made. Even if transactions are at arm's length, the disclosure of related party transactions is useful because it is likely that future transactions may be affected by such relationships. The main issues in determining such disclosures are the identification of related parties, the types of transactions and arrangements and the information to be disclosed.

It can be seen that information about related parties can be an important element of any investment decision and regulatory authorities consider disclosure of such information to be of paramount importance.

The following specific comments relate to the list of transactions with connected persons which you supplied to us.

### Sale of goods to directors

Related party transactions need only be disclosed where they are material. An important aspect of IAS 24 is the assessment of both the materiality and significance of the transactions to the reporting enterprise. Additionally, transactions are material where the users of financial statements might reasonably be influenced by such a transaction. Thus it is not possible to avoid disclosing such items on the grounds that they are not numerically large enough. Where the related party is a director then the transaction could be viewed in relation to its materiality to that director. The standard requires disclosure of contracts with key personnel and sales of assets to directors where control exists. Also the standard requires disclosure of related party relationships where control exists irrespective of whether there have been any transactions. Contracts of significance with directors may also require disclosure by local Stock Exchanges.

In this case your director (Mr Satay) has purchased $600,000 (12 months × $50,000) of goods from the company and a car for $45,000 with a market value of $80,000. Mr Satay effectively controls Engina. Although neither of these transactions is material or significant to the company or the directors, IAS 24 and the spirit of good corporate governance would dictate that any transactions with directors are extremely sensitive and we would recommend disclosure of such transactions.

### Hotel property

International Financial Reporting Standards generally require any element of a transaction necessary for an understanding of the financial statements to be disclosed. The hotel property sold to the brother of the Managing Director is a related party transaction which appears to have been undertaken at below market price. The disclosure of simply this fact would not reflect the reality of your company's position. Disclosure of the substance of the transaction is an important element of IAS 24. The carrying value of the hotel needs to be adjusted as it has become impaired. The hotel should have been shown in your records under IAS 36 *Impairment of assets* at the lower of carrying value ($5 million) and the recoverable amount (higher of net selling price ($4.3 million – $0.2 million, i.e. $4.1 million, and value in use $3.6 million). Thus the hotel should have been recorded at $4.1 million.

Thus the property has been sold at $100,000 below the impaired value and this is the nature of the disclosure which should be made, thus reflecting more closely the nature of the property market in your country and the nature of the transaction.

**Group structure**

Local Companies Acts and Stock Exchange rules often contain requirements to disclose directors' interests in the share capital of a company. Mr Satay controls Engina through his ownership of 80% of the share capital of Wheel.

Any transactions of Engina with either Car or Wheel will have to be disclosed as each of Car, Wheel and Enigma are under the common control of Mr Satay.

We hope that the above explanations are of use to you and realise that culturally and politically they may seem unacceptable. However, if you wish for a quotation on a recognised Stock Exchange, then the disclosure requirements set out above will almost certainly have to be adhered to.

Yours faithfully,

Brice and Partners

| ACCA marking scheme | |
|---|---|
| | *Marks* |
| Style of letter/report | 4 |
| Reasons | 8 |
| Goods to directors | 4 |
| Property | 5 |
| Group | 4 |
| | —— |
| Total | 25 |
| | —— |

## 29 NORMAN (JUN 08 EXAM)  *Online question assistance*

(a) Upon adoption of IFRS 8 *Operating segments*, the identification of Norman's segments may or may not change depending on how segments were identified previously. IFRS 8 requires operating segments to be identified on the basis of internal reports about the components of the entity that are regularly reviewed by the chief operating decision maker in order to allocate resources to the segment and to assess its performance. Formerly companies identified business and geographical segments using a risks and rates of return approach with one set of segments being classed as primary and the other as secondary. IFRS 8 states that a component of an entity that sells primarily or exclusively to other operating segments of the entity meets the definition of an operating segment if the entity is managed that way. IFRS 8 does not define segment revenue, segment expense, segment result, segment assets, and segment liabilities but does require an explanation of how segment profit or loss, segment assets, and segment liabilities are measured for each segment. This will give entities some discretion in determining what is included in segment profit or loss but this will be limited by their internal reporting practices. The core principle is that the entity should disclose information to enable users to evaluate the nature and financial effects of the types of business activities in which it engages and the economic environments in which it operates.

IFRS 8 *Operating segments* defines an operating segment as follows. An operating segment is a component of an entity:

- that engages in business activities from which it may earn revenues and incur expenses (including revenues and expenses relating to transactions with other components of the same entity)

- whose operating results are reviewed regularly by the entity's chief operating decision makers to make decisions about resources to be allocated to the segment and assess its performance; and for which discrete financial information is available

IFRS 8 requires an entity to report financial and descriptive information about its reportable segments. Reportable segments are operating segments that meet specified criteria:

- the reported revenue, from both external customers and intersegment sales or transfers, is 10% or more of the combined revenue, internal and external, of all operating segments; or

- the absolute measure of its reported profit or loss is 10% or more of the greater, in absolute amount, of (i) the combined reported profit of all operating segments that did not report a loss, and (ii) the combined reported loss of all operating segments that reported a loss; or

- its assets are 10% or more of the combined assets of all operating segments.

If the total external revenue reported by operating segments constitutes less than 75% of the entity's revenue, additional operating segments must be identified as reportable segments (even if they do not meet the quantitative thresholds set out above) until at least 75% of the entity's revenue is included in reportable segments. There is no precise limit to the number of segments that can be disclosed.

As the key performance indicators are set on a city by city basis, there may be information within the internal reports about the components of the entity which has been disaggregated further. Also the company is likely to make decisions about the allocation of resources and about the nature of performance on a city basis because of the individual key performance indicators.

In the case of the existing segments, the European segment meets the criteria for a segment as its reported revenue from external and inter segment sales ($203 million) is more than 10% of the combined revenue ($1,010 million). However, it fails the profit/loss and assets tests. Its results are a loss of $10 million which is less than 10% of the greater of the reported profit or reported loss which is $165 million. Similarly its segment assets of $300 million are less than 10% of the combined segment assets ($3,100 million). The South East Asia segment passes all of the threshold tests. If the company changes its business segments then the above tests will have to be reperformed. A further issue is that the current reported segments constitute less than 75% of the company's external revenue (50%), thus additional operating segments must be identified until 75% of the entity's revenue is included in reportable segments.

Norman may have to change the basis of reporting its operating segments. Although the group reports to management on the basis of three geographical regions, it is likely that management will have information which has been further disaggregated in order to make business decisions. Therefore, the internal reports of Norman will need to be examined before it is possible to determine the nature of the operating segments.

(b) Property is sometimes sold with a degree of continuing involvement by the seller so that the risks and rewards of ownership have not been transferred. The nature and extent of the buyer's involvement will determine how the transaction is accounted for. The substance of the transaction is determined by looking at the transaction as a whole and IAS 18 *Revenue* requires this by stating that where two or more transactions are linked, they should be treated as a single transaction in order to understand the commercial effect (IAS 18 paragraph 13). In the case of the sale of the hotel, theme park and casino, Norman should not recognise a sale as the company continues to enjoy substantially all of the risks and rewards of the businesses, and still operates and manages them. Additionally the residual interest in the business reverts back to Norman. Also Norman has guaranteed the income level for the purchaser as the minimum payment to Conquest will be $15 million a year. The transaction is in substance a financing arrangement and the proceeds should be treated as a loan and the payment of profits as interest.

The principles of IAS 18 and IFRIC 13 *Customer loyalty programmes* require that revenue in respect of each separate component of a transaction is measured at its fair value. Where vouchers are issued as part of a sales transaction and are redeemable against future purchases, revenue should be reported at the amount of the consideration received/receivable less the voucher's fair value. In substance, the customer is purchasing both goods or services and a voucher. The fair value of the voucher is determined by reference to the value to the holder and not the cost to the issuer. Factors to be taken into account when estimating the fair value, would be the discount the customer obtains, the percentage of vouchers that would be redeemed, and the time value of money. As only one in five vouchers are redeemed, then effectively the hotel has sold goods worth ($300 + $4) million, i.e. $304 million for a consideration of $300 million. Thus allocating the discount between the two elements would mean that (300 ÷ 304 × $300m) i.e. $296.1 million will be allocated to the room sales and the balance of $3.9 million to the vouchers. The deferred portion of the proceeds is only recognised when the obligations are fulfilled.

(Note that, although IFRIC 13 has been removed from the ACCA P2 syllabus from 2011, the principle it applies is still relevant and may still be examined.)

The recognition of government grants is covered by IAS 20 *Accounting for government grants and disclosure of government assistance*. The accruals concept is used by the standard to match the grant received with the related costs. The relationship between the grant and the related expenditure is the key to establishing the accounting treatment. Grants should not be recognised until there is reasonable assurance that the company can comply with the conditions relating to their receipt and the grant will be received. Provision should be made if it appears that the grant may have to be repaid.

There may be difficulties of matching costs and revenues when the terms of the grant do not specify precisely the expense towards which the grant contributes. In this case the grant appears to relate to both the building of hotels and the creation of employment. However, if the grant was related to revenue expenditure, then the terms would have been related to payroll or a fixed amount per job created. Hence it would appear that the grant is capital based and should be matched against the depreciation of the hotels by using a deferred income approach or deducting the grant from the carrying value of the asset (IAS 20). Additionally the grant is only to be repaid if the cost of the hotel is less than $500 million which itself would seem to indicate that the grant is capital based. If the company feels that the cost will not reach $500 million, a provision should be made for the estimated liability if the grant has been recognised.

| ACCA marking scheme | | |
|---|---|---|
| | | *Marks* |
| (a) | Identification of segments | 2 |
| | Definition | 2 |
| | Reporting information | 2 |
| | Norman applicability | 5 |
| | | ─── |
| | | 11 |
| (b) | Sale of businesses | 4 |
| | Vouchers | 4 |
| | Grant income | 4 |
| | Quality of discussion | 2 |
| | | ─── |
| | | 14 |
| | | ─── |
| | Total | 25 |
| | | ─── |

**Examiner's comments**

This question dealt with segmental reporting and the application of the principles to a given scenario's second part of the question dealt with income recognition in three different scenarios. The first part of the question was quite well answered by candidates. However in the International papers, many students confused IFRS 8 with the requirements of IAS 14. There are some significant differences between the two standards particularly in the definition of a segment. Candidates did apply the principles of the standard quite well to the scenario. The second part of the question required candidates to discuss the accounting treatment of a financing arrangement, the treatment of discount vouchers and government grants. The treatment of customer loyalty programmes is the subject of IFRIC 13. The examination will require candidates to have knowledge of certain IFRIC's to supplement the accounting treatment required by the standard. Candidates performed quite well on this part of the question and applied their knowledge of IAS 18 very well to the cases in point. This type of question will appear regularly in the paper with candidates having to apply their knowledge to small scenarios with a common theme.

## 30    WADER (JUN 07 EXAM)

**Key answer tips**

This question tests in detail the way impairments of current and non-current assets have to be dealt with and when reorganisation provisions should be recognised. The fact that non-specific allowances against receivables are no longer permissible and the way in which the impairment of revalued assets is accounted for can be quite tricky, otherwise it should be possible to score good marks.

(a)   Trade receivables are financial assets normally designated to be measured at amortised cost, provided both the business model test and cash flow characteristics test can be complied with per IFRS 9 *Financial instruments*. According to this standard, loans and receivables are measured at amortised cost using the effective interest rate method. Initially, they will be carried at fair value at the time of recognition, which in the case of trade receivables will be the invoice amount.

The effective interest rate method spreads the interest income or expense over the life of the financial asset or liability. Obviously, such a method does not seem to be relevant to trade receivables where normally there is no interest payment to spread. IFRS 9 therefore, allows short-term receivables with no stated interest rate to be measured at the original invoice amount, if the effect of discounting is immaterial. This would apply to trade receivables and, therefore, they will still be carried at the invoice amount.

An entity must assess at the end of each reporting period whether there is any objective evidence that a financial asset or group of financial assets is impaired. If there is objective evidence that an impairment loss on the financial assets has been incurred, the loss must be recognised in profit or loss. Since trade receivables are financial assets, annual impairment assessments must be performed. The amount of the loss is determined by looking at the carrying value of the trade receivable and comparing it with the present value of the estimated cash flows discounted at the effective interest rate. As previously outlined, trade receivables will not normally be discounted and will not normally have an effective interest rate.

A formulaic approach is not acceptable unless the formula can be shown to produce an estimate sufficiently close to the method specified in IFRS 9 that requires an estimate of the cash that will actually be received. The recognition of future losses based on possible or expected future trends is not in accordance with the IASB *Framework* and IAS 37 *Provisions, contingent liabilities and contingent assets*. A general allowance would therefore not be allowed as the historical experience is zero and it is unlikely to produce an acceptable estimate of the cash flows to be received.

Impairment of individually significant balances must be separately assessed and an allowance made when it is probable that the cash due will not be received in full. Where there is no objective evidence of impairment, the individual asset is included in a group of financial assets of similar credit risk and the group assessed for impairment. Therefore provision must be made for the impairment of Tray, and Milk will be included with other receivables for the purpose of assessing the impairment of a general portfolio of receivables.

In the case of Wader, therefore, the basis of the impairment loss is flawed. The general allowance will not be allowed. As the due date for the receipt of cash from Tray is one year hence, then it could be argued that discounting should be used to calculate any impairment loss. The impairment will be calculated as follows:

|  | Balance ($m) | Cash ($m) |
|---|---|---|
| Tray ($4.1m discounted at 5%) | 4.0 | 3.9 |
| Milk and other receivables | 7.0 | 6.6 |
|  | 11.0 | 10.5 |

Wader would show a balance of $500,000 on the allowance account, or simply reduce trade receivables by the impairment loss of $500,000.

(b)    Wader has to estimate the net realisable value (NRV) of the inventory and compare this to its cost as IAS 2 Inventories requires inventory to be valued at the lower of cost and NRV.

NRV is the estimated selling price in the ordinary course of business, less the estimated cost of completion and the estimated costs necessary to make the sale (IAS 2 para 6). Any write-down should be recognised in profit or loss in the period in which the write down occurs. Any reversal should be recognised in profit or loss in the period in which the reversal occurs (IAS 2 para 34).

The list selling price should be reduced by the customer discounts as this represents the proceeds to be received when the sale is made. The warehouse overhead costs will be incurred regardless of how long the inventory is held and are not necessarily incurred to effect the sale. It is appropriate to include personnel costs in the estimate of NRV but only where they are necessary. In this case the variable component of personnel salaries (commissions) will be taken into account but not the fixed salaries as they are normal overheads and do not influence the sale of the product.

|  | $ |
|---|---|
| List price | 50 |
| Customer discounts | (2.5) |
| Commissions – sale | (10.0) |
| Net realisable value | 37.5 |
| Cost | 35.0 |

No write down of this product is, therefore, required.

(c)    IAS 16 *Property, plant and equipment* requires the increase in the carrying amount of an asset to be recognised in other comprehensive income and accumulated in equity under the heading 'revaluation surplus'. The increase should be recognised in profit or loss to the extent that it reverses a revaluation decrease of the same asset previously recognised in profit or loss. If an asset's carrying amount is decreased as a result of a revaluation, the decrease shall be recognised in profit or loss. However, the decrease is recognised in other comprehensive income as a reduction in the revaluation surplus accumulated within equity to the extent of any credit balance existing in revaluation surplus in respect of that asset. The buildings would be accounted for as follows:

|  | *Year-ended* | | |
|---|---|---|---|
|  | *31 May 20X6* | *31 May 20X7* | |
|  | $m | $m | |
| Cost/valuation | 10.0 | 8.00 | |
| Depreciation ($10m/20) | (0.5) | (0.42) | ($8m ÷ 19) |
|  | 9.5 | 7.58 | |
| Impairment to profit or loss | (1.5) | | |
| Reversal of impairment loss to profit or loss | | 1.42 | |
| Gain on revaluation – revaluation surplus | | 2.00 | |
| Carrying amount | 8.0 | 11.00 | |

The gain on revaluation in 20X7 has been recognised in profit or loss to the extent of the revaluation loss charged in 20X6 as adjusted for the additional depreciation (1.5 ÷ 19, i.e. $0.08m) that would have been recognised in 20X7 had the opening balance been $9.5 million, and the loss of $1.5 million not been recognised. This adjustment for depreciation is not directly mentioned in IAS 16, but is a logical consequence of the application of the matching principle and would be against the principle of IAS 16 if not carried out.

(d) A provision under IAS 37 *Provisions, contingent liabilities and contingent assets* can only be made in relation to the entity's restructuring plans where there is both a detailed formal plan in place and the plans have been announced to those affected. The plan should identify areas of the business affected, the impact on employees and the likely cost of the restructuring and the timescale for implementation. There should be a short timescale between communicating the plan and starting to implement it. A provision should not be recognised until a plan is formalised.

A decision before the end of the reporting period to restructure is not sufficient in itself for a provision to be recognised. A formal plan should be announced prior to the end of the reporting period. A constructive obligation should have arisen. It arises where there has been a detailed formal plan and this has raised a valid expectation in the minds of those affected. The provision should only include direct expenditure arising from the restructuring. Such amounts do not include costs associated with ongoing business operations. Costs of retraining staff or relocating continuing staff or marketing or investment in new systems and distribution networks, are excluded. It seems as though in this case a constructive obligation has arisen as there have been detailed formal plans approved and communicated thus raising valid expectations. The provision can be allowed subject to the exclusion of the costs outlined above.

Although executory contracts are outside IAS 37, it is permissible to recognise a provision that is onerous. Onerous contracts can result from restructuring plans or on a standalone basis. A provision should be made for the best estimate of the excess unavoidable costs under the onerous contract. This estimate should assess any likely level of future income from new sources. Thus in this case, the rental income from sub-letting the building should be taken into account. The provision should be recognised in the period in which it was identified and a cost recognised in profit or loss. Recognising an onerous contract provision is not a change in accounting policy under IAS 8 *Accounting policies, changes in accounting estimates and errors*.

The provision will be the lower of:

**Scenario 1**

|  | 20X8 $ | 20X9 $ | Total |
|---|---|---|---|
| Rent | 150,000 | 150,000 | |
| Discount rate | 1.05 | 1.052 | |
| Present value | 142,857 | 136,054 | |
| Sub-let income | (100,000) | (95,238) | |
| | 42,857 | 40,816 | 83,673 |

**Scenario 2**

|  | 20X8 | 20X9 | Total |
|---|---|---|---|
| Rent | 270,000 | | |
| Discount rate | 1.05 | | |
| Present value | 257,142 | | |
| Sub-let income | (100,000) | | |
| | 157,142 | | |

Therefore, the provision would be $83,673 as this course of action would be more beneficial to the company.

| ACCA marking scheme | |
|---|---|
| | *Marks* |
| Impairment | 7 |
| Inventory | 4 |
| Property, plant & equipment | 7 |
| Restructuring | 7 |
| | — |
| Total | 25 |
| | — |

## 31 ROUTER (JUN 07 EXAM)  *Online question assistance*

**Key answer tips**

Part (a) is straightforward, but there are tricky little bits in each of the other parts. Don't worry too much about these, but just focus on gaining the marks for the easier elements.

(a) Under IAS 18 *Revenue*, revenue on a service contract is recognised when the outcome of the transaction can be measured reliably. For revenue arising from the rendering of services, provided that all of the following criteria are met, revenue should be recognised by reference to the stage of completion of the transaction at the end of the reporting period (the percentage-of-completion method) (IAS 18 para 20):

(i) the amount of revenue can be measured reliably

(ii) it is probable that the economic benefits will flow to the seller

(iii) the stage of completion at the end of the reporting period can be measured reliably;

(iv) the costs incurred and to be incurred in respect of the transaction can be measured reliably.

When the above criteria are not met, revenue arising from the rendering of services should be recognised only to the extent of the expenses recognised that are recoverable. Because the only revenue which can be measured reliably is the fee for making the film ($5 million), this should therefore be recognised as revenue in the year to 31 May 20X7 and matched against the cost of the film of $4 million. Only when the television company shows the film should any further amounts of $100,000 be recognised as there is an outstanding performance condition in the form of the editing that needs to take place before the television company will broadcast the film. The costs of the film should not be carried forward and matched against anticipated future income unless they can be deemed to be an intangible asset under IAS 38 *Intangible assets*. Additionally, when assessing revenue to be recognised in future years, the costs of the editing and Router's liability for these costs should be assessed.

(b) IAS 16 *Property, plant and equipment* permits assets to be revalued on a class by class basis. The different characteristics of the buildings allow them to be classified separately. Different measurement models can, therefore, be used for the office buildings and the film studios. However, IAS 8 *Accounting policies, changes in accounting estimates and errors* says that once an entity has decided on its accounting policies, it should apply them consistently from period to period and across all relevant transactions. An entity can change its accounting policies but only in specific circumstances. These circumstances are:

(i) where there is a new accounting standard or interpretation or changes to an accounting standard

(ii) where the change results in the financial statements providing reliable and more relevant information about the effects of transactions, other events or conditions on the entity's financial position, financial performance, or cash flows.

Voluntary changes in accounting policies are quite uncommon but may occur when an accounting policy is no longer appropriate. Router will have to ensure that the change in accounting policy meets the criteria in IAS 8. Additionally, depreciated historical cost will have to be calculated for the film studios at the commencement of the period and the opening balance on the revaluation reserve and any other affected component of equity adjusted. The comparative amounts for each prior period should be presented as if the new accounting policy had always been applied. There are limits on retrospective application on the grounds of impracticability.

It is surprising that the lease of the land is considered to be a finance lease under IAS 17 *Leases*. Land is considered to have an indefinite life and should, therefore normally be classified as an operating lease unless ownership passes to the lessee during the lease term. The lease of the land should be separated out from the lease and treated individually. The value of the land so determined would be removed from the statement of financial position in terms of the liability and asset and the lease payments treated as rentals in profit or loss. A prior period adjustment should also be made. The buildings would continue to be treated as property, plant and equipment (PPE) and the carrying amount not adjusted. However, the remaining useful life of the building should be revised to reflect the shorter lease term. This will result in the carrying amount being depreciated over the shorter period. This change to the depreciation policy is applied prospectively not retrospectively. A change in the estimated depreciation charge would be regarded as a change in accounting estimate and not a change of accounting policy.

The lease liability must be assessed for derecognition under IFRS 9 *Financial instruments*, because of the revision of the lease terms, in order to determine whether the new terms are substantially different from the old. The purpose of this is to determine whether the change in terms is a modification or an extinguishment. The change seems to constitute a 'modification' because there is little change to the terms. The lease liability is, therefore, amended by deducting the one off payment ($10 million) from the carrying amount (after adjustment for the lease of land) together with any transaction costs. The lease liability is then remeasured to the present value of the revised future cash flows, discounted using the original effective interest rate. Any adjustment made in remeasuring the lease liability will be recognised in profit or loss.

(c) The investment in Wireless is currently accounted for using the equity method of accounting under IAS 28 (revised) *Investments in associates and joint ventures*. On the sale of a 15% holding, the interest in an associate will be derecognised, with a gain or loss on derecognition calculated for inclusion in profit or loss for the year. Router should recognise a gain on the sale of the holding in Wireless of $8 million (W1). The gain comprises the following:

(i) the disposal value or proceeds on the shares sold, plus

(ii) the fair value of the residual shareholding in Wireless, less

(iii) the carrying value of the associate at the date of disposal.

The residual holding of a 10% interest will be accounted for in accordance with IFRS 9. An equity instrument must be measured at fair value at the point of initial recognition, and thereafter at each reporting date until derecognition occurs. Normally, equity investments are classified as fair value through profit or loss (FVTPorL), with any change in fair value taken to profit or loss each year. Alternatively, it is possible to designate the investment to be classified as fair value through other comprehensive income (FVTOCI) upon initial recognition. If this is the case, all movements in fair value, including the impact of any impairment, will be taken to other comprehensive income each year.

Therefore, at 1 January 20X7, the investment will be recorded at fair value. At 31 May 20X7 a further gain of $(26 − 23) million, i.e. $3 million will be recorded. The gain of $3 million will be recorded in either profit or loss or other comprehensive income for the year, depending upon how the investment was classified at initial recognition.

(d) IFRS 10 *Consolidated financial statements*, identifies three elements of determining whether one entity has control of another as follows:

(i) power over the investee, and

(ii) exposure, or rights, to variable returns from its investment with the investee, and

(iii) ability to use its power over the investee to affect the amount of the investor's returns.

Para 12 of IFRS 10 identifies that any power by one entity to control another must be based upon current ability to direct activities which affect variable returns. At first sight, it would therefore appear that Router currently controls Playtime as it owns 60% of the issued equity capital of that entity.

The matter is complicated by the fact that a competitor entity holds warrants which are currently exercisable and which, if exercised, would result in the competitor gaining control of Playtime. As the warrants are currently exercisable, this means that there could be a change in control of Playtime which Router cannot do anything about.

Para 8 of IFRS 10 requires that all relevant facts should be considered in determining whether one entity has control of another, and that this should be subject to reassessment if relevant facts and circumstances change.

*It can therefore be argued that, based upon available information, Router is able to control Playtime only because the competitor entity permits it to do so. In this situation, control is really being exercised in a passive way by the competitor who retains the ability to take more active control of Playtime, irrespective of what Router may want or prefer.*

One party only can control Playtime and, therefore, the competitor company should consolidate Playtime. In coming to this decision all the facts and circumstances that affect potential voting rights (except the intention of management and the financial ability to exercise or convert) should be considered. It seems, however, that there is a prima facie case for Router not consolidating Playtime but accounting for it under IAS 28 or IFRS 9. Normally, if one entity controls another, it would not normally be possible for a third party to also exercise significant influence in the controlled entity. However, due to the unusual nature of the rights of both Router and the competitor relating to Playtime, this may be the case.

**(W1) Gain on sale of Wireless**

|  | $m |
|---|---|
| Sale proceeds | 40 |
| Plus the fair value of the residual investment | 23 |
|  | 63 |
| Less: CV of interest in associate at disposal date | (55) |
|  | 8 |

| ACCA marking scheme | |
|---|---|
|  | *Marks* |
| Revenue recognition | 5 |
| Studios and office | 10 |
| Film distribution company | 6 |
| Playtime | 4 |
| Available / maximum | 25 |

**32 KEY (DEC 09 EXAM)**  *Walk in the footsteps of a top tutor*

**Key answer tips**

This two-part question deals with non-current assets and impairment. Part (a) requires a general discussion of factors relevant when impairment testing during a period of limited availability of credit from banks. Part (b) develops this theme and requires specific impairment testing and supporting discussion of a specific scenario. This requires the use of present value information and extracts of discount tables have been provided in the question.

*A good starting point is to state and explain the definition of what impairment is, together when an impairment test may be required.*

(a) IAS 36 *Impairment of assets* states that an asset is impaired when its carrying amount will not be recovered from its continuing use or from its sale. An entity must determine at each reporting date whether there is any indication that an asset is impaired. If an indicator of impairment exists then the asset's recoverable amount must be determined and compared with its carrying amount to assess the amount of any impairment. Accounting for the impairment of non-financial assets can be difficult as IAS 36 *Impairment of assets* is a complex accounting standard. The turbulence in the markets and signs of economic downturn will cause many companies to revisit their business plans and revise financial forecasts. As a result of these changes, there may be significant impairment charges. Indicators of impairment may arise from either the external environment in which the entity operates or from within the entity's own operating environment. Thus the current economic downturn is an obvious indicator of impairment, which may cause the entity to experience significant impairment charges.

Assets should be tested for impairment at as low a level as possible, at individual asset level where possible. However, many assets do not generate cash inflows independently from other assets and such assets will usually be tested within the cash-generating unit (CGU) to which the asset belongs. Cash flow projections should be based on reasonable assumptions that represent management's best estimate of the range of economic conditions that will exist over the remaining useful life of the asset. The discount rate used is the rate, which reflects the specific risks of the asset or CGU.

*Here is the basic principle for the carrying value of assets in the statement of financial position, together with a definition of recoverable amount.*

The basic principle is that an asset may not be carried in the statement of financial position at more than its recoverable amount. An asset's recoverable amount is the higher of:

- the amount for which the asset could be sold in an arm's length transaction between knowledgeable and willing parties,

- net of costs of disposal (fair value less costs to sell); and

- the present value of the future cash flows that are expected to be derived from the asset (value in use). The expected future cash flows include those from the asset's continued use in the business and those from its ultimate disposal. Value in use (VIU) is explicitly based on present value calculations.

This measurement basis reflects the economic decisions that a company's management team makes when assets become impaired from the viewpoint of whether the business is better off disposing of the asset or continuing to use it.

Note that, where a fair value measurement is required, IFRS 13 will normally apply unless specifically excluded. IFRS 13 formalises the procedure to determine a fair value measurement when required, so that observable inputs as used as far as possible to support a fair value measurement. As such, it is a market-based measurement based upon the value at which an asset would be disposed of or a liability transferred between willing parties on an arm's length basis.

Therefore, The assumptions used in arriving at the recoverable amount need to be 'reasonable and supportable' regardless of whether impairment calculations are based on fair value less costs to sell or value in use. The acceptable range for such assumptions will change over time and forecasts for revenue growth and profit margins are likely to have fallen in the economic climate. The assumptions made by management should be in line with the assumptions made by industry commentators or analysts. Variances from market will need to be justified and highlighted in financial statement disclosures.

*This part of the answer considers market evidence and the reaction of the market to when impairment losses may or may not have been recognised.*

Whatever method is used to calculate the recoverable amount; the value needs to be considered in the light of available market evidence. If other entities in the same sector are taking impairment charges, the absence of an impairment charge have to be justified because the market will be asking the same question.

It is important to inform the market about how it is dealing with the conditions, and be thinking about how different parts of the business are affected, and the market inputs they use in impairment testing. Impairment testing should be commenced as soon as possible as an impairment test process takes a significant amount of time. It includes identifying impairment indicators, assessing or reassessing the cash flows, determining the discount rates, testing the reasonableness of the assumptions and benchmarking the assumptions with the market. Goodwill does not have to be tested for impairment at the year-end; it can be tested earlier and if any impairment indicator arises at the reporting date, the impairment assessment can be updated. Also, it is important to comply with all disclosure requirements, such as the discount rate and long-term growth rate assumptions in a discounted cash flow model, and describe what the key assumptions are and what they are based on.

It is important that the cash flows being tested are consistent with the assets being tested. The forecast cash flows should make allowance for investment in working capital if the business is expected to grow. When the detailed calculations have been completed, the company should check that their conclusions make sense by comparison to any market data, such as share prices and analysts reports. Market capitalisation below net asset value is an impairment indicator, and calculations of recoverable amount are required. If the market capitalisation is lower than a value-in-use calculation, then the VIU assumptions may require reassessment. For example, the cash flow projections might not be as expected by the market, and the reasons for this must be scrutinised. Discount rates should be scrutinised in order to see if they are logical. Discount rates may have risen too as risk premiums rise. Many factors affect discount rates in impairment calculations. These include corporate lending rates, cost of capital and risks associated with cash flows, which are all increasing in the current volatile environment and can potentially result in an increase of the discount rate.

*Here is the application of the impairment review, including discounting of expected future cashflows to their present value at the date of the impairment review.*

(b)   An asset's carrying amount may not be recovered from future business activity. Wherever indicators of impairment exist, a review for impairment should be carried out. Where impairment is identified, a write-down of the carrying value to the recoverable amount should be charged as an immediate expense in profit or loss. Using a discount rate of 5%, the value in use of the non-current assets is:

| Year to 31 May: | 2010 | 2011 | 2012 | 2013 | Total |
|---|---|---|---|---|---|
| Discounted cash flows ($000) | 267 | 408 | 431 | 452 | 1,558 |

The carrying value of the non-current assets at 31 May 2009 is $3 million – depreciation of $600,000. i.e. $2.4 million. Therefore the assets are impaired by $842,000 ($2.4m – $1.558m).

IAS 36 requires an assessment at each reporting date whether there is an indication that an impairment loss may have decreased. This does not apply to goodwill or to the unwinding of the discount. In this case, the increase in value is due to the unwinding of the discount as the same cash flows have been used in the calculation. Compensation received in the form of reimbursements from governmental indemnities is recorded in the statement of comprehensive income when the compensation becomes receivable according to IAS 37 *Provisions, contingent liabilities and contingent assets*. It is treated as separate economic events and accounted for as such. At this time the government has only stated that it may reimburse the company and therefore credit should not be taken of any potential government receipt.

*Having identified the extent of any impairment, accounting for it depends upon whether the asset is carried at cost or at revalued amount.*

For a revalued asset, the impairment loss is treated as a revaluation decrease. The loss is first set against any revaluation surplus and the balance of the loss is then treated as an expense in profit or loss. The revaluation gain and the impairment loss would be treated as follows:

|  | Depreciated historical cost | Revalued carrying value |
|---|---|---|
|  | $m | $m |
| 1 December 2006 | 10.0 | 10.0 |
| Depreciation (2 years) | (2.0) | (2.0) |
| Revaluation |  | (0.8) |
|  | 8.0 | 8.8 |
| Depreciation | (1.0) | (1.1) |
| Impairment loss | (1.5) | (2.2) |
| 30 November 2009 after impairment loss | 5.5 | 5.5 |

The impairment loss of $2.2 million is charged to equity until the carrying amount reaches depreciated historical cost and thereafter it goes to profit or loss. It is assumed that the company will transfer an amount from revaluation surplus to retained earnings to cover the excess depreciation of $0.1 million as allowed by IAS 16. Therefore the impairment loss charged to equity would be $(0.8 – 0.1) million i.e. $0.7 million and the remainder of $1.5 million would be charged to profit or loss.

*Consideration now turns to IFRS 5 and whether assets may be regarded as held for sale.*

A plan by management to dispose of an asset or group of assets due to under utilisation is an indicator of impairment. This will usually be well before the held for sale criteria under IFRS 5 *Non-current assets held-for-sale and discontinued activities* are met. Assets or CGUs are tested for impairment when the decision to sell is made. The impairment test is updated immediately before classification under IFRS 5. IFRS 5 requires an asset held for sale to be measured at the lower of its carrying amount and its fair value less costs to sell. Non-current assets held for sale and disposal groups are re-measured at the lower of carrying amount or fair value less costs to sell at every balance sheet date from classification until disposal. The measurement process is similar to that which occurs on classification as held for sale. Any excess of carrying value over fair value less costs to sell is a further impairment loss and is recognised as a loss in the statement of comprehensive income in the current period. Fair value less costs to sell in excess of carrying value is ignored and no gain is recorded on classification. The non-current assets or disposal group cannot be written up past its previous (pre-impairment) carrying amount, adjusted for depreciation that would have been applied without the impairment. The fact that the asset is being marketed at a price in excess of its fair value may mean that the asset is not available for immediate sale and therefore may not meet the criteria for 'held for sale'.

| | **ACCA marking scheme** | |
|---|---|---:|
| | | *Marks* |
| (a) | Impairment process | 4 |
| | General considerations | 4 |
| | Professional marks | 2 |
| | | |
| (b) | Non-current asset at cost | 6 |
| | Non-current asset at valuation | 6 |
| | Non-current assets held for sale | 3 |
| | | — |
| Total | | 25 |
| | | — |

**Examiner's comments**

This question dealt with the subject of impairment. Candidates were asked to discuss the main considerations which an entity should take into account when impairment testing non-current assets in a climate where there were credit limitations. The second part of the question required candidates to set out how to account for any potential impairment in given circumstances. The first part of the question was very well answered although the main weakness in candidates' answers related to the fact that many candidates simply set out the rules of impairment testing without relating it to the economic climate set out in the question. The second part of the question was quite well answered. Candidates found some difficulties in discounting future cash flows and the treatment of the impairment loss and revaluation gain. Candidates did not discuss the key issues in sufficient depth. The question asked for a discussion but many candidates simply calculated the accounting adjustments without sufficient discussion of the issues.

## 33    MARRGRETT (DEC 08 EXAM)  *Walk in the footsteps of a top tutor*

**Key answer tips**

This question requires discussion and application of accounting treatments to proposed transactions, specifically IFRS 3 (Revised) and IFRS 10. This is an indication from the examiner that new or recently revised reporting standards are considered to be examinable and that he expects ACCA P2 students to be up to date with current developments. Although there is a single requirement for twenty-five marks, there are several issues to be considered. The best way to approach this question is to deal with each issue separately and to identify the specific accounting requirements for each issue. Having done that, the accounting treatment should then be applied to the specific information in the question,

IFRS 3 (Revised) is a further development of the acquisition model and represents a significant change in accounting for business combinations. The consideration is the amount paid for the business acquired and is measured at fair value. Consideration will include cash, assets, contingent consideration, equity instruments, options and warrants. It also includes the fair value of all equity interests that the acquirer may have held previously in the acquired business.

*Focus on identifying the key principles to apply from IFRS 3 Revised.*

The principles to be applied are that:

(a)    a business combination occurs only in respect of the transaction that gives one entity control of another

(b)    the identifiable net assets of the acquiree are re-measured to their fair value on the date of the acquisition

(c)    NCI are measured on the date of acquisition under one of the two options permitted by IFRS 3 (Revised).

IFRS 10 *Consolidated financial statements* was issued in 2011 and replaces those parts of IAS 27 which previously dealt with consolidated financial statements. IFRS 10 identifies three elements to determine whether one entity has control over as follows:

(a)    power over the investee, where one party has the current ability to direct activities that significantly affect its returns, and

(b)    exposure, or rights to, variable returns from involvement in the investee, and

(c)    the ability to use power over the investee to affect the level of returns.

In most cases, this will be quite evident from one entity owning the majority of the equity capital of another entity. However, the approach to determining whether or not control is exercised is principles-based, which recognises that control may be exercised in a range of circumstances, other than by ownership of equity capital. IFRS 10 requires that the judgement of whether or not one entity controls another should be subject to regular review.

*Here is a change introduced by IFRS 3 Revised.*

An equity interest previously held in the acquiree which qualified as an associate under IAS 28 *Investments in associates and joint ventures* is similarly treated as if it were disposed of and reacquired at fair value on the acquisition date. Accordingly, it is re-measured to its acquisition date fair value, and any resulting gain or loss compared to its carrying amount under IAS 28 is recognised in profit or loss for the year. Thus the 30% holding in the associate previously held will be included in the consideration. If the carrying amount of the interest in the associate is not held at fair value at the acquisition date, the interest should be measured to fair value and the resulting gain or loss should be recognised in profit or loss. The business combination has effectively been achieved in stages.

Thus the 30% holding in the associate previously held will be included in the consideration. If the carrying amount of the interest in the associate is not held at fair value at the acquisition date, the interest should be measured to fair value and the resulting gain or loss should be recognised in profit or loss. The business combination has effectively been achieved in stages.

*Here is a change introduced by IFRS 3 Revised.*

The fees payable in transaction costs are not deemed to be part of the consideration paid to the seller of the shares. They are not assets of the purchased business that are recognised on acquisition. Therefore, they should be expensed as incurred and the services received. Transaction costs relating to the issue of debt or equity, if they are directly attributable, will not be expensed but deducted from debt or equity on initial recognition.

It is common for part of the consideration to be contingent upon future events. Marrgrett wishes some of the existing shareholders/employees to remain in the business and has, therefore, offered share options as an incentive to these persons. The issue is whether these options form part of the purchase consideration or are compensation for post-acquisition services. The conditions attached to the award will determine the accounting treatment. In this case there are employment conditions and, therefore, the options should be treated as compensation and valued under IFRS 2 *Share-based payment*. Thus a charge will appear in post-acquisition earnings for employee services as the options were awarded to reward future services of employees rather than to acquire the business.

*Here is a change introduced by IFRS 3 Revised.*

The additional shares to a fixed value of $50,000 are contingent upon the future returns on capital employed. Marrgrett only wants to make additional payments if the business is successful. All consideration should be fair valued at the date of acquisition, including the above contingent consideration. The contingent consideration payable in shares where the number of shares varies to give the recipient a fixed value ($50,000) meets the definition of a financial liability under IAS 32 *Financial instruments: presentation*. As a result the liability will have to be fair valued and any subsequent remeasurement will be recognised in profit or loss. There is no requirement under IFRS 3 (Revised) for the payments to be probable.

*Here is a change introduced by IFRS 3 Revised.*

Intangible assets should be recognised on acquisition under IFRS 3 (Revised). These include trade names, domain names, and non-competition agreements. Thus these assets will be recognised and goodwill effectively reduced. The additional clarity in IFRS 3 (Revised) could mean that more intangible assets will be recognised on acquisition. As a result of this, the post-combination statement of profit or loss may have more charges for amortisation of the intangibles than was previously the case.

*Here is a change introduced by IFRS 3 Revised.*

The revised standard gives entities the option, on a transaction by transaction basis, to measure non-controlling interests (NCI) at the fair value of the proportion of identifiable net assets or at full fair value. The first option results in measurement of goodwill on consolidation which would normally be little different from the previous standard. The second approach records goodwill on the NCI as well as on the acquired controlling interest. Goodwill is the residual but may differ from that under the previous standard because of the nature of the valuation of the consideration as previously held interests are fair valued and also because goodwill can be measured in the above two ways (full goodwill and partial goodwill). The standard gives entities a choice for each separate business combination of recognising full or partial goodwill. Recognising full goodwill will increase reported net assets and may result in any future impairment of goodwill being of greater value. Measuring NCI at fair value may have some difficulties but goodwill impairment testing may be easier under full goodwill as there is no need to gross-up goodwill for partly-owned subsidiaries. The type of consideration does not affect goodwill regardless of how the payment is structured. Consideration is recognised in total at its fair value at the date of acquisition. The form of the consideration will not affect goodwill but the structure of the payments can affect post-acquisition profits. Contingent payments which are deemed to be debt instruments will be remeasured at each reporting date with the change going to profit or loss.

Marrgrett has a maximum period of 12 months to finalise the acquisition accounting but will not be able to recognise the re-organisation provision at the date of the business combination. The ability of the acquirer to recognise a liability for reducing or changing the activities of the acquiree is restricted. A restructuring provision can only be recognised in a business combination when the acquiree has at the acquisition date, an existing liability which complies with IAS 37 *Provisions, contingent liabilities and contingent assets*. These conditions are unlikely to exist at the acquisition date. A restructuring plan that is conditional on the completion of a business combination is not recognised in accounting for the acquisition but the expense will be met against post-acquisition earnings.

*Impact of IFRS 10 and IAS 28 (revised).*

IFRS 10 uses the economic entity model whereas previous practice used the parent company approach. The economic entity model treats all providers of equity capital as shareholders of the entity even where they are not shareholders in the parent. A partial disposal of an interest in a subsidiary in which control is still retained is regarded as a treasury transaction and accounted for in equity. It does not result in a gain or loss but an increase or decrease in equity. This will arise by comparison of the disposal proceeds received from the share disposal with the increased interest that non-controlling interest shareholders have in the net assets and unimpaired goodwill of the subsidiary at that date. However, where a partial disposal in a subsidiary results in a loss of control but the retention of an interest in the form of an associate, then a gain or loss is recognised in the whole interest. A gain or loss is recognised on the portion that has been sold, and a holding gain or loss is recognised on the interest retained being the difference between the book value and fair value of the interest. Both gains/losses are recognised in profit or loss.

Note that for an interest in another entity to be accounted for as an associate, it must meet the definition of an associate from IAS 28 (Revised); an entity is regarded as an associate if an investor is able to exercise significant influence over it. IAS 28 (Revised) then defines significant influence as power to participate in the financial and operating policy decisions of an investee, but which is not control or joint control as defined by IFRS 10 and IFRS 11 respectively.

| ACCA marking scheme | |
|---|---|
| | *Marks* |
| Consideration | 6 |
| IFRS 3 and consideration | 5 |
| Consideration | 2 |
| Intangible assets | 2 |
| Non-controlling interests | 5 |
| Finalisation and reorganisation provision | 2 |
| IFRS 10 and IAS 28 (revised) | 3 |
| | — |
| Total | 25 |
| | — |

**Examiner's comments**

This question required candidates to discuss the accounting practice and principles relating mainly to business combinations. The question was based around a case study which included acquisition accounting, equity accounting, share based payment and provisioning. In most jurisdictions, this involved dealing with IFRS 3 (Revised) and IFRS 10, which replaces substantial parts of IAS 27. The question required knowledge of accounting for purchase consideration, transaction costs, contingent consideration, intangible assets, non–controlling interests and reorganisation provisions. Candidates generally gave quite good answers to the question but the main issue was that candidates found it difficult to assimilate relevant information. If the question outlines the specific information, which is required then candidates seem to be able to construct good answers. However when candidates are asked to essentially advise a client given certain information, then the quality of the answers deteriorates.

Candidates should practice questions where advice to clients is required. It is also important for candidates to keep up to date with current developments by reading relevant articles in on-line journals and other publications. Particular issues included failing to recognise that the existing 30% interest in the associate should be fair valued when control of the subsidiary is gained, also dealing with the payments to the subsidiary's directors created a problem and a minority of candidates stated that the full goodwill method was mandatory.

## 34    TYRE (JUN 06 EXAM)

**Key answer tips**

This is a typical discussion question where you are asked to deal with a number of accounting issues. The first three are relatively straightforward and you will have come across them before. The last one is trickier, but you need to think of it in terms of IAS 37 and whether or not a provision is required.

**Advice on sundry accounting issues: year-ended 31 May 20X6**

The following details the nature of the advice relevant to the accounting issues.

**Revenue recognition**

(i)     **Sale to customers**

IAS 18 *Revenue* requires that revenue relating to the sale of goods is recognised when the significant risks and rewards are transferred to the buyer. Also the company should not retain any continuing managerial involvement associated with ownership or control of the goods. Additionally the revenue and costs must be capable of reliable measurement and it should be probable that the economic benefits of the transaction will go to the company.

Although the deposit is non refundable on cancellation of the order by the customer, there is a valid expectation that the deposit will be repaid where the company does not fulfil its contractual obligation in supplying the vehicle. The deposit should, therefore, only be recognised in revenue when the vehicle has been delivered and accepted by the customer. It should be treated as a liability up to this point. At this point also, the balance of the sale proceeds will be recognised. If the customer does cancel the order, then the deposit would be recognised in revenue at the date of the cancellation of the order.

The appendix to IAS 18, although not part of the standard, agrees that revenue is recognised when goods of this nature are delivered to the buyer.

**Sale of fleet cars**

The company has not transferred the significant risks and rewards of ownership as required by IAS 18 as the buyback option is expected to occur. The reason for this conclusion is that the company has retained the risk associated with the residual value of the vehicles. Therefore, the transaction should not be treated as a sale. The vehicles should be treated as an operating lease as essentially only 60% of the purchase price will be received by Tyre. Ownership of the assets are not expected to be transferred to Hub, the lease term is arguably not for the major part of the assets' life, and the present value of the minimum lease payments will not be substantially equivalent to the fair value of the asset. Therefore it is an operating lease (IAS 17). No 'outright sale profit' will be recognised as the risks and rewards of ownership have been retained and no sale has occurred. The vehicles will be shown in property, plant and equipment at their carrying amount. The lease income should be recognised on a straight line basis over the lease term of three years unless some other basis is more representative. The vehicles will be depreciated in accordance with IAS 16 *Property, plant and equipment*. If there is any indication of impairment then the company will apply IAS 36 *Impairment of assets*. As the discount given is normal for this type of transaction, it will not be taken into account in estimating the fair value of the assets.

The buyback option will probably meet the definition of a financial liability and will be accounted for under IAS 39 *Financial instruments: recognition and measurement*. The liability should be measured at fair value and subsequently at amortised cost unless designated at the outset as being at fair value through profit or loss.

(ii) **Former administrative building**

The land and buildings of the former administrative centre are accounted for as separate elements. The demolition of the building is an indicator of the impairment of the property under IAS 36. The building will not generate any future cash flows and its recoverable amount is zero. Therefore, the carrying value of the building will be written down to zero and the loss charged to profit or loss in the year to 31 May 20X6 when the decision to demolish the building was made. The land value will be in excess of its carrying amount as the company uses the cost model and land prices are rising. Thus no impairment charge is recognised in respect of the land.

The demolition costs will be expensed when incurred and a provision for environmental costs recognised when an obligation arises, i.e. in the financial year to 31 May 20X7. It may be that some of these costs could be recognised as site preparation costs and be capitalised under IAS 16.

The land will not meet the criteria set out in IFRS 5 *Non-current assets held for sale and discontinued operations* as a non-current asset that is held for sale. IFRS 5 says that a non-current asset should be classified as held for sale if its carrying amount will be recovered principally through a sale transaction rather than through continuing use. However, the non-current asset must be available for immediate sale and must be actively marketed at its current fair value (amongst other criteria) and these criteria have not been met in this case.

When the building has been demolished and the site prepared, the land could be considered to be an investment property and accounted for under IAS 40 *Investment property* where the fair value model allows gains (or losses) to be recognised in profit or loss for the period.

(iii) **Retail outlets**

The two new long lease agreements have been separately classified as an operating lease and a finance lease. The lease premium paid for a finance lease should be capitalised and recognised as an asset under the lease. IAS 17 *Leases* says that costs identified as directly attributable to a finance lease are added to the amount recognised as an asset. It will be included in the present value calculation of the minimum lease payments. The finance lease will be recognised at its fair value or if lower the present value of the minimum lease payments. The premium will be depreciated as part of the asset's value over the shorter of the lease term and the asset's useful life. Initially, a finance lease liability will be set up which is equal to the value of the leased asset.

The operating lease premium will be spread over the lease term on a straight line basis unless some other method is more representative. The premium will be effectively treated as a prepayment of rent and is amortised over the life of the agreement.

(iv) **Car accessories**

An obligation should not be recognised for the coupons and no provision created under IAS 37 *Provisions, contingent liabilities and contingent assets*. A provision should only be recognised where there is an obligating event. There has to be a present obligation (legal or constructive), the probability of an outflow of resources and the ability to make a reliable estimate of the amount of the obligation. These conditions do not seem to have been met. Until the vehicle is purchased the accessories cannot be obtained. That is the point at which the present obligation arises, the outflow of resources occurs and an estimate of the amount of the obligation can be made. When the car is purchased, the accessories become part of the cost of the sale. The revenue recognised will be the amount received from the customer (the sales price). The revenue will not be grossed up to include the value of the accessories.

| ACCA marking scheme | |
|---|---|
| | *Marks* |
| Revenue recognition | 8 |
| Administrative building | 7 |
| Lease agreements | 5 |
| Car accessories | 5 |
| | ——— |
| Total | 25 |
| | ——— |

## 35 PROCHAIN (JUN 06 EXAM)

**Key answer tips**

Another discussion paper covering a number of accounting issues. You are given marks for each segment of the question, so always answer the part of the question you are most comfortable with first. You don't need to attempt the question in order.

**Model areas**

The cost of the model areas should be accounted for as property, plant and equipment in accordance with IAS 16 *Property, plant and equipment* (PPE). PPE are tangible assets that are held for use in the production or supply of goods or services, for rental to others or for administrative purposes, and are expected to be utilised in more than one period (IAS 16.6). The model areas meet this definition because they are used in more than one accounting period, and customers will be able to view the fashion goods in those areas. The costs of the model areas should be depreciated over their expected useful life to their expected residual value which in this case is zero.

Prochain, after initial recognition, could use the cost model or revaluation model for the measurement of the model areas. However, it would be difficult to adopt the revaluation model as it would not be possible to measure fair value reliably. Normally market based information is used.

Prochain has an obligation to dismantle the model areas after two years. The company should assess whether it has a present obligation as a result of a past event. The assessment should be carried out in accordance with IAS 37 *Provisions, contingent liabilities and contingent assets*. In this case it would seem that a provision should be set up and the amount added to the cost of the asset. The costs of dismantling to be recognised are an initial estimate of the obligations which arise when PPE is acquired and as a consequence of using the asset. In this case the costs of dismantling the model areas are estimated at 20% of the construction cost. The approximate age of the PPE is eight months. Thus the cost shown in the statement of financial position at 31 May 20X6 should be ($20 million + (20% of $20 million discounted for two years at 5.5%)), i.e. $23.6 million and the accumulated depreciation should be ($23.6m × 8/24), i.e. **$7.9 million**. The discount is unwound over the two year period as a finance cost in the statement of comprehensive income (3.6 × 5.5% × 8/12, i.e. **$0.13 m**).

A provision for the dismantling costs will be set up for $3.6 million plus the unwound discount of $0.13, i.e. **$3.73 million**.

**Purchase of Badex**

IFRS 3 *Business combinations* deals with such acquisitions and this standard was revised in January 2008. Where part of the consideration is cash and deferred, fair value should be assessed by discounting amounts payable to their present value. In the previous IFRS 3 directly related acquisition costs such as professional fees (legal, accounting, valuation etc) could be included as part of the cost of the acquisition. This has now been stopped and such costs must be expensed. Accordingly the legal fees of $2 million are not part of the cost of the investment.

The previous version of IFRS 3 required contingent consideration to be accounted for only if it was probable that it would become payable.

The revised Standard requires the acquirer to recognise the acquisition-date fair value of contingent consideration as part of the consideration for the acquiree. This 'fair value' approach is consistent with how other forms of consideration are valued and fair value is defined as: 'The amount for which an asset could be exchanged, or a liability settled, between knowledgeable, willing parties in an arm's length transaction.'

With regard to changes in the fair value of any contingent consideration after the acquisition date, if the change is due to additional information obtained after the acquisition date that affects the facts or circumstances as they existed at the acquisition date this is treated as a 'measurement period adjustment' and the liability (and goodwill) are remeasured. This is effectively a retrospective adjustment and is rather similar to an adjusting event under IAS 10 *Events after the reporting period*. This is very unlikely.

However, what is more likely, is that changes will be due to events after the acquisition date (for example, meeting an earnings target which triggers a higher payment than was provided for at acquisition) are not remeasured. Its subsequent settlement shall be accounted for within equity (e.g. Cr share capital/share premium Dr retained earnings) if the contingent consideration is to be settled in the form of shares, but if it is a liability then the difference will be recognised in profit or loss.

The purchase consideration is $100 million plus the present value of the guaranteed minimum payment of $10 million ÷ $1.055^2$ ($9 million), plus the fair value of the contingent consideration of $5 million i.e. $114 million. The cost of the investment will be $114 million and a provision will be created for the deferred consideration of $9 million. The discount of $1 million is a finance cost and will be recorded as an interest expense over the two year period.

The acquirer is required to recognise separately an intangible asset of the acquiree company at the acquisition date if it meets the definition of an intangible asset in IAS 38 *Intangible assets* and its fair value can be measured reliably. IAS 38's criteria are separability or having arisen from a contractual or other legal right. The separate recognition of an intangible asset is not dependent on the acquiree's business having recognised the asset. The cost of internally generating the brand name 'Badex' will not be recognised on Badex's statement of financial position but may be recognised indirectly on Prochain's statement of financial position on acquisition. No active market will exist for the brand name but there may be sufficient information available to reasonably expect that the brand name can be measured reliably. Brand names are specifically mentioned in IAS 38 as being an example of a separate class of intangible assets. It seems that the many types of intangible assets set out in IAS 38 will lead to separate recognition of several intangible assets. Companies have to disclose why an intangible asset's fair value could not be measured reliably and why it was not recognised separately. Thus it would seem that the IASB envisage that most intangible assets will be separately accounted for.

As the fair value of the brand name appears to be capable of reliable measurement there will be separate recognition of the intangible at its value of $20 million. The intangible asset is separate, it has been sold and the purchase price will be a reliable measure of cost.

**Research and development expenditure**

IAS 38 *Intangible assets* provides guidance on the recognition of internally generated intangible assets, particularly on the expenditure on research and development of products. During the research phase, a project is not deemed to be far enough advanced for an entity to be able to demonstrate that it is probable that economic benefits will be generated. Therefore all expenditure incurred during this phase should be expensed immediately in the statement of comprehensive income. Where economic benefits can realistically be expected to be generated from development activities, then an intangible asset can be recognised subject to meeting the following recognition criteria:

(i)    technical feasibility of project

(ii)   intention to complete the intangible asset and use or sell it

(iii)  the ability to use or sell the intangible

(iv)   generation of probable future economic benefits

(v)    availability of adequate technical, financial and other resources to complete the development and to use or sell it

(vi)   ability to reliably measure the expenditure attributable to the intangible.

For a company to recognise an intangible asset in the statement of financial position, it should be probable that the expected future economic benefits generated from the asset will flow to the entity and the cost of the asset should be capable of reliable measurement. Costs that should be recognised as part of the intangible asset are those that are directly attributable to preparing the asset for its intended use. These costs will include employee costs and design costs. Work undertaken to establish whether there is a market for a product is deemed not to be directly attributable to bringing the intangible asset into a condition for its intended use. Staff training costs are specifically excluded from the component costs of an internally generated intangible asset. The costs of upgrading the existing machinery can be capitalised as property, plant and equipment. IAS 36 *Impairment of assets* will be used to establish whether future economic benefits will be generated. Thus the costs incurred will be dealt with as follows:

|  | Profit or loss | SOFP Intangible assets | Tangible assets |
|---|---|---|---|
|  | $m | $m | $m |
| Research as to extent of market | 3 |  |  |
| Prototype clothing and goods design |  | 4 |  |
| Employee costs |  | 2 |  |
| Development work |  | 5 |  |
| Production and launch – machinery |  |  | 3 |
| market research | 2 |  |  |
| training costs | 1 |  |  |
|  | 6 | 11 | 3 |

Intangible assets should be carried using either the cost model or the revaluation model.

There is an element of subjectivity involved in determining the value of any intangible asset to arise from the above expenditure and it is up to the company to demonstrate that the recognition criteria are explicitly met. In this case, it would appear that the company would recognise $11 million. The project has advanced to a stage where it is probable that future economic benefits will arise.

**Apartments**

The apartments are occupied by persons who are contracted to the company and are essentially employees. The lease terminates with the termination of the contract because they are essentially owner occupied. The apartments should be classified as property, plant and equipment (IAS 40.9). The rent is below market rate but there is no employee benefit cost to the company. The difference between the market rent and the actual rent is an opportunity cost which will not be recognised. To recognise it would involve also the recognition of notional income which is not allowed under IFRSs. The cost recognised would be the depreciation of the apartments. Therefore, the property should not be designated as investment property nor the difference between the market and actual rental shown as an employee benefit expense.

| ACCA marking scheme | |
|---|---|
|  | Marks |
| Model areas | 7 |
| Purchase of Badex | 8 |
| Research and development | 6 |
| Apartments | 4 |
| Total | 25 |

## 36    MARGIE (DEC 10 EXAM)     *Walk in the footsteps of a top tutor*

**Key answer tips**

This is a multi-part question which focuses upon application of IFRS 2 and other reporting standards. Each part is self-contained, so can be answered in the order you prefer. Remember to clearly identify which part you are answering, particularly if you are answering them out of order. The mark allocations for each part of the question give a good indication of the amount of time that should be spent on each part.

*Determine whether or not the transaction falls within the scope of IFRS 2. If not, explain why not and then continue by explaining the required accounting treatment.*

(a)    The arrangement is not within the scope of IFRS 2 '*Share-based payment*' because the contract may be settled net and has not been entered into in order to satisfy Margie's expected purchase, sale or usage requirements. Margie has not purchased the wheat but has entered into a financial contract to pay or receive a cash amount. IFRS 9 '*Financial Instruments*' requires derivatives to be measured at fair value through profit or loss, unless it is part of a hedging arrangement when the provisions of IAS 39 '*Financial Instrument: recognition and measurement*' apply until IFRS 9 is updated.

Contracts to buy or sell non-financial items are within the scope of IFRS 9 if they can be settled net in cash or another financial asset and are not entered into and held for the purpose of the receipt or delivery of a non-financial item in accordance with the entity's expected purchase, sale, or usage requirements. Contracts to buy or sell non-financial items are inside the scope if net settlement occurs. The following situations constitute net settlement:

(a)    the terms of the contract permit either counterparty to settle net;

(b)    there is a past practice of net settling similar contracts;

(c)    there is a past practice, for similar contracts, of taking delivery of the underlying and selling it within a short period after delivery to generate a profit from short-term fluctuations in price, or from a dealer's margin; or

(d)    the non-financial item is readily convertible to cash.

The contract will be accounted for as a derivative and should be valued at fair value (asset or liability at fair value) through profit or loss. Initially the contract should be valued at nil as under the terms of a commercial contract the value of 2,500 shares should equate to the value of 350 tonnes of wheat. At each period end the contract would be remeasured to fair value and it would be expected that differences will arise between the values of wheat and Margie shares as their respective market values will be dependent on a number of differing factors. The net difference should be taken to profit or loss.

As Margie has no intention of taking delivery of the wheat this does not appear to be a hedging contract as no firm commitment exists to purchase neither is this a highly probable forecast transaction.

*Determine how the award should be accounted for on acquisition of Antalya. You should consider both the original award made by Antalya and also the award made by Margie upon acquisition of the subsidiary.*

(b)   Share-based payment awards exchanged for awards held by the acquiree's employees are measured in accordance with IFRS 2 'Share-based payment'. If the acquirer is obliged to replace the awards, some or all of the fair value of the replacement awards must be included in the consideration. The amount not included in the consideration will be recognised as a compensation expense. If the acquirer is not obliged to exchange the acquiree's awards, the acquirer does not adjust the consideration even if the acquirer does replace the awards.

A portion of the fair value of the award granted by Margie is accounted for under IFRS 3 and a portion under IFRS 2, even though no post-combination services are required. The amount included in the cost of the business combination is the fair value of Antalya's award at the acquisition date ($20 million). Any additional amount, which in this case is $2 million, is accounted for as a post-combination expense under IFRS 2. This amount is recognised immediately as a post-combination expense because no post-combination services are required.

*This part of the question contains two separate issues – ensure that you address both issues in turn.*

(c)   The shares issued to the employees were issued in their capacity as shareholders and not in exchange for their services. The employees were not required to complete a period of service in exchange for the shares. Thus the transaction is outside the scope of IFRS 2.

As regards the purchase of the building, Grief did not act in its capacity as a shareholder as Margie approached the company with the proposal to buy the building. Grief was a supplier of a building and as such the transaction comes under IFRS 2. The building is valued at fair value with equity being credited with the same amount.

*This part of the question considers how to account for a share-based payment scheme when the vesting period is uncertain at the grant date. When the scheme is measured for the first time for inclusion in the financial statements, the cost should be spread over the expected vesting period at that date. Subsequent treatment will depend upon whether the actual vesting period is shorter or longer than the expected vesting period.*

(d) Where the vesting period is linked to a market performance condition, an entity should estimate the expected vesting period. If the actual vesting period is shorter than estimated, the charge should be accelerated in the period that the entity delivers the cash or equity instruments to the counterparty. When the vesting period is longer, the expense is recognised over the originally estimated vesting period. The effect of a vesting condition may be to change the length of the vesting period. In this case, paragraph 15 of IFRS 2 'Share based payment' requires the entity to presume that the services to be rendered by the employees as consideration for the equity instruments granted will be received in the future, over the expected vesting period. Hence, the entity will have to estimate the length of the expected vesting period at grant date, based on the most likely outcome of the performance condition. If the performance condition is a market condition, the estimate of the length of the expected vesting period must be consistent with the assumptions used in estimating the fair value of the share options granted and is not subsequently revised.

Margie expects the market condition to be met in 2011 and thus anticipates that it will charge $1 million per annum until that date (100 × 4,000 × $10 divided by 4 years). As the market condition has been met in the year to 30 November 2010, the expense charged in the year would be $2 million ($4 million − $2 million already charged) as the remaining expense should be accelerated and charged in the year.

| ACCA marking scheme | | |
|---|---|---|
| | | *Marks* |
| (a) | Discussion IAS 39 | 5 |
| | Conclusion | 2 |
| (b) | Discussion of IFRS 3/IFRS 2 | 4 |
| | Calculation | 2 |
| (c) | Discussion | 4 |
| (d) | Discussion | 4 |
| | Calculation | 2 |
| | Professional | 2 |
| | | ——— |
| Total | | 25 |
| | | ——— |

**Examiner's comments**

This question was a case study type question based around share-based transactions. The question was not totally related to IFRS 2 but also to other standards where shares are exchanged in a transaction.

The first scenario dealt with a contract to purchase a commodity with shares .The purchase price was to be settled in cash at an amount equal to the value of an amount of the entity's shares. The entity wished to treat the transaction as a share based payment transaction under IFRS 2 'Share-based Payment'. Many candidates did not recognise the fact that the transaction should be dealt with under IAS39. This type of transaction has been examined recently but candidates did not seem to recognise the nature of the transaction.

In part b the entity acquired 100% of the share capital of another entity in a business combination and this entity had previously granted a share-based payment to its employees. A replacement award was issued a replacement award that did not require post-combination services. Candidates had to understand the interaction of IFRS 2 and IFRS 3 in order to answer the question. The question was not well answered although candidates did seem to realise that there was a post combination expense to be taken into account.

In part c, the entity issued shares during the financial year which were subscribed for by employees who were existing shareholders, and some were issued to an entity for the purchase of a building. Candidates often felt that the first transaction was within the scope of IFRS 2 and the second was not. Unfortunately this assumption was incorrect with the correct answer being that the first transaction was outside the scope and the second was within scope.

In part d the entity granted share options to each of its employees with the options vesting in the future provided the employee has remained in the company's service until that time. The terms and conditions of the options had a market condition. Candidates generally seemed to understand the effect of a market condition and answered this part of the question very well. Overall this question was not as well answered as the other questions on the paper.

## 37 VIDENT (JUN 05 EXAM)

**Key answer tips**

This question requires a detailed knowledge of accounting for share-based payments as per IFRS 2. This is a key area of the syllabus so you should spend plenty of time on this question. Make sure that as well as calculating the effect of a share-based payment transaction, you can deal with the deferred tax effect as well. This question also includes a prior period adjustment as it deals with accounting for share-based payments for the first time by the company.

**Report to the Directors of Vident, a public limited company**

(a)    **IFRS 2 *Share-based payment***

The arguments put forward by the Directors for not recognising the remuneration expense have been made by many opponents of the IFRS.

The argument that the share options do not have a cost to the company and, therefore, should not be recognised, is not one which is consistent with the way that other share issues are dealt with. An accounting entry is required to recognise the resources received as consideration for the shares issued, just as occurs when shares are issued in a business acquisition. The expense recognised represents the consumption of the resources received, just as depreciation will be charged on the non-current assets acquired in a business acquisition. The consumption of the resources in the case of share options is immediate and may be spread over a period of time.

The question as to whether the expense arising from share options meets the definition of an expense as set out in the *Framework* is problematical. The *Framework* requires an outflow of assets or a liability to be incurred before an expense is created. Services do not normally meet the definition of an asset and, therefore, consumption of those services does not represent an outflow of assets. However, share options are issued for valuable consideration, that is the employee services and the benefits of the asset received results in an expense. The main reason why the creation of the expense is questioned is that the receipt of the asset and its consumption in the form of employee services occur at virtually the same time. The conclusion must, therefore, be that the recognition of the expense arising from share-based payment transactions is consistent with the *Framework*.

The argument that any cost from share-based payment is already recognised in the dilution of earnings per share (EPS) is not appropriate as the impact of EPS reflects the two economic events that have occurred. The company has issued share options with the subsequent effect on the diluted EPS and it has consumed the resources that it received for awarding those options, thereby decreasing earnings. Those two different effects on EPS are counted once each.

It is probably true that IFRS 2 may discourage companies from introducing or continuing with employee share plans. However, the main reason for the non-continuation of such schemes could be that the true economic consequences of such plans are being revealed rather than the situation where resources are consumed by issuing share options without accounting properly for those transactions. The role of accounting is to report in a neutral manner and not to distort the financial position.

(b)  **Accounting in the financial statements for the year-ended 31 May 20X5**

IFRS 2 requires an expense to be recognised for the share options granted to the directors with a corresponding amount shown in equity. Where options do not vest immediately but only after a period of service, then there is a presumption that the services will be rendered over the vesting period. The fair value of the services rendered will be measured by reference to the fair value of the equity instruments at the date that the equity instruments were granted. Fair value should be based on market prices. The treatment of vesting conditions depends on whether or not the conditions relate to the market price of the instruments. Market conditions are effectively taken into account in determining the fair value of the instruments and therefore can be ignored for the purposes of estimating the number of equity instruments that will vest. For other conditions such as remaining in the employment of the company, the calculations are carried out based on the best estimate of the number of instruments that will vest. The estimate is revised when subsequent information is available.

Note that the requirements of IFRS 13 *Fair value measurement* do not apply to situations where IFRS 2 applies.

The share options are valued as follows:

|  | Prior to 1 June 20X4 Remuneration expense $ | Year-ended 31 May 20X5 Remuneration expense $ |
|---|---|---|
| J. Van Heflin | | |
| 20,000 options × $5 × ½ | 50,000 | 50,000 |
| R. Ashworth | | |
| 50,000 options × $6 × 1/3 | | 100,000 |
| | 50,000 | 150,000 |

The conditions set out in performance condition A and the service conditions by the director have been met. The expense is spread over two years up to the vesting date of 1 June 20X5.

The increase in the share price to above $13.50 in condition B has not been met but IFRS 2 says that the services received should be recognised irrespective of whether the market condition is satisfied. Additionally the director has to work for the company for three years for the options to vest and, therefore, the expense is spread over three years.

The opening balance of retained earnings at 1 June 20X4 would be reduced by $50,000 and equity (separate component) increased by $50,000.

Directors' remuneration relating to share options of $150,000 would be recognised in profit or loss in the year ended 31 May 20X5 and equity (separate component) would be increased by the same amount.

(c) **Deferred tax implications**

IAS 12 (para 58) requires the deferred tax on the share options to be recognised in profit or loss for the period. The difference between the tax base of the services received (that is the amount of the tax allowance in future periods) and the carrying value of zero will be a deductible temporary difference that results in a deferred tax asset. IFRS 2 says that the estimated future tax deduction should be based on the option's intrinsic value at the year-end as the value at the exercise date will not be known. The intrinsic value is the difference between the fair value (market price) of the share and the exercise price of the option.

**Prior to 1 June 20X4**

Deferred tax asset and income

20,000 options × ($12.50 − $4.50) (intrinsic value) × 1/2 (first year) × 30% tax rate i.e. $24,000

All of this deferred tax income will be recognised in the opening statement of financial position (subject to the rules of IAS 12 *Income taxes*).

If the amount of the tax deduction exceeds the amount of the accumulated remuneration expense, then this indicates that the tax deduction relates to equity as well as to the remuneration expense. The remuneration expense is $50,000 prior to 1/06/04 and the eligible tax deduction will be 20,000 × intrinsic value ($8) × 1/2 i.e. $80,000. Therefore of the deferred tax income ($80,000 − $50,000) × 30% will go to equity, i.e. $9,000.

|  | *Year to 31 May 20X5* |
|---|---|
|  | $ |
| Deferred tax asset at year-end |  |
| 20,000 options × ($12 – $4.50) × 30% | 45,000 |
| 50,000 options × ($12 – $6) × 30% × 1/3 | 30,000 |
|  | ——— |
|  | 75,000 |
| Less recognised in opening balance | (24,000) |
|  | ——— |
| Deferred tax income for year to profit or loss | 51,000 |
|  | ——— |

As above the total remuneration expense to date must be compared to the amount of the tax deduction. The total remuneration expense is $200,000 and the eligible tax deduction is $150,000 (20,000 × $12 – $4.50) + $100,000 (50,000 × $6 × 1/3) i.e. $250,000. Therefore of the deferred tax income $50,000 × 30%, i.e. $15,000 should go to equity. In 20X4, $9,000 of this figure has already gone to equity and therefore of the deferred tax income for 20X5 ($51,000), $6,000 should go to equity.

Thus a deferred tax asset will arise in your first financial statements using IFRS 2.

It is hoped that the above is useful.

| ACCA marking scheme | | |
|---|---|---|
|  |  | *Marks* |
| (a) | Discussion | 9 |
| (b) | Computation and discussion | 9 |
| (c) | Computation and discussion | 7 |
|  |  | — |
| Total |  | 25 |
|  |  | — |

## 38   ASHLEE (JUN 05 EXAM)

**Key answer tips**

This question covers reorganisation and impairment – a regularly examined topic. Don't forget to discuss all the relevant standards – IFRS 5, IAS 36 and IAS 37, making specific comments about each in turn. Any reorganisation question, will normally involve these three standards.

There are several matters to be considered when looking at the implications of the information regarding Ashlee's financial statements.

The mistakes that have been found in the financial statements would have to be adjusted before the financial statements could be approved and published. Additionally, because the loan covenant agreements have been breached then the assets of the group should be reviewed for impairment and any impairment recognised in the financial statements for the year-ended 31 March 20X5.

The fact that loan covenants were breached would require Ashlee to determine whether the going concern assumption in the financial statements is appropriate. As the loan creditors appear to have come to an arrangement with Ashlee, then the going concern position may not be affected. If the situation had been so severe that the whole business was to be closed, then provision would be made in the financial statements to 31 March 20X5 and a fundamental change in the basis of accounting would occur.

**Pilot**

The reorganisation costs cannot be included in the financial statements for the year-ended 31 March 20X5 because the decision to reorganise was not made or announced before the year-end and there was no formal plan at the year-end (IAS 37 *Provisions, contingent liabilities and contingent assets*). The provision should be made in the year to 31 March 20X6. Disclosure should be made in the financial statements for the year ended 31 March 20X5 of the intended reorganisation, as a disclosable non-adjusting event under IAS 10 *Events after the reporting period*.

Pilot's net assets (along with those of Ashlee and Gibson) are required to be tested for impairment under IAS 36 *Impairment of assets* at 31 March 20X5 as a significant reorganisation is deemed to indicate possible impairment. The reorganisation provision should not be taken into account in determining the net assets at the year-end and therefore any figure for the recoverable amount should be based upon projections which do not take the reorganisation into account. The costs and benefits of the reorganisation should be taken out of the projections.

|  | With reorganisation | Without reorganisation |
|---|---|---|
|  | $m | $m |
| Net assets | 85 | 85 |
| Less reorganisation costs | (4) |  |
|  | 81 | 85 |
| Recoverable amount | 84 | 82 |
| Impairment | N/A | 3 |

Therefore there is an impairment of Pilot's net assets at 31 March 20X5 of $3 million. This will be written off goodwill. Given the benefit of the reorganisation, this impairment loss may be reversed in future years. However, IAS 36 does not allow an impairment loss relating to goodwill to be reversed.

**Gibson**

IFRS 5 *Non-current assets held for sale and discontinued operations* establishes two classifications, which are held for sale non-current assets and a disposal group. A disposal group is a collection of assets and liabilities that are to be disposed of in a single transaction. Non-current assets classified as held for sale must be available for immediate sale in their present condition, the sale of the asset must be highly probable and, with limited exception, the sale must be completed within one year. In the case of a disposal group, the measurement basis required for non-current assets classified as held for sale is applied to the group as a whole. Any resultant impairment loss is allocated using IAS 36. Disposal groups classified as held for sale, are measured at the lower of the carrying amount and fair value less costs to sell. Disposal groups are not depreciated.

Gibson will be classified as a disposal group as the decision had been made prior to the year-end and negotiations were occurring at the time of the preparation of the financial statements. Gibson thus was available for immediate sale. The carrying amount of the net assets ($450 million) will be compared to the fair value of the net assets ($415 million) less the estimated costs of selling ($5 million). Thus an impairment loss of $40 million will arise which will be allocated as follows:

|  | $m | Allocated impairment loss $m | Carrying amount after impairment $m |
|---|---|---|---|
| Goodwill | 30 | (30) | – |
| PPE – cost | 120 | (4) | 116 |
| – valuation | 180 | (6) | 174 |
| Inventory | 100 | – | 100 |
| Net current assets | 20 | – | 20 |
|  | 450 | (40) | 410 |

The impairment loss reduces the goodwill to zero and then the residual loss is allocated to the other non-current assets on a prorate basis (IFRS 5/IAS 36). Even if Gibson had not been classified as a disposal group, an impairment review would have occurred because of the reorganisation. IAS 36 does not require an impairment review because of a decision to sell.

The impairment loss reduces the goodwill to zero and then the residual loss is allocated to the other non-current assets on a prorate basis (IFRS 5/IAS 36). Even if Gibson had not been classified as a disposal group, an impairment review would have occurred because of the reorganisation. IAS 36 does not require an impairment review because of a decision to sell.

**Ashlee**

If the shares in Race were acquired principally for the purpose of selling them in the near term, then they should be classified as held for trading and therefore at fair value through profit and loss. On initial recognition the shares would be valued at 150,000 × $20, i.e. $3 million. The transaction costs would be recognised in profit or loss. Subsequently, any gain or loss should be recognised in profit or loss. This includes unrealised holding gains and losses. Thus a profit of 150,000 × ($25 – $20) i.e. $750,000 would also be recognised for the current year in profit or loss.

If the shares were acquired for any other reason, they should be classified as fair value through other comprehensive income. Any designation as fair value through comprehensive income must be made upon initial recognition of the financial asset. The transaction costs would be included as part of the initial measurement of the financial asset which would be recognised at $3.1 million. Any subsequent unrealised gain or loss is recognised in other comprehensive income and held in equity. Dividend income would be recognised in profit or loss each year. Impairment losses would be accounted for within any change in the fair value of the shares and would not be recycled to profit or loss for the year. When the asset is sold, the gain or loss on disposal is calculated by comparing the disposal proceeds against carrying value; there is no recycling of any amounts previously taken to equity to determine the total gain or loss (including amounts held in equity) on disposal in profit or loss for the year. Thus the gain for the year of ($3.75 – $3.1m) i.e. $650,000 would be recognised in other comprehensive income and held in equity.

Both methods would result in the asset being valued at $3.75 million at 31 March 20X5.

It would appear that if loan covenant agreements have been breached, then there may be impairment of the holding company's net assets as the impairment suffered by the subsidiary companies would appear not to affect loan covenant agreements unless they were particularly serious. There is an issue over the revenue recognition policy of Ashlee. As the development properties are essentially 'inventory' then IFRS 5 does not apply as regards being held for sale, as all inventories are essentially for resale. The change of accounting policy is questionable and goes against IAS 18 *Revenue* (Appendix A) that indicates that in the case of real estate sales, revenue is recognised when legal title passes to the buyer. Thus the profit of $10 million on the sale should not be included in the financial statements. IAS *40 Investment property* does not apply when property is intended for sale in the ordinary course of business.

The above circumstances should be taken into account when redrafting the financial statements for the year-ended 31 March 20X5.

| ACCA marking scheme | |
|---|---|
| | *Marks* |
| Introduction | 3 |
| Pilot | 9 |
| Gibson | 8 |
| Ashlee | 6 |
| | —— |
| Available | 26 |
| | —— |
| Total | 25 |
| | —— |

**39** **GREENIE (DEC 10 EXAM)**  *Walk in the footsteps of a top tutor*

**Key answer tips**

As this is a discussion question dealing with several issues, you should deal with each in turn, clearly identifying which part of the question requirement you are dealing with, particularly if you answer the various parts out of order. Whilst some marks will be available for stating definitions from reporting standards, additional credit will be earned for application of the definitions to the circumstances outlined within the question. As a final point, remember that you will earn appropriate credit for discussing relevant issues and points, even if you arrive at a different conclusion to the suggested answer, so ensure that you apply good exam technique and answer all parts of the question requirement.

*A good starting point is a definition from a relevant reporting standard, which can then be applied to the scenario within the question.*

(a)    IAS 37 paragraph 14, states that an entity must recognise a provision if, and only if:

      (i)    a present obligation (legal or constructive) has arisen as a result of a past event (the obligating event),

      (ii)    payment to settle the obligation is probable ('more likely than not'), and

      (iii)    the amount can be estimated reliably.

An obligating event is an event that creates a legal or constructive obligation and, therefore, results in an enterprise having no realistic alternative but to settle the obligation [IAS 37.10].

At the date of the financial statements, there was no current obligation for Greenie. In particular, no action had been brought in connection with the accident. It was not yet probable that an outflow of resources would be required to settle the obligation. Thus no provision is required.

*Again, state the relevant definition and apply it to the circumstances within the question.*

Greenie may need to disclose a contingent liability. IAS 37 defines a contingent liability as:

(a)    a possible obligation that has arisen from past events and whose existence will be confirmed by the occurrence or not of uncertain future events; or

(b)    a present obligation that has arisen from past events but is not recognised because:

      (i)    it is not probable that an outflow of resources will occur to settle the obligation; or

      (ii)    the amount of the obligation cannot be measured with sufficient reliability.

IAS 37 requires that entities should not recognise contingent liabilities but should disclose them, unless the possibility of an outflow of economic resources is remote. It appears that Greenie should disclose a contingent liability. The fact that the real nature and extent of the damages, including whether they qualify for compensation and details of any compensation payments remained to be established all indicated the level of uncertainty attaching to the case. The degree of uncertainty is not such that the possibility of an outflow of resource could be considered remote. Had this been the case, no disclosure under IAS 37 would have been required.

Thus the conditions for establishing a liability are not fulfilled. However, a contingent liability should be disclosed as required by IAS 37.

The possible recovery of these costs from the insurer gives rise to consideration of whether a contingent asset should be disclosed. Given the status of the expert report, any information as to whether judicial involvement is likely will not be available until 2011. Thus this contingent asset is more possible than probable. As such no disclosure of the contingent asset should be included.

*This part of the question deals with application of knowledge relating to circumstances when significant influence or control may be exercised. You should state and apply relevant definitions within your answer. As the question requirement is for a discussion, you should try to consider all relevant circumstances, and try to avoid writing a 'one-sided' justification of your conclusion.*

(b)    Greenie appears to have significant influence over Manair, and therefore, it should be accounted for as an associate. According to paragraph 2 of IAS 28 'Investments in Associates', significant influence is the power to participate in the financial and operating decisions of the investee but is not control or joint control over the policies. Where an investor holds 20% or more of the voting power of the investee, it is presumed that the investor has significant influence unless it can be clearly demonstrated that this is not the case. If the investor holds less than 20% of the voting power of the investee, it is presumed that the investor does not have significant influence, unless such influence can be clearly demonstrated (IAS 28, paragraph 6).

In certain cases, whether significant influence exists should also be assessed when an investor holds less than 20% especially where it appears that the substance of the arrangement indicates significant influence. Greenie holds 19.9% of the voting shares and it appears as though there has been an attempt to avoid accounting for Manair as an associate. The fact that one investor holds a majority share of the voting power can indicate that other investors do not have significant influence. A substantial or majority ownership by an investor does not, however, necessarily preclude other investors from having significant influence (IAS 28 paragraph 6). IAS 28 paragraph 7 states that the existence of significant influence by an investor is usually evidenced in one or more of the following ways:

(i)     representation on the board of directors or equivalent governing body of the investee;

(ii)    participation in the policy-making process;

(iii)   material transactions between the investor and the investee;

(iv)   interchange of managerial personnel; or

(v)    provision of essential technical information.

The shareholders' agreement allows Greenie to participate in some decisions. It needs to be determined whether these include financial and operating policy decisions of Manair, although this is very likely. The representation on the board of directors combined with the additional rights Greenie had under the shareholders' agreement, give Greenie the power to participate in some policy decisions. Additionally, Greenie had sent a team of management experts to give business advice to the board of Manair.

In addition, there is evidence of material transactions between the investor and the investee and indications that Greenie provided Manair with maintenance and technical services. Both these facts are examples of how significant influence might be evidenced.

Based on an assessment of all the facts, it appears that Greenie has significant influence over Manair and that Manair should be considered an associate and accounted for using the equity method of accounting.

Finally as it is likely that Manair is an associated undertaking of Greenie the transactions themselves would be deemed related party transactions. Greenie would need to disclose within its own financial statements the relationship, an outline of the transactions including their total value, outstanding balances including any debts deemed irrecoverable or doubtful (IAS 24 para 17).

*This part of the question requires discussion of two issues – recognition of the franchise right and classification of irredeemable preference shares. You should ensure that you address both issues to maximise the marks earned. Remember that, even if you arrive at the wrong conclusion, you will still earn marks for discussion of relevant issues within your answer.*

(c) The franchise right should be recognised using the principles in IFRS 2 'Share based payment'. The asset should be recognised at the fair value of the rights acquired and the existence of exchange transactions and prices for similar franchise rights means that a fair value can be established. The franchise right should therefore be recorded at $2.3 million. If the fair value had not been reliably measurable then the franchise right would have been recorded at the fair value of the equity instruments issued i.e. $2.5 million.

Normally irredeemable preference shares would be classified as equity. The contractual obligation to pay the fixed cash dividend creates a liability component and the right to participate in ordinary dividends creates an equity component. If Greenie were to comply with IAS 32 'Financial instruments: Presentation', it would require the preference shares to be treated as compound financial instruments with both an equity and liability component. The value of the equity component is the residual amount after deducting the separately determined liability component from the fair value of the instrument as a whole.

Under IAS 32, it would seem that substantially all of the carrying value of Greenie's preference shares would be allocated to the liability component because of the dividend elements and the fixed net cash dividend would be treated as a finance cost.

IAS 1 'Presentation of financial statements' requires departure from a requirement of a standard only in the extremely rare circumstances where management conclude that compliance would be so misleading that it would conflict with the objective of financial statements set out in the Framework. Greenie's argument that the presentation of the preference shares in accordance with IAS 32 would be misleading is not acceptable. The fact that it would not reflect the nature of the instruments as having characteristics of permanent capital providing participation in future profits is not a valid argument. IAS 1 requires additional disclosures when compliance with the specific requirements in IFRS is insufficient to enable a user to understand the impact of particular transactions or conditions on financial position and financial performance. A fair presentation would be achieved by complying with IAS 32 and providing additional disclosures to explain the characteristics of the preference shares.

| ACCA marking scheme | | Marks |
|---|---|---|
| (a) | Provision discussion | 3 |
| | Contingent liability discussion | 3 |
| (b) | Significant influence discussion and application | 10 |
| (c) | Intangible assets | 3 |
| | Preference shares | 4 |
| | Professional | 2 |
| | | ___ |
| Total | | 25 |
| | | ___ |

**Examiner's comments**

This question dealt with real world scenarios taken from corporate financial statements. It is important that the exam paper reflects actual issues in financial statements and those candidates can apply their knowledge to these scenarios.

A public limited company which developed and operated airports was involved in litigation over an accident at one of the airports and the issues was whether a provision or contingent liability should be provided for. In this case it was important for candidates to justify their conclusion by discussing the nature of a provision and contingency. This part of the question was well answered although many candidates came to the incorrect conclusion.

In part b, candidates had to determine the relationship between an entity and a company that it had invested in. There was a need to discuss the relationship between the two entities in order to determine what the relationship constituted. Many candidates did not again use the scenario and in this question it was critical to discuss the facts in the question. However the question was well answered.

In part c the entity issued shares for the acquisition of franchise rights at a local airport and showed irredeemable preference shares as equity instruments in its statement of financial position. Candidates had to determine the correct accounting treatment for these items. This part of the question was not well answered with candidates not understanding how to account for the irredeemable preference shares. Understanding the nature of equity and liability is a key element of the syllabus. Overall the question was well answered.

## 40 NETTE (JUN 04 EXAM)

**Key answer tips**

The *Conceptual Framework for Financial Reporting 2010* contains an ideal set of theoretical principles, while individual accounting standards cover practical rules for dealing with practical situations. Although not directly relevant to the question, note that the Framework is currently the subject of a long-term review project, which should result in the publication of an updated document which will be adopted by both the IASB and US FASB. Don't be nervous about pointing out possible inconsistencies between the *Framework* and individual standards; that is what this question is all about, particularly in the areas of provisioning, accounting for grants and accounting for deferred tax.

(a)   The *Framework for the preparation and presentation of financial statements* provides a conceptual underpinning for the International Financial Reporting Standards (IFRSs). IFRSs are based on the *Framework* and its aim is to provide a framework for the formulation of accounting standards. If accounting issues arise which are not covered by accounting standards then the *Framework* can provide a basis for the resolution of such issues. The *Framework* deals with several areas:

(i)     the objective of financial statements

(ii)    the underlying assumptions

(iii)   the qualitative characteristics of financial information

(iv)   the elements of financial statements

(v)    recognition in financial statements

(vi)   measurement in financial statements

(vii)  concepts of capital and capital maintenance.

The *Framework* adopts an approach which builds corporate reporting around the definitions of assets and liabilities and the criteria for recognising and measuring them in the statement of financial position. This approach views accounting in a different way to most companies. The notion that the measurement and recognition of assets and liabilities is the starting point for the determination of the profit of the business does not sit easily with most practising accountants who see the transactions of the company as the basis for accounting. The *Framework* provides a useful basis for discussion and is an aid to academic thought. However, it seems to ignore the many legal and business roles that financial statements play. In many jurisdictions, the financial statements form the basis of dividend payments, the starting point for the assessment of taxation, and often the basis for executive remuneration. A statement of financial position, fair value system that the IASB seems to favour would have a major impact on the above elements, and would not currently fit the practice of accounting. Very few companies take into account the principles embodied in the *Framework* unless those principles themselves are embodied in an accounting standard. Some International Accounting Standards are inconsistent with the *Framework* primarily because they were issued earlier than the *Framework*. The *Framework* is a useful basis for financial reporting but a fundamental change in the current basis of financial reporting will be required for it to have any practical application. The IASB seems intent on ensuring that this change will take place.

Note that there is a long-term joint project between the IASB and US FASB to develop a common conceptual framework. Currently, the definitions of the various elements of the financial statements have been adopted from the previous edition of the Framework document. As at November 2011, the Conceptual Framework for Financial Reporting 2010 project comprises eight phases which, once complete, will lead to the withdrawal of the current Framework document.

IAS 8 *Accounting policies, changes in accounting estimates and errors*) makes reference to the use of the *Framework* where there is no IFRS or IFRIC in issue.

(b)   (i)   **Situation 1**

Under IAS 37 *Provisions, contingent liabilities and contingent assets*, a provision should be made at the end of the reporting period for the discounted cost of the removal of the extraction facility because of the following reasons:

(i)     The installation of the facility creates an obligating event.

(ii)    The operating licence creates a legal obligation that is likely to occur

(iii)   80% of the costs of removal will have to be incurred irrespective of the future operations of the company and cannot be avoided

(iv)    A transfer of economic benefits (i.e. the costs of removal) will be required to settle the obligation

(v)     A reasonable estimate of the obligation can be made although it is difficult to estimate a cost which will be incurred in twenty years time (IAS 37 says that only in exceptional circumstances will it not be possible to make some estimate of the obligation).

The cost to be incurred will be treated as part of the cost of the facility to be depreciated over its production life. However, the costs relating to the damage caused by the extraction should not be included in the provision until the gas is extracted. This would be 20% of the total discounted provision. The accounting for the provision is as follows:

|  | $m |
|---|---|
| Present value of obligation at 1 June 20X3 | 50 |
| Provision for decommissioning 80% × $50m | 40 |
| Provision for damage through extraction (20% × $50m × $1.05^{20}$) | 1.33 |

**Statement of financial position at 31 May X4 (extracts)**

| Property, plant and equipment: | $m |
|---|---|
| Cost of extraction facility | 200 |
| Provision for decommissioning | 40 |
|  | 240 |
| *less* depreciation (240 ÷ 20 years) | (12) |
| Carrying value | 228 |

| Other provisions: | $m |
|---|---|
| Provision for decommissioning | 40 |
| Unwinding of discount ($40m × 5%) | 2 |

**Statement of comprehensive income**

|  | $m |
|---|---|
| Depreciation | 12.00 |
| Provision for damage | 1.33 |
| Unwinding of discount (finance cost) | 2.00 |

**Statement of financial position extracts at 31 May X4**

|  | $m |
|---|---|
| Property. plant & equipment | 200 |
| Cost of extraction facility | 40 |
|  | 240 |
| Less: depreciation (240/20 yrs) | (12) |
|  | 228 |

|  | $m |
|---|---|
| Provision for decommissioning: | 40.00 |
| Unwinding of discount: ($40m × 5%) | 2.00 |
|  | 42.00 |
| Provision for damage | 1.33 |
|  | 43.33 |

**Statement of Comprehensive income**

|  | $m |
|---|---|
| Depreciation | 12.00 |
| Provision for damage | 1.33 |
| Unwinding of discount (finance cost) | 2.00 |

A simple straight line basis has been used to calculate the required provision for damage. A more complex method could be used whereby the present value of the expected cost of the provision ($10m) is provided for over 20 years and the discount thereon is unwound over its life. This would give a charge in the year of $0.5m + ($10m × 5%), i.e. **$1m**.

**Situation 2**

A provision for deferred tax should be made under IAS 12 *Income taxes* as follows:

| Building: | | $m | Temporary difference $m |
|---|---|---|---|
| Tax written down value | (75% × $8m) | 6.0 | |
| Net book value | $9m | | |
| Less deferred credit | ($1.8m) | 7.2 | |
| | | | 1.2 |
| Deferred tax liabilities – temporary differences | | | 40.0 |
| Total temporary differences – deferred tax liabilities | | | 41.2 |
| Warranty | | | 4 |
| Tax losses | | | 70 |
| Total temporary differences – deferred tax assets | | | 74 |

The company would recognise a deferred tax asset of at least $41.2 million of the temporary differences of $74 million at the tax rate of 30%. If the company could prove that suitable taxable profits were available in the future or that tax planning opportunities were available to create suitable taxable profits, then the balance of the deferred tax asset ($32.8 million at tax rate of 30%) could be recognised.

(ii) The International Accounting Standards Board's *Framework* would require recognition of the full discounted liability for the decommissioning. The problem is that this can only be achieved by creating an asset on the statement of financial position. This asset struggles to meet the *Framework*'s definition of an asset and is somewhat dubious by nature. An asset is a resource controlled by the company as a result of past events and from which future economic benefits are expected to flow. It is difficult to see how a future cost can meet this definition. The other strange aspect to the treatment of this item is that depreciation (and hence part of the provision) will be treated as an operating cost and the unwinding of the discount could be treated as a finance cost. This latter treatment could fail any qualitative test in terms of the relevance and reliability of the information.

A liability is defined in the *Framework* as a present obligation arising from past events, the settlement of which is expected to result in an outflow of economic benefits. The idea of a constructive obligation utilised in IAS 37 is also included as a requirement in the *Framework*. Assets and liabilities are essentially a collection of rights and obligations. The provision for deferred taxation does not meet the criteria for a liability (or an asset) as set out in the *Framework*. The only tax liability (present obligation as a result of past events) is in fact the current tax due to the tax authorities. A deferred tax liability can be avoided, for example, if a company makes future losses, and with suitable tax planning strategies it may never result in taxable amounts.

A deferred tax asset is dependent upon the certainty of future profits or tax planning opportunities. It can be argued that a deferred tax asset does not confer any 'right' to future economic benefits as future profits are never certain.

Additionally the grant of $2 million has been treated as a liability in the financial statements. Unless there are circumstances in which the grant has to be repaid, it is also unlikely to meet the definition of a liability.

## 41   ARON (JUN 09 EXAM)      *Walk in the footsteps of a top tutor*

### Key answer tips

This question deals with recognition and measurement of financial instruments. Part (a) is concerned with the use of fair values, particularly if there is no reliable or active market to help determine fair value. Part (b) of the requirement deals with accounting for four financial instruments, including a convertible bond and an interest-free loan, together with supporting calculations, comment and explanation. Accounting for one of the financial instruments also required knowledge of accounting for foreign currency transactions.

(a)   **Discussion of fair value and its relevance**

IFRS 13 *Fair value measurement* now formalises the basis upon which a fair value measurement is determined. This should help to bring consistency to the determination of a fair value measurement, both by an entity over time, and also between entities, to enhance constancy and comparability of information. It should also enhance transparency and understanding.

The fair value of an asset is defined as the price that would be received to sell and asset, or paid to transfer a liability in an orderly transaction between market participants at the measurement date. If available, a quoted market price in an active market for an identical asset or liability is the best evidence of fair value and should be used as the basis for the measurement. IFRS 13 refers to this as 'Level 1 inputs'. Level 2 inputs comprise observable inputs, other than those within Level 1, such as prices in an active market for similar, though not identical, assets or liabilities. Such fair value measurements will require assessment as to whether they require any adjustment to arrive at a reliable fair value measurement. Level 3 inputs are not directly observable and will typically comprise management estimates and judgements, including the use of pricing or other appropriate models, to arrive at a fair value measurement.

Fair values should also reflect the assumption that market entrants have had adequate time to undertake reasonable marketing activity. In addition, it is also assumed that any transaction is not based upon a distress or forced basis. Transactions costs are ignored as they are regarded as a feature of the transaction, not of the asset or liability to be measured.

The IASB has concluded that fair value is the most relevant measure for most financial instruments. Fair value measurements provide more transparency than historical cost based measurements. Reliability is as important as relevance because relevant information that is not reliable is of no use to an investor. Fair value measurements should be reliable and computed in a manner that is faithful to the underlying economics of the transaction. Measuring financial instruments at fair value should not necessarily mean abandoning historical cost information.

However, market conditions will affect fair value measurements. In many circumstances, quoted market prices are unavailable. As a result, difficulties occur when making estimates of fair value. It is difficult to apply fair value measures in illiquid markets and to decide how and when models should be used for fair valuation. Fair value information can provide a value at the point in time that it is measured but its relevance will depend on the volatility of the market inputs and whether the instruments are actively traded or are held for the long term. Fair value provides an important indicator of risk profile and exposure but to fully understand this and to put it into context, the entity must disclose sufficient information. IFRS 13 requires significant disclosures relating to how fair value measurements have been determined for inclusion in the financial statements, including the categorisation of inputs used to determine such measurements.

(b)    (i)    **Convertible bond**

Some compound instruments have both a liability and an equity component from the issuer's perspective. In this case, IAS 32 *Financial instruments: presentation* requires that the component parts be accounted for and presented separately according to their substance based on the definitions of liabilities and equity. The split is made at issuance and not revised for subsequent changes in market interest rates, share prices, or other events that changes the likelihood that the conversion option will be exercised. (IAS 32.28)

A convertible bond contains two components. One is a financial liability, namely the issuer's contractual obligation to pay cash in the form of interest or capital, and the other is an equity instrument, which is the holder's option to convert into shares. When the initial carrying amount of a compound financial instrument is required to be allocated to its equity and liability components, the equity component is assigned the residual amount after deducting from the fair value of the instrument as a whole the amount separately determined for the liability component. (IAS 32.31)

In the case of the bond, the liability element will be determined by discounting the future stream of cash flows which will be the interest to be paid and the final capital balance assuming no conversion. The discount rate used will be 9% which is the market rate for similar bonds without the conversion right. The difference between cash received and the liability component is the value of the option.

|  | $000 |
|---|---|
| Present value of interest at end of: | |
| Year 1 (31 May 2007) ($100m × 6%) ÷ 1.09 | 5,505 |
| Year 2 (31 May 2008) ($100m × 6%) ÷ 1.092 | 5,050 |
| Year 3 (31 May 2009) ($100m + ($100m × 6%))÷ 1.093 | 81,852 |
| | |
| Total liability component | 92,407 |
| Total equity element | 7,593 |
| | |
| Proceeds of issue | 100,000 |

The issue cost will have to be allocated between the liability and equity components in proportion to the above proceeds.

|  | $000 Liability | $000 Equity | $000 Total |
|---|---|---|---|
| Proceeds | 92,407 | 7,593 | 100,000 |
| Issue cost | (924) | (76) | (1,000) |
| | | | |
| | 91,483 | 7,517 | 99,000 |

The credit to equity of $7,517 would not be re-measured. The liability component of $91,483 would be measured at amortised cost using the effective interest rate of 9.38%, as this spreads the issue costs over the term of the bond. The interest payments will reduce the liability in getting to the year end. The initial entries would have been:

| Financial instrument | $000 | Interest | $000 |
|---|---|---|---|
| Dr Cash | 100,000 | Cr Cash | 1,000 |
| Cr Liability | 92,407 | Dr Liability | 924 |
| Cr Equity | 7,593 | Dr Equity | 76 |

The liability component balance on 31 May 2009 becomes $100,000 as a result of the effective interest rate of 9.38% being applied and cashflows at 6% based on nominal value.

| B/fwd | Eff int 9.38% | Cashflow 6% | C/fwd |
|---|---|---|---|
| 91,483 | 8,581 | (6,000) | 94,064 |
| 94,064 | 8,823 | (6,000) | 96,887 |
| 96,887 | 9,088 | (6,000) | (100,000) |

On conversion of the bond on 31 May 2009, Aron would issue 25 million ordinary shares of $1 and the original equity component together with the balance on the liability will become the consideration.

|  | $000 |
|---|---|
| Share capital – 25 million at $1 | 25,000 |
| Share premium | 82,517 |
|  | |
| Equity and liability components (100,000 + 7,593 – 76) | 107,517 |

(ii) **Shares in Smart**

In this situation Aron has to determine if the transfer of shares in Smart qualifies for derecognition. The criteria are firstly to determine that the asset has been transferred, and then to determine whether or not the entity has transferred substantially all of the risks and rewards of ownership of the asset. If substantially all the risks and rewards have been transferred, the asset is derecognised. If substantially all the risks and rewards have been retained, derecognition of the asset is precluded.

In this case the transfer of shares qualifies for derecognition as Aron no longer retains any risks and rewards of ownership. In addition Aron obtains a new financial asset which is the shares in Given which should be recognised at fair value. The transaction will be accounted for as follows:

|  | $m |
|---|---|
| Proceeds – FV of shares received in Given | 5.5 |
| Carrying amount of shares in Smart | 5.0 |
|  | |
| Gain to profit or loss | 0.5 |

The shares in Given should be recognised at fair value of $5.5 million; presumably there will be a designation upon initial recognition to account for this new financial asset at fair value through other comprehensive income if it is to be held on a continuing basis.

In addition, Aron may choose to make a transfer within equity of the cumulative gain recognised up to disposal date of $400,000.

(iii) **Foreign Subsidiary**

In this situation, IFRS 9 will apply to the debt instrument in the foreign subsidiary's financial statements and IAS 21 *The effects of changes in foreign exchange rates* will apply in translating the financial statements of the subsidiary for inclusion in the group financial statements. Under IAS 21, all exchange differences resulting from translation are recognised in equity until disposal of the subsidiary, when they are recycled to profit or loss as part of the gain or loss on disposal of the subsidiary.

As the debt instrument is held for trading it will be carried at fair value through profit or loss in Gao's financial statements. Thus at 31 May 2009, there will be a fair value gain of 2 million zloti which will be credited to profit or loss of Gao. In the consolidated financial statements, the carrying value of the debt at 1 June 2008 would have been $3.3 million (10 million zloti ÷ 3). At the year end this carrying value will have increased to $6 million (12 million zloti ÷ 2). Aron will translate the statement of profit or loss of Gao using the average rate of 2.5 zloti to the dollar. Although the fair value of the debt instrument has increased by $2.7 million, Aron will only recognise 2 million zloti ÷ 2.5, i.e. $800,000 of this in the consolidated statement of profit or loss with the remaining increase in value of ($2.7 − $0.8) million, i.e. $1,900,000 being classified as other comprehensive income and taken to equity until the disposal of the foreign subsidiary.

|  | $m |
|---|---|
| Opening balance at 1 December 2008 | 3.3 |
| Increase in year | 2.7 |
| | |
| Closing balance at 30 November 2009 | 6.0 |

| | |
|---|---|
| Dr Debt instrument | 2.7 |
| Cr Consolidated profit or loss | 0.8 |
| Cr Equity | 1.9 |

(iv)  **Interest Free Loans**

When a financial asset is recognised initially, IFRS 9 requires it to be measured at fair value, plus transaction costs in certain situations. Normally the fair value is the fair value of the consideration given. However, the fair value of an interest free loan may not necessarily be its face amount. The instrument's fair value may be evidenced by comparison with other market transactions in the same instrument. In this case, the fair value may be estimated as the discounted present value of future receipts using the market interest rate. If the interest-free loans are to be measured at amortised cost, they must comply with the requirements of both the business model test and the cash flow characteristics test. The first test requires that the financial asset is held to collect the contractual cash flows associated with the asset. The second test requires that the cash flows consist solely of repayment of interest and capital relating to the financial asset. This would appear to be the case; if this was not the case, the financial asset would need to be accounted for as fair value through profit or loss.

The difference between the fair value of the loan and the face value of the loan will be treated as employee remuneration under IAS 19 *Employee benefits*.

|  | $m |
|---|---|
| Fair value of loan at 1 June 2008 ($10/(1.06^2)$) | 8.9 |
| Employee compensation | 1.1 |
| | |
| Closing balance at 30 November 2009 | 10.0 |

The employee compensation would be charged to profit or loss over the two-year period. As the company wishes to classify the asset as loans and receivables, it will be measured at 31 May 2009, at amortised cost using the effective interest method. In this case the effective interest rate will be 6% and the value of the loan in the statement of financial position will be ($8.9 million × 1.06) i.e. $9.43 million. Interest of $0.53 million will be credited to profit or loss.

At 1 June 2008:

| | |
|---|---:|
| Dr Loan | 8.9 |
| Dr Employee compensation | 1.1 |
| Cr Cash | 10.0 |

At 31 May 2009:

| | |
|---|---:|
| Dr Loan | 0.53 |
| Cr Profit or loss – interest | 0.53 |

| **ACCA marking scheme** | | | |
|---|---|---|---:|
| | | | *Marks* |
| (a) | Fair value – IFRS 13 subjective | | 4 |
| | | | |
| (b) | Convertible bond | explanation | 2 |
| | | calculation | 4 |
| | Shares in Smart | explanation | 2 |
| | | calculation | 2 |
| | Foreign subsidiary | explanation of principle | 2 |
| | | accounting treatment | 3 |
| | Interest free loan | explanation of principle | 2 |
| | | Accounting treatment | 2 |
| | Quality of explanation | | 3 |
| | | | —— |
| | | | 21 |
| | | | —— |
| Total | | | 25 |
| | | | —— |

**Examiner's comments**

This question required a brief discussion of how the fair value of financial instruments is determined with a comment on the relevance of fair value measurements for financial instruments where markets are volatile and illiquid. This part of the question was quite well answered although the answers were quite narrow and many candidates simply described the classification of financial instruments in loans and receivables, available for sale etc. The second part of the question required candidates to discuss the accounting for four different financial instruments. The requirement was to discuss the accounting but many candidates simply showed the accounting entries without any discussion. If the accounting entries were incorrect then it was difficult to award significant marks for the attempt. If however there is a discussion of the principles, then it is easier to award marks for a discussion which has a subjective element to it rather than a calculation which is normally correct or incorrect. The financial instruments ranged from a convertible bond to transfer of shares to a debt instrument in a foreign subsidiary to interest free loans. The treatment of the convertible bond was quite well done except for the treatment of the issue costs and the conversion of the bond. This part of the question often gained good marks. Again the treatment of the transfer of shares and interest free loans was well done but the exchange and fair value gains were often combined and not separated in the case of the debt instrument of the foreign subsidiary. Generally speaking this was the best-answered question in part B of the paper.

## 42 JOHAN (DEC 08 EXAM)  *Walk in the footsteps of a top tutor*

**Key answer tips**

This question requires discussion and application of accounting treatments applicable to intangible assets, property, plant and equipment, leases, inventory and revenue recognition. The question requirement is broken down into smaller requirements, each with a mark allocation which should help you with time management during the examination. The best way to approach this question is to deal with each issue separately and to identify the specific accounting requirements for each issue. Having done that, the accounting treatment should then be applied to the specific information in the question.

*Here is a definition of an intangible asset which can then be applied to information in the question.*

An intangible asset meets the identifiability criterion when it is separable or it arises from contractual or other legal rights (IAS 38 *Intangible assets*). Additionally intangible assets are recognised where it is probable that the future economic benefits attributable to the asset will flow to the entity and the asset's cost can be reliably measured. Where intangible assets are acquired separately, the asset's cost or fair value reflects the estimations of the future economic benefits that are expected to flow to the entity. The licence will, therefore, meet the above criteria for recognition as an intangible asset at cost. Subsequent to initial recognition, IAS 38 permits an entity to adopt the cost or revaluation model as its accounting policy. The revaluation model can only be adopted if intangible assets are traded in an active market. As the licence cannot be sold, the revaluation model cannot be used.

*Here is an accounting policy for intangible assets using the cost model.*

The cost model requires intangible assets to be carried at cost less amortisation and impairment losses (IAS 38, para 74). Amortisation is the systematic allocation of the depreciable amount of an intangible asset over its useful life. The depreciable amount is the asset's cost less its residual value. The licence will have no residual value. The depreciable amount should be allocated on a systematic basis over its useful life. The method of amortisation should reflect the pattern in which the asset's economic benefits are expected to be consumed. If that pattern cannot be determined reliably, the straight line method of amortisation must be used. The licence does not suffer wear and tear from usage, that is the number of customers using the service. The economic benefits of the licence relate to Johan's ability to benefit from the use of the licence. The economic benefits relate to the passage of time and the useful life of the licence is now shorter. Therefore, the asset depletes on a time basis and the straight line basis is appropriate. The licence should be amortised from the date that the network is available for use; that is from 1 December 2007. In accordance with IAS 36, an impairment review should have been undertaken at 30 November 2007 when the licence was not being amortised. Although the licence is capable of being used on the date it was purchased, it cannot be used until the associated network assets and infrastructure are available for use. Johan expects the regulator to renew the licence at the end of the initial term and thus consideration should be given to amortising the licence over the two licence periods, i.e. a period of 11 years (five years and six years) as the licence could be renewed at a nominal cost. However, Johan has no real experience of renewing licences and cannot reliably determine what amounts, if any, would be payable to the regulator. Therefore, the licence should be amortised over a five year period, that is $24 million per annum.

*Like other assets, intangibles should be subject to an impairment review if there is an indication of possible impairment.*

There are indications that the value of the licence may be impaired. The market share for the year to 30 November 2008 is disappointing and competition is fierce in the sector, and retention of customers difficult. Therefore, an impairment test should be undertaken. Johan should classify the licence and network assets as a single cash generating unit (CGU) for impairment purposes. The licence cannot generate revenue in its own right and the smallest group of assets that generates independent revenue will be the licence and network assets. The impairment indicators point to the need to test this cash generating unit for impairment.

**Costs incurred in extending network**

The cost of an item of property, plant and equipment should be recognised when

(i)     it is probable that future economic benefits associated with the item will flow to the entity, and

(ii)    the cost of the item can be measured reliably (IAS 16 *Property, plant and equipment (PPE)*)

It is necessary to assess the degree of certainty attaching to the flow of economic benefits and the basis of the evidence available at the time of initial recognition. The cost incurred during the initial feasibility study ($250,000) should be expensed as incurred, as the flow of economic benefits to Johan as a result of the study would have been uncertain.

*Here is a definition of what can be capitalised as part of cost of PP&E per IAS 16.*

IAS 16 states that the cost of an item of PPE comprises amongst other costs, directly attributable costs of bringing the asset to the location and condition necessary for it to be capable of operating in a manner intended by management (IAS 16, para 16). Examples of costs given in IAS 16 are site preparation costs, and installation and assembly costs. The selection of the base station site is critical for the optimal operation of the network and is part of the process of bringing the network assets to a working condition. Thus the costs incurred by engaging a consultant ($50,000) to find an optimal site can be capitalised as it is part of the cost of constructing the network and depreciated accordingly as planning permission has been obtained.

*Here is a definition of a lease which can then be applied to the information in the question.*

Under IAS 17 *Leases*, a lease is defined as an agreement whereby the lessor conveys to the lessee, in return for a payment or series of payments, the right to use an asset for an agreed period of time. A finance lease is a lease that transfers substantially all the risks and rewards incidental to ownership of the leased asset to the lessee. An operating lease is a lease other than a finance lease. In the case of the contract regarding the land, there is no ownership transfer and the term is not for the major part of the asset's life as it is land which has an indefinite economic life. Thus substantially all of the risks and rewards incidental to ownership have not been transferred. The contract should be treated, therefore, as an operating lease. The payment of $300,000 should be treated as a prepayment in the statement of financial position and charged to profit or loss over the life of the contract on the straight line basis. The monthly payments will be expensed and no value placed on the lease contract in the statement of financial position.

**Handsets and revenue recognition**

*Here is a definition of inventory which can then be applied to the information in the question.*

The inventory of handsets should be measured at the lower of cost and net realisable value (IAS 2 *Inventories*, para 9). Johan should recognise a provision at the point of purchase for the handsets to be sold at a loss. The inventory should be written down to its net realisable value (NRV) of $149 per handset as they are sold both to prepaid customers and dealers. The NRV is $51 less than cost. Net realisable value is the estimated selling price in the normal course of business less the estimated selling costs.

*Here is a definition for revenue which can then be applied to the information in the question.*

IAS 18 *Revenue*, requires the recognition of revenue by reference to the stage of completion of the transaction at the reporting date. Revenue associated with the provision of services should be recognised as service as rendered. Johan should record the receipt of $21 per call card as deferred revenue at the point of sale. Revenue of $18 should be recognised over the six month period from the date of sale. The unused call credit of $3 would be recognised when the card expires as that is the point at which the obligation of Johan ceases. Revenue is earned from the provision of services and not from the physical sale of the card.

IAS 18 does not deal in detail with agency arrangements but says the gross inflows of economic benefits include amounts collected on behalf of the principal and which do not result in increases in equity for the entity. The amounts collected on behalf of the principal are not revenue. Revenue is the amount of the 'commission'. Additionally where there are two or more transactions, they should be taken together if the commercial effect cannot be understood without reference to the series of transactions as a whole.

As a result of the above, Johan should not recognise revenue when the handset is sold to the dealer, as the dealer is acting as an agent for the sale of the handset and the service contract. Johan has retained the risk of the loss in value of the handset as they can be returned by the dealer and the price set for the handset is under the control of Johan. The handset sale and the provision of the service would have to be assessed as to their separability. However, the handset cannot be sold separately and is commercially linked to the provision of the service. Johan would, therefore, recognise the net payment of $130 as a customer acquisition cost which may qualify as an intangible asset under IAS 38, and the revenue from the service contract will be recognised as the service is rendered. The intangible asset would be amortised over the 12 month contract. The cost of the handset from the manufacturer will be charged as cost of goods sold ($200).

| ACCA marking scheme | | Marks |
|---|---|---|
| Intangible assets | Licence | 2 |
| | Amortisation | 2 |
| | Impairment | 2 |
| | Renewal | 2 |
| | | 8 |
| Property, plant and equipment | | |
| | Cost | 1 |
| | Feasibility study | 1 |
| | Location and condition | 1 |
| | Capitalised costs | 1 |
| Leases | Operating lease | 2 |
| | Prepayment | 1 |
| | | 7 |
| Inventory | | 2 |
| IAS 18 *Revenue* | recognition | 2 |
| | agency | 2 |
| | separability | 2 |
| | | 8 |
| Discussion | | 2 |
| Total | | 25 |

**Examiner's comments**

This question required candidates to discuss the issues and accounting practices relating to the telecommunications industry. The case study did not involve relevant knowledge of the industry or require discussion of complex technical issues but the application of fundamental accounting knowledge to the case in question. The key knowledge areas were intangible assets, impairment, PPE, leases, inventories, and revenue recognition. The question was not well answered with candidates failing to recognise the key accounting principles required. Again the question was framed as if candidates were giving general advice to a client but in this case the requirements were broken down into sections to facilitate candidates' answers. This question was not well answered by candidates because of the lack of a capability to apply knowledge.

The main areas where candidates had problems was determining when the intangible asset should be recognised, determining the amortisation period for the asset, recognising that there was a lease and not a contingent liability, allocating the lease premium, determining when the revenue should be recognised on the sale of the handsets on the agency agreement and recognising the write down of inventory. This type of question will continue in the future and therefore candidates should again practice the application of fundamental knowledge to a particular industry. One of the issues seemed to be that candidates did not appear to be able to draft answers where the main purpose of the question is to advise clients. Candidates seemed to be able to produce definitions without having the capability of applying those definitions.

## 43 CARPART (JUN 09 EXAM)  *Walk in the footsteps of a top tutor*

**Key answer tips**

This is a multi-topic question within a scenario of a motor vehicle parts manufacturer and who also purchases vehicles from the manufacturer to sell on to customers. The principal issues dealt with in the question include revenue recognition (IAS 18), property, plant and equipment (IAS 16) and leases (IAS 17).

(i) **Vehiclex**

*Revenue recognition principles require that elements or components should be accounted for separately for revenue recognition purposes.*

A transaction may contain separately identifiable components that should be accounted for separately. IAS 18 *Revenue* says that it is necessary to apply the recognition criteria to each separately identifiable component of a single transaction in order to reflect the substance of the transaction. In assessing the substance, the transaction should be viewed from the customer's perspective and not the seller. If the customer views the purchase as one product, then it is likely that the recognition criteria should be applied to the transaction as a whole. If there are a number of elements to the transaction, then the revenue recognition criteria should be applied to each element separately. In this case there is no contract to sell the machinery to Vehiclex and thus no revenue can be recognised in respect of the machinery. The machinery is for the use of Carpart and the contract is not a construction contract under IAS 11 *Construction contracts*. The machinery is accounted for under IAS 16 *Property, plant and equipment* and depreciated assuming that the future economic benefits of the machinery will flow to Carpart and the cost can be measured reliably. Carpart should conduct impairment reviews to ensure the carrying amount is not in excess of recoverable amount whenever there is deemed to be an indication of impairment. Seat orders not covering the minimum required would be an example of an impairment indicator. The impairment review of the machine would most probably need to be conducted with the machinery forming part of a cash generating unit. The contract to manufacture seats is not a service or construction contract but is a contract for the production of goods. The contract is a contract to sell goods and IAS 18 is applicable with revenue recognised on sale.

(ii)    **Autoseat**

*Consider whether an arrangement contains a lease – if so, then the lease should be accounted for in accordance with IAS 17.*

Companies often enter into agreements that do not take the legal form of a lease but still convey the right to use an asset in return for payment. IFRIC 4 *Determining whether an arrangement contains a lease* provides guidance on when such arrangements are leases. If it is determined that the arrangement constitutes a lease, then it is accounted for under IAS 17 *Leases*. IFRIC 4 sets out when the assessment should be made and how to deal with the payments. Under IFRIC 4, a lease is based on the substance of the arrangement which means assessing if:

(i)    fulfilment of the contract is dependent upon the use of a specified asset; and

(ii)    the contract conveys the right to use the asset. This means by operating the asset, controlling physical access, or if there is only a remote possibility that parties other than the purchaser will take more than a significant amount of the assets' output and the price the purchaser will pay is neither fixed per unit of output nor equal to the current market price.

In this case it seems that the contract contains a lease for the following reasons:

(i)    The completion of the contract depends upon the construction and use of a specific asset which is the specialised machinery which is dedicated to the production of the seats and cannot be used for other production. All of the output is to be sold to Autoseat who can inspect the seats and reject defective seats before delivery;

(ii)    The contract allows Autoseat the right to use the asset because it controls the underlying use as it is remote that any other party will receive any more than an insignificant amount of its production. The only customer is Autoseat who sets the levels of production and has a purchase option at any time;

(iii)   The price of the production is not fixed as it is a 'take or pay' contract as Autoseat is committed to fully repay the cost of the machinery, nor is it equal to the current market price because the supply is not marked to market during the contract;

(iv)   The payments for the lease are separable from any other elements in the contract (IFRIC 4) as Carpart will recover the cost of the machinery through a fixed price per seat over the life of the contract.

The contract contains a finance lease in the financial statements of Carpart because of the specialised nature of the machinery and because the contract is for the life of the asset (three years). The payments under the contract will be separated between the lease element and the revenue for the sale of the car seats. Carpart will recognise a lease receivable equal to the net present value of the minimum lease payments. Carpart does not normally sell machinery nor recognises revenue on the sale of machinery and, therefore, no gain or loss should be recognised on recognition and the initial carrying amount of the receivable will equal the production cost of the machinery (IAS 17, 43). Lease payments will be split into interest income and receipt of the lease receivables.

(Note that, although IFRIC 4 has been removed from the ACCA P2 syllabus from 2011, the principle it applies is still relevant and may still be examined.)

(iii)   **Car sales**

*Examine sale and repurchase agreements closely so that the underlying commercial purpose can be identified and accounted for.*

IAS 18 states that a sale and repurchase agreement for a non-financial asset must be analysed to determine if the seller has transferred the risks and rewards of ownership to the buyer. If this has occurred then revenue is recognised. Where the seller has retained the risks and rewards of ownership, the transaction is a financial arrangement even if the legal title has been transferred.

In the case of vehicles sold and repurchased at the end of the contract period, Carpart should recognise revenue on the sale of the vehicle. The residual risk that remains with Carpart is not significant at 20% of the sale price as this is thought to be significantly less than the market price. The agreed repurchase period also covers most of the vehicle's economic life. The car has to be maintained and serviced by the purchaser and must be returned in good condition. Thus the transfer of the significant risks and rewards of ownership to the buyer would appear to have taken place.

In the case of the sale with an option to repurchase, Carpart has not transferred the significant risks and rewards of ownership at the date of the transaction. The repurchase price is significant and the agreed repurchase period is less than substantially all of the economic life of the vehicle. The repurchase price is above the fair value of the vehicle and thus the risks of ownership have not been transferred. Also the company feels that the option will be exercised. The transaction is accounted for as an operating lease under IAS 17. The cars will be accounted for as operating leases until the option expires. The vehicles will be taken out of the inventory and debited to 'assets under operating lease' and depreciated over two years taking into account the estimated residual value. The cash received will be split between rentals received in advance (30%) and long-term liabilities (70%) which will be discounted. The rental income will be recognised in profit or loss over the two-year period.

**Demonstration vehicles**

*This is a relatively straightforward classification of cost as a capital item in accordance with IAS 16.*

The demonstration vehicles should be taken out of inventory and capitalised as property, plant and equipment (PPE) at cost. They meet the recognition criteria as they are held for demonstration purposes and are expected to be used in more than one accounting period. They should be depreciated whilst being used as demonstration vehicles and when they are to be sold they are reclassified from PPE to inventory and depreciation ceased.

| ACCA marking scheme | | |
|---|---|---|
| | | *Marks* |
| Vehicles | IAS 18 | 2 |
| | IAS 11 | 1 |
| | IAS 16 | 1 |
| Autoseat | IFRIC 4 | 3 |
| | Discussion | 3 |
| | Finance lease | 3 |
| Sale of vehicles | IAS 18 | 3 |
| | Repurchase 4 years | 2 |
| | Repurchase 2 years | 3 |
| | Demonstration | 2 |
| Professional marks | | 2 |
| | | — |
| Total | | 25 |
| | | — |

**Examiner's comments**

This question required candidates to discuss certain transactions of a vehicle part manufacturer, which sells vehicles purchased from itself. Additionally a discussion of certain supply arrangements for the supply of car seats to two local companies was required. The question required knowledge of IAS 18 *Revenue*, IAS 16 *Property, plant and equipment*, IFRIC 4 *Determining whether an arrangement contains a lease* and IAS 17 *Leases*. Candidates were required to apply the general principles in the standards to the scenario. Candidates found this quite difficult and often did not identify the nature of the transactions particularly the finance lease in part b of the question. Candidates could score good marks without any detailed knowledge of IFRIC 4 by simply applying the principles of IAS 17 or the Framework. Again the nature of the risks and rewards of ownership and the principles it embodies is essential to any P2 examination candidates often could not apply this principle to the question. Detailed knowledge of IFRIC 4 would have been useful but if candidates had applied the basic principles of the standards above, then they would have scored good marks. This did not always happen with the result that this question was the poorest answered on the paper.

## 44 BURLEY (DEC 09 EXAM)  *Walk in the footsteps of a top tutor*

**Key answer tips**

This three-part question is set in a scenario of an entity operating in the energy sector. Part (i) deals with revenue recognition (a topic regularly examined), together with inventory and associated issues for 10 marks. Part (ii) deals with issues mainly covered by IFRS 11 *Joint arrangements* to classify the situations therein as either joint ventures or joint operations, or something else, as appropriate. Part (iii) deals with the recognition and accounting for an intangible asset. Within each of the three parts there are relatively easy marks to be gained by stating and applying definitions and accounting treatments.

*Begin with stating the criteria for recognition of revenue relating to the sale of goods per IAS 18.*

(i) Revenue arising from the sale of goods should be recognised when all of the following criteria have been satisfied: [IAS 18 Para 14]

    (a) The seller has transferred to the buyer the significant risks and rewards of ownership;

    (b) The seller retains neither continuing managerial involvement to the degree usually associated with ownership nor effective control over the goods sold;

(c)     The amount of revenue can be measured reliably;

(d)     It is probable that the economic benefits associated with the transaction will flow to the seller; and

(e)     The costs incurred or to be incurred in respect of the transaction can be measured reliably.

*Develop your answer by applying the definition to the specific information within the question.*

Burley should recognise a purchase from Slite for the amount of the excess amount extracted (10,000 barrels × $100). The substance of the transaction is that Slite has sold the oil to Burley at the point of production at market value at that time. Burley should recognise all of the oil it has sold to the third parties as revenue including that purchased from Slite as the criteria in IAS 18 are met. The amount payable to Slite will change with movements in the oil price. The balance at the year-end is a financial liability, which should reflect the best estimate of the amount of cash payable, which at the year-end would be $1,050,000. The best estimate will be based on the price of oil on 30 November 2009. At the year-end there will be an expense of $50,000 as the liability will have increased from $1 million. The amount payable will be revised after the year-end to reflect changes in the price of oil and would have amounted to $950,000. Thus giving a gain of $100,000 to profit or loss in the following accounting period.

*Develop your answer by defining and applying the principles of IAS 10 Events after the reporting period, and IAS 2 Inventories*

Events after the reporting period are events, which could be favourable or unfavourable, and occur between the end of the reporting period and the date that the financial statements are authorised for issue. [IAS 10 Para 3]

An adjusting event is an event after the reporting period that provides further evidence of conditions that existed at the end of the reporting period, including an event that indicates that the going concern assumption in relation to the whole part or part of the enterprise is not appropriate. A non-adjusting event is an event after the reporting period that is indicative of a condition that arose after the end of the reporting period. [IAS 10 Para 3]

Inventories are required to be stated at the lower of cost and net realisable value (NRV). [IAS 2 Para 9] NRV is the estimated selling price in the ordinary course of business, less the estimated cost of completion and the estimated costs necessary to make the sale. Any write-down to NRV should be recognised as an expense in the period in which the write-down occurs. Estimates of NRV are based on the most reliable evidence available at the time the estimates are made. These estimates consider fluctuations in price directly relating to events occurring after the end of the financial period to the extent that they confirm conditions at the end of the accounting period.

Burley should calculate NRV by reference to the market price of oil at the reporting date. The price of oil changes frequently in response to many factors and therefore changes in the market price since the reporting date reflect events since that date. These represent non-adjusting events. Therefore the decline in the price of oil since the date of the financial statements will not be adjusted in those statements. The inventory will be valued at cost of $98 per barrel as this is lower than NRV of $(105 – 2) i.e. $103 at the year-end.

**Workings 1**

|  |  | DR($000) | CR($000) |
|---|---|---|---|
| Purchases/inventory | (10,000 × 100) | 1,000 | |
| Slite – financial liability | | | 1,000 |
| At year end: | | | |
| Expense | (10,000 × ($105 – 100)) | 50 | |
| Slite – financial liability | | | 50 |
| After year end | | | |
| Slite – financial liability | (10,000 × ($105 – 95)) | 100 | |
| Profit or loss | | | 100 |

Cash paid to Slite is $950,000 on 12 December 2009

(ii)

*Begin by stating and applying the relevant definitions from IFRS 11 Joint arrangements. Continue by explaining the permitted accounting treatments.*

A joint arrangement is defined by IFRS 11 *Joint arrangements*, (which supersedes IAS 31 Interests in joint ventures) as "an arrangement of which two or more parties have joint control" (para 4). Joint control is identified as being "contractually agreed sharing of control which....require...unanimous consent of the parties sharing control" (para 7). Joint arrangements are then classified into being either a joint operation or a joint venture.

Based upon the information in the question, it states that decision-making related to Wells can be made by a majority of the three equity-holders. Consequently, it would appear that the investment in Wells cannot be regarded as being a joint arrangement within the definition of IFRS 11.

As Burley, Jorge and Heavy Wells have an interest in Wells which does not meet the definition of a joint arrangement, it would appear that they are each able to exercise significant influence over Wells; consequently, they should each regard the investment in Wells as an associate and apply equity accounting when accounting for their respective interest in Wells.

The intention of Burley to apply proportionate consolidation is therefore inappropriate. Proportionate consolidation was permitted by IAS 31 in specific circumstances where there was a jointly controlled entity, but this accounting treatment is not permitted by IFRS 11.

One of the key differences between decommissioning costs and other costs of acquisition is the timing of costs. Decommissioning costs will not become payable until some future date. Consequently, there is likely to be uncertainty over the amount of costs that will be incurred. Management should record its best estimate of the entity's obligations. [IAS 16.16]

Discounting is used to address the impact of the delayed cash flows. The amount capitalised, as part of the assets will be the amount estimated to be paid, discounted to the date of initial recognition. The related credit is recognised in provisions. An entity that uses the cost model records changes in the existing liability and changes in discount rate are added to, or deducted from, the cost of the related asset in the current period. [IFRIC 1.5]

Thus in the case of Wells, the accounting for the decommissioning is as follows.

The carrying amount of the asset will be:

|  |  | $m |
|---|---|---|
| Carrying amount at 1 Dec 08 | (240 – dep'n 60 – 14.1 decrease In decommissioning costs) | 165.9 |
| *Less* depreciation | 165.9 ÷ 30 years | (5.5) |
| Carrying amount at 30 Nov 2009 |  | 160.4 |
| Finance cost | ($32.6 million – $14.1 million) @7% | 1.3 |
| Decommissioning liability will be: | ($32.6m – $14.1m) | 18.5 |
| Decommissioning liability at 30 Nov 09 |  | 19.8 |

The pipeline is identified as being a jointly-controlled asset between Burley and other entities. If this is the case, all parties must act in concert together to make unanimous decisions regarding the relevant activities (i.e. financial and operating policies) relating to that asset. This arrangement meets the definition of a joint operation from IFRS 11 in that "the parties that have joint control of the arrangement have rights to the assets and obligations for the liabilities, relating to the arrangement" (App A IFRS 11)

Consequently, jointly controlled assets involve the joint control, and often the joint ownership, of assets dedicated to the joint venture. Each venturer may take a share of the output from the assets and each bears a share of the expenses incurred. The pipeline is a jointly controlled asset. Therefore, Burley should not show the asset as an investment but as property, plant and equipment. Any liabilities or expenses incurred should be shown also.

(iii)

*Begin by stating the definition of an asset from the Framework document and develop your answer by referring to the definition of an intangible asset from IAS 38.*

An asset is a resource controlled by the enterprise as a result of past events and from which future economic benefits are expected to flow to the enterprise. [Framework. Para 49(a)] An asset is recognised in the statement of financial position when it is probable that the future economic benefits will flow to the enterprise and the asset has a cost or value that can be measured reliably. [Framework Para 89]

IAS 38 *Intangible assets* also requires an enterprise to recognise an intangible asset, whether purchased or self-created (at cost) if, and only if: [IAS 38]

(a)   it is probable that the future economic benefits that are attributable to the asset will flow to the enterprise; and

(b)   the cost of the asset can be measured reliably.

This requirement applies whether an intangible asset is acquired externally or generated internally.

The probability of future economic benefits must be based on reasonable and supportable assumptions about conditions that will exist over the life of the asset. [IAS 38] The probability recognition criterion is always considered to be satisfied for intangible assets that are acquired separately or in a business combination. [IAS 38] IAS 36 *Impairment of assets* also says that at each balance sheet date, an entity should review all assets to look for any indication that an asset may be impaired (its carrying amount may be in excess of the greater of its net selling price and its value in use). IAS 36 has a list of external and internal indicators of impairment. If there is an indication that an asset may be impaired, then the asset's recoverable amount should be calculated. [IAS 36] Thus the licence can be capitalised and if the exploration of the area does not lead to the discovery of oil, and activities are discontinued in the area, then an impairment test will be performed.

| ACCA marking scheme | |
|---|---|
| | *Marks* |
| Revenue recognition | 4 |
| Inventory | 3 |
| Events after reporting period | 2 |
| Joint arrangements | 3 |
| Accounting for entity | 2 |
| Decommissioning | 5 |
| Asset definition/IAS 38/IAS 36 | 4 |
| Professional marks | 2 |
| | —— |
| Total | 25 |
| | —— |

**Examiner's comments**

This question was a case study type question based around a company in the oil industry. It involved knowledge of revenue recognition principles, events after the reporting period, inventory, accounting for jointly controlled entities, decommissioning costs and intangible assets. The question was quite well answered with candidates setting out the principles of revenue recognition quite well. The application of the knowledge was not quite of the same standard. The answers to the second part of the question require determining the relationship between the entity and another entity. The interest in the entity was that of an equity interest but many candidates felt that the entity was jointly controlled and that proportionate consolidation could be used instead of equity accounting. The accounting for decommissioning costs was quite well answered with many students gaining the correct answer for the decommissioning liability. The final part required candidates to apply IAS 38 *Intangible assets* to a scenario. Again, the answers were of a good standard, although the main weakness was in the application of the knowledge.

## 45 SHIRES PROPERTY CONSTRUCTION

**Key answer tips**

This three-part question is a good question to help you work through the process of applying a reconstruction scheme. It is unlikely that you would be asked to prepare journal entries, but this may help you to work through the process logically and they are provided for reference. Much of the revised statement of financial position can be compiled from information provided about new carrying values, without necessarily preparing a reconstruction account, although this may be required as part of your workings for the finished answer. The last two parts of the question involve explanation and comment, so don't regard this type of question as purely a 'number crunching' exercise; questions in part (b) of the exam paper invariably have a written element.

(a) **Shires Property Construction**

**Statement of financial position at 1 January 2010 (after reconstruction)**

| | $ | |
|---|---|---|
| Non-current assets: | | |
| Land at valuation | | 90,000 |
| Building at valuation | | 80,000 |
| Equipment at valuation | | 10,000 |
| | | ——— |
| | | 180,000 |
| Current assets: | | |
| Inventories at valuation | 50,000 | |
| Trade receivables ($70,692 × 90%) | 63,623 | |
| Cash at bank (W5) | 46,287 | 159,910 |
| | ——— | ——— |
| | | 339,910 |
| | | ——— |
| Equity and liabilities | | |
| Equity shares @ $0.25 (W4) | | 142,500 |
| Share premium | | 17,500 |
| Retained earnings | | nil |
| Capital reconstruction reserve (W1) | | 5,663 |
| | | ——— |
| | | 165,663 |
| Non-current liabilities: | | |
| 9.5% Debenture 2013 | 89,000 | |
| 8.0% Unsecured loan | 35,000 | |
| | ——— | 124,000 |
| Current liabilities: | | |
| Trade payables | | 50,247 |
| | | ——— |
| | | 339,910 |
| | | ——— |

### (b) Division of pre-tax profit

| Interested parties | | Before reconstruction | After reconstruction |
|---|---|---|---|
| Debenture holders | | $ | $ |
| Gross interest | (W2) | 6,400 | 8,455 |
| 5,000 equity shares | (W4) | | 1,360 |
| | | 6,400 | 9,815 |
| Unsecured loan | | | |
| Gross interest | (W3) | 3,500 | 2,800 |
| 35,000 equity shares | (W4) | | 9,516 |
| | | | 12,316 |
| Directors | (W4) | | 680 |
| Balance to equity shareholders | (W4) | 40,100 | 27,189 |
| | | 50,000 | 50,000 |

The allocation of profit, both before and after the reconstruction, reflects respective interests of those who provide the long-term finance or the entity: the debenture holders, the unsecured loan holders and providers of equity finance.

The providers of loan finance will increase their share of available profit after the reconstruction. This could be regarded as reasonable as their continued support is required if the reconstruction is to be successful. Similarly, the proportion of available profit to which equity holders would be entitled has fallen, reflecting their relatively weak position before the reconstruction is implemented.

### (c) Comments on the capital structure

Gearing is: ($35,000 + $89,000) / ($165,663 = $124,000) = 42.8%

Whether gearing is viewed as high or not depends upon the current economic climate. It will however reduce when the debenture loan is paid off in 2013. Indeed, dividends on equity shares will have to be very restrained if cash is to be available to redeem the debentures. Alternatively, debenture holders might agree to exchange them for equity shares.

The shareholders' equity almost covers approximately 92% of the carrying value of the non-current assets. The capital structure is reasonably satisfactory.

The debenture holders have done very well. Their interest has been increased by 1.5% and the redemption date has not been changed.

The providers of the unsecured loan have also received an increase in the rate of interest to be charged on that loan.

*Workings*

(W1) **Trial balance after reconstruction**

| | $ | $ |
|---|---|---|
| Land | 90,000 | |
| Buildings | 80,000 | |
| Equipment | 10,000 | |
| Inventories | 50,000 | |
| Trade receivables | 63,623 | |
| Cash | 46,287 | |
| Equity shares @$0.25 | | 142,500 |
| Share premium | | 17,500 |
| 8% Unsecured loan | | 35,000 |
| 9.5% debenture loan 2013 | | 89,000 |
| Trade payables | | 50,247 |
| Reconstruction account (bal fig) | | 5,663 |
| | 339,910 | 339,910 |

| Reconstruction account: | $ | $ |
|---|---|---|
| Retained earnings deficit | 39,821 | |
| Brand w/off | 60,000 | |
| Receivables w/off | 7,069 | |
| Redesignation of equity shares to $0.25 | | 150,000 |
| Land revalued | 66,000 | |
| Building revalued | | 52,754 |
| Equipment revalued | 754 | |
| Inventory revalued | 70,247 | |
| Deb interest arrears cancelled | | 7,800 |
| Directors loans cancelled | | 6,000 |
| Gain on disposal of financial assets | | 33,000 |
| Capital reconstruction reserve (bal fig) | 5,663 | |
| | 249,554 | 249,554 |

(W2) **Debenture loan interest gross**

Before    8% × $80,000 = $6,400

After    9.5% × $89,000 = $8,455

This does, of course, include interest on capitalised interest.

(W3) **Unsecured loan interest gross**

Before    5% × $70,000 = $3,500

After    8% × $35,000 = $2,800

(W4) **The balance of the retained earnings of $50,000 belongs to the equity shareholders**

|  | $ | $ |  | $ | $ |
|---|---|---|---|---|---|
| **Before** |  | 50,000 | **After** | 50,000 |  |
| Less: Deb interest | (6,400) |  |  | (8,455) |  |
| Unsecured loan interest | (3,500) |  |  | (2,800) |  |
|  |  | (9,900) |  |  | (11,255) |
| Available for equity shareholders |  | 40,100 |  |  | 38,745 |

| After reconstruction: | Shares @ $0.25 No. | Shares @ $0.25 $ | Share premium $ |
|---|---|---|---|
| Debenture holders | 20,000 | 5,000 |  |
| Unsecured loan | 140,000 | 35,000 |  |
| Directors' shares | 10,000 | 2,500 | 7,500 |
| Other shareholders | 400,000 | 100,000 | 10,000 |
|  | 570,000 | 142,500 | 17,500 |

| Profits available to pay dividends |  | $ |
|---|---|---|
| Debenture holders | 20,000/570,000 × $38,745 | 1,360 |
| Unsecured loan | 140,000/570,000 × $38,745 | 9,516 |
| Directors | 10,000/570,000 × $38,745 | 680 |
| Original equity holders | 400,000/570,000 × $38,745 | 27,189 |
|  |  | 38,745 |

(W5) **Bank balance:**

| Note ref |  | $ |
|---|---|---|
|  | Overdraft brought forward | (36,713) |
| 3 | Share issue @ $0.30 | 60,000 |
| 4 | Additional debenture loan | 9,000 |
| 7 | Disposal proceeds of financial assets | 60,000 |
| 9 | Payment to trade payables | (46,000) |
|  | Closing bank balance | 46,287 |

**Journal entries (for reference only)**

|  |  | Dr | Cr |
|---|---|---|---|
|  |  | $ | $ |
| (1) | Equity shares of $1 each | 200,000 |  |
|  | Equity shares of $0.25 each |  | 50,000 |
|  | Reconstruction account |  | 150,000 |

Re-designation of issued equity share capital as $0.25 shares (formerly $1 shares) and transferring excess nominal value to reconstruction account.

| (2) | 5% unsecured loan | 70,000 |  |
|---|---|---|---|
|  | 8% unsecured loan |  | 35,000 |
|  | Equity shares of $0.25 each |  | 35,000 |

Exchange of 5% unsecured loan for 8% unsecured loan and 140,000 equity shares of $0.25 each.

| (3) | Cash | 60,000 |  |
|---|---|---|---|
|  | Equity shares of $0.25 each – 200,000 |  | 50,000 |
|  | Share premium account $0.05 – 200,000 |  | 10,000 |

Issue of 200,000 $0.25 equity shares at an issue price of $0.30 to the original equity shareholders.

| (4)(a) | Interest payable on debentures | 12,800 |  |
|---|---|---|---|
|  | Equity shares of $0.25 each – 20,000 |  | 5,000 |
|  | Reconstruction account |  | 7,800 |

Issue of shares and capitalisation of unpaid debenture interest

| (4)(b) | 8% Debenture loan 2013 | 80,000 |  |
|---|---|---|---|
|  | 9.5% Debenture loan 2013 |  | 80,000 |

Increase in interest rate on 2013 Debenture loan to 9.5%.

| (4)(c) | Cash | 9,000 |  |
|---|---|---|---|
|  | 9.5% Debenture 2013 |  | 9,000 |

Issue of $9,000 debentures at par value for cash.

| (5) | Loans from directors | 16,000 |  |
|---|---|---|---|
|  | Equity shares of $0.25 each – 10,000 |  | 2,500 |
|  | Share premium |  | 7,500 |
|  | Reconstruction account |  | 6,000 |

Capitalisation and writing off of directors' loans.

| (6) | Reconstruction account | 99,821 |  |
|---|---|---|---|
|  | Intangible asset – brand |  | 60,000 |
|  | Retained earnings |  | 39,821 |

Brand and deficit on retained earnings written off.

| (7) | Cash | 60,000 |  |
|---|---|---|---|
|  | Financial assets at FVTPorL |  | 27,000 |
|  | Reconstruction account |  | 33,000 |

Sale of financial assets at a profit of $33,000.

| (8) | No journal entry required. |  |  |
|---|---|---|---|

| (9) | Trade payables | 46,000 |  |
|---|---|---|---|
|  | Cash |  | 46,000 |

Payment made to trade payables.

|  | | | |
|---|---|---|---|
| (10) | Reconstruction account | 7,069 | |
| | Trade receivables | | 7,069 |
| | Write-off of bad debts. | | |
| (11) | Land | | 66,000 |
| | Building | 52,754 | |
| | Equipment | | 754 |
| | Inventories | | 70,247 |
| | Reconstruction account | 84,247 | |
| | Revaluation of non-current assets. | | |
| | | 137,001 | 137,001 |

| ACCA marking scheme | | |
|---|---|---|
| | | Marks |
| (a) | Statement of financial position | 12 |
| (b) | Division of operating profits | 8 |
| (c) | Comments on capital structure | 5 |
| Total | | 25 |

## 46 BOOMERANG

**Key answer tips**

This question has several requirements, which are mainly narrative, which reflects the expectation that question format within Section B of the examination paper will be mainly narrative. The answer to this question is perhaps longer than could reasonably be produced under examination conditions; however, the comprehensive answer is a good learning tool. You should try to answer each part of the question requirement, applying the respective legal rights of the various interest groups to ensure appropriate allocation of assets and/or profits based upon their respective legal entitlement.

(a) **MEMORANDUM**

To:     Finance Director – Boomerang

From:   Advisor

Re:     Draft proposals for scheme of capital reduction and reorganisation of Boomerang

("the scheme") as at 31 October 2012

Thank you for a copy of the draft scheme.

In our view, one of the key considerations for the court and the various parties whose rights are being varied is whether the scheme is fair to all parties.

We have therefore reviewed the scheme as a whole and particularly from the perspective of each of the interested parties, including whether they would be likely to approve the scheme as required.

**Liquidation:**

Upon liquidation, the assets are realised and liabilities settled, with any surplus remaining going to the equity shareholders. If the company is insolvent, they are unlikely to receive any payment upon liquidation.

Creditors are paid off based upon their relative priority. A fixed charge holder is paid from the proceeds of the asset(s) subject to that charge. If the fixed charge asset(s) are insufficient to repay the charge holder, the charge holder becomes an unsecured creditor the balance still outstanding.

Floating charge holders are paid from the proceeds of the assets subject to that charge, subject to first paying out preferential creditors such as unpaid wages. If the floating charge holder has not been repaid in full, that charge-holder becomes an unsecured creditor for the balance outstanding.

If the amounts following reconstruction are used as a guide to realisable values of the various assets and liabilities (this many not necessarily be the case), the following is an indication of the likely outcome:

|  | $ | $ |
|---|---|---|
| Freehold property disposed of | | 700,000 |
| Leasehold property | | 370,000 |
| Plant and equipment | | 675,000 |
| Inventory – subject to floating charge | 400,000 | |
| Receivables – subject to floating charge | 225,000 | |
| Less: preferential creditors - wages | (260,000) | |
| Less: preferential creditors – professional fees | (40,000) | |
| Balance –available to floating charge holder | 325,000 | |
| 8% debenture | (540,000) | |
| Balance as unsecured creditor | (215,000) | 1,745,000 |
| Other unsecured creditors: | | |
| 4% debenture | (170,000) | |
| Corporate tax liabilities | (190,000) | |
| Trade payables | (576,000) | |
| Bank overdraft | (494,000) | (1,645,000) |
| Available for equity holders | | 100,000 |

The preferential creditors for unpaid wages and professional fees associated with liquidation would be paid in full from realisation of inventory and receivables. However, there would be insufficient funds from those assets to fully repay the 8% debenture holder. The unpaid balance would then be classified as an unsecured creditor.

All of the unsecured creditors would rank equally for repayment from the remaining assets – there would appear to be just enough realisable proceeds from the remaining assets. In effect, there would be a negligible dividend (i.e. return of capital) to the equity shareholders. Note that if any of the realisable values of the assets were significantly less than the amounts used above, the unsecured creditors would bear the loss on a pro rata basis.

(b) **Overview of the scheme**

One of the principal issues facing Boomerang at present is the accumulated deficit on retained earnings following several years of unprofitable trading. This means that, even if Boomerang were to commence trading profitably, the deficit would need to be cleared before there was any possibility of a dividend being paid to the equity shareholders. How long this may take would depend upon profitability and would require the continued patience of equity shareholders.

Another principal issue is the extent of the bank overdraft which is approximately $500,000 and which the bank has requested that steps be taken to reduce it. As the 8% debenture is secured against the inventory and receivables, the overdraft would only be repaid if there were sufficient assets to meet all claims of unsecured creditors. If the 8% debenture could not be repaid from the proceeds of realising the inventory and receivables, any unpaid amount would rank as an unsecured creditor and potentially increase the risk of less than full recovery of the overdraft by the bank.

Additionally, the 4% debenture is due for repayment in early 2013 and there is currently little prospect of being able to repay this as the bank is unwilling to increase the overdraft facility and there are likely to be problems finding significant additional sources of equity finance.

**The immediate future:**

If the profit forecast by Boomerang is reliable, the following is likely to result:

|  | $ |
|---|---|
| Profit before interest and tax | 200,000 |
| Less: interest 8% × $540,000 | (43,200) |
|  |  |
| Profit before tax | 156,800 |
| Tax @ 25% | (39,200) |
|  |  |
| Profit after tax for the year | 117,600 |

The consequences of implementing the scheme can be summarised as follows:

(i) The bank overdraft would be reduced, but not cleared in the short term.

(ii) The 4% debenture due for repayment in 2013 would be paid in full.

(iii) There is a significant commercial risk that trade creditors and other providers of finance may not be willing to continue supporting the business if they are unlikely to receive repayment of interest and/or capital on normal due dates.

(iv) The possibility of raising additional finance for working capital in 2015, whether in the form of an issue of shares or increased loan finance, would be subject to considerable uncertainty.

(v) At this level of annual profit, all other factors remaining unchanged, it would take approximately (340,000 / 117,600) three years to clear the deficit on retained earnings and offer the possibility of a dividend from profits to equity shareholders.

(vi) This This level of profit equates to earnings per share of (117,600 / 2,100,000) 5.6 cents per share.

**Holder of 10% of the equity before reconstruction**

Following reconstruction, the shareholder will own (135,000 / 2,100,000) approximately 6.4% of the equity shares in issue. The proportionate voting power will be reduced if the reconstruction scheme is implemented. In addition, due to the increase in the number of shares in issue, profits available for distribution in the form of a dividend will need to be spread across an increased number of shareholders.

Even if the scheme is implemented, as there is still a deficit on retained earnings, this will need to be cleared before dividends could be paid. If the forecast level of profit is reliable, it would take three years before shareholders would potentially receive a dividend.

If Boomerang was liquidated, equity shareholders would receive a minimal amount. Arguably, the shareholder has nothing to lose by approving the reconstruction. They may benefit from some future return for no further outlay.

**8% debenture holder**

If Boomerang was liquidated, the 8% debenture holder would be repaid in full if the estimate of realisable values was reliable. The assets subject to the floating charge are, on their own, insufficient to ensure recovery of the amount due to the debenture holder. The debenture holder would rank as an unsecured creditor for part of the amount due, as preferential creditors must be paid in priority to floating charge holders.

The debenture holder may be tempted to take full recovery now, rather than risk less than full recovery at some later date if future trading is less profitable than expected. The debenture holder may be encouraged to support the scheme if the floating charge is extended to cover the business as a whole, providing more security to the debenture holder. Another factor that may encourage the debenture holder to support the scheme would be to increase the rate of interest they receive so as to counteract any increase in risk they are accepting.

**The bank**

The bank is a primary source of working capital for Boomerang, and it is likely that Boomerang would not be able to continue in business without this support.

The bank, as an unsecured creditor, is in a relatively weak position to recover the amount outstanding in the event of liquidation or upon breach of the terms and conditions of the overdraft agreement.

Based upon the available information, in the event of liquidation, the bank would fully recover the amounts advanced to Boomerang. In common with the position of the debenture holder as an unsecured creditor, full recovery is dependent upon realisation of assets for at least the values expected. If this did not happen, unsecured creditors would bear any shortfall on a pro rata basis.

The bank overdraft would be substantially reduced if the scheme was implemented. This would ease some of the concerns raised by the bank, but would still leave it exposed to potential future losses if future trading following reconstruction was not profitable or did not generate sufficient cash inflows to pay liabilities.

The bank may be willing to consider reclassifying part of their overdraft as a long-term loan, with an agreed schedule of repayments. This would also ease part of the immediate pressure on liquidity currently faced by Boomerang, with a beneficial impact upon liquidity ratios and short-term working capital management.

The bank may be encouraged to support any reconstruction scheme by having a charge against some or all of the assets not already subject to a charge. This could be problematical as there are only limited assets available and numerous competing interests (debenture holder, preferential creditors, other unsecured creditors) who would all like to reduce their exposure to risk by having amounts due to them secured.

### Trade creditors

Currently, all trade creditors, who will be unsecured creditors, would be repaid in full if Boomerang was to be liquidated.

Whether they can be persuaded to support the scheme, rather than simply recovering what is due to them now, may not be a straightforward judgement for them to make.

Clearly, if Boomerang were to continue trading and make a profit, that would mean continued sales revenue for the suppliers. If future trading was not profitable, trade creditors would be at risk of not recovering all of the amounts due to them.

As individual creditors, they could take protective action, such as selling to Boomerang on a cash basis only, or by factoring receivables where sales have been made to Boomerang on credit. They could also impose lower credit limits than has previously been the case and strictly enforce the terms of business with Boomerang to minimise their risk of loss.

(c) **Additional tax liabilities**

The decision of the tax authorities is an adjusting event as defined by IAS 10 *Events after the reporting period*. Therefore, at the reporting date, it would appear that a provision is required in accordance with IAS 37 *Provisions, contingent liabilities and contingent assets* for the additional tax liabilities as they relate to past transactions and events and it is probable that they cannot be avoided.

If the decision to appeal is considered, application of IAS 10 suggests that this is a non-adjusting event as the decision to appeal only arises following the decision of the tax authorities communicated on 5 November - it does not affect the situation at the reporting date. As a non-adjusting event, the financial statements should not be adjusted to reflect this information. It is not relevant that an independent professional advisor considers that it is likely the decision of the tax authorities will be overturned.

There should be disclosure only of the decision to appeal, unless the ability to continue as a going concern is threatened.

| ACCA marking scheme | | Marks |
|---|---|---|
| (a) | Liquidation of Boomerang | 7 |
| (b) | Reconstruction – overview and interested parties | 15 |
| (c) | Additional tax liabilities | 3 |
| | | —— |
| Total | | 25 |
| | | —— |

**Note:** the marking scheme is a suggested allocation of marks. Appropriate credit should be given where reasonable comments have been made.

# CURRENT ISSUES

## 47 TRANSITION (JUN 08 EXAM)

(a) The transition to International Financial Reporting Standards (IFRS) involves major change for companies as IFRS introduces significant changes in accounting practices that often were not required by national GAAPs. For example financial instruments and share-based payment plans in many instances have appeared on the statements of financial position of companies for the first time in recent years. As a result IFRS financial statements are often significantly more complex than financial statements based on national GAAP. This complexity is caused by the more extensive recognition and measurement rules in IFRS and a greater number of disclosure requirements. Because of this complexity, it can be difficult for users of financial statements which have been produced using IFRS to understand and interpret them, and thus can lead to inconsistency of interpretation of those financial statements.

The form and presentation of financial statements is dealt with by IAS 1 *Presentation of financial statements*. This standard sets out alternative forms or presentations of financial statements. Additionally local legislation often requires supplementary information to be disclosed in financial statements, and best practice as to the form or presentation of financial statements takes time to emerge internationally. As a result companies moving to IFRS have tended to adopt IFRS in a way which minimises the change in the form of financial reporting that was applied under national GAAP. For example UK companies have tended to present a statement of recognised income and expense, and a separate statement of changes in equity whilst French companies tend to present a single statement of changes in equity.

It is possible to interpret standards in different ways and in some standards there is insufficient guidance. For example there are different acceptable methods of classifying financial assets under IFRS 9 *Financial instruments* in the statement of financial position as at fair value through profit or loss or (subject to certain conditions) at amortised cost.

IFRSs are not based on a consistent set of principles, and there are conceptual inconsistencies within and between standards.

To some extent, this source of inconsistency is being reduced as a result of:

- the drive towards convergence of IFRS and US GAAP, and
- the development of the Conceptual Framework for Financial Reporting 2010, which is part of the convergence process between IFRS and US GAAP.

Recently issued reporting standards which increase the degree of convergence between IFRS and US GAAP include IFR3 10 *Consolidated financial statements* which specifies criteria to determine whether one entity controls another and should therefore be included within consolidated financial statements. IFRS 11 *Joint arrangements* has removed the accounting policy choice previously permitted by its predecessor IAS 31, and now requires a more standardised form of accounting, depending upon whether a joint operation or a joint venture is being accounted for. IFRS 13 *Fair value measurement* now specifies a definitive definition of what constitutes a fair value measurement and how this may be determined when preparing financial statements.

Certain standards allow alternative accounting treatments, and this is a further source of inconsistency amongst financial statements. Companies may tend to use the method which was used under national GAAP. Another example of choice in accounting methods under IFRS is IAS 16 *Property, plant and equipment* where the cost or revaluation model can be used for a class of property, plant and equipment. Also there is very little industry related accounting guidance in IFRS. As a result judgement plays an important role in the selection of accounting policies. In certain specific areas this can lead to a degree of inconsistency and lack of comparability. It is also true to say that some of the more recently issued or revised reporting standards reduce the range or number of permitted accounting treatments; for example revision of IAS 23 *Borrowing costs* requires capitalisation of borrowing costs if they meet specified criteria, rather than allowing a choice of accounting treatment.

IFRS 1 *First time adoption of International Financial Reporting Standards*, allows companies to use a number of exemptions from the requirements of IFRS. These exemptions can affect financial statements for several years. For example, companies can elect to recognise all cumulative actuarial gains and losses relating to post-employment benefits at the date of transition to IFRS but use the 'corridor' approach thereafter. Thus the effect of being able to use a 'one off write off' of any actuarial losses could benefit future financial statements significantly, and affect comparability. Additionally after utilising the above exemption, companies can elect to recognise subsequent gains and losses outside profit or loss in 'other comprehensive income' in the period in which they occur and not use the 'corridor' approach thus affecting comparability further.

Additionally IAS 18 *Revenue* allows variations in the way revenue is recognised. For example some telecom operations defer part of the revenue received from customers where future benefits have been granted to customers under loyalty programmes, whilst others make a provision for the cost of the scheme. The identification of the functional currency under IAS 21 *The effects of changes in foreign exchange rates*, can be subjective. For example the functional currency can be determined by the currency in which the commodities that a company produces are commonly traded, or the currency which influences its operating costs, and both can be different.

Another source of inconsistency is the adoption of new standards and interpretations earlier than the due date of application of the standard. With the IASB currently developing new or revised reporting standards, early adoption or lack of it could affect comparability although IAS 8 *Accounting policies, changes in accounting estimates and errors* requires a company to disclose the possible impact of a new standard on its initial application. For example, IFRS 9 *Financial instruments*, issued in November 2009, is effective for all accounting periods commencing on or after 1 January 2013, with early adoption permitted. The standard also includes an element of transitional relief from restatement of comparatives for early adoption. It is not hard to see that, until IFRS 9 is fully implemented by all entities, there may be a lack of comparability in reported results during this transition period. Many companies make very little reference to the future impact of new standards.

(b) Management judgement may have a greater impact under IFRS than generally was the case under national GAAP. IFRS utilises fair values extensively. Management have to use their judgement in selecting valuation methods and formulating assumptions when dealing with such areas as onerous contracts, share-based payments, pensions, intangible assets acquired in business combinations and impairment of assets. Differences in methods or assumptions can have a major impact on amounts recognised in financial statements. IAS 1 expects companies to disclose the sensitivity of carrying amounts to the methods, assumptions and estimates underpinning their calculation where there is a significant risk of material adjustment to their carrying amounts within the next financial year. Often management's judgement is that there is no 'significant risk' and they often fail to disclose the degree of estimation or uncertainty and thus comparability is affected.

In addition to the IFRSs themselves, a sound financial reporting infrastructure is required. This implies effective corporate governance practices, high quality auditing standards and practices, and an effective enforcement or oversight mechanism. Therefore, consistency and comparability of IFRS financial statements will also depend on the robust nature of the other elements of the financial reporting infrastructure.

Many preparers of financial statements will have been trained in national GAAP and may not have been trained in the principles underlying IFRS and this can lead to unintended inconsistencies when implementing IFRS especially where the accounting profession does not have a CPD requirement. Additionally where the regulatory system of a country is not well developed, there may not be sufficient market information to utilise fair value measurements and thus this could lead to hypothetical markets being created or the use of mathematical modelling which again can lead to inconsistencies because of lack of experience in those countries of utilising these techniques. This problem applies to other assessments or estimates relating to such things as actuarial valuations, investment property valuations, impairment testing, etc.

The transition to IFRS can bring significant improvement to the quality of financial performance and improve comparability worldwide. However, there are issues still remaining which can lead to inconsistency and lack of comparability with those financial statements.

| | ACCA marking scheme | Marks |
|---|---|---|
| (a) | Changes from national GAAP | 2 |
| | Complexity | 1 |
| | Recognition, measurement, disclosure | 2 |
| | Alternative forms of presentation | 1 |
| | Inconsistent principles | 2 |
| | Alternate accounting treatments | 3 |
| | Little industry related guidance | 1 |
| | IFRS 1 | 2 |
| | Interpretation of IFRS | 2 |
| | Adoption date | 1 |
| | | 17 |
| (b) | Management judgments | 2 |
| | Disclosure of sensitivity | 1 |
| | Regulatory infrastructure | 2 |
| | Training/markets | 1 |
| | Communication | 2 |
| | | 8 |
| Total | | 25 |

**Examiner's comments**

This question dealt with the transition to IFRS, whether this has brought greater consistency to financial statements and also in some papers whether consistency between local GAAP and IFRS is important. The second part of the question dealt with the importance of management judgement and the local regulatory framework in ensuring that confidence can be placed in financial statements. Surprisingly few candidates answered this question but those that did scored well. Candidates' answers dealt with the inconsistencies in the standards, lack of appropriate guidance, choice of accounting practice and problems with implementation of the standards. The part of the question dealing with management judgement and the regulatory framework was not as well answered but generally the answers dealt with issues surrounding fair values and the use of assumptions.

## 48 FRAMEWORK (DEC 07 EXAM)

(a)   The IASB wish their standards to be 'principles-based' and in order for this to be the case, the standards must be based on fundamental concepts. These concepts need to constitute a framework which is sound, comprehensive and internally consistent. Without agreement on a framework, standard setting is based upon the personal conceptual frameworks of the individual standard setters which may change as the membership of the body changes and results in standards that are not consistent with each other. Such a framework is designed not only to assist standard setters, but also preparers of financial statements, auditors and users.

A common goal of the IASB is to converge their standards with national standard setters. The IASB will encounter difficulties converging their standards if decisions are based on different frameworks. The IASB has been pursuing a number of projects that are aimed at achieving short term convergence on certain issues with national standard setters as well as major projects with them. Convergence will be difficult if there is no consistency in the underlying framework being used.

Frameworks differ in their authoritative status. The IASB's Framework, introduced in 1989, requires management to expressly consider the Framework if no standard or interpretation specifically applies or deals with a similar and related issue. However, certain frameworks have a lower standing. For example, entities are not required to consider the concepts embodied in certain national frameworks in preparing financial statements. Thus the development of an agreed framework would eliminate differences in the authoritative standing of conceptual frameworks and lead to greater consistency in financial statements internationally.

The existing concepts within most frameworks are quite similar. However, these concepts need revising to reflect changes in markets, business practices and the economic environment since the concepts were developed. The existing frameworks need developing to reflect these changes and to fill gaps in the frameworks. For example, the IASB's Framework does not contain a definition of the reporting entity. An agreed international framework could deal with this problem, especially if priority was given to the issues likely to give short-term standard setting benefits.

Many standard setting bodies attempted initially to resolve accounting and reporting problems by developing accounting standards without an accepted theoretical frame of reference. The result has been inconsistency in the development of standards both nationally and internationally. The frameworks were developed when several of their current standards were in existence. In the absence of an agreed conceptual framework the same theoretical issues are revisited on several occasions by standard setters. The result is inconsistencies and incompatible concepts. Examples of this are substance over form and matching versus prudence. Some standard setters such as the IASB permit two methods of accounting for the same set of circumstances. An example is the accounting for joint ventures where the equity method and proportionate consolidation are allowed.

Additionally there have been differences in the way that standard setters have practically used the principles in the framework. Some national standard setters have produced a large number of highly detailed accounting rules with less emphasis on general principles. A robust framework might reduce the need for detailed rules although some companies operate in a different legal and statutory context than other entities. It is important that a framework must result in standards that account appropriately for actual business practice.

An agreed framework will not solve all accounting issues, nor will it obviate the need for judgement to be exercised in resolving accounting issues. It can provide a framework within which those judgements can be made.

A framework provides standard setters with both a foundation for setting standards, and concepts to use as tools for resolving accounting and reporting issues. A framework provides a basic reasoning on which to consider the merits of alternatives. It does not provide all the answers, but narrows the range of alternatives to be considered by eliminating some that are inconsistent with it. It, thereby, contributes to greater efficiency in the standard setting process by avoiding the necessity of having to re-debate fundamental issues and facilitates any debate about specific technical issues. A framework should also reduce political pressures in making accounting judgements. The use of a framework reduces the influence of personal biases in accounting decisions.

However, concepts statements are by their nature very general and theoretical in their wording, which leads to alternative conclusions being drawn. Whilst individual standards should be consistent with the Framework, in the absence of a specific standard, it does not follow that concepts will provide practical solutions. IAS 8 *Accounting policies, changes in accounting estimates and errors* sets out a hierarchy of authoritative guidance that should be considered in the absence of a standard. In this case, management can use its judgement in developing and applying an accounting policy, albeit by considering the IASB Framework, but can also use accounting standards issued by other bodies. Thus an international framework may not totally provide solutions to practical accounting problems.

(b) There are several issues which have to be addressed if an international conceptual framework is to be successfully developed. These are:

(i) **Objectives**

Agreement will be required as to whether financial statements are to be produced for shareholders or a wide range of users and whether decision usefulness is the key criteria or stewardship. Additionally there is the question of whether the objective is to provide information in making credit and investment decisions. The Conceptual Framework for Financial Reporting 2010, issued in September 2010, has made little or no change to the objectives of general purpose financial reporting.

(ii) **Qualitative characteristics**

The qualities to be sought in making decisions about financial reporting need to be determined. The decision usefulness of financial reports is determined by these characteristics. There are issues concerning the trade-offs between relevance and reliability. An example of this concerns the use of fair values and historical costs. It has been argued that historical costs are more reliable although not as relevant as fair values. Additionally there is a conflict between neutrality and the traditions of prudence or conservatism. These characteristics are constrained by materiality and benefits that justify costs.

The Conceptual Framework for Financial Reporting 2010 ('the 2010 Framework') identified two fundamental qualitative characteristics, relevance and faithful representation. Relevance is regarded as information capable to making a difference in decisions made by users, which is supported by issues of materiality. Faithful representation requires that information should be complete, neutral and free form error. This would suggest that it is without bias or manipulation and is clearly described. In addition to the two fundamental qualitative characteristics, there are four enhancing characteristics; comparability, verifiability, timeliness and understandability

(iii) **Definitions of the elements of financial statements**

The principles behind the definition of the elements need agreement. There are issues concerning whether 'control' should be included in the definition of an asset or become part of the recognition criteria. Also the definition of 'control' is an issue particularly with financial instruments. For example, does the holder of a call option 'control' the underlying asset? Some of the IASB's standards contravene its own conceptual framework. IFRS 3 requires the capitalisation of goodwill as an asset despite the fact that it can be argued that goodwill does not meet the definition of an asset in the Framework. IAS 12 requires the recognition of deferred tax liabilities that do not meet the liability definition. Similarly equity and liabilities need to be capable of being clearly distinguished. Certain financial instruments could either be liabilities or equity, for example obligations settled in shares.

At September 2010, although issued, the 2010 Framework is not yet in final form. Draft definitions within the 2010 Framework include:

- An *asset* of an entity is a present economic resource to which the entity has either a right or other access that others do not have

- A *liability* of an entity is a present economic obligation for which the entity is the obligor

The principal reasons for reviewing and potentially changing these definitions are as follows:

1   The definitions place too much emphasis on identifying the future inflow or outflow of economic benefits, instead of focusing on the item that presently exists, an economic resource or economic obligation.

2   The definitions place undue emphasis on identifying the past transactions or events that gave rise to the asset or the liability, instead of focusing on whether the entity has an economic resource or obligation at the reporting date.

3   It is unclear how the definitions apply to contractual obligations.

(iv) **Recognition and de-recognition**

The principles of recognition and de-recognition of assets and liabilities need reviewing. Most frameworks have recognition criteria, but there are issues over the timing of recognition. For example, should an asset be recognised when a value can be placed on it or when a cost has been incurred? If an asset or liability does not meet recognition criteria when acquired or incurred, what subsequent event causes the asset or liability to be recognised? Most frameworks do not discuss de-recognition. (The IASB's Framework does not discuss the issue.) It can be argued that an item should be de-recognised when it does not meet the recognition criteria, but financial instruments standards (IAS 39) require other factors to occur before financial assets can be de-recognised. Different attributes should be considered such as legal ownership, control, risks or rewards.

(v) **Measurement**

More detailed discussion of the use of measurement concepts, such as historical cost, fair value, current cost, etc are required and also more guidance on measurement techniques. Measurement concepts should address initial measurement and subsequent measurement in the form of revaluations, impairment and depreciation which in turn gives rise to issues about classification of gains or losses in income or in equity. Selection of bases of measurement should be related to the qualitative requirements of that information.

(vi) **Reporting entity**

Issues have arisen over what sorts of entities should issue financial statements, and which entities should be included in consolidated financial statements. A question arises as to whether the legal entity or the economic unit should be the reporting unit. Complex business arrangements raise issues over what entities should be consolidated and the basis upon which entities are consolidated. For example, should the basis of consolidation be 'control' and what does 'control' mean?

(vii) **Presentation and disclosure**

Financial reporting should provide information that enables users to assess the amounts, timing and uncertainty of the entity's future cash flows, its assets, liabilities and equity. It should provide management explanations and the limitations of the information in the reports. Discussions as to the boundaries of presentation and disclosure are required.

**Additional comments:**

Note that a new Conceptual Framework for Financial Reporting was issued in 2010, which, initially has adopted the definitions of the various elements of the financial statements from the previous Framework document. As at November 2011, only chapters 1 and 3 of the 2010 Framework document have been adopted by both the IASB and US FASB. In principle, there is no change within chapter 1 to the underlying objectives of the 2010 Framework, to provide financial information which is relevant to users of that information.

Chapter 3 of the 2010 Framework considers the qualitative characterises of information – relevance and faithful representation are identified as fundamental qualitative characteristics, which are enhanced by the further qualitative characteristics of comparability, verifiability, timeliness and understandability.

The remaining chapters and content of the 2010 Framework to be updated or agreed as appropriate form part of a long-term project between the IASB and US FASB. Many of the issues involved will not be easily resolved, otherwise it is a reasonable assumption that they would have been dealt with at an earlier stage. They are likely to involve discussion, negotiation, compromise and change on the part of both parties.

| ACCA marking scheme | | Marks |
|---|---|---|
| (a) | Subjective | 13 |
| | | 13 |
| (b) | Up to 2 marks per key issue | 10 |
| | (i)  Objectives | |
| | (ii)  Qualitative characteristics | |
| | (iii)  Definitions | |
| | (iv)  Recognition and de-recognition | |
| | (v)  Measurement | |
| | (vi)  Reporting entity | |
| | (vii)  Presentation and disclosure | |
| | Appropriateness and quality of discussion | 2 |
| | | 12 |
| Total | | 25 |

**Examiner's comments**

This question required candidates to discuss the need for an agreed conceptual framework and the key issues to be addressed in determining the components of such a framework. Considering that the IASB and FASB, and the ASB see the current conceptual framework project as being a key current development, it was surprising that more candidates did not answer this question better as there has been a significant amount of coverage in the accountancy press. It is important that candidates read the accountancy press in order to gain an insight into current issues. The answers to part a) were often quite narrow with little discussion of the practical use of a framework. Candidates who considered the reasons for differences in accounting practice often produced a reasonable answer. The answers to part b) generally did not consider the key elements of a conceptual framework such as the objectives, recognition and derecognition, measurement etc. These key issues are those of all frameworks both local and international .The professional marks were awarded for considering, discussing and combining ideas and information to arrive at a broader understanding of the issues. Candidates found this process quite difficult.

## 49 CORPORATE REPORTING (DEC 08 EXAM)  *Walk in the footsteps of a top tutor*

**Key answer tips**

This question requires explanation of the importance of accounting standards together with discussion of costs and benefits to users of increased disclosure in financial statements. The question requirement is separated into two specific parts, each with a mark allocation which should help you with time management during the examination, plus two marks for quality of discussion and reasoning. The best way to approach this question is to deal with each requirement separately and to make specific, supported, comments.

(a) It could be argued that the marketplace already offers powerful incentives for high-quality reporting as it rewards such by easing or restricting access to capital or raising or lowering the cost of borrowing capital depending on the quality of the entity's reports. However, accounting standards play an important role in helping the market mechanism work effectively.

*Several reasons regarding the need for accounting standards can be identified – focus upon fundamental issues such as comparability, reliability and cost-benefit factors.*

Accounting standards are needed because they:

- Promote a common understanding of the nature of corporate performance and this facilitates any negotiations between users and companies about the content of financial statements. For example, many loan agreements specify that a company provide the lender with financial statements prepared in accordance with generally accepted accounting principles or International Financial Reporting Standards. Both the company and the lender understand the terms and are comfortable that statements prepared according to those standards will meet certain information needs. Without standards, the statements would be less useful to the lender, and the company and the lender would have to agree to create some form of acceptable standards which would be inefficient and less effective.

- Assist neutral and unbiased reporting. Companies may wish to portray their past performance and future prospects in the most favourable light. Users are aware of this potential bias and are sceptical about the information they receive. Standards build credibility and confidence in the capital marketplace to the benefit of both users and companies.

- Improve the comparability of information across companies and national boundaries. Without standards, there would be little basis to compare one company with others across national boundaries which is a key feature of relevant information.

- Create credibility in financial statements. Auditors verify that information is reported in accordance with standards and this creates public confidence in financial statements

- Facilitate consistency of information by producing data in accordance with an agreed conceptual framework. A consistent approach to the development and presentation of information assists users in accessing information in an efficient manner and facilitates decision-making.

(b) Increased information disclosure benefits users by reducing the likelihood that they will misallocate their capital. This is obviously a direct benefit to individual users of corporate reports. The disclosure reduces the risk of misallocation of capital by enabling users to improve their assessments of a company's prospects.

*Benefits of increased information disclosure can also be identified from the earlier points made – focus upon cost-benefit factors and fundamental issues.*

This creates three important results.

(i) Users use information disclosed to increase their investment returns and by definition support the most profitable companies which are likely to be those that contribute most to economic growth. Thus, an important benefit of information disclosure is that it improves the effectiveness of the investment process.

(ii) The second result lies in the effect on the liquidity of the capital markets. A more liquid market assists the effective allocation of capital by allowing users to reallocate their capital quickly. The degree of information asymmetry between the buyer and seller and the degree of uncertainty of the buyer and the seller will affect the liquidity of the market as lower asymmetry and less uncertainty will increase the number of transactions and make the market more liquid. Disclosure will affect uncertainty and information asymmetry.

(iii) Information disclosure helps users understand the risk of a prospective investment. Without any information, the user has no way of assessing a company's prospects. Information disclosure helps investors predict a company's prospects. Getting a better understanding of the true risk could lower the price of capital for the company. It is difficult to prove however that the average cost of capital is lowered by information disclosure, even though it is logically and practically impossible to assess a company's risk without relevant information. Lower capital costs promote investment, which can stimulate productivity and economic growth.

However although increased information can benefit users, there are problems of understandability and information overload.

*Several reasons regarding costs and benefits of information disclosure can be identified.*

Information disclosure provides a degree of protection to users. The benefit is fairness to users and is part of corporate accountability to society as a whole.

The main costs to the preparer of financial statements are as follows:

(i)      the cost of developing and disseminating information,

(ii)     the cost of possible litigation attributable to information disclosure,

(iii)    the cost of competitive disadvantage attributable to disclosure.

The costs of developing and disseminating the information include those of gathering, creating and auditing the information.

Additional costs to the preparers include training costs, changes to systems (for example on moving to IFRS), and the more complex and the greater the information provided, the more it will cost the company.

Although litigation costs are known to arise from information disclosure, it does not follow that all information disclosure leads to litigation costs. Cases can arise from insufficient disclosure and misleading disclosure. Only the latter is normally prompted by the presentation of information disclosure. Fuller disclosure could lead to lower costs of litigation as the stock market would have more realistic expectations of the company's prospects and the discrepancy between the valuation implicit in the market price and the valuation based on a company's financial statements would be lower. However, litigation costs do not necessarily increase with the extent of the disclosure. Increased disclosure could reduce litigation costs.

Disclosure could weaken a company's ability to generate future cash flows by aiding its competitors. The effect of disclosure on competitiveness involves benefits as well as costs. Competitive disadvantage could be created if disclosure is made relating to strategies, plans, (for example, planned product development, new market targeting) or information about operations (for example, production-cost figures). There is a significant difference between the purpose of disclosure to users and competitors. The purpose of disclosure to users is to help them to estimate the amount, timing, and certainty of future cash flows. Competitors are not trying to predict a company's future cash flows, and information of use in that context is not necessarily of use in obtaining competitive advantage. Overlap between information designed to meet users' needs and information designed to further the purposes of a competitor is often coincidental. Every company that could suffer competitive disadvantage from disclosure could gain competitive advantage from comparable disclosure by competitors. Published figures are often aggregated with little use to competitors.

Companies bargain with suppliers and with customers, and information disclosure could give those parties an advantage in negotiations. In such cases, the advantage would be a cost for the disclosing entity. However, the cost would be offset whenever information disclosure was presented by both parties, each would receive an advantage and a disadvantage.

There are other criteria to consider such as whether the information to be disclosed is about the company. This is both a benefit and a cost criterion. Users of corporate reports need company-specific data, and it is typically more costly to obtain and present information about matters external to the company. Additionally, consideration must be given as to whether the company is the best source for the information. It could be inefficient for a company to obtain or develop data that other, more expert parties could develop and present or do develop at present.

There are many benefits to information disclosure and users have unmet information needs. It cannot be known with any certainty what the optimal disclosure level is for companies. Some companies through voluntary disclosure may have achieved their optimal level. There are no quantitative measures of how levels of disclosure stand with respect to optimal levels. Standard setters have to make such estimates as best they can, guided by prudence, and by what evidence of benefits and costs they can obtain.

| ACCA marking scheme | | Marks |
|---|---|---|
| (a) | Common understanding | 2 |
| | Neutral, unbiased | 2 |
| | Comparability | 1 |
| | Credibility | 2 |
| | Consistency | 2 |
| | | ___ |
| | | 9 |
| | | ___ |
| (b) | Investment process | 4 |
| | Risk | 2 |
| | Protection | 2 |
| | Costs | 2 |
| | Competitive disadvantage | 2 |
| | Other criteria | 2 |
| | | ___ |
| | | 14 |
| | | ___ |
| Professional marks | | 2 |
| | | ___ |
| Total | | 25 |
| | | ___ |

**Examiner's comments**

This question required candidates to discuss the reason why accounting standards are required to keep the market mechanism working effectively and additionally to discuss the costs and benefits to users of financial information of increased disclosure in financial statements. There were a variety of answers from candidates, which were quite good, but very few candidates made reference to the Framework. The Framework is always a useful reference point for answers to discursive questions. In answering the part of the question dealing with the costs and benefits of disclosure, very few candidates mentioned possible litigation and competitive disadvantage and advantage. Also information asymmetry and its link with the liquidity of the market were seldom mentioned. Particularly in these current times, this point has particular relevance. Future questions in this area may have a calculation element. Candidates answered this question very well producing answers which demonstrated a good understanding of the usefulness of accounting standards and the cost and benefits of disclosure.

**50   WORLD ENERGY (JUN 04 EXAM)**

**Key answer tips**

This is a very typical discussion question on social and environmental accounting. Since there is little in the way of standards on these topics, your comments can be as wide-ranging and general as you want but make sure that they are relevant to the precise question that has been asked.

(a)   The way in which companies manage their social and environmental responsibilities is a high level strategic issue for management. Companies that actively manage these responsibilities can help create long term sustainable performance in an increasingly competitive business environment. Greater transparency in this area will benefit organisations and their stakeholders. These stakeholders will have an interest in knowing that the company is attempting to adopt best practice in the area. Institutional investors will see value in the 'responsible ownership' principle adopted by the company. Although there is no universal 'best practice' there seems to be growing consensus that high performance is linked with high quality practice in such areas as recruitment, organisational culture, training and reduction of environmental risks and impact. Companies that actively reduce environmental risks and promote social disclosures could be considered to be potentially more sustainable, profitable, valuable and competitive. Many companies build their reputation on the basis of social and environmental responsibility and go to substantial lengths to prove that their activities do not exploit their workforce or any other section of society.

Governments are encouraging disclosure by passing legislation, for example in the area of anti-discrimination and by their own example in terms of the depth and breadth of reporting (also by requiring companies who provide services to the government to disclose such information). External awards and endorsements, such as environmental league tables and employer awards, encourage companies to adopt a more strategic approach to these issues. Finally, local cultural and social pressures are causing greater demands for transparency of reporting.

There are arguments for giving organisations the freedom to determine the contents of such reports and for encouraging common practices and measures. Standardised reports may fail to capture important information in individual organisations and may lead to 'compliance' rather than 'relevance'. At the same time, best practice would encourage consistency, comparability and reliability, providing a common framework which companies and stakeholders might find useful.

(b)   **Corporate environmental governance**

The reporting of corporate environmental governance by World Energy could be improved by including the following information in the financial statements:

(i)    a statement of the environmental policy covering all aspects of business activity

(ii)   the management systems which reduce and minimise environmental risks (reference should be made to internationally recognised environmental management systems)

(iii)  details of environmental training and expertise

(iv) a report on their environmental performance including disclosing verified emissions to air/land and water, and how they are seeking to reduce these and other environmental impacts. Operating site reports could be prepared for local communities for businesses with high environmental impacts

(v) details of any environmental offence that resulted in enforcement action, fine, etc, and any serious pollution incident (vi) a report on historical trends for key indicators and a comparison with the corporate targets

(vii) a simple environmental statement of comprehensive income and statement of financial position including income and value derived from the environment, expenditure on natural resources, licences etc, investment in anti-pollution equipment.

The environmental performance statements and report should be audited and verified to recognise environmental and auditing standards, and companies should perhaps have a health, safety and environment committee.'

(c) The reporting of 'Human Capital Management' (HCM) varies worldwide. Legal requirements tend to determine the information which is currently disclosed, with multinational companies being more proactive in publishing information especially where they feel it will help them recruit talented employees and build up their employer brand image. Legislation generally requires the disclosure of workforce demographics, remuneration, information on disabled employees, etc.

In order to improve the understanding of the link between corporate performance and employees, reports on HCM should have a more strategic focus by communicating the links between the item practices, its business strategies and its performance. Information on the following aspects could enhance this focus:

(i) size and composition of the workforce

(ii) retention and motivation of employees

(iii) skills necessary for success, training, remuneration and fair employment practices

(iv) leadership and succession planning.

Information disclosed should be comparable over time by using consistent and commonly accepted definitions.

The Management Discussion and Analysis (MDA) could be used for these additional disclosures as this document contains an analysis and discussion of the main trends and factors likely to affect the company's performance. Key indicators and definitions need to be developed in order to ensure comparability of disclosure. In addition to reporting in published financial statements, internal reports can be made to employees, employee newsletters and website bulletins can be issued. Specific corporate social responsibility reports can be published externally and planned media releases can be made.

| ACCA marking scheme | | | |
|---|---|---|---|
| | | | *Marks* |
| (a) | Strategic issue | | 1 |
| | Sustainable performance | | 1 |
| | Transparency | | 1 |
| | Best practice | | 1 |
| | Responsible ownership | | 1 |
| | Performance | | 1 |
| | Reduction of risks | | 1 |
| | Reputation | | 1 |
| | Exploitation | | 1 |
| | Governments | | 1 |
| | External awards | | 1 |
| | Cultural/Social pressures | | 1 |
| | | | — |
| | Available | | 12 |
| | Maximum | | 10 |
| (b) | 1 mark per point up to a maximum | | 7 |
| | | | — |
| (c) | Nature of current information | | 4 |
| | Visibility | | 4 |
| | | | — |
| | | | 8 |
| | | | — |
| Available | | | 27 |
| **Maximum** | | | **25** |

## 51 GLOWBALL (PILOT 01)

**Key answer tips**

This question requires knowledge of environmental reporting and makes the link between environmental liabilities and IAS 37. Don't forget that environmental liabilities will only be seen in the financial statements if they meet the definition of a liability.

### Report to the Directors of Glowball – Environmental Reporting

### Introduction

The following report details the current reporting requirements and guidelines relating to Environmental Reporting and specific comments on 'environmental events' occurring in the period.

### Current reporting requirements and guidelines

The initial goal of environmental reporting was simply to demonstrate a company's commitment to the environment. However, the debate has moved on and the central objective of any environmental report is now to communicate environmental performance.

Wider ranging objectives may also be attributed to the report, such as acknowledging shared responsibility for the environment, differentiating the company from its competitors, obtaining social approval for operating practices and demonstrating regulatory compliance. Reports in practice vary from a simple public relations statement to a detailed examination of the company's environmental performance.

Environmental accounting disclosure is an assortment of mandatory and voluntary requirements. Not all companies report on environmental performance and those that do report often focus on only selected aspects of performance. It is typically only the leaders in environmental reporting that report in a comprehensive manner. In the UK, environmental reporting is voluntary although disclosure of environmental matters such as the business's impact on the environment is encouraged in a company's 'Operating and Financial Review' by the ASB's Reporting Statement on best practice on the operating and financial review. Accounting standards on non-current assets, provisions, and research and development costs mention the need to disclose environmental effects.

This voluntary position contrasts with the situation in Denmark and the Netherlands, which have passed legislation making environmental disclosure mandatory for the larger companies. In the USA, the SEC/FASB environmental accounting standards are obligatory, although the standards may not be policed as closely as other accounting standards. The International Accounting Standards Board has not as yet issued a standard in this area. However, IAS 37 *Provisions, contingent liabilities and contingent assets* requires disclosure of potential environmental liabilities in certain circumstances.

There is a range of codes of practice and environmental reporting guidelines that have been published. Examples of these documents are as follows:

(i) The Global Reporting Initiative's Sustainability Reporting Guidelines. These are published by the Coalition of Environmentally Responsible Economies (CERES) and its set of principles for investors and others to assess environmental performance has become the de facto standard worldwide.

(ii) The UNCTAD Report on 'Environmental Financial Accounting and Reporting at the Corporate level'.

(iii) The ACCA Guide to environment and energy reporting.

There is a whole range of governmental, academic, professional body and international agencies that have published reports and guidelines that can be accessed and downloaded from the Web. Under the Eco Management and Audit Scheme (EMAS), companies can sign up to agree to a specific code of practice, but the report must be validated by an accredited environmental verifier.

The Companies Act 2006 now requires the directors of UK quoted companies to report on environmental matters, the company's employees and social/community issues.

In summary, environmental reports can enhance a company's reputation and standing, and the use of environmental reporting will expand. Currently, except in a few specific countries, this form of activity reporting is voluntary and, therefore, the extent of disclosure varies significantly. However, until regulation and standards are developed, the completeness and consistency of environmental reports will not be achieved. Similarly best practice in the attestation of the reports also needs establishing. However, environmental reporting is important to large companies as it is no passing phase. The main question is as to the form and content of the environmental report.

**Comments on specific events**

All of the specific events could be included in an environmental report but certain events will require disclosure or a provision in the financial statements.

(i)   Glowball has a reputation for ensuring the preservation of the environment and this fact, together with specific examples of the restoration of land, could be included in the environmental report. Additionally, however, provisions for environmental liabilities should be recognised when the company becomes obliged legally or constructively to rectify environmental damage or perform restorative work (IAS 37). The mere existence of the need for restorative work does not of itself give rise to a specific obligation. There is no legal obligation to carry out the work but there is a constructive obligation because of the company's conduct in the past and there is a valid expectation that the company will restore the farmland. It is a difficult concept but given the information currently provided by yourselves, it would seem that a provision of $150 million would be required in the financial statements.

(ii)  In evaluating the environmental performance of the company, it would be useful to set out how many tests have been carried out by the regulatory authorities and how many times the company has passed the tests. Additionally, it appears that the number of times the company is prosecuted for infringements of environmental laws is reducing year by year. Thus this fact, together with the number of prosecutions in 20X4 and 20X5, could be presented in a small table.

An estimate of the fine to be imposed should be made and a provision recognised for $5 million in the financial statements. The amount of the fine would also be disclosed in the environmental report together with the circumstances surrounding it.

(iii) The company should produce a report showing the environmental impact of the processes thus creating a measure of the overall environmental impact. The emissions should be categorised into:

(a)   acidity to air and water

(b)   hazardous air emissions

(c)   aquatic oxygen demand and ecotoxicity.

In each category, the reduction of emissions over the years should be set out and compared with target reductions. In the case of (c) above accurate measurements of emissions is not possible and this should be stated. The environmental report should not misstate the facts as this will affect the credibility of the report. The planned expenditure of $70 million on research should be mentioned in the environmental report but will not be provided for in the financial statements as the expenditure is avoidable and an obligation does not exist.

(iv)  The fact that the company sites and constructs its gas installations in an environmentally friendly way can be disclosed in the section of the report dealing with direct environment impacts. Details of such policies can be explained in detail in this section of the report, setting out the criteria used for the sitings.

Similarly the policy of dismantling the installations rather than sinking them can be set out together with the costs involved.

However, IAS 37 has a significant impact on decommissioning activities. The company is building up the required provision over the useful life of the installation but IAS 37 requires the full provision to be established as soon as the obligation exists.

Thus the decommissioning costs of $407 million (undiscounted) will have to be provided for and brought onto the statement of financial position at the discounted amount and a corresponding asset created.

We hope that the above explanations are helpful and that we can assist you in the formal preparation of the environmental report.

| ACCA marking scheme | | |
|---|---|---|
| | | *Marks* |
| (a) | Current reporting requirements | 10 |
| (b) | Restoration | 5 |
| | Infringement of law | 4 |
| | Emissions | 4 |
| | Decommissioning activities | 4 |
| Report | | 4 |
| | | ─── |
| Available | | 31 |
| **Maximum** | | **25** |
| | | ─── |

## 52 FAIR VALUE MEASUREMENT (JUN 07 EXAM)  *Walk in the footsteps of a top tutor*

**Key answer tips**

This question is potentially quite tricky, because there is no scenario within which to discuss fair value measurement, so there are no numbers to hang your arguments on. However it is an important current issue and you should be well-informed about these principles happy with preparing entirely discursive answers.

*Reliability and measurement are key issues relating to how amounts are arrived at for inclusion within the financial statements.*

(a) **Reliability and measurement**

Fair value can be defined as the price that would be received to sell an asset or paid to transfer a liability. The fair value can be thought of as an 'exit price'. A fair value measurement assumes that the transaction to sell the asset or transfer the liability occurs in the principal market for the asset or liability or, in the absence of a principal market, the most advantageous market for the asset or liability which is the market in which the reporting entity would sell the asset or transfer the liability with the price that maximises the amount that would be received or minimises the amount that would be paid. IAS 39 *Financial instruments: recognition and measurement* requires an entity to use the most advantageous active market in measuring the fair value of a financial asset or liability when multiple markets exist whereas IAS 41 *Agriculture* requires an entity to use the most relevant market. Thus there can be different approaches for estimating exit prices. Additionally valuation techniques and current replacement cost could be used.

A hierarchy of fair value measurements would have to be developed in order to convey information about the nature of the information used in creating the fair values. For example quoted prices (unadjusted) in active markets would provide better quality information than prices which reflect the reporting entity's own thinking about the assumptions that market participants would use in pricing the asset or liability. Enron made extensive use of what it called 'mark-to-market' accounting that was based on valuation techniques and estimates. IFRSs currently do not have a single hierarchy that applies to all fair value measures. Instead individual standards indicate preferences for certain inputs and measures of fair value over others, but this guidance is not consistent among all IFRSs.

Some companies, in order to effectively manage their businesses, have already developed models for determining fair values. Businesses manage their operations by managing risks. A risk management process often requires measurement of fair values of contracts, financial instruments, and risk positions.

If markets were liquid and transparent for all assets and liabilities, fair value accounting clearly would give reliable information which is useful in the decision making process. However, because many assets and liabilities do not have an active market, the inputs and methods for estimating their fair value are more subjective and, therefore, the valuations are less reliable. Fair value estimates can vary greatly, depending on the valuation inputs and methodology used. Where management uses significant judgment in selecting market inputs when market prices are not available, reliability will continue to be an issue.

Management can use significant judgment in the valuation process. Management bias, whether intentional or unintentional, may result in inappropriate fair value measurements and consequently misstatements of earnings and equity capital. Without reliable fair value estimates, the potential for misstatements in financial statements prepared using fair value measurements will be even greater.

Consideration must be given to revenue recognition issues in a fair value system. It must be ensured that unearned revenue is not recognised early as it recently was by certain high-tech companies.

As the variety and complexity of financial instruments increases, so does the need for independent verification of fair value estimates. However, verification of valuations that are not based on observable market prices is very challenging. Users of financial statements will need to place greater emphasis on understanding how assets and liabilities are measured and how reliable these valuations are when making decisions based on them.

**IFRS 13 update note:**

IFRS 13 *Fair value measurement* was issued in June 2011 to standardise the definition and the basis upon which fair value measurements are made for inclusion in financial statements. The basic definition is the value at which an asset could be sold or a liability transferred in an active market between willing parties on an arm's length basis. Such a definition excludes transactions costs as they are a characteristic of the transaction, and not the asset or liability under consideration.

It is assumed that such transactions would be based in the principal market for that asset or liability. Where there is no principal market, the most advantageous market that an entity could access should be used.

IFRS 13 also identifies a hierarchy of inputs to the measurement process; Level 1 inputs are the most reliable and consist of values for an identical asset or liability being traded in an active market at the measurement date. Level 2 inputs comprise prices in an active market, for a similar, although not identical asset or liability; such measurements are likely to require modification for application as a fair value measurement in financial statements. Level 3 inputs comprise other inputs used in the measurement process, such as estimations and assumptions regarding future profits or cash flows used in the measurement process for an asset or liability. The idea behind the hierarchy is to provide greater consistency in how fair value measurements are arrived at, and a greater degree of transparency for users of that information to understand how those measurements have been arrived at.

*Adequate disclosure of amounts, and the basis on which those amounts have been determined, are essential in corporate reports.*

**Disclosure**

Fair values reflect point estimates and do not result in transparent financial statements. Additional disclosures are necessary to bring meaning to these fair value estimates. These disclosures might include key drivers affecting valuations, fair-value range estimates, and confidence levels. Another important disclosure consideration relates to changes in fair value amounts.

For example, changes in fair values on securities can arise from movements in interest rates, foreign-currency rates, and credit quality, as well as purchases and sales from the portfolio. For users to understand fair value estimates, they must be given adequate disclosures about what factors caused the changes in fair value. It could be argued that the costs involved in determining fair values may exceed the benefits derived there from. When considering how fair value information should be presented in the financial statements, it is important to consider what type of financial information investors want. There are indications that some investors desire both fair value information and historical cost information. One of the issues affecting the credibility of fair value disclosures currently is that a number of companies include 'health warnings' with their disclosures indicating that the information is not used by management. This language may contribute to users believing that the fair value disclosures lack credibility.

**IFRS 13 update note:**

IFRS 13 requires extensive disclosures to explain to users of financial statements how any fair value measurements included within financial statements have been arrived at.

(b)     The main disagreement over a shift to fair value measurement is the debate over relevance versus reliability. It is argued that historical cost financial statements are not relevant because they do not provide information about current exchange values for the entity's assets that to some extent determine the value of the shares of the entity. However, the information provided by fair values may be unreliable because it may not be based on arm's-length transactions. Proponents of fair value accounting argue that this measurement is more relevant to decision makers even if it is less reliable and would produce statements of financial position that are more representative of a company's value. However it can be argued that relevant information that is unreliable is of no use to an investor. One advantage of historical cost financial information is that it produces earnings numbers that are not based on appraisals or other valuation techniques. Therefore, the profit or loss for the period is less likely to be subject to manipulation by management. In addition, historical cost statement of financial position figures comprise actual purchase prices, not estimates of current values that can be altered to improve various financial ratios. Because historical cost statements rely less on estimates and more on 'hard' numbers, it can be said that historical cost financial statements are more reliable than fair value financial statements. Furthermore, fair value measurements may be less reliable than historical costs measures because fair value accounting provides management with the opportunity to manipulate the reported profit for the period. Developing reliable methods of measuring fair value so that investors trust the information reported in financial statements is critical.

Fair value measurement could be said to be more relevant than historical cost as it is based on market values and not entity specific measurement on initial recognition, so long as fair values can be reliably measured. Generally the fair value of the consideration given or received (effectively historical cost) also represents the fair value of the item at the date of initial recognition. However there are many cases where significant differences between historical cost and fair value can arise on initial recognition.

Historical cost does not purport to measure the value received. It cannot be assumed that the price paid can be recovered in the market place. Hence the need for some additional measure of recoverable value and impairment testing of assets. Historical cost can be an entity specific measurement. The recorded historical cost can be lower or higher than its fair value. For example the valuation of inventory is determined by the costing method adopted by the entity and this can vary from entity to entity. Historical cost often requires the allocation of costs to an asset or liability. These costs are attributed to assets, liabilities and expenses, and are often allocated arbitrarily. An example of this is self constructed assets. Rules set out in accounting standards help produce some consistency of historical cost measurements but such rules cannot improve representational faithfulness.

Another problem with historical cost arises as regards costs incurred prior to an asset being recognised. Historical costs recorded from development expenditure cannot be capitalised if they are incurred prior to the asset meeting the recognition criteria in IAS 38 *Intangible assets*. Thus the historical cost amount does not represent the fair value of the consideration given to create the asset.

The relevance of historical cost has traditionally been based on a cost/revenue matching principle. The objective has been to expense the cost of the asset when the revenue to which the asset has contributed is recognised. If the historical cost of the asset differs from its fair value on initial recognition then the matching process in future periods becomes arbitrary. The measurement of assets at fair value will enhance the matching objective. Historical cost may have use in predicting future net reported income but does not have any necessary implications for future cash flows. Fair value does embody the market's expectations for those future cash flows.

However, historical cost is grounded in actual transaction amounts and has existed for many years to the extent that it is supported by practical experience and familiarity. Historical cost is accepted as a reliable measure especially where no other relevant measurement basis can be applied.

As part of the long-term convergence project with US GAAP, an ED was issued in June 2010 dealing with fair value measurement. Reasons for the issue of the ED include the fact that guidance on measuring fair value is distributed across many IFRSs, and it is not always consistent. Additionally, the current guidance is incomplete, in that it provides neither a clear measurement objective nor a robust measurement framework. The IASB believes that this adds unnecessary complexity to IFRSs and contributes to diversity in practice.

The IASB's objectives in the fair value measurement project are to:

- establish a single source of guidance for all fair value measurements;
- clarify the definition of fair value and related guidance;
- enhance disclosures about fair value measurements; and
- increase convergence of IFRS and US GAAP.

| ACCA marking scheme | |
|---|---|
| | *Marks* |
| Reliability and measurement | 10 |
| Disclosures | 3 |
| Market value | 3 |
| Value received | 2 |
| Entity specific | 4 |
| Matching | 2 |
| Pre-acquisition costs | 2 |
| Reliable and relevant | 3 |
| | ⎯⎯ |
| Available | 29 |
| **Maximum** | **25** |
| | ⎯⎯ |

## 53 MANAGEMENT COMMENTARY

**Key answer tips**

Part (a) should be straightforward if you have studied this topic, but part (b) requires some more imagination. Search through the information in the question very carefully, and try to include every bit in your answer.

(a) **Purpose of the Management Commentary (MC)**

The Management Commentary (MC) is a narrative report that provides a context within which to interpret the financial position, financial performance and cash flows of an entity. **(0.5 marks)**

Management are able to explain its objectives and its strategies for achieving those objectives. **(0.5 marks)**

Users routinely use the type of information provided in management commentary to help them evaluate an entity's prospects and its general risks, as well as the success of management's strategies for achieving its stated objectives. **(1.0 marks)**

For many entities, management commentary is already an important element of their communication with the capital markets, supplementing as well as complementing the financial statements. **(1.0 marks)**

The MC is a Practice Statement (PS), rather than a mandatory reporting standard. The reason for this is that, not every entity may be required to prepare such a statement, due to factors such as:

- national business law **(0.5 marks)**

- relevant business practice regulation, such as corporate governance requirements **(0.5 marks)**

- the size of the entity, in financial terms and/or the nature and extent of business activities **(0.5 marks)**

No two entities will be alike in all respects, so it would be difficult to be prescriptive or definitive on issues which will vary considerably between different entities. **(0.5 marks)**

This PS helps management to provide useful commentary to financial statements prepared in accordance with IFRS information. The users are identified as existing and potential members, together with lenders and creditors, which is similar to the principal users of annual financial reports.

It can be adopted by entities, where applicable, any time from the date of issue in December 2010.

(b)   **Framework for presentation of management commentary**

The following principles should be applied when a management commentary is prepared:

1    to provide management's view of the entity's performance, position and progress; and **(1.0 marks)**

2    to supplement and complement information presented in the financial statements. **(1.0 marks)**

Consequently, the MC should include information which is both forward-looking and adheres to the qualitative characteristics of information as described in the 2010 Conceptual Framework for Financial Reporting. The fundamental qualitative characteristics are identified as relevance and faithful representation, which are supported by further enhancing characteristics of comparability, verifiability, timeliness and understandability. **(1.5 marks)**

The MC should provide information to help users of the financial reports to assess the performance of the entity and the actions of its management relative to stated strategies and plans for progress. **(1.5 marks)**

That type of commentary will help users of the financial reports to understand risk exposures and strategies of the entity, relevant non-financial factors and other issues not otherwise included within the financial statements. This clearly indicates that the MC should consist of information which is additional to information already contained within the IFRS financial statements, rather than simply a repeat or rearrangement of such information. **(1.5 marks)**

The MC should provide management's perspective of the entity's performance, position and progress. MC should derive from the information that is important to management in managing the business. This will typically include both backward-looking information and supporting commentary, together with forward-looking information and commentary. This latter component is often deficient or lacking within narrative components of financial statements as they are prepared at present as it is normally regarded as being commercially sensitive. **(2.0 marks)**

It could be argued that some of the content to be included within a MC is already included within the directors' report or, for examples, the chief executive's review. However, PS 1 provides a consistent basis for relevant commentary and supporting data which may not be included elsewhere within the annual financial statements. Additionally, the content of the MC should be linked to previous, and future, MC by identifying and explaining changes in strategy, expected and actual results and other issues supported by financial and non-financial measures and indicators of performance. **(1.5 marks)**

(c) **Elements of management commentary**

Although the particular focus of MC will depend on the facts and circumstances of each individual entity, it should include information that is essential to an understanding of:

(i) the nature of the business; – this may include not only the nature and extent of current activities, but changes that may take place at some future date, together with factors that may influence whether such changes are implemented. **(1.0 marks)**

(ii) management's objectives and its strategies for meeting those objectives; – the objectives may include both financial objectives (such as growth in the equity dividend paid or earnings per share) and non-financial factors (such as improving health and safety performance or minimising environmental damage). The important issue is that they should be clearly stated, measurable and evaluated over time for performance or achievement of targets. This is likely to include information which may not have been published in the past.

As such, it may take time for managers to determine which information they should provide within the MC and how that information should be reported. **(3.0 marks)**

(iii) the entity's most significant resources, risks and relationships; – this may include information relating to relationships with principal customers and/or suppliers. Other factors which may be relevant include whether there are any factors which may undermine those relationships, such as volatility of exchange rates, government policy or regulation which may affect the entity, or even its customers and suppliers **(2.0 marks)**

(iv) the results of operations and prospects; and **(1.0 marks)**

(v) the critical performance measures and indicators that management uses to evaluate the entity's performance against stated objectives. This will include financial and non-financial information. There is likely to be qualitative information, together with supporting narrative and disclosures. The performance measures and indicators should be reported consistently each year, to enable comparison and evaluation to take place. Where performance measures and indicators are amended, this should be made clear within the commentary, including reasons for any amendment, together with restated information to enable evaluation of the revised data. **(3.0 marks)**

| ACCA marking scheme | | |
|---|---|---|
| | | *Marks* |
| (a) | Purpose of MC | 5 |
| (b) | Principles and framework | 10 |
| (c) | Elements to include | 10 |
| | | —— |
| Total | | 25 |
| | | —— |

## 54 IFRS FOR SME (JUN 06 EXAM)

**Key answer tips**

This question covers IFRSs and Small and Medium Entities (SMEs). This is an important topic due to the publication of IFRS for SME in July 2009 so the question requires knowledge of the issue. It is a difficult question to answer as it is harder to think of specific points when you are not presented with a scenario. Make sure you review the answer carefully.

(a) IFRSs were not designed specifically for listed companies. However, in many countries the main users of IFRSs are listed companies. Currently SMEs who adopt IFRSs have to follow all the requirements, but not all SMEs take exception to applying IFRSs because it gives their financial statements enhanced reliability, relevance and credibility, and results in fair presentation. However, other SMEs will wish to comply with IFRSs for consistency and comparability purposes within their own country and internationally but wish to apply simplified or different standards relevant to SMEs on the grounds that some IFRSs are unnecessarily demanding and some of the information produced is not used by users of SME financial statements.

The objectives of general purpose financial statements are basically appropriate for SMEs and publicly listed companies alike. Therefore there is an argument that there is a need for only one set of IFRSs that could be used nationally and internationally. However, some SMEs require different financial information than listed companies. For example expanded related party disclosures may be useful as SMEs often raise capital from shareholders, directors and suppliers. Additionally directors often offer personal assets as security for bank finance.

The cost burden of applying the full set of IFRSs may not be justified on the basis of user needs. The purpose and usage of the financial statements, and the nature of the accounting expertise available to the SME, will not be the same as for listed companies. These circumstances themselves may provide justification for a separate set of IFRSs for SMEs. A problem which might arise is that users become familiar with IFRSs as opposed to local GAAP thus creating a two tier system which could lead to local GAAP being seen as an inferior or even a superior set of accounting rules.

One course of action would be for GAAP for SMEs to be developed on a national basis with IFRSs being focused on accounting for listed company activities. The main issue here would be that the practices developed for SMEs may not be consistent and may lack comparability across national boundaries. This may mean that where SMEs subsequently wish to list their shares on a capital market, the transition to IFRSs may be difficult. It seems that national standards setters are strongly supportive of the development of IFRSs for SMEs.

(b) There are several issues which need to be addressed when developing IFRSs for SMEs:

(i) **The purpose of the standards and type of entity**

The principal aim of the development of an accounting framework for SMEs is to provide a framework which generates relevant, reliable and useful information. The standards should provide high quality and understandable accounting standards suitable for SMEs globally. Additionally they should meet the needs set out in (a) above, for example reducing the financial reporting burden for SMEs. It is unlikely that one of the objectives would be to provide information for management or meet the needs of the tax authorities as these bodies will have specific requirements which would be difficult to meet in an accounting standard. If the standards for SMEs were to be a modified version of the full IFRSs and not an independently developed set of standards (i.e. if they were based on the same conceptual framework), this would allow easier transition to full IFRSs if the SME grows or decides to become a publicly listed entity.

It is important to define the type of entity for which the standards are intended. Companies who have issued shares to the public would be expected to use full IFRSs. The question arises as to whether SME standards should apply to all unlisted entities or just those listed entities below a certain size threshold. The difficulty with size criteria is that it would have to apply worldwide and it would be very difficult to specify such criteria. Additionally some unlisted companies, for example public utilities, have a reporting obligation that is equivalent to that of a listed company and should follow full IFRSs.

The main characteristic which distinguishes SMEs from other entities is the degree of public accountability. Thus the definition of what constitutes an SME could revolve around those entities that do not have public accountability. Indicators of public accountability will have to be developed. For example, a listed company or companies holding assets in a fiduciary capacity (bank), or a public utility, or an entity with economic significance in its country. Thus all entities that do not have public accountability may be considered as potential users of IFRSs for SMEs.

Size may not be the best way to determine what may be regarded as a SME. SMEs could be defined by reference to ownership and the management of the entity. SMEs are not necessarily just smaller versions of public companies.

(ii)   **The development of IFRSs for SMEs as a modification of existing IFRSs**

Most SMEs have a narrower range of users than listed entities. The main groups of users are likely to be the owners, suppliers and lenders. In deciding upon the modifications to make to IFRSs, the needs of the users will need to be taken into account as well as the costs and other burdens imposed upon SMEs by the IFRSs. There will have to be a relaxation of some of the measurement and recognition criteria in IFRSs in order to achieve the reduction in the costs and the burdens. Some disclosure requirements, such as segmental reports and earnings per share, are intended to meet the needs of listed entities, or to assist users in making forecasts of the future. Users of financial statements of SMEs often do not make such kinds of forecasts. Thus these disclosures may not be relevant to SMEs, and a review of all of the disclosure requirements in IFRSs will be required to assess their appropriateness for SMEs.

The difficulty is determining which information is relevant to SMEs without making the information disclosed meaningless or too narrow/restricted. It may mean that measurement requirements of a complex nature may have to be omitted.

There are, however, rational grounds for justifying different treatments because of the different nature of the entities and the existence of established practices at the time of the issue of an IFRS.

(iii)  **The treatment of items not dealt with by an IFRS for SMEs**

IFRSs for SMEs would not necessarily deal with all the recognition and measurement issues facing an entity but the key issues should revolve around the nature of the recognition, measurement and disclosure of the transactions of SMEs. In the case where the item is not dealt with by the standards there are three alternatives:

(1)   the entity can look to the full IFRS to resolve the issue

(2)   management's judgement can be used with reference to the *Framework* and consistency with other IFRSs for SMEs

(3)   existing practice could be used.

The first approach is more likely to result in greater consistency and comparability. However, this approach may also increase the burden on SMEs as it can be argued that they are subject to two sets of standards.

An SME may wish to make a disclosure required by a full IFRS which is not required by the SME standard, or a measurement principle is simplified or exempted in the SME standard, or the IFRS may give a choice between two measurement options and the SME standard does not allow choice. Thus the issue arises as to whether SMEs should be able to choose to comply with a full IFRS for some items and SME standards for other items, allowing an SME to revert to IFRSs on a principle by principle basis. The problem that will arise will be a lack of consistency and comparability of SME financial statements.

(iv)   In February 2007, the IASB published for public comment the exposure draft of its International Financial Reporting Standard for Small and Medium-sized Entities (IFRS for SMEs). The IFRS for SME was subsequently issued in July 2009.

The aim of the new standard is to provide a simplified, self-contained set of accounting principles that are appropriate for smaller, non-listed companies and are based on full International Financial Reporting Standards (IFRSs), developed primarily for listed companies.

As compared with IFRSs, the IFRS for SMEs:

- removes choices for accounting treatment; for example, the cost model must be used for property, plant and equipment and for investment properties

- eliminates topics that are not generally relevant to SMEs; for example lessor accounting for finance leases (not a big concession, when lessors are normally large institutions which would not be eligible for the IFRS for SMEs) and accounting in a hyperinflationary environment

- simplifies methods for recognition and measurement; for example, there are only two categories of financial assets and all development expenditure must be recognised as an expense.

Where the IFRS for SMEs does not specifically address a transaction, event, or condition, an SME is required to look to the requirements and guidance elsewhere in the IASB Standard for SMEs dealing with similar and related issues (that is, select an appropriate accounting policy by analogy). Failing that, the SME is required to adopt an accounting policy which results in relevant and reliable information; in doing so, it may (but is not required to) look to the requirements and guidance in IFRSs dealing with similar and related issues.

As a result the new standard reduces the volume of accounting guidance applicable to SMEs by more than 85 per cent when compared with the full set of IFRSs.

Although the publication of IFRS for SME has been looked upon favourably by businesses and regulators, it typically requires approval from national governments or regulators for it to be adopted in a particular country. South Africa became the first country to adopt the IFRS for SME in August 2009. Application of IFRS for SME in the UK will commence from accounting periods beginning on or after 1 January 2013.

Adoption of the IFRS for SME appears to be more enthusiastic in developing and emerging economies. Some major economies, such as France and Germany, are less enthusiastic to adopt the IFRS for SME. The principal reason would appear to be that there is reliance upon their accounting systems for the collection of tax.

(v)   The subject matter of several reporting standards has been omitted from the IFRS for SME as follows:

- Earnings per share (IAS 33)
- Interim reporting(IAS 34)
- Segmental reporting (IFRS 8)
- Assets held for sale (IFRS 5)
- Insurance contracts

The subject matter of other reporting standards has been simplified for inclusion within the IFRS for SME. In principle, many of the recognition and measurement principles have been simplified, resulting in the elimination of choice where that was possible within IFRS, to apply the most straight-forward treatment such as:

- R & D always expensed
- Goodwill amortised (10 years)
- No revaluation of property, plant and equipment
- Simplification in accounting for financial assets
- Finance costs never capitalised
- Simplified method of accounting for defined benefit plan obligations
- Cost model of accounting for associates and joint ventures is permitted
- Proportionate consolidation of jointly controlled assets is disallowed.

| ACCA marking scheme | Marks |
|---|---|
| (a)   Subjective | 5 |
| (b)   Purpose | 5 |
| How to modify | 5 |
| Item not dealt with | 5 |
| Exposure draft | 5 |
| Omitted standards | 5 |
| Simplified standards | 5 |
| | — |
| Total | 35 |
| | — |

## 55   HOLCOMBE (JUN 10 EXAM)  *Walk in the footsteps of a top tutor*

**Key answer tips**

This two-part question considers theoretical and conceptual issues associated with accounting for leases. Part (a) comprises two discussion-based elements; the first relates to whether the current reporting standard is conceptually flawed, and the second deals with whether the operating lease in the scenario meets the definition of an asset and liability from the Framework document. A sound knowledge of the reporting standard, together with logical application of the definition of an asset and liability should enable you to achieve a good mark for part (a) of the question. Part (b) of the question requires accounting for a sale and leaseback transaction if the operating lease was to be accounted for as an asset, together with accounting for an inflation adjustment. The last element of part (b) may put some students off, but the first element for six marks, should be a source of marks for most students for straight-forward application of accounting for derecognition of the office building and recognition of an operating lease asset and obligation. Within this question, there are also 2 professional marks available for clarity and quality of discussion within your answer, so ensure that you use appropriate presentation and professional language to gain these marks.

*Begin by identifying and explaining the weaknesses with the current accounting standard dealing with leasing. IAS 17; specific criticisms will earn more marks than vague or general comments.*

(a)   (i)   The existing accounting model for leases has been criticised for failing to meet the needs of users of financial statements. It can be argued that operating leases give rise to assets and liabilities that should be recognised in the financial statements of lessees. Consequently, users may adjust the amounts recognised in financial statements in an attempt to recognise those assets and liabilities and reflect the effect of lease contracts in profit or loss. The information available to users in the notes to the financial statements is often insufficient to make reliable adjustments to the financial statements.

The existence of two different accounting methods for finance leases and operating leases means that similar transactions can be accounted for very differently. This affects the comparability of financial statements. Also current accounting standards provide opportunities to structure transactions so as to achieve a specific lease classification. If the lease is classified as an operating lease, the lessee obtains a source of financing that can be difficult for users to understand, as it is not recognised in the financial statements.

Existing accounting methods have been criticised for their complexity. In particular, it has proved difficult to define the dividing line between the principles relating to finance and operating leases. As a result, standards use a mixture of subjective judgments and rule based criteria that can be difficult to apply.

The existing accounting model can be said to be conceptually flawed. On entering an operating lease contract, the lessee obtains a valuable right to use the leased item. This right meets the Framework's definition of an asset. Additionally the lessee assumes an obligation to pay rentals that meet the Framework's definition of a liability. However, if the lessee classifies the lease as an operating lease, that right and obligation are not recognised.

There are significant and growing differences between the accounting methods for leases and other contractual arrangements. This has led to inconsistent accounting for arrangements that meet the definition of a lease and similar arrangements that do not. For example leases are financial instruments but they are scoped out of IAS 32/IFRS 9.

*Begin by stating the definition of an asset and liability from the Framework document. This can then be applied to the specific information in the question, before coming to an opinion on whether or not the lease meets the definition of an asset or liability.*

(ii)   An asset is a resource controlled by the entity as a result of past events and from which future economic benefits are expected to flow to the entity. Holcombe has the right to use the leased plant as an economic resource because the entity can use it to generate cash inflows or reduce cash outflows. Similarly, Holcombe controls the right to use the leased item during the lease term because the lessor is unable to recover or have access to the resource without the consent of the lessee or unless there is a breach of contract. The control results from past events, which is the signing of the lease contract and the receipt of the plant by the lessee. Holcombe also maintains the asset.

Unless the lessee breaches the contract, Holcombe has an unconditional right to use the leased item. Future economic benefits will flow to the lessee from the use of the leased item during the lease term. Thus it could be concluded that the lessee's right to use a leased item for the lease term meets the definitions of an asset in the Framework.

A liability is a present obligation of the entity arising from past events, the settlement of which is expected to result in an outflow from the entity of resources embodying economic benefits. The obligation to pay rentals is a liability.

Unless Holcombe breaches the contract, the lessor has no contractual right to take possession of the item until the end of the lease term. Equally, the entity has no contractual right to terminate the lease and avoid paying rentals. Therefore the lessee has an unconditional obligation to pay rentals. Thus the entity has a present obligation to pay rentals, which arises out of a past event, which is the signing of the lease contract and the receipt of the item by the lessee. Finally the obligation is expected to result in an outflow of economic benefits in the form of cash.

Thus the entity's obligation to pay rentals meets the definition of a liability in the Framework.

*This part of the question requirement deals with accounting for a sale and leaseback arrangement; in particular, derecognition of an office building and capitalising rights and obligations under an operating lease, with the gain on disposal deferred and released over the operating lease term.*

(b)   (i)   On sale of the building, Holcombe will recognise the following in the financial statements to 30 April 2010:

| | | |
|---|---|---|
| Dr | Cash | $150m |
| Cr | Office building | $120m |
| Cr | Deferred Income (SOFP) | $30m |

Recognition of gain on the sale of the building

| | | |
|---|---|---|
| Dr | Deferred Income (SOFP) | $6m |
| Cr | Deferred Income (I/S) | $6m |

Release of the gain on sale of the building ($30m/5 years)

Dr    Operating lease asset         $63.89m

Cr    Obligation to pay rentals      $63.89m

Recognition of the leaseback at net present value of lease payments using 8% discount rate

In the first year of the leaseback, Holcombe will recognise the following:

Dr    Lease obligation – rentals     $16m

Cr    Cash                           $16m

Recognition of payment of rentals

Dr    Interest expense               $5.11m

Cr    ease obligation                $5.11m

Recognition of interest expense ($63.89m * 8%)

Dr    Depreciation expense           $12.78m

Cr    Right-of-use asset             $12.78m

Recognition of depreciation of operating lease asset over five years ($63.89m/5 years).

The statement of financial position will show a carrying value of $51.11m being cost of $63.89m less depreciation of $12.78m.

(ii)    Inflation adjustments should be recognised in the period in which they are incurred as they are effectively contingent rent and are not included in any minimum lease calculations. A contingent rent according to IAS 17 is 'that part of the rent that is not fixed in amount but is based on the future amount of a factor that changes other than with the passage of time.' Thus in this case, Holcombe would recognise operating rentals of $5 million in year 1, $5 million in year 2 plus the inflation adjustment at the beginning of year 2, and $5 million in year 3 plus the inflation adjustment at the beginning of year 2 plus inflation adjustment at the beginning of year 3. Based on current inflation, the rent will be $5.2 million in year 2 and $5.408 million in year 3

| ACCA marking scheme | | | |
|---|---|---|---|
| | | | Marks |
| (a) | (i) | Subjective | 7 |
| | (ii) | Subjective | 7 |
| | | Professional marks | 2 |
| | | | |
| (b) | (i) | Recognition of gain | 1 |
| | | Recognition of the leaseback | 1 |
| | | Recognition of the payment of rentals | 2 |
| | | Recognition of interest expense and depreciation | 2 |
| | (ii) | Contingent rentals | 3 |
| | | | ─── |
| Total | | | 25 |
| | | | ─── |

**Examiner's comments**

This question required candidates to discuss the reasons why the current lease accounting standards may fail to meet the needs of users and could be said to be conceptually flawed. The second part of the question required a discussion of a plant operating lease in the financial statements met the definition of an asset and liability as set out in the 'Framework for the Preparation and Presentation of Financial Statements.' Candidates' answers were quite narrow in their discussion of the weaknesses in the accounting standards. The definitions of asset and liability were well rehearsed and candidates scored well on this part of the question. It is apparent that very few candidates read widely. This question always deals with current issues which mean that a wider reading base is required to achieve a good mark. Accounting and Business, and the student accountant are just two examples of magazines that provide wider exposure to current issues.

The final part of the question required candidates to show the accounting entries in the year of the sale and lease back assuming that an operating lease was recognised as an asset in the statement of financial position and to state how an inflation adjustment on a short term operating lease should be dealt with in the financial statements of an entity. The purpose of this question was to show how a change in the current accounting standards (by recognising operating leases in the statement of financial position) would affect their accounting treatment. The question was well answered and candidates scored well generally on this question.

## 56    FINANCIAL INSTRUMENTS (DEC 09 EXAM)  *Walk in the footsteps of a top tutor*

**Key answer tips**

As with many of the theoretical and conceptual questions on this topic, a good approach is to state and explain the basic accounting treatment associated with accounting for financial instruments. You should then try to highlight circumstances where there may be more than one basis of measurement for a financial asset or a financial liability, stating that this may lead to complexity or confusion, for both the preparer and the user of financial statements. The second element of part (a) should enable you to earn further marks by explaining that, if there is only one basis of measurement, this would improve consistency and comparability of financial statements. Part (b) is a small numerical element requiring you to calculate and explain how financial liabilities would be measured on both a fair value and amortised cost basis which you should be able to attempt and earn some marks.

*A good start to this question would be to identify situations where financial assets and liabilities are subject to different methods of measurement.*

(a)  (i)    Financial instruments can be measured under IFRS in a variety of ways. For example financial assets utilise the equity method for associates, fair value with gains and losses in earnings, fair value with gains and losses in other comprehensive income. Financial liabilities can also utilise different measurement methods including fair value with gains and losses in earnings and amortised cost. The measurement methods used under IFRS sometimes portray an estimate of current value and others may portray original cost if this is an acceptable basis for approximation to fair value. Some of the measurements include the effect of impairment losses, which are recognised differently under IFRS. For example financial assets at fair value through profit/loss (FVTPL) and those financial assets measured at amortised cost recognise changes in value in earnings, whilst those classified as fair value through other comprehensive income (FVTOCI) are measured at fair value with changes, including impairment losses, in other comprehensive income.

The above can result in two identical instruments being measured or accounted for differently by the same entity because management's intentions for realising the value of the instrument may determine the way it is measured (FVTPL compared to either FVTOCI or amortised cost, provided the appropriate conditions have been complied with for this designation). Therefore management also has the accounting policy decision of valuing a financial asset per IFRS 9 at FVTPL or FVTOCI (if it is an equity instrument) or at amortised cost (in the case of loans and receivables). Additionally, the percentage of the ownership interest acquired will determine how the holding is accounted for (associate – equity method, subsidiary – acquisition method).

The different ways in which financial instruments can be measured creates problems for preparers and users of financial statements because of the following:

(a)    The criteria for deciding which instrument can be measured in a certain way are complex and difficult to apply. It is sometimes difficult to determine whether an instrument is equity or a liability and the criteria can be applied in different ways as new types of instruments are created.

(b)    Management can choose how to account for an instrument or can be forced into a treatment that they would have preferred to avoid. For example if it is not clear at the time of initial recognition whether a loan or receivable has complied with both the business model test and the contractual cash flows characteristics test, then it must be accounted for as FVTPL, rather than amortised cost.

(c)    Different gains or losses resulting from different measurement methods may be combined in the same line item in the statement of comprehensive income.

(d)    It is not always apparent which measurement principle has been applied to which instrument and what the implications are of the difference. Comparability is affected and the interpretation of financial statements is difficult and time consuming.

*Develop your answer to explain why use of fair value may reduce complexity in the recognition and measurement of financial instruments, and then deal separately with the issue of why this may lead to uncertainty in financial statements.*

(ii)    There are several approaches that can be taken to solve the measurement and related problems. There is pressure to develop standards, which are principle-based and less complex. It has been suggested by IASB members that the long-term solution is to measure all financial instruments using a single measurement principle thus making reported information easier to understand and allowing comparisons between entities and periods. If fair value was used for all types of financial instrument then:

(a)    There would be no need to 'classify' financial instruments

(b)    There would be no requirement to report how impairment losses have been quantified

(c)    There would be no need for rules as regards transfers between measurement categories

(d)    There would be no measurement mismatches between financial instruments and the need for fair value hedge accounting would be reduced

(e)    Identification and separation of embedded derivatives would not be required (this may be required for non-financial instruments)

(f)    A single measurement method would eliminate the confusion about which method was being used for different types of financial instruments

(g)    Entities with comparable credit ratings and obligations will report liabilities at comparable amounts even if borrowings occurred at different times at different interest rates. The reverse is true also. Different credit ratings and obligations will result in the reporting of different liabilities

(h)    Fair value would better reflect the cash flows that would be paid if liabilities were transferred at the re-measurement date

Fair value would result in an entity reporting the same measure for security payment obligations with identical cash flow amounts and timing. At present different amounts are likely to be reported if the two obligations were incurred at different times if market interest rates change.

There is uncertainty inherent in all estimates and fair value measurements, and there is the risk that financial statements will be seen as more arbitrary with fair value because management has even more ability to affect the financial statements. Accountants need to be trained to recognise biases with respect to accounting estimates and fair value measurements so they can advise entities. It is important to demonstrate consistency in how an entity has applied the fair value principles and developed valuations to ensure credibility with investors, lenders and auditors. Although entities may select which assets and liabilities they wish to value under IAS 39 and IFRS 9, outside parties will be looking for consistency in how the standard was applied. Circumstances and market conditions change. Markets may become illiquid and the predicative models may not provide an ongoing advantage for the entity.

IFRS 9 *Financial instruments* reduces the number of classifications of financial assets from four (as previously measured under IAS 39) to three. Additionally, there is increased emphasis upon fair value as being the required or appropriate basis of measurement for financial assets, with measurement at amortised cost only possible where appropriate conditions have been complied with. Further, IFRS 9 reduces opportunity or scope to measure financial assets at historic cost, again citing fair value as the required basis of measurement. This reporting standard also reduces opportunity or scope for reclassification of financial assets by management.

*This requires measurement of a liability using both fair value and amortised cost, together with explanatory comment. Measurement at amortised cost should be easy marks for application of a familiar principle. Where fair value of a loan (or receivable) is required, use the current market rate of interest to discount the future cash flows to present value. Note that this differs from measurement by amortised cost which discounts the future cash flows at the original effective rate of interest.*

(b) Using amortised cost, both financial liabilities will result in single payments, which are almost identical at the same point in time in the future amounting to $59.9 million, i.e. $47m × 1.05 for 5 years and $45m × 1.074 for 4 years.

However, the carrying amounts at 30 November 2009 would be different. The initial loan would be carried at $47 million plus interest of $2.35 million, i.e. $49.35 million, whilst the new loan would be carried at $45 million even though the obligation at 30 November 2013 would be approximately the same.

If the two loans were carried at fair value, then the initial loan would be carried at $45 million thus showing a net profit of $2 million (interest expense of $2.35 million and unrealised gain of $4.35 million). This arises as, at the reporting date, the total amount due to be repaid on 31 November 2013 of $59.9 million is discounted back to present value at 30 November 2009 using the current market rate of interest: i.e. $59.9m × 0.75151 = $45 million, where 0.7515 is the discount factor 1/1.074 discounted for four years.

| ACCA marking scheme | | | Marks |
|---|---|---|---|
| (a) | (i) | 1 mark per point up to maximum | 9 |
| | (ii) | 1 mark per point up to maximum | 9 |
| | Professional marks | | 2 |
| | | | |
| (b) | Identical payment | | 2 |
| | Carrying amount | | 1 |
| | Fair value | | 2 |
| | | | — |
| Total | | | 25 |
| | | | — |

**Examiner's comments**

This question required candidates to discuss the measurement issues relating to financial instruments and how these issues would be alleviated if fair value were used for all financial instruments. The second part of the question asked candidates to compare two loans which were to result in almost identical payments in the future but which were being carried at different amounts currently. Candidates answered the question quite well. Many candidates simply quoted the measurement rules relating to financial instruments without setting out how these rules created confusion and complexity for users. In addition, many candidates simply set out the advantages and disadvantages of fair value accounting rather than discussing how the use of fair value might result in less complexity in financial statements. The calculations in part b of the question were quite well done although very few candidates saw that the redemption amounts were the same but the carrying amounts were quite different.

**57 IFRS FOR SME APPLIED (DEC 10 EXAM)**  *Walk in the footsteps of a top tutor*

**Key answer tips**

This question is typical of the format of the more recently examined current issues questions. It requires technical knowledge and understanding, together with an applied element. Part (a) included discussion of the development of IFRS for SME, together with examples from that reporting standard of some key reporting requirements. Part (b) included application of two different accounting policies, together with explanation and comment upon the results of comparing the two treatments. This part of the question also included a computational element, which was a point flagged by the Examiner during the February 2009 Teachers' Conference.

*Focus on the key requirements of the question, including definitions and explaining the accounting treatment required.*

(a) (i) There were several approaches, which could have been taken in developing standards for SMEs. One course of action would have been for GAAP for SMEs to be developed on a national basis, with IFRS focusing on accounting for listed company activities. The main issue would have been that the practices developed for SMEs may not have been consistent and may have lacked comparability across national boundaries. Additionally, if a SME had wished to list its shares on a capital market, the transition to IFRS would have been more difficult.

Another approach would have been to detail the exemptions given to smaller entities in the mainstream IFRS. In this case, an appendix would have been included within the standard detailing the exemptions given to smaller enterprises.

A third approach would have been to introduce a separate set of standards comprising all the issues addressed in IFRS, which are relevant to SMEs.

However, the IFRS for SMEs is a self-contained set of accounting principles that are based on full IFRSs, which have been simplified so that they are suitable for SMEs. The Standard is organised by topic with the intention that the standard would be helpful to preparers and users of SME financial statements. The IFRS for SMEs and full IFRSs are separate and distinct frameworks. Entities that are eligible to apply the IFRS for SMEs, and that choose to do so, must apply that Standard in full and cannot choose the most suitable accounting policy from full IFRS or IFRS for SMEs.

However, the IFRS for SMEs is naturally a modified version of the full standards, and not an independently developed set of standards. It is based on recognised concepts and principles which should allow easier transition to full IFRS if the SME decides to become a public listed entity.

Note that the intention is for IFRS for SME to be updated at periodic intervals, approximately every three years. When this occurs, it is likely to increase the extent of comparability with full IFRS within which individual standards are revised, withdrawn or issued based upon the IASB work programme.

(ii) In deciding on the modifications to make to IFRS, the needs of the users have been taken into account, as well as the costs and other burdens imposed upon SMEs by IFRS. Relaxation of some of the measurement and recognition criteria in IFRS has been made in order to achieve the reduction in these costs and burdens. Some disclosure requirements in full IFRS are intended to meet the needs of listed entities, or to assist users in making forecasts of the future. Users of financial statements of SMEs often do not need such detailed information.

*Make specific comments regarding which accounting requirements are excluded from IFRS for SME.*

Small companies have different strategies, with survival and stability rather than profit maximisation being their goals. The stewardship function is often absent in small companies thus there are a number of accounting practices and disclosures which may not provide relevant information for the users of SME financial statements. As a result the standard does not address the following topics:

(i) earnings per share;

(ii) interim financial reporting;

(iii) segment reporting;

(iv) insurance (because entities that issue insurance contracts are not eligible to use the standard); and

(v) assets held for sale.

In addition there are certain accounting treatments, which are not allowable under the standard. Examples of these disallowable treatments are the revaluation model for property, plant and equipment and intangible assets. Generally there are simpler and more cost effective methods of accounting available to SMEs than those accounting practices, which have been disallowed. Additionally the Standard eliminates the 'available-for-sale' and 'held-to maturity' classifications of financial assets as permitted by IAS 39, 'Financial Instruments: Recognition and measurement'. Note that this issue is of reduced significance as IAS 39 is in the course of being replaced by IFRS 9 *'Financial Instruments'*, with the effective date for IFRS 9 currently stated to be for accounting periods commencing on or after 1 January 2015. IFRS 9 has not adopted the 'available-for-sale' classifications and there are conditions attached to using amortised cost for measurement of financial assets. All financial instruments are measured at amortised cost using the effective interest method except that investments in non-convertible and non-puttable ordinary and preference shares that are publicly traded or whose fair value can otherwise be measured reliably are measured at fair value through profit or loss. All amortised cost instruments must be tested for impairment. At the same time the Standard simplifies the hedge accounting and de-recognition requirements.

---

*Make specific comments regarding which accounting requirements have been simplified by IFRS for SME.*

---

Additionally the IFRS for SMEs makes numerous simplifications to the recognition, measurement and disclosure requirements in full IFRSs. Examples of these simplifications are:

(i) goodwill and other indefinite-life intangibles are amortised over their useful lives, but if useful life cannot be reliably estimated, then the useful life is presumed to be 10 years

(ii) a simplified calculation is allowed if measurement of defined benefit pension plan obligations (under the projected unit credit method) involves undue cost or effort

(iii) the cost model is permitted for investments in associates and joint ventures.

As a result of the above, SMEs do not have to comply with over 90% of the volume of accounting requirements applicable to listed companies. If an entity opts to use the IFRS for SMEs, it must follow the standard in its entirety and it cannot cherry pick between the requirements of the IFRS for SMEs and those of full IFRSs.

There is no universally agreed definition of a SME and a single definition cannot capture all the dimensions of a SME, or cannot be expected to reflect the differences between firms, sectors, or countries at different levels of development. Most definitions based on size use measures such as number of employees, net asset total, or annual turnover. However, none of these measures apply well across national borders. The IFRS for SMEs is intended for use by entities that have no public accountability (i.e. its debt or equity instruments are not publicly traded).

The decision regarding which entities should use the IFRS for SMEs remains with national regulatory authorities and standard-setters. These bodies often specify more detailed eligibility criteria.

*Part (b) tests your knowledge in relation to three specific accounting issues. You should deal with each situation in turn, explaining both the IFRS requirement and the full IFRS requirement from the appropriate reporting standard(s).*

(b) (i) **Defined benefit scheme**

The accounting policy currently applied by Whitebirk is consistent with IFRS for SME. Note that IFRS for SME also permits actuarial gains and losses to be recognised in profit or loss; this is no longer permitted by IAS 19. The entity shall apply its chosen accounting policy consistently to all of its defined benefit plans and all of its actuarial gains and losses. Actuarial gains and losses recognised in other comprehensive income shall also be presented within other components of equity on the statement of financial position.

Note: it is likely that, when the IFRS for SME is updated, this accounting policy choice may be removed to require all actuarial gains and losses to be taken to other comprehensive income. This would increase consistency with IAS 19 as amended in 2011.

(ii) **Business combination**

The IFRS states that the acquirer shall, at the acquisition date:

(a) recognise goodwill acquired in a business combination as an asset, and

(b) initially measure that goodwill at its cost, being the excess of the cost of the business combination over the acquirer's interest in the net fair value of the identifiable assets, liabilities and contingent liabilities.

After initial recognition, the acquirer shall measure goodwill acquired in a business combination at cost less accumulated amortisation and accumulated impairment losses. If an entity is unable to make a reliable estimate of the useful life of goodwill, the life is presumed to be ten years. There is no choice of accounting method for non controlling interests and therefore the partial goodwill method would be used.

Goodwill will be $5.7 million less 90% of $6 million i.e. $0.3 million. This will then be amortised over ten years at a value of $30,000 per annum.

(iii)   **Research and development expenditure**

The IFRS states that an entity shall recognise expenditure incurred internally on an intangible item, including all expenditure for both research and development activities, as an expense when it is incurred unless it forms part of the cost of another asset that meets the recognition criteria in this IFRS. Thus the expenditure of $1.5 million on research and development should all be written off to profit or loss.

<table>
<tr><td colspan="4" align="center">**ACCA marking scheme**</td><td></td></tr>
<tr><td></td><td></td><td></td><td></td><td>*Marks*</td></tr>
<tr><td>(a)</td><td>(i)/(ii)</td><td colspan="2">Subjective assessment including professional</td><td>16</td></tr>
<tr><td>(b)</td><td>(i)</td><td colspan="2">Defined benefit scheme</td><td>3</td></tr>
<tr><td></td><td>(Ii)</td><td colspan="2">Business combination</td><td>4</td></tr>
<tr><td></td><td>(iii)</td><td colspan="2">Research and development expenditure</td><td>2</td></tr>
<tr><td></td><td></td><td></td><td></td><td>———</td></tr>
<tr><td>Total</td><td></td><td></td><td></td><td>25</td></tr>
<tr><td></td><td></td><td></td><td></td><td>———</td></tr>
</table>

**Examiner's comments**

In part a, candidates had to comment on the different approaches which could have been taken by the International Accounting Standards Board in developing the 'IFRS for Small and Medium-sized Entities' explaining the approach finally taken by the IASB. Additionally candidates had to discuss the main differences and modifications to IFRS which the IASB made to reduce the burden of reporting for SME's. Specific examples had to be given and also a discussion of how the Board had dealt with the problem of defining an SME. This part of the question was very well answered. The subject had been very topical and been the subject of articles in the accountancy press.

In part b candidates had to discuss how the certain transactions should be dealt with in the financial statements of an entity with reference to the 'IFRS for Small and Medium-sized Entities'. The answers to this part of the question were quite variable. The three topic areas chosen were defined benefit, the purchase of an entity and research and development expenditure. Candidates were generally unclear about how to account for the transactions and many used full IFRS. The main issue was that candidates automatically assumed that the corridor approach would be used for defined benefit schemes which was incorrect. This question was generally well answered.

# UK GAAP FOCUS

## 58 KEY (DEC 09 EXAM) (UK GAAP FOCUS)

(a) FRS 11 *Impairment of fixed assets and goodwill* states that an asset is impaired when its carrying amount will not be recovered from its continuing use or from its sale. An entity must determine at each reporting date whether there is any indication that an asset is impaired. If an indicator of impairment exists then the asset's recoverable amount must be determined and compared with its carrying amount to assess the amount of any impairment. Accounting for the impairment of fixed assets can be difficult as FRS 11 is a complex accounting standard. The turbulence in the markets and signs of economic downturn will cause many companies to revisit their business plans and revise financial forecasts. As a result of these changes, there may be significant impairment charges. Indicators of impairment may arise from either the external environment in which the entity operates or from within the entity's own operating environment. Thus the current economic downturn is an obvious indicator of impairment, which may cause the entity to experience significant impairment charges.

Assets should be tested for impairment at as low a level as possible, at individual asset level where possible. However, many assets do not generate cash inflows independently from other assets and such assets will usually be tested within the income-generating unit (IGU) to which the asset belongs. Cash flow projections should be based on reasonable assumptions that represent management's best estimate of the range of economic conditions that will exist over the remaining useful life of the asset. The discount rate used is the rate which reflects the specific risks of the asset or IGU.

The basic principle is that an asset may not be carried in the balance sheet at more than its recoverable amount. An asset's recoverable amount is the higher of:

(a) the amount for which the asset could be sold in an arm's length transaction between knowledgeable and willing parties, net of costs of disposal (fair value less costs to sell); and

(b) the present value of the future cash flows that are expected to be derived from the asset (value in use). The expected future cash flows include those from the asset's continued use in the business and those from its ultimate disposal. Value in use (VIU) is explicitly based on present value calculations.

This measurement basis reflects the economic decisions that a company's management team makes when assets become impaired from the viewpoint of whether the business is better off disposing of the asset or continuing to use it. The assumptions used in arriving at the recoverable amount need to be 'reasonable and supportable' regardless of whether impairment calculations are based on fair value less costs to sell or value in use. The acceptable range for such assumptions will change over time and forecasts for revenue growth and profit margins are likely to have fallen in the economic climate. The assumptions made by management should be in line with the assumptions made by industry commentators or analysts. Variances from market will need to be justified and highlighted in financial statement disclosures. Whatever method is used to calculate the recoverable amount; the value needs to be considered in the light of available market evidence. If other entities in the same sector are taking impairment charges, the absence of an impairment charge has to be justified because the market will be asking the same question. It is important to inform the market about how it is dealing with the conditions, and be thinking about how different parts of the business are affected, and the market inputs they use in impairment testing. Impairment testing should be commenced as soon as possible as an impairment test process takes a significant amount of time. It includes identifying impairment indicators, assessing or reassessing the cash flows, determining the discount rates, testing the reasonableness of the assumptions and benchmarking the assumptions with the market. Goodwill does not have to be tested for impairment at the year-end; it can be tested earlier and if any impairment indicator arises at the balance sheet date, the impairment assessment can be updated. Also it is important to comply with all disclosure requirements such as the discount rate and long-term growth rate assumptions in a discounted cash flow model and describe what the key assumptions are and what they are based on.

It is important that the cash flows being tested are consistent with the assets being tested. The forecast cash flows should make allowance for investment in working capital if the business is expected to grow. When the detailed calculations have been completed, the company should check that their conclusions make sense by comparison to any market data such as share prices and analysts reports. Market capitalisation below net asset value is an impairment indicator, and calculations of recoverable amount are required. If the market capitalisation is lower than a value-in-use calculation, then the VIU assumptions may require reassessment. For example, the cash flow projections might not be as expected by the market, and the reasons for this must be scrutinised. Discount rates should be scrutinised in order to see if they are logical. Discount rates may have risen too as risk premiums rise. Many factors affect discount rates in impairment calculations. These include corporate lending rates, cost of capital and risks associated with cash flows, which are all increasing in the current volatile environment and can potentially result in an increase of the discount rate.

(b) An asset's carrying amount may not be recovered from future business activity. Wherever indicators of impairment exist, a review for impairment should be carried out. Where impairment is identified, a write-down of the carrying value to the recoverable amount should be charged as an immediate expense in profit or loss. Using a discount rate of 5%, the value in use of the non-current assets is:

| Year to | 31 May 2010 | 31 May 2011 | 31 May 2012 | 31 May 2013 | Total |
|---|---|---|---|---|---|
| Discounted cash flows: | ($000) | ($000) | ($000) | ($000) | ($000) |
| | 267 | 408 | 431 | 452 | 1,558 |

The carrying value of the non-current assets at 31 May 2009 is $3 million – depreciation of $600,000. i.e. $2.4 million. Therefore the assets are impaired by $842,000 ($2.4m – $1.558m).

FRS 11 requires an assessment at each balance sheet date whether there is an indication that an impairment loss may have decreased. This does not apply to goodwill. FRS 11 states that increase in value in use should not be recognised if they arise from the unwinding of the discount or the occurrence of forecast cash flows. In this case, the increase in value will be due to the unwinding of the discount and the increase in the cash flows used in the calculation. Compensation received in the form of reimbursements from governmental indemnities is recorded in the profit and loss account when the compensation becomes receivable. It is treated as a separate economic event and accounted for as such. At this time the government has only stated that it may reimburse the company and therefore credit should not be taken for any potential government receipt.

For a revalued asset, FRS 11 distinguishes two types of impairment. These are impairments arising from a clear consumption of economic benefits and other impairments of revalued fixed assets. The former should be recognised in the profit and loss account as it is effectively depreciation whilst other impairments should be recognised in the statement of total recognised gains and losses (STRGL) until the carrying amount reaches depreciated historical cost. Any balance of the loss is then treated as an expense in the profit and loss account. This latter category is intended to cover impairments caused by a general fall in prices such as would occur in the present economic climate experienced by the company. Thus the revaluation gain and the impairment loss would be treated as follows:

| Depreciated historical cost | $m | Revalued carrying value | $m |
|---|---|---|---|
| 1 Dec 06 | 10 | | 10 |
| Depreciation (2 years) | (2) | | (2) |
| Revaluation | | | 0.8 |
| 1 Dec 08 | 8 | | 8.8 |
| Depreciation | (1) | | (1.1) |
| Impairment loss | (1.5) | | (2.2) |
| 30 Nov 09 after impairment loss | 5.5 | | 5.5 |

The impairment loss of $2.2 million is charged to equity until the carrying amount reaches depreciated historical cost and thereafter it goes to profit or loss. It is assumed that the company will transfer an amount from revaluation surplus to retained earnings to cover the excess depreciation of $0.1 million as allowed by company law. Therefore the impairment loss charged to STRGL would be $(0.8 – 0.1) million i.e. $0.7 million and the remainder of $1.5 million would be charged to profit or loss.

A plan by management to dispose of an asset or group of assets due to underperformance could be deemed to be an indicator of impairment. Where a decision is made to sell a subsidiary, the amounts expected to be received would provide a basis for measuring the recoverable amount of the entity. It seems that the subsidiary's assets are impaired because their carrying amount is not recoverable from the proceeds of sale. FRS 3 *Reporting financial performance* and FRS 12 *Provisions, contingent liabilities and contingent assets* prohibit recognition of provisions for liabilities in respect of sales or terminations of businesses until there is a binding sale contract or constructive obligation. Provisions do not include amounts written off fixed assets and both FRS 3 and FRS 12 refer to the need to review assets for impairment before any provisions are recognised.

Thus an impairment loss of $5 million ($17m + $3m – $15m) should be recognised as soon as a disposal is envisaged. The impairment loss would be allocated first to write off goodwill of $3 million and then to write down the subsidiary's fixed assets by $2 million.

## 59    BURLEY (DEC 09 EXAM) (UK GAAP FOCUS)

(i)     The basic principle of revenue recognition is that a seller should recognise revenue when it obtains the right to consideration in exchange for performance (FRS 5 Application Note G). Revenue should be measured at the fair value of the consideration. Burley should recognise a purchase from Slite for the amount of the excess amount extracted (10,000 barrels × $100). The substance of the transaction is that Slite has sold the oil to Burley at the point of production at market value at that time. Burley should recognise all of the oil it has sold to the third parties as revenue including that purchased from Slite as the criteria above are met. The amount payable to Slite will change with movements in the oil price. The balance at the year-end is a financial liability, which should reflect the best estimate of the amount of cash payable, which at the year-end would be $1,050,000.

The best estimate will be based in the price of oil on 30 November 2009. At the year end there will be an expense of $50,000 as the liability will have increased from $1 million. The amount payable will be revised after the year-end to reflect changes in the price of oil and would have amounted to $950,000. Thus giving a gain of $100,000 to profit or loss in the following accounting period.

Events after the balance sheet date are events, which could be favourable or unfavourable and occur between the end of the reporting period and the date that the financial statements are authorised for issue. [FRS 21 Para 3] An adjusting event is an event after the reporting period that provides further evidence of conditions that existed at the end of the reporting period, including an event that indicates that the going concern assumption in relation to the whole part or part of the enterprise is not appropriate. A non-adjusting event is an event after the reporting period that is indicative of a condition that arose after the end of the reporting period. [FRS 21 Para 3]

Stock is required to be stated at the lower of cost and net realisable value (NRV). NRV is the estimated selling price in the ordinary course of business, less the estimated cost of completion and the estimated costs necessary to make the sale. Any write-down to NRV should be recognised as an expense in the period in which the write-down occurs. Estimates of NRV are based on the most reliable evidence available at the time the estimates are made. These estimates consider fluctuations in price directly relating to events occurring after the end of the financial period to the extent that they confirm conditions at the end of the accounting period.

Burley should calculate NRV by reference to the market price of oil at the balance sheet date. The price of oil changes frequently in response to many factors and therefore changes in the market price since the balance sheet date reflect events since that date. These represent non-adjusting events therefore the decline in the price of oil since the date of the financial statements will not be adjusted in those statements. The stock will be valued at cost of $98 per barrel as this is lower than NRV of $(105 – 2) i.e. $103 at the year-end.

***Workings 1***

|  |  | DR ($) | CR ($) |
|---|---|---|---|
| Purchases/stock | (10,000 × 100) | 1m |  |
| Slite – financial liability |  |  | 1m |
| At year end: |  |  |  |
| Expense |  | 50,000 |  |
| Slite – financial liability | (10,000 × $(105 – 100)) |  | 50,000 |
| After year end: |  |  |  |
| Slite financial liability | (10,000 × $(105 – 95)) | 100,000 |  |
| Profit and loss account |  |  | 100,000 |

Cash paid to Slite is $950,000 on 12 December 2009

(ii)   FRS 9 *Associates and joint ventures* states that a joint venture is:

An entity in which the reporting entity holds an interest on a long-term basis and is jointly controlled by the reporting entity and one or more other venturers under a contractual arrangement.

Joint control is present where none of the entities alone can control that entity but all together can do so and decisions on financial and operating policy essential to the activities, economic performance and financial position of that venture require each venturer's consent. Joint control implies that each venturer should play an active role in setting the operating and financial policies of the joint venture, at least at general strategy level. The effect of this requirement is that each venturer has a veto on high-level strategic decisions. A joint venture must be a separate entity actually carrying on a business of its own. Where this is not the case, it is a joint arrangement that is not an entity. Accounting for joint ventures in the consolidated financial statements joint ventures should be included under the gross equity method.

Thus Burley cannot use the gross equity method, as Wells is not jointly controlled. A decision can be made by gaining the approval of two thirds of the venturers and not by unanimous agreement. Two out of the three venturers can make the decision. Thus each investor must account for their interest in the entity as an associate since they have significant influence but not control. Equity accounting will be used.

One of the key differences between decommissioning costs and other costs of acquisition is the timing of costs. Decommissioning costs will not become payable until some future date. Consequently, there is likely to be uncertainty over the amount of costs that will be incurred. Management should record its best estimate of the entity's obligations.

Discounting is used to address the impact of the delayed cash flows. The amount capitalised, as part of the assets will be the amount estimated to be paid, discounted to the date of initial recognition. The related credit is recognised in provisions. The entity would record changes in the existing liability due to changes in discount rate and these changes are added to, or deducted from, the cost of the related asset in the current period.

Thus in the case of Wells, the accounting for the decommissioning is as follows.

| | | $m |
|---|---|---|
| The carrying amount of the asset will be | | |
| Carrying amount at 1 December 2008 | (240 – depreciation 60 – 14.1 decrease in decommissioning costs) | 165.9 |
| *Less* depreciation | 165.9 ÷ 30 years | (5.5) |
| Carrying amount at 30 November 2009 | | 160.4 |
| Finance cost | ($32.6 million – $14.1 million) at 7% | 1.3 |
| Decommissioning liability will be: | ($32.6m – $14.1m) | 18.5 |
| Decommissioning liability at 30 November 2009 | | 19.8 |

A 'joint arrangement' that is not an entity is defined by FRS 9 as a contractual arrangement under which the participants engage in joint activities that do not create an entity because it would not be carrying on a trade or business of its own. Thus cost sharing or risk taking arrangements are joint arrangements and the standard gives shared production facilities as an example of a joint arrangement. Thus the pipeline is an example of a joint arrangement.

FRS 9 requires that the venturer should recognise in its financial statements its share of the joint assets, liabilities and cash flows, measured according to the terms of the agreement. Therefore Burley should not show the asset as an investment but as fixed assets. Any joint liabilities or expenses incurred should be shown also.

(iii) An asset is a right or other access to future economic benefits controlled by an entity as a result of past transactions or events (*Statement of Principles*). An asset should be recognised when there is sufficient evidence that there has been a change in assets or liabilities, which can be measured with sufficient reliability.

FRS 10 *Goodwill and intangible assets* defines intangible assets as 'non-financial fixed assets that do not have physical substance but are identifiable and are controlled by the entity through custody or legal rights'. Separability is a key element of the definition of an intangible asset. Some intangibles are more clearly separable than others but determining where this point lies is quite subjective. Another component is control. FRS 5 defines control as the ability to obtain future economic benefits relating to an asset and to restrict the access of others to those benefits. In the context of intangible assets, FRS 10 states that control must be exercised through custody or legal rights. Thus in the case of the licence, control is exercised by legal rights that restrict the access of others.

Thus the licence can be capitalised at cost and amortised. If the exploration of the area does not lead to the discovery of oil, and activities are discontinued in the area, then an impairment test will be performed.

## 60    CATE (JUN 10 EXAM) (UK GAAP FOCUS)

(a)    A deferred tax asset should be recognised if it is more likely than not that it will be recovered. A key requirement of FRS 19 *Deferred tax* is that deferred tax assets should only be 'recognised' to the extent that, on the basis of all available evidence, it can be regarded as more likely than not that there will be suitable profits from which the future reversal of the underlying timing differences can be deducted. The recognition of deferred tax assets on losses carried forward does not seem to be in accordance with FRS 19. Cate is not able to provide convincing evidence that sufficient taxable profits will be generated against which the unused tax losses can be offset. According to FRS 19 the existence of unused tax losses is strong evidence that future taxable profit may not be available against which to offset the losses. Therefore when an entity has a history of recent losses, the entity recognises deferred tax assets arising from unused tax losses only to the extent that the entity has evidence that there will be suitable taxable profits from which the future reversal of the underlying timing differences can be deducted. As Cate has a history of recent losses and as it does not have sufficient taxable temporary differences, Cate needs to provide convincing other evidence that sufficient taxable profit would be available against which the unused tax losses could be offset. The unused tax losses in question did not result from identifiable causes, which were unlikely to recur as the losses are due to ordinary business activities. Additionally there are no tax planning opportunities available to Cate that would create taxable profit in the period in which the unused tax losses could be offset (FRS 19).

Thus at 31 May 2010 it is unlikely that the entity would generate taxable profits before the unused tax losses expired. The improved performance in 2010 would not be indicative of future good performance as Cate would have suffered a net loss before tax had it not been for the non-operating gains.

Cate's anticipation of improved future trading could not alone be regarded as meeting the requirement for strong evidence of future profits. When assessing the use of carry-forward tax losses, weight should be given to revenues from existing orders or confirmed contracts rather than those that are merely expected from improved trading. Thus the recognition of deferred tax assets on losses carried forward is not in accordance with FRS 19 as Cate is not able to provide convincing evidence that sufficient taxable profits would be generated against which the unused tax losses could be offset.

(b)    **Investment**

Cate's position for an investment where the investor has significant influence and its method of calculating fair value can be challenged.

An asset's recoverable amount represents its greatest value to the business in terms of its cash flows that it can generate i.e. the higher of net realisable value (which is what the asset can be sold for less direct selling expenses) and value in use (the cash flows that are expected to be generated from its continued use including those from its ultimate disposal). The assets recoverable amount is compared with its carrying value to indicate any impairment. Both net realisable value and value in use can be difficult to determine. However, it is not always necessary to calculate both measures, as if the NRV or value in use is greater than the carrying amount, there is no need to estimate the other amount.

It should be possible in this case to calculate a figure for the recoverable amount. Cate's view that market price cannot reflect the fair value of significant holdings of equity such as an investment in an associate is incorrect as FRS 11 *Impairment of fixed assets and goodwill* prescribes the method of conducting the impairment test in such circumstances by stating that if there is no binding sale agreement but an asset is traded in an active market, fair value less costs to sell is the asset's market price less the costs of disposal. Further, the appropriate market price is usually the current bid price.

Additionally investments in associates generate discrete cash flows and should be considered individually. Their value in use should normally be based on the future cash flows of the underlying entities that are attributable to the group's interest rather than on the dividend cash flows. Investments in associates come within the scope of FRS 11. Estimates of future cash flows should be produced. These cash flows are then discounted to present value hence giving value in use.

It seems as though Cate wishes to avoid an impairment charge on the investment.

(c) **FRS 3 *Reporting financial performance***

An undertaking will cease to be a subsidiary when a group sells or reduces its percentage interest in the undertaking below 50%. Similarly a parent may lose control because of changes in the rights it holds or those held by another party in that undertaking. A reduction in the percentage interest may arise from a direct disposal or from an indirect disposal, for example the exercise of share options by another party or the subsidiary issues shares to other non-group parties as in the case of Cate. A gain or loss will normally arise in both cases. A partial disposal of an interest in a subsidiary in which the parent company loses control but retains an interest as an associate or trade investment creates the recognition of a gain or loss on the interest disposed of. The profit or loss should be calculated as the difference between the carrying amount of the net assets of the subsidiary attributable to the group's interest before the reduction and the carrying amount of the net assets of the subsidiary attributable to the group's interest after the reduction including any proceeds received. The net assets include any related goodwill not written off. In this case, Cate should stop consolidating Date on a line-by-line basis from the date that control was lost. Further investigation is required into whether the holding is treated as an associate or trade investment. The agreement that Cate is no longer represented on the board or able to participate in management would suggest loss of significant influence despite the 35% of voting rights retained.

FRS 3 requires the profit or loss on sale of an asset to be calculated by reference to the carrying value of that asset and conflicts with FRS 2 calculation above as goodwill is used in the calculation. Also the important components, which FRS 3 requires to be highlighted, are:

(a)    the results of continuing operations (separately highlighting the results of acquisitions in the year, if material);

(b)    the results of discontinued operations;

(c)    the results of exceptional transactions – analysed over continuing and discontinued operations.

FRS 3 defines a discontinued operation as an operation that is sold or terminated and that satisfies all of the following conditions:

(a)    the sale or termination is completed either in the period or before the earlier of three months after the commencement of the subsequent period or the date on which the financial statements are approved;

(b)     if a termination, the former activities have ceased permanently;

(c)     the sale or termination has a material effect on the nature and focus of the reporting entity's operations and represents a material reduction in its operating facilities resulting either from its withdrawal from a particular market (whether class of business or geographical) or from a material reduction in turnover in continuing markets;

(d)     the assets, liabilities, results of operations and activities are clearly distinguishable, physically and operationally and for financial reporting purposes.

Cate has not met all of the conditions of FRS 3 but it could be argued that the best presentation in the financial statements is that set out in FRS 3 for the following reasons.

The decision not to subscribe to the issue of new shares of Date is clearly a change in the strategy of Cate. Further by deciding not to subscribe to the issue of new shares of Date, Cate agreed to the dilution and the loss of control, which could be argued, is similar to a decision to sell shares while retaining a continuing interest in the entity. Also Date represents a separate distinguishable line of business, which is a determining factor in FRS 3, and information disclosed on FRS 3 principles highlights the impact of Date on Cate's financial statements. Finally, the agreement between Date's shareholders confirms that Cate has lost control over its former subsidiary.

The results of Date should be classified as discontinued if the retained interest is not being subject to significant influence by the group.

(d)     **Defined benefit plan**

The Plan is not a defined contribution plan because Cate has a legal or constructive obligation to pay further contributions if the fund does not have sufficient assets to pay all employee benefits relating to employee service in the current and prior periods (FRS 17 Para's 2, 20). All other post-employment benefit plans that do not qualify as a defined contribution plan are, by definition therefore defined benefit plans. Defined benefit plans may be unfunded, or they may be wholly or partly funded. Also FRS 17 indicates that Cate's plan is a defined benefit plan as it shows that an entity's obligation is not limited to the amount that it agrees to contribute to the fund. An example of a constructive obligation is a practice of granting annual increases to pensions in payment and deferred pensions that are discretionary but are in practice granted as a measure of protection against inflation. The cost of the increases should be factored into the annual service cost and scheme liability. According to the terms of the Plan, if Cate opts to terminate, Cate is responsible for discharging the liability created by the Plan. FRS 17 says that an entity should account not only for its legal obligation under the formal terms of a defined benefit plan, but also for any constructive obligation that arises from the enterprise's informal practices. Informal practices give rise to a constructive obligation where the enterprise has no realistic alternative but to pay employee benefits. Even if the Plan were not considered to be a defined benefit plan under FRS 17, Cate would have a constructive obligation to provide the benefit, having a history of paying benefits. The practice has created a valid expectation on the part of employees that the amounts will be paid in the future. Therefore Cate should account for the Plan as a defined benefit plan in accordance with FRS 17. Cate has to recognise, at a minimum, its net present liability for the benefits to be paid under the Plan.

## 61   NORMAN (JUN 08 EXAM) (UK GAAP FOCUS)

**Segment Reporting**

SSAP 25 *Segmental reporting* supports the provisions of the Companies Acts by saying that it is the directors' responsibility to determine the analysis of the segments. The standard aims to provide guidance on factors which should influence the definition of segments. Such factors include operations which are subject to different degrees of risk or return on capital employed, have experienced different rates of growth, and have different potential for future development. Having established that a segment is distinguishable based on the above criteria, it is necessary to consider whether a segment is significant enough to warrant separate disclosure. A segment will normally be significant if:

(a)     its turnover from third parties is 10% or more of the total third party turnover, or

(b)     its segment result (profit or loss) is 10% or more of the combined result of all segments in profit or of all segments in loss, whichever combined result is the greater, or

(c)     its net assets are 10% or more of the total net assets of the entity

A class of business is defined as a distinguishable component of an entity that provides a separate product or resource. To identify reportable classes of business, directors should consider the nature of products, processes, markets distribution channels, the organisation of the entity and any legal factors.

The segmental information needs to reflect the company's risk and returns profile, and to inform users of the nature of that profile. Thus in determining business or geographical segments, products or services with significantly different risks, rewards, and future prospects should not be combined together to create a reportable segment. SSAP 25 explains the criteria for identifying whether separate segments exist but this explanation is only for guidance purposes. The directors have to exercise their judgement in this area. It would appear that separate business segments do not exist for Norman but that separate geographical segments do exist. The standard's definition of a geographical segment is 'a geographical area comprising an individual country or group of countries in which an entity operates, or to which it supplies products or services' (SSAP 25 para 31). In addition it emphasises that geographical analysis needs to consider two distinct aspects:

(i)     analysis by operating location (origin basis)

(ii)    analysis by destination of sale or service (destination basis).

Different risk environments are an important factor in determining segments.

In the case of the existing segments the European segment meets the criteria for a segment as its reported revenue from external sales ($210 million) is more than 10% of the combined revenue ($1,010 million). However, it fails the profit/loss and net asset tests. Its results are a profit of $10 million which is less than 10% of the greater of the reported profit or reported loss. The profit reported is $175 million. Similarly its segment net assets of $100 million are less than 10% of the combined segment assets $1,200 million). The South East Asia segment passes all of the threshold tests. If the company changes its segments then the above tests will have to be re-performed.

There may be other regions which might fall under the definition of a segment and Norman should review the risk profile of the 'other regions' segment. The fact that performance indicators are set for each hotel will not affect the determination of the geographical segments under SSAP 25.

## 62 ENGINA (PILOT 01) (UK GAAP FOCUS)

Brice and Partners

Brice Lane

Bridlington

(Date)

The Directors

Engina and Co.

Orange Lane

Edmond

Dear Sirs

**Related Party Transactions**

We are writing to explain the reasons why it is important to disclose 'Related Party Transactions' while at the same time explaining the nature of the disclosure required under current UK regulations. We appreciate the cultural and political sensitivity of the disclosure of such transactions in your country and the fact that such opinions will not change in the short term. However, a key factor in your thoughts about the disclosure of 'Related Party Transactions' is the fact that in addition to the requirements of the accounting standard (FRS 8 *Related party disclosures*) and the Companies Act, the Stock Exchange imposes additional disclosures on companies which require a listing. We hope that the following general discussion and specific comments on the transactions undertaken in your company will assist your understanding of quite a complex and sensitive area.

Related party relationships are part of the normal business process. Entities operate the separate parts of their business through subsidiaries and associates, and acquire interests in other enterprises for investment or commercial reasons. Thus control or significant influence can be exercised over the investee by the investing company. These relationships can have a significant effect on the financial position and operating results of the company and lead to transactions which would not normally be undertaken. For example, a company may sell a large proportion of its production to its parent company because it cannot and could not find a market elsewhere. Additionally the transactions may be effected at prices which would not be acceptable to unrelated parties.

Even if there are no transactions between the related parties, it is still possible for the operating results and financial position of an enterprise to be affected by the relationship. A recently acquired subsidiary can be forced to finish a relationship with a company in order to benefit group companies. Transactions may be entered into on terms different from those applicable to an unrelated party. For example, a holding company may lease equipment to a subsidiary on terms unrelated to market rates for equivalent leases.

In the absence of contrary information, it is assumed that the financial statements of an entity reflect transactions carried out on an arm's length basis and that the entity has independent discretionary power over its actions and pursues its activities independently.

If these assumptions are not justified because of related party transactions, then disclosure of this fact should be made. Even if transactions are at arm's length, the disclosure of related party transactions is useful because it is likely that future transactions may be affected by such relationships. The main issues in determining such disclosures are the identification of related parties, the types of transactions and arrangements and the information to be disclosed.

It can be seen that information about related parties can be an important element of any investment decision and the regulatory authorities in the UK consider disclosure of such information to be of paramount importance.

The following specific comments relate to the list of transactions with connected persons which you supplied to us.

**Sale of goods to directors**

Related party transactions need only be disclosed where they are material. These transactions are material where the users of financial statements might reasonably be influenced by such a transaction. Thus it is not possible to avoid disclosing such items on the grounds that they are not numerically large enough. Additionally, where the related party is a director then the transaction should be viewed in relation to its materiality to that director. Contracts of significance with directors also require disclosure by the Stock Exchange.

In this case your director (Mr Satay) has purchased $600,000 (12 months × $50,000) of goods from the company and a car for $45,000 with a market value of $80,000. Although neither of these transactions is material or significant to the company or the directors, the spirit of good corporate governance would dictate that any transactions with directors are extremely sensitive and we would recommend disclosure of such transactions.

**Hotel property**

Accounting standards (FRS 8 *Related party disclosures*) require 'any other elements of the transactions necessary for an understanding of the financial statements' to be disclosed. The hotel property sold to the brother of the Managing Director is a related party transaction which appears to have been undertaken at below market price. The disclosure of simply this fact would not reflect the reality of your company's position. The carrying value of the hotel needs to be adjusted as it has become impaired. The hotel should have been shown in your records under UK accounting standards at the lower of carrying value ($5 million) and the recoverable amount (higher of net realisable value ($4.3 million − $0.2 million, i.e. $4.1 million) and value in use $3.6 million). Thus the hotel should have been recorded at $4.1 million.

Thus the property has been sold at $100,000 below the impaired value and this is the nature of the disclosure which should be made, thus reflecting more closely the nature of the property market in your country and the nature of the transaction.

**Group structure**

The Companies Acts and Stock Exchange rules contain requirements to disclose directors interests in the share capital of a company. Mr Satay owns 10% of the share capital of Engina directly and controls 90% of its share capital through his 80% ownership of Wheel Ltd.

Current rules in the UK (FRS 8) give exemptions to disclosures of transactions with group members (Wheel Ltd) in the accounts of 90% (or more) owned subsidiaries. Thus Engina need not disclose transactions with Wheel Ltd (assuming that Wheel Ltd prepares group accounts). However, the transactions with Car Ltd will have to be disclosed as both Car and

Engina are under the common control of Mr Satay and Car is not an investee of the Wheel group. We realise that the above disclosure requirements seem a little inconsistent but this is due to the current requirements of the accounting standards.

We hope that the above explanations are of use to you and realise that culturally and politically they may seem unacceptable. However, if you wish for a quotation on the Stock Exchange in the UK, then the disclosure requirements set out above will have to be adhered to.

Yours faithfully,

Brice and Partners

## 63 GHORSE (DEC 07 EXAM) (UK GAAP FOCUS)

Under SSAP 21 *Accounting for leases and hire purchase contracts*, operating lease payments should be recognised as an expense in the profit and loss account over the lease term on a straight-line basis, unless another systematic basis is more representative of the time pattern of the user's benefit.

The provisions of the lease have changed significantly and would need to be reassessed.

The lease term is now for the major part of the economic life of the assets, and at the inception of the lease, the present value of the minimum lease payments is more than 90% (97.4%) of the fair value of the leased asset. (Fair value $35 million, NPV of lease payments $34.1 million) Even if title is not transferred at the end of the lease the lease can still be a finance lease. Any change in the estimate of the length of life of a lease would not change its classification but where the provisions of the lease have changed, re-assessment of its classification takes place. Thus it would appear that the lease is now a finance lease, and it would be shown in the balance sheet at the present value of the lease payments as this is lower than the fair value. This change in classification will not affect ROCE but it will increase tangible fixed assets by $34.1 million and liabilities by the same amount.

**Effect on ROCE**

|  | $m |
|---|---|
| Operating profit before tax and interest | 30 |
| *Less* profit on discontinued operations | (1) |
| Impairment | (3.5) |
|  | 25.5 |

|  | $m |
|---|---|
| Capital employed | 220 |
| *Less* impairment | (3.5) |
| Profit on sale of Cee | 3 |
| Deferred tax asset (4.5 + 2.7) | 7.2 |
|  | 226.7 |

ROCE will fall from 13.6% to 11.2% (25.5/226.7) and thus the directors' fears that a ROCE would be adversely affected are justified.

## 64 GRANGE (DEC 09 EXAM) (UK GAAP FOCUS)

**(a)** **Disposal of equity interest in Sitin**

The loss recognised in the profit and loss account would be as follows:

|  | $m |
|---|---|
| Fair value of consideration | 23.0 |
| Less net assets and goodwill derecognized net assets (60% of 36) | (21.6) |
| Goodwill ($39 – $32 million) x 60% | (4.2) |
| Loss on disposal | (2.8) |

Sitin will be treated as an associate and will be valued at (40% × ($36m + $7m) i.e. $17.2 million.

**(b)** **Grange plc**

**Consolidated Balance Sheet at 30 November 2009**

|  | $m |
|---|---|
| Fixed Assets: | |
| Tangible assets (W6) | 775.47 |
| Investment property (W7) | 8.0 |
| Goodwill (32.8 + 8 – 2) | 38.8 |
| Intangible assets (10 – 3) | 7.0 |
| Investment in Sitin (part (a)) | 17.2 |
|  | 846.47 |
| | |
| Current assets | 926.0 |
| Creditors: amounts falling due within one year | |
| Trade creditors | (354.0) |
| Provisions for liabilities | (52.0) |
|  | (406.0) |
| Net current assets | 520.0 |
| Total assets less current liabilities | 1,366.47 |
| Creditors: amounts falling due after more than one year | (334.0) |
| Net assets | 1,032.47 |
| | |
| Capital and reserves | |
| Called up share capital | 430.0 |
| Profit and loss reserve (W3) | 426.25 |
| Other reserves (W3) | 38.4 |
|  | 894.65 |
| Non-controlling interest (i.e. minority interest) | 137.82 |
| Capital employed | 1,032.47 |

*Workings*

(W1) **Park Goodwill and subsequent acquisition**

|  | $m |
|---|---|
| Fair value of consideration for 60% interest | 250 |
| Fair value of identifiable net assets acquired (60% of 360) | (216) |
| Franchise right (60% of 10) | (6) |
| | |
| Goodwill | 28 |

Depreciation of Franchise right

1 June 2008 to 30 November 2009 – $10m divided by 5 years multiplied by 1.5 years is $3 million

Dr Profit for loss $3 million

Cr Franchise right $3 million

|  | $m |
|---|---|
| Fair value of consideration for 20% interest | 90 |
| Fair value of identifiable net assets acquired (20% of 414) | (82.8) |
| Fair value of land (20% of 5) | (1) |
| Franchise right (20% of 7) | (1.4) |
| | |
| Goodwill | 4.8 |
| | |
| Total goodwill is $(28 + 4.8)m i.e. | $32.8m |

(W2) **Fence goodwill and disposal**

|  | $m |
|---|---|
| Fair value of consideration | 214 |
| Fair value of net assets held | (202) |
| Increase in value of PPE | (4) |
| | |
| Goodwill | 8 |

|  | $m |
|---|---|
| Sale of equity interest in Fence | |
| Fair value of consideration received | 80.0 |
| Less (Net Assets per question at 30 November 2009 232 – provision created 25 + Fair value of PPE at acquisition 4 – depreciation of fair value adjustment 0.53) | |
| (4 × 16/12 × 1/10) × 25% | (52.62) |
| Goodwill (8 × 25%) | (2.0) |
| | |
| Gain on sale to the group | 25.38 |

Because a provisional fair value had been recognised and the valuation for the fixed asset was received within 12 months of the date of the acquisition, the fair value of the net assets at acquisition is adjusted thus affecting goodwill.

At the date of acquisition the liability was a contingent liability and it was only events in the post acquisition period that has resulted in the liability crystallising. The contingent liability consolidation adjustment is reversed and a provision created accordingly. No adjustment will be made to goodwill arising on acquisition.

At acquisition 31 July 2008

| | |
|---|---|
| Dr Retained earnings | $30 million |
| Cr Contingent liability | $30 million |

In the period to 30 November 2009

| | |
|---|---|
| Dr Contingent Liability/provisions | $5 million |
| Cr Profit or Loss | $5 million |

(W3) **Profit and loss account reserve and other reserves**

| Retained earnings | $m |
|---|---|
| Grange - balance at 30 November 2009 | 410.0 |
| Associate profits Sitin (post acquisition profit 4 x 100%) | 4.0 |
| Loss on disposal of Sitin | (2.8) |
| Impairment | (31.0) |
| Provision for legal claims | (7.0) |
| Post acquisition reserves: Park (60% x (year end retained earnings 170 – acquisition profit 115 – franchise amortisation 3)) | 31.2 |
| Fence (100% × (year end retained earnings 65 – acquisition retained earnings 73 + conversion of contingent liability and reduction 5 – FV PPE depreciation 0.53)) | (3.53) |
| Fence – profit on sale | 25.38 |
| | 426.25 |

| Other reserves | $m |
|---|---|
| Balance at 30 November 2009 | 22 |
| Post acqn reserves – Park (60% x (14 – 10)) | 2.4 |
| – Fence (17 – 9) | 8 |
| Revaluation surplus – foreign property | 4 |
| Investment property – gain | 2 |
| | 38.4 |

**(W4) Provisions**

|  | $m |
|---|---|
| Balance at 30 November 2009 Grange | 10 |
| Park | 6 |
| Fence | 4 |
|  | 20 |
| Contingency | 30 |
| Cancellation of contingency and introduction of provision | (5) |
| Provision for environmental claims | 7 |
|  | 52 |

**(W5) Non-controlling interest (i.e. minority interest)**

|  | $m |
|---|---|
| Park (20% of (414 + land 5 + franchise 7)) | 85.20 |
| Fence (W2) | 52.62 |
| Total | 137.82 |

**(W6) Fixed assets**

|  | $m | $m |
|---|---|---|
| Grange | 251 | |
| Park | 311 | |
| Fence | 238 | 800 |
| Increase in value of land – Park (360 – 230 – 115 – 10) | | 5 |
| Investment property – reclassified | | (6) |
| Impairment – Grange (W9) | | (31) |
| Increase in value of fixed assets – Fence | | 4 |
| Less: increased depreciation ($4 \times 16/12 \div 10$) | | (0.53) |
| Revaluation surplus – foreign property | | 4 |
|  | | 775.47 |

**(W7)** The land should be classified as an investment property. Although Grange has not decided what to do with the land, it is being held for capital appreciation. SSAP 19 *Investment property* states that land held for investment potential is an investment property. The land will be measured at open market value. The fall in value of the investment property after the year-end will not affect its year-end valuation as the uncertainty relating to the regeneration occurred after the year-end.

| Dr Investment property | $6 million |
|---|---|
| Cr Tangible assets | $6 million |
| Dr Investment property | $2 million |
| Cr Other reserves | $2 million |

No depreciation will be charged

**(W8) Provision for environmental claims**

The environmental obligations of $1 million and $6 million (total $7 million) arise from past events but the costs of $4 million relating to the improvement of the manufacturing process relate to the company's future operations and should not be provided for.

| | |
|---|---|
| Dr Profit and loss account | $7 million |
| Cr Provision | $7 million |

**(W9) Restructuring**

A provision for restructuring should not be recognised, as a constructive obligation does not exist. A constructive obligation arises when an entity both has a detailed formal plan and makes an announcement of the plan to those affected. The events to date do not provide sufficient detail that would permit recognition of a constructive obligation. Therefore no provision for reorganisation should be made and the costs and benefits of the plan should not be taken into account when determining the impairment loss. Any impairment loss can be allocated to non-current assets, as this is the area in which the directors feel that loss has occurred.

| | $m |
|---|---|
| Carrying value of Grange's net assets | 862 |
| Revaluation surplus | 4 |
| Provision for legal claims | (7) |
| Investment property | 2 |
| | 861 |
| Value-in-use (pre-restructuring) | 830 |
| Impairment to fixed assets | (31) |

**(W10) Foreign property**

| | $m |
|---|---|
| Value at 30 November 2009 (12m dinars/1.5) | 8 |
| Value at acquisition 30 November 2008 | 4 |
| Revaluation surplus to equity | 4 |
| Change in fair value (4m dinars at 1.5) | 2.67 |
| Exchange rate change | 1.33 |
| (8m dinars at 2 minus 12 million dinars at 1.5) | 4 |

## 65    ASHANTI (JUN 10 EXAM) (UK GAAP FOCUS)

Ashanti Group: Profit and Loss Account for the year ended 30 April 2010 (see working 1)

|  | Ashanti $m |
|---|---|
| Turnover | 1,096 |
| Cost of sales | (851) |
| Gross profit | 245 |
| Distribution costs | (64) |
| Administration expenses | (94.71) |
| Other operating income | 54 |
| Operating profit before interest | 140.29 |
| Loss on sale of operations | (9.44) |
| Profit from associate | 2.1 |
| Net interest costs | (26.00 |
| Profit on ordinary activities before tax | 106.95 |
| Taxation | (49.00) |
| Profit on ordinary activities after taxation | 57.95 |
| Non-controlling interest (i.e. minority interest) (W8) | (8.66) |
| Profit on ordinary activities after attributable to | 49.29 |
|  | 57.95 |

Statement of total recognised gains and losses:

| | |
|---|---|
| Profit for financial year | 57.95 |
| Gains (net) on fixed assets revaluation | 18.60 |
| Actuarial losses on defined benefit plan | (14.00) |
| Total Recognised Gains and Losses for year | 62.55 |

| Total Recognised Gains and Losses attributable to: | $m |
|---|---|
| Equity holders of the parent | 52.09 |
| Non-controlling interest (i.e. minority interest) (W8) | 10.46 |
|  | 62.55 |

KAPLAN PUBLISHING

*Workings*

(W1)

| | Ashanti $m | Bochem $m | Ceram $m | Adjusts $m | Total $m |
|---|---|---|---|---|---|
| Turnover | 810 | 235 | 71 | (15) | |
| Revenue from illiquid customer (W5) | (5) | | | | 1,096 |
| Intercompany profit ($5m × 20%) | (1) | | | | |
| Cost of sales | (686) | (137) | (42) | 15 | (851) |
| | | | | | |
| Gross profit | 118 | 98 | 29 | | 245 |
| Distribution costs | (30) | (21) | (13) | | (64) |
| Administrative expenses | (55) | (29) | (6) | | |
| Mis-selling accrual (W7) | (0.21) | | | | |
| Depreciation (W2) | | (2) | | | |
| Loss on revaluation of plant and machinery (W6) | (0.6) | | | | |
| Impairment of goodwill (W2) | (1.9) | | | | (94.71) |
| Other income | 31 | 17 | 6 | | 54 |
| Impairment of bond (W4) | (5.00) | | | | |
| Impairment of trade receivable (W5) | (3) | | | | |
| Net interest costs | (8) | (6) | (4) | | (26.00) |
| Sale of equity interest (W2) | 8.06 | | | | |
| Loss on sale of Ceram (W3) | | (17.5) | | | (9.44) |
| Share of profits of associate (W3) | | 2.1 | | | 2.1 |
| | | | | | |
| Profit before tax | 53.35 | 41.6 | 12 | | 106.95 |
| Income tax expense | (21.00) | (23.00) | (5) | | (49.00) |
| | | | | | |
| Profit for the year | 32.35 | 18.60 | 7 | | 57.95 |
| Statement of total recognised gains and losses: | | | | | |
| Gains on property revaluation | 12 | 6 | – | | |
| Revaluation adjustment (W6) | 0.6 | | | | 18.6 |
| Actuarial losses on defined benefit plan | (14) | – | – | | (14.0) |
| | | | | | |
| Recognised gains and losses | (1.4) | 6.00 | – | | 4.6 |
| | | | | | |
| Total recognised gains and losses | 30.95 | 24.60 | 7 | | 62.55 |

(W2)  **Bochem**

|  | $m |
|---|---|
| Fair value of consideration for 70% interest | 150 |
| Fair value of identifiable net assets acquired (70% of $160m) | (112) |
| **Goodwill** | 38 |

| Depreciation of plant |  |
|---|---|
| Fair value of identifiable net assets | 160 |
| Book value ($55m + $85m + $10m) | (150) |
| **Plant revaluation** | 10 |

| Dr Profit or loss ($10 × 1/5) | 2.0 |
|---|---|
| Dr Retained earnings | 2.0 |
| Cr Accumulated depreciation | 4.0 |
| Goodwill impairment |  |
| Up to 30 April 2009, $38m × 15% | $5.7 m |
| Further impairment up to 30 April 2010, $38 × 5% | $1.9 m |
| **Total impairment** | $8.6 m |

| Sale of equity interest in Bochem | $m |
|---|---|
| Fair value of consideration received | 34 |
| Less Net assets disposed (Net assets per question at year end $210m + Fair value of PPE at acquisition $10m – depreciation of fair value adjustment $4m) × 10% | (21.6) |
| Goodwill (38 – 7.6) × 10/70 | (4.34) |
| **Gain on disposal** | 8.06 |

(W3)  **Ceram**

|  | $m | $m |
|---|---|---|
| Fair value of consideration for 80% interest | 136 |  |
| Indirect holding in Ceram – MI (30% of 136) | (40.8) | 95.2 |
| Fair value of identifiable net assets acquired (56% × $115m) |  | (64.4) |
| **Goodwill** |  | 30.8 |

The fair value of the consideration held in Ceram represents the 80% shareholding purchased by Bochem. The 30% element that belongs to the MI of Bochem needs to be deducted thereby giving the net balance representing the effective 56% (70% of 80%) shareholding from the group viewpoint.

As Bochem has sold a controlling interest in Ceram, a gain or loss on disposal should be calculated. Additionally, the results of Ceram should only be consolidated in the profit and loss account for the six months to 1 November 2009. Thereafter Ceram should be equity accounted. However, goodwill could be calculated from the entity's perspective which would give a significantly different goodwill and gain/loss on disposal figure.

The loss recognised in the profit and loss account would be as follows:

|  |  | $m |
|---|---|---|
| Fair value of consideration |  | 90 |
| Less: | net assets and goodwill derecognised |  |
|  | net assets (160 × 50%) | (80) |
|  | goodwill (30.8 × 50/56) | (27.5) |
| Loss on disposal to profit or loss |  | (17.5) |

The loss above has been calculated from Bochem's viewpoint and therefore a portion of this loss belongs to the MI of Bochem.

The share of the profits of the associate would be 30% of a half years' profit ($7m) i.e. $2.1 million.

(W4) **Bond at fair value through profit or loss**

As the bond is classified at fair value through profit or loss, the expected future cashflows are discounted using the current market rate of interest as follows:

| Date | Cashflow ($000) | 10% discount factor | $000 |
|---|---|---|---|
| 30.04.11 | 1,600 | 0.909 | 1,454 |
| 30.04.12 | 1,400 | 0.826 | 1,156 |
| 30.04.13 | 16,500 | 0.751 | 12,391 |
|  |  |  | 15,001 |
|  | Impairment |  | 4,999 |
|  | Carrying value |  | 20,000 |

(W5) Ashanti should not record the revenue of $5 million, as it is not probable that economic benefit relating to the sale will flow to Ashanti. The revenue will be recorded when the customer pays for the goods. The cost of the goods will remain in the financial statements and the allowance for doubtful debts will be reduced to $3 million.

(W6) **Plant and machinery**

|  | $m |
|---|---|
| Carrying value at 1 May 2009 | 13 |
| Less depreciation for year | (1.44) |
|  | 11.56 |
| Fall in value to depreciated historical cost to STRGL | (1.96) |
| Depreciated historical cost at end of year to April 2010 | 9.6 |
| Fall in value to recoverable amount to P/L | (0.6) |
|  | 9 |
| Fall in value – revaluation to STRGL | (1) |
| Value in balance sheet | 8 |

The above treatment is applied where there is no obvious consumption of economic benefits as regards the fixed assets.

At 30 April 2009, a revaluation gain of ($13m – $12m – depreciation $1.2m) $2.2 million would be recorded in equity for the plant and machinery. At 30 April 2010, the value of the PPE would be $13m – depreciation of $1.44m i.e. $11.56m. Thus there will be a revaluation loss of $11.56m – $8m i.e. $3.56m. Of this amount $2.96 million ($1.96m + $1m) will be charged against revaluation surplus in reserves and $0.6 million will be charged to profit or loss.

(W7) A provision should be made under FRS 12 for the mis-selling obligation as the costs clearly arise from a past event which was the sale of goods to the customers. Ashanti should provide for the fine and the amount anticipated to be paid to customers. The costs to improve the company's system and the training costs relate to the company's future operations and are not provided for.

Accrual is therefore $40,000 + $170,000 = $0.21m

(W8) **Non-controlling interest (i.e. minority interest) (MI)**

| | |
|---|---|
| MI in profits for year is (30% of $18.6m + 44% of $7 million) = | $8.66m |
| MI in other recognised income is (30% × $6.0 million) = | $1.80m |
| | $10.46m |

## 66 MARRGRETT (DEC 08 EXAM) (UK GAAP FOCUS)

The Companies Act and FRS 7 'Fair values in acquisition accounting' state that the acquisition cost of a subsidiary is made up of cash consideration, fair value of other consideration and expenses of acquisition. The consideration is the amount paid for the business acquired and is measured at fair value. Consideration will include cash, shares, assets, contingent consideration, equity instruments, options and warrants. When an associate becomes a subsidiary, a proportion of the associate's results have already been dealt with in the consolidated profit and loss account and balance sheet. Goodwill will already have been calculated on the acquisition of the interest in the associate and will have been amortised. The method of accounting for goodwill set out in the Companies Act still applies and goodwill should be calculated by taking the difference between the fair value of the group's share of the net assets and the total acquisition cost of the interests. Under this method the group's share of the post acquisition profits of the associate become reclassified as goodwill, thus reducing goodwill. FRS 2 recognises that this accounting treatment is inconsistent with the way the investment was previously treated and this could lead to failure to give a true and fair view. Therefore FRS 2 requires that goodwill should be calculated as the sum of goodwill arising on each purchase adjusted for any subsequent diminution in value.

The fees payable in transaction costs need to be analysed into two elements. Costs of raising capital for the acquisition and fees incurred directly in making an acquisition. Costs relating to issuing shares should be charged against reserves and the share premium account would be available for this. Other costs which may be capitalised are defined in FRS 7 as 'fees and other costs incurred directly in making an acquisition'. These costs must not include internal costs, but may include the costs of lawyers and bankers. The work carried out by advisors is likely to overlap the work on raising capital and so reasonable allocations may have to be made.

It is common for part of the consideration to be contingent upon future events. Marrgrett wishes some of the existing shareholders/employees to remain in the business and has, therefore, offered share options as an incentive to these persons. The issue is whether these options form part of the purchase consideration or are compensation for post acquisition services. The conditions attached to the award will determine the accounting treatment. In this case there are employment conditions and, therefore, the options should be treated as compensation and valued under FRS 20 'Share based payment'. Thus a charge will appear in post acquisition earnings for employee services as the options were awarded to reward future services of employees rather than to acquire the business.

The additional shares to a fixed value of £50,000 are contingent upon the future returns on capital employed. Marrgrett only wants to make additional payments if the business is successful. All consideration should be fair valued at the date of acquisition, including the above contingent consideration. The contingent consideration payable in shares where the number of shares varies to give the recipient a fixed value (£50,000) meets the definition of a financial liability under FRS 25 'Financial Instruments: Disclosure and Presentation'. As a result the liability will have to be fair valued and any subsequent remeasurement will be recognised in the income statement. There is no requirement for the payments to be probable.

Intangible assets acquired as part of a business acquisition should be capitalised separately if their value can be measured reliably on initial recognition. The normal principles for valuing assets acquired in an acquisition will apply to intangible assets. FRS 7 states that where an intangible is recognised, its fair value should be based on its replacement cost which is normally estimated market value. FRS 10 requires reliable measurement also.

Intangible assets that have a readily obtainable market value are quite rare. However if the company regularly buys and sells intangibles such as trade names, then, Marrgrett may have developed valuation techniques which allow them to be capitalised separately from goodwill. If valuation techniques have not been developed by the company as regards the trade and internet domain names, then the value of the intangibles will be subsumed within goodwill.

Uniform accounting policies should be used to determine the amounts to be included in the consolidated financial statements. Problems can arise where subsidiaries are subject to different tax law as it may not be practicable to require subsidiaries to change their accounting policies as there may be local regulation which requires certain treatments in the financial statements. In order to comply with FRS 2, an adjustment must be made on consolidation to the depreciation charge and the accumulated depreciation in order to bring it into line with group practice. An adjustment to deferred taxation may also be required.

FRS 7 requires the fair value exercise to be complete in time for the publication of Marrgrett's first post acquisition financial statements. If it cannot be completed by this time, provisional values should be included which should be amended in the next financial statements with any corresponding adjustment to goodwill. The company will not be able to recognise the re-organisation provision at the date of the business combination. The ability of the acquirer to recognise a liability for reducing or changing the activities of the acquiree is restricted under FRS 7. A restructuring provision can only be recognised in a business combination when the acquiree has at the acquisition date already committed to the expenditure or course of action. These conditions are unlikely to have existed at the acquisition date. A restructuring plan that is conditional on the completion of a business combination is not recognised in accounting for the acquisition but the expense will be met against post acquisition earnings.

Where a group reduces its stake in a subsidiary, any profit or loss should be calculated as the difference between the carrying amount of the net assets of the subsidiary before the reduction in holding and the carrying amount attributable to the group's interest after the reduction together with any proceeds received. The net assets compared should include any related goodwill not previously written off through the profit and loss account. Where the undertaking continues to be subsidiary after the disposal, the minority interests in the subsidiary are increased by the carrying amount of the net assets that are now attributable to the minority because of the decrease in the company's stake. No amount of goodwill is attributable to the minority.

As regards the disposal of the second subsidiary to its management, it is necessary to decide whether Marrgrett has the power to exercise or actually exercises dominant influence or manages the subsidiary on a unified basis. If this is the case, then the company will remain a subsidiary. If Marrgrett does not have dominant influence, then a view will have to be taken as to whether it is probable that the profit target will be met. If it is considered probable that they will be met, the company would not be a subsidiary and would not be consolidated. Full details of the conversion rights would be disclosed in the financial statements.

# Section 3

# PILOT PAPER EXAM QUESTIONS

## SECTION A

1   The following draft financial statements relate to Zambeze, a public limited company:

**Draft group statements of financial position at 30 June**

|  | 2006 $m | 2005 $m |
|---|---|---|
| Assets: | | |
| Non-current assets: | | |
| Property, plant and equipment | 1,315 | 1,005 |
| Goodwill | 32 | 25 |
| Investment in associate | 270 | 290 |
| | 1,617 | 1,320 |
| Current assets: | | |
| Inventories | 650 | 580 |
| Trade receivables | 610 | 530 |
| Cash at bank and cash equivalents | 50 | 140 |
| | 1,310 | 1,250 |
| Total assets | 2,927 | 2,570 |
| Equity and liabilities: | | |
| Share capital | 100 | 85 |
| Share premium account | 30 | 15 |
| Revaluation reserve | 50 | 145 |
| Retained earnings | 254 | 250 |
| | 434 | 495 |
| Non controlling interest | 62 | 45 |
| Total equity | 496 | 540 |
| Non-current liabilities | 850 | 600 |
| Current liabilities | 1,581 | 1,430 |
| Total liabilities | 2,431 | 2,030 |
| Total equity and liabilities | 2,927 | 2,570 |

**Draft group statement of profit or loss and other comprehensive income for the year ended 30 June 2006**

|  | $m |
|---|---|
| Revenue | 4,700 |
| Cost of sales | (3,400) |
| Gross profit | 1,300 |
| Distribution and administrative expenses | (600) |
| Finance costs (interest payable) | (40) |
| Share of profit in associate | 30 |
| Profit before tax | 690 |
| Income tax expense (including tax on income from associate $10 million) | (210) |
| Profit for the period | 480 |
| Other comprehensive income: |  |
| Foreign exchange difference of associate | (5) |
| Impairment losses on property, plant and equipment offset against revaluation surplus | (95) |
| Total comprehensive income | 380 |

| Attributable to: |  |
|---|---|
| Equity holders of the parent | 355 |
| Non-controlling interest | 25 |
| Total comprehensive income | 380 |

**Draft statement of changes in equity for the year ended 30 June 2006**

|  | $m |
|---|---|
| Total comprehensive income | 355 |
| Dividends paid | (446) |
| New shares issued | 30 |
| Total movement during the year | (61) |
| Shareholders' funds at 1 July 2005 | 495 |
| Shareholders' funds at 30 June | 434 |

The following relates to Zambeze:

(i)   Zambeze acquired a seventy per cent holding in Damp, a public limited company, on 1 July 2005. The fair values of the net assets acquired were as follows:

|  | $m |
|---|---|
| Property, plant and equipment | 70 |
| Inventories and work in progress | 90 |
|  | 160 |

The purchase consideration was $100 million in cash and $25 million (discounted value) deferred consideration which is payable on 1 July 2006. The difference between the discounted value of the deferred consideration ($25 million) and the amount payable ($29 million) is included in 'interest payable'. Zambeze wants to set up a provision for reconstruction costs of $10 million retrospectively on the acquisition of Damp. This provision has not yet been set up.

(ii) There had been no disposals of property, plant and equipment during the year. Depreciation for the period charged in cost of sales was $60 million.

(iii) Current liabilities comprised the following items:

|  | 2006 $m | 2005 $m |
|---|---|---|
| Trade payables | 1,341 | 1,200 |
| Interest payable | 50 | 45 |
| Taxation | 190 | 185 |
|  | 1,581 | 1,430 |

(iv) Non-current liabilities comprised the following:

|  | 2006 $m | 2005 $m |
|---|---|---|
| Deferred consideration – purchase of Damp | 29 | – |
| Liability for the purchase of Property, plant and equipment | 144 | – |
| Loans repayable | 621 | 555 |
| Provision for deferred tax | 30 | 25 |
| Retirement benefit liability | 26 | 20 |
|  | 850 | 600 |

(v) The defined benefit liability comprised the following:

|  | $m |
|---|---|
| Movement in year: |  |
| Liability at 1 July 2005 | 20 |
| Current and past service costs charged to income statement | 13 |
| Contributions paid to retirement benefit scheme | (7) |
| Liability 30 June 2006 | 26 |

There was no remeasurement gains or losses in the year.

(vi) Goodwill is calculated using the full goodwill method. At the date of acquisition, the fair value of the non-controlling interest was $50 million. Goodwill was impairment tested on 30 June 2006 and any impairment was included in the financial statements for the year ended 30 June 2006.

(vii) The Finance Director has set up a company, River, through which Zambeze conducts its investment activities. Zambeze has paid $400 million to River during the year and this has been included in dividends paid. The money was invested in a specified portfolio of investments. Ninety-five per cent of the profits and one hundred per cent of the losses in the specified portfolio of investments are transferred to Zambeze. An investment manager has charge of the company's investments and owns all of the share capital of River. An agreement between the investment manager and Zambeze sets out the operating guidelines and prohibits the investment manager from obtaining access to the investments for the manager's benefit. An annual transfer of the profit/loss will occur on 30 June annually and the capital will be returned in four years' time. The transfer of $400 million cash occurred on 1 January 2006 but no transfer of profit/loss has yet occurred. The statement of financial position of River at 30 June 2006 is as follows:

**River – statement of financial position at 30 June 2006**

|  | $m |
|---|---|
| Investment at fair value through profit or loss | 390 |
|  | 390 |
| Share capital | 400 |
| Retained earnings | (10) |
|  | 390 |

**Required:**

(a)  Prepare a group cash flow statement for the Zambeze Group for the year ended 30 June 2006 using the indirect method.   **(35 marks)**

(b)  Discuss the issues which would determine whether River should be consolidated by Zambeze in the group financial statements.   **(9 marks)**

(c)  Discuss briefly the importance of ethical behaviour in the preparation of financial statements and whether the creation of River could constitute unethical practice by the finance director of Zambeze.   **(6 marks)**

Two marks are available for the quality of the discussion of the issues regarding the consolidation of River and the importance of ethical behaviour.

**(Total: 50 marks)**

## SECTION B – TWO QUESTIONS ONLY TO BE ATTEMPTED

**2**   Electron, a public limited company, operates in the energy sector. The company has grown significantly over the last few years and is currently preparing its financial statements for the year ended 30 June 2006.

Electron buys and sells oil and currently has a number of oil trading contracts. The contracts to purchase oil are treated as non-current assets and amortised over the contracts' durations. On acceptance of a contract to sell oil, fifty per cent of the contract price is recognised immediately with the balance being recognised over the remaining life of the contract. The contracts always result in the delivery of the commodity.   **(4 marks)**

Electron has recently constructed an ecologically efficient power station. A condition of being granted the operating licence by the government is that the power station be dismantled at the end of its life which is estimated to be 20 years. The power station cost $100 million and began production on 1 July 2005. Depreciation is charged on the power station using the straight line method. Electron has estimated at 30 June 2006, it will cost $15 million (net present value) to restore the site to its original condition using a discount rate of five per cent. Ninety-five per cent of these costs relate to the removal of the power station and five per cent relates to the damage caused through generating energy.

**(7 marks)**

Electron has leased another power station which was relatively inefficient, to a rival company on 30 June 2006. The beneficial and legal ownership remains with Electron and in the event of one of Electron's power stations being unable to produce energy, Electron can terminate the agreement. The leased power station is being treated as an operating lease with the net present value of the income of $40 million being recognised in profit or loss. The fair value of the power station is $70 million at 30 June 2006. A deposit of $10 million was received on 30 June 2006 and it is included in the net present value calculation.

**(5 marks)**

The company has a good relationship with its shareholders and employees. It has adopted a strategy of gradually increasing its dividend payments over the years. On 1 August 2006, the board proposed a dividend of 5c per share for the year ended 30 June 2006. The shareholders will approve the dividend along with the financial statements at the general meeting on 1 September 2006 and the dividend will be paid on 14 September 2006. The directors feel that the dividend should be accrued in the financial statements for the year ended 30 June 2006 as a 'valid expectation' has been created.   **(3 marks)**

The company granted share options to its employees on 1 July 2005. The fair value of the options at that date was $3 million. The options vest on 30 June 2008. The employees have to be employed at the end of the three year period for the options to vest and the following estimates have been made:

**Estimated percentage of employees leaving during vesting period at:**

Grant date 1 July 2005         5%

30 June 2006                   6%                                          **(4 marks)**

Effective communication to the directors.                               **(2 marks)**

**Required:**

**Draft a report suitable for presentation to the directors of Electron which discusses the accounting treatment of the above transactions in the financial statements for the year ended 30 June 2006, including relevant calculations.**

**(Total: 25 marks)**

3    The following statement of financial position relates to Kesare Group, a public limited company at 30 June 2006:

| | $000 |
|---|---|
| Assets: | |
| Non-current assets: | |
| Property, plant, and equipment | 10,000 |
| Goodwill | 6,000 |
| Other intangible assets | 5,000 |
| Financial assets (cost) | 9,000 |
| | 30,000 |
| | |
| Trade receivables | 7,000 |
| Other receivables | 4,600 |
| Cash and cash equivalents | 6,700 |
| | 18,300 |
| | |
| Total assets | 48,300 |
| | |
| Equity and liabilities | |
| Share capital | 9,000 |
| Other reserves | 4,500 |
| Retained earnings | 9,130 |
| | |
| Total equity | 22,630 |
| | |
| Non-current liabilities | |
| Long term borrowings | 10,000 |
| Deferred tax liability | 3,600 |
| Employee benefit liability | 4,000 |
| | |
| Total non-current liabilities | 17,600 |
| | |
| Current tax liability | 3,070 |
| Trade and other payables | 5,000 |
| | |
| Total current liabilities | 8,070 |
| | |
| Total liabilities | 25,670 |
| | |
| Total equity and liabilities | 48,300 |

The following information is relevant to the above statement of financial position:

(i) The financial assets are classified as 'fair value through other comprehensive income' but are shown in the above statement of financial position at their cost on 1 July 2005, including transactions costs of $0.5 million. The market value of the assets is $10.5 million on 30 June 2006. Taxation is payable on the sale of the assets.

(ii) The stated interest rate for the long term borrowing is 8 per cent. The loan of $10 million represents a convertible bond which has a liability component of $9.6 million and an equity component of $0.4 million. The bond was issued on 30 June 2006.

(iii) The defined benefit plan had a rule change on 1 July 2005. Kesare estimate that of the past service costs of $1 million, 40 per cent relates to vested benefits and 60 per cent relates to benefits that will vest over the next five years from that date. The past service costs have not been accounted for.

(iv) The tax bases of the assets and liabilities are the same as their carrying amounts in the statement of financial position at 30 June 2006 except for the following:

|  | $000 |
|---|---|
| (a) |  |
| Property, plant, and equipment | 2,400 |
| Trade receivables | 7,500 |
| Other receivables | 5,000 |
| Employee benefits | 5,200 |

(b) Other intangible assets were development costs which were all allowed for tax purposes when the cost was incurred in 2005.

(c) Trade and other payables includes an accrual for compensation to be paid to employees. This amounts to $1 million and is allowed for taxation when paid.

(v) Goodwill is not allowable for tax purposes in this jurisdiction.

(vi) Assume taxation is payable at 30%.

**Required:**

(a) Discuss the conceptual basis for the recognition of deferred taxation using the temporary difference approach to deferred taxation. **(7 marks)**

(b) Calculate the provision for deferred tax at 30 June 2006 after any necessary adjustments to the financial statements showing how the provision for deferred taxation would be dealt with in the financial statements. (Assume that any adjustments do not affect current tax. Candidates should briefly discuss the adjustments required to calculate the provision for deferred tax). **(18 marks)**

Two marks will be awarded for the quality of the discussion of the conceptual basis of deferred taxation in (a).

**(Total: 25 marks)**

**4**   A significant number of entities and countries around the world have adopted International Financial Reporting Standards (IFRS) as their basis for financial reporting, often regarding these as a means to improve the quality of information on corporate performance. However, while the advantages of a common set of global reporting standards are recognised, there are a number of implementation challenges at the international and national levels if the objective of an improved and harmonised reporting system is to be achieved.

**Required:**

(a)   Discuss the implementation challenges faced by the International Accounting Standards Board (IASB) if there is to be a successful move to International Financial Reporting Standards.                                                              **(18 marks)**

(b)   In January 2008 the International Accounting Standards Board issued IFRS 3 *Business combinations* which replaced a previous standard of the same name and revised and amended IAS 27 *Consolidated and separate financial statements*. These changes radically change the basis of reporting business combinations and transactions with minority interests (non-controlling interests).

Discuss how the changes introduced above will fundamentally affect the existing accounting practices for business combinations.                       **(7 marks)**

Two marks will be awarded for the quality of the discussion of the ideas and information.

**(Total: 25 marks)**

# Section 4

# ANSWERS TO PILOT PAPER EXAM QUESTIONS

**1   ZAMBEZE GROUP**

(a)   **Zambeze Group**

   **Group Statement of Cash Flows for the year ended 30 June 2006**

|                                              | $m    | $m    |
|----------------------------------------------|-------|-------|
| Cash flows from operating activities:        |       |       |
| Net profit before taxation                   |       | 690   |
| Adjustments for:                             |       |       |
| Share of profit in associate                 | (30)  |       |
| Depreciation                                 | 60    |       |
| Impairment of goodwill (W2)                  | 8     |       |
| Interest expense                             | 40    |       |
| Retirement benefit expense                   | 13    |       |
|                                              |       | 91    |
| Operating profit before working capital changes: |  | 781   |
| Increase in trade receivables                | (80)  |       |
| Decrease in inventories (650 – 580 – 90)     | 20    |       |
| Increase in trade payables                   | 141   |       |
|                                              |       | 81    |
| Cash generated from operations:              |       | 862   |
| Interest paid (Working 5)                    | (31)  |       |
| Income taxes paid (W4)                       | (190) |       |
| Cash paid to retirement benefit scheme       | (7)   |       |
|                                              |       | (228) |

|  | $m | $m |
|---|---|---|
| Net cash from operating activities: |  | 634 |
| Cash flows from investing activities |  |  |
| Acquisition of subsidiary | (100) |  |
| Purchase of property, plant and equipment (W1) | (251) |  |
| Dividends received from Associate (W3) | 35 |  |
| Investment in River | (400) |  |
| Net cash used in investing activities |  | (716) |
| Cash flows from financing activities: |  |  |
| Proceeds from issue of share capital | 30 |  |
| Increase in long-term borrowings | 66 |  |
| Dividends paid (W6) | (46) |  |
| Non-controlling interest dividends (W2) | (58) |  |
| Net cash used in financing activities |  | (8) |
| Net decrease in cash and cash equivalents |  | (90) |
| Cash and cash equivalents at beginning of period |  | 140 |
| Cash and cash equivalents at the end of period |  | 50 |

**Workings**

| (W1) | $m |
|---|---|
| Non-current assets |  |
| Balance at 1 July 2005 | 1,005 |
| Impairment losses | (95) |
| Depreciation | (60) |
| Purchases (by deduction) | 395 |
| Acquisition – Damp | 70 |
| Closing balance | 1,315 |

Cash flow is $395 million minus the liability for Property, plant and equipment of $144 million, i.e. $251 million.

| (W2) | $m |
|---|---|
| Purchase of subsidiary: |  |
| Consideration paid (100 + 25) | 125 |
| Fair value of NCI at acquisition | 50 |
|  | 175 |
| Fair value of net assets at acquisition | 160 |
| Goodwill at acquisition | 15 |

|  | $m |
|---|---|
| Goodwill: |  |
| Balance at 1 July 2005 | 25 |
| Goodwill on acquisition of subsidiary | 15 |
| Impairment (by deduction) | (8) |
| Balance at 30 June 2006 | 32 |

|  | $m |
|---|---|
| Non-controlling interest |  |
| Balance at 1 July 2005 | 45 |
| FV of NCI at acquisition of Damp | 50 |
| Profit for year | 25 |
| Dividend (by deduction) | (58) |
| Balance at 30 June 2006 | 62 |

|  |  | $m |
|---|---|---|
| **(W3)** |  |  |
| Dividend from associate: |  |  |
| Balance at 1 July 2005 |  | 290 |
| Income (net of tax) (30 – 10) |  | 20 |
| Foreign exchange loss |  | (5) |
| Dividends received  (by deduction) |  | (35) |
| Balance at 30 June 2006 |  | 270 |

|  |  | $m | $m |
|---|---|---|---|
| **(W4)** |  |  |  |
| Taxation: |  |  |  |
| Balance at 1 July 2005 | Income tax |  | 185 |
| Deferred tax |  |  | 25 |
| Income statements (210 – 10) |  |  | 200 |
| Tax paid  (by deduction) |  |  | (190) |
| Balance at 30 June 2006 | Income tax | 190 |  |
| Deferred tax |  | 30 |  |
|  |  |  | 220 |

| (W5) | $m |
|---|---|
| Interest paid: | |
| Balance at 1 July 2005 | 45 |
| Income statement | 40 |
| Unwinding of discount on purchase | (4) |
| Cash paid (by deduction) | (31) |
| | |
| Closing balance at 30 June 2006 | 50 |

(W6) The cash payment to River should be shown as 'investing activities' of $400 million and the dividend paid will then be $(446,400) million, i.e. $46 million.

(b) The definition of 'control' underpins the definition of the parent and subsidiary relationship. IFRS 10 *Consolidated financial statements* identifies control as the sole basis for consolidation which comprises three elements as follows:

(i) power over the investee, where the investor has current ability to direct activities that significantly affect the investee's returns, and

(ii) exposure, or rights to, variable returns from involvement in the investee, and.

(iii) the ability to use power over the investee to affect the amount of the investors returns.

IFRS 10 adopts a principles-based approach to determining whether or not control is exercised. As a result an entity has control over another entity when it has the ability to exercise that power, regardless of whether control is actively demonstrated or passive in nature.

Under IIFRS 10 control of an entity effectively comprises the ability to control the entity's decision making with a view to obtaining benefits from the entity. The ability to control decision making alone is not normally sufficient to establish control for accounting purposes but would normally be accompanied by the objective of obtaining benefits from the entity's activities. If a company obtains the benefits of ownership, is exposed to the risks of ownership, and can exercise decision making powers to obtain those benefits, then the company must control the third party.

Consequently, IFRS 10 requires that Zambeze should consolidate River as Zambeze controls it through the operating guidelines. Zambeze also receives 95% of the profits and suffers all the losses of River. The guidelines were set up when River was formed and, therefore, the company was set up as a vehicle with the objective of keeping certain transactions off the statement of financial position of Zambeze. The investment manager manages the investments of River within the guidelines and incurs no risk and receives 5% of the profits for the management services.

(c) Ethics in accounting is of utmost importance to accounting professionals and those who rely on their services. Accounting professionals know that people who use their services, especially decision makers using financial statements, expect them to be highly competent, reliable, and objective. Those who work in the field of accounting must not only be well qualified but must also possess a high degree of professional integrity. A professional's good reputation is one of his or her most important assets.

There is a very fine line between acceptable accounting practice and management's deliberate misrepresentation in the financial statements. The financial statements must meet the following criteria:

(i)   Technical compliance: A transaction must be recorded in accordance with generally accepted accounting principles (GAAP).

(ii)  Economic substance: The resulting financial statements must represent the economic substance of the event that has occurred.

(iii) Full disclosure and transparency: Sufficient disclosure must be made so that the effects of transactions are transparent to the reader of the financial statements.

In the case of River it could be argued that the first criterion may be met because the transaction is apparently recorded in technical compliance with IFRS, but technical compliance alone is not sufficient. The second criterion is not met because the transaction as recorded does not reflect the economic substance of the event that has occurred.

Accounting plays a critical function in society. Accounting numbers affect human behaviour especially when it affects compensation, and to deliberately mask the nature of accounting transactions could be deemed to be unethical behaviour.

River was set up with the express purpose of keeping its activities off the statement of financial position. The Finance Director has an ethical responsibility to the shareholders of Zambeze and society not to mask the true nature of the transactions with this entity. Further, if the transaction has been authorised by the Finance Director without the authority or knowledge of the Board of Directors, then a further ethical issue arises. Showing the transfer of funds as a dividend paid is unethical and possibly illegal in the jurisdiction. The transfer should not be hidden and River should be consolidated.

| ACCA marking scheme | | Marks |
|---|---|---|
| (a) | Operating activities | 6 |
| | Retirement benefit | 3 |
| | Associate | 3 |
| | Subsidiary treatment | 4 |
| | Property, plant and equipment | 3 |
| | Goodwill | 2 |
| | Non-controlling interest | 3 |
| | Taxation | 3 |
| | Dividend paid | 3 |
| | Interest | 2 |
| | River | 2 |
| | Issue of shares | 1 |
| | Maximum | 35 |
| (b) | Issues | 9 |
| (c) | Ethical discussion | 3 |
| | River | 3 |
| Total | | 50 |

## 2    ELECTRON

**REPORT TO DIRECTORS OF ELECTRON**

**Terms of reference**

This report sets out the nature of the accounting treatment and concerns regarding the following matters:

- Oil contracts

- Power station

- Operating leases

- Proposed dividend

- Share options.

**Oil Contracts**

The accounting policy adopted for the agreements relating to the oil contracts raises a number of concerns. The revenue recognition policy currently used is inflating revenue in the first year of the contract with 50% of the revenue being recognised, but a smaller proportion of the costs are recognised in the form of depreciation. Over the life of the contract, costs and revenues are equally matched but in the short term there is a bias towards a more immediate recognition of revenue against a straight line cost deferral policy. Additionally oil sales result in revenue while purchases of oil result in a tangible non-current asset. IAS 18 *Revenue* states that revenue and expenses that relate to the same transaction or event should be recognised simultaneously and the 'Framework' says that the 'measurement and display of the financial effect of like transactions must be carried out in a consistent way'. Accounting policies should provide a framework to ensure that this occurs. The current accounting practice seems to be out of line with IAS 18 and the *Framework*.

However, the election of the company to use some form of deferral policy for its agreements is to be commended as it attempts to bring its revenue recognition policy in line with the length of the agreements. The main problem is the lack of a detailed accounting standard on revenue recognition.  The result is the current lack of consistency in accounting for long-term agreements. However, it may be advisable to adopt a deferral policy in terms of this type of revenue. The contracts always result in the delivery of the oil in the normal course of business and are not, therefore, accounted for as financial instruments as they qualify as normal sale and purchase contracts.

**Power Station**

Under IAS 37 *Provisions, contingent liabilities and contingent assets*, a provision should be made at the reporting date for the discounted cost of the removal of the power station because of the following reasons:

(i)     the installation of the power station creates an obligating event

(ii)    the operating licence creates a legal obligation which is likely to occur

(iii)   the costs of removal will have to be incurred irrespective of the future operations of the company and cannot be avoided

(iv)    a transfer of economic benefits (i.e. the costs of removal) will be required to settle the obligation

(v)     a reasonable estimate of the obligation can be made although it is difficult to estimate a cost which will be incurred in twenty years time (IAS 37 says that only in exceptional circumstances will it not be possible to make some estimate of the obligation).

The costs to be incurred will be treated as part of the cost of the facility to be depreciated over its production life. However, the costs relating to the damage caused by the generation of energy should not be included in the provision, until the power is generated which in this case would be 5% of the total discounted provision. The accounting for the provision is shown in Appendix 1.

**Operating leases**

It may be necessary to consider whether a leasing agreement meets the definition of a lease in IAS 17 *Leases* and how a company should account for any fee that it might receive. A lease is classified as a finance lease if it transfers substantially all the risks and rewards 'incident' to ownership. All other leases are classified as operating leases. In this case, the beneficial and legal ownership remains with Electron and Electron can make use of the power station if it so wishes. Also for a lease asset to be a finance lease the present value of the minimum lease payments should be substantially all of the fair value of the leased asset. In this case this amounts to 57.1% ($40 million ÷ $70 million) which does not constitute 'substantially all'. Thus there does not seem to be any issue over the classification of the lease as an operating lease. The immediate recognition as income of the future benefit at net present value is a little more problematical. IAS 17 says that lease income from operating leases should be recognised on a straight line basis over the lease term unless another systematic basis is more representative. If a fee is received as an 'up front' cash payment then IAS 18 *Revenue* (para 20) should be applied. If there is future involvement required to earn the fee, or there are retained risks or risk of the repayment of the fee, or any restrictions on the lessor's use of the asset, then immediate recognition is inappropriate. The present policy of recognising the total lease income as if it were immediate income which it is not, would be difficult to justify. Similarly, as regards the deposit received, revenue should only be recognised when there is performance of the contract. Thus as there has been no performance under the contract, no revenue should be accrued in the period.

**Proposed dividend**

The dividend was proposed after the reporting date and the company, therefore, did not have a liability at that date. No provision for the dividend should be recognised. The approval by the directors and the shareholders are enough to create a valid expectation that the payment will be made and give rise to an obligation. However, this occurred after the current year end and, therefore, will be charged against the profits for the year ending 30 June 2007.

The existence of a good record of dividend payments and an established dividend policy does not create a valid expectation or an obligation. However, the proposed dividend will be disclosed in the notes to the financial statements as the directors approved it prior to the authorisation of the financial statements.

**Share options**

Equity-settled transactions with employees would normally be expensed on the basis of their fair value at the grant date. Fair value should be based on market prices wherever possible. Many shares and share options will not be traded on an active market. In this case, valuation techniques, such as the option pricing model, would be used. IFRS 2's objective for equity-based transactions with employees is to determine and recognise compensation costs over the period in which the services are rendered. In this case, the company has granted to employees share options that vest in three years' time on the condition that they remain in the entity's employ for that period. These steps will be taken:

(i)    the fair value of the options will be determined at the date on which they were granted

(ii)   this fair value will be charged to the income statement equally over the three year vesting period with adjustments made at each accounting date to reflect the best estimate of the number of options that eventually will vest.

Shareholders' equity will be increased by an amount equal to the income statement charge. The charge in the income statement reflects the number of options that are likely to vest, not the number of options granted or the number of options exercised. If employees decide not to exercise their options because the share price is lower than the exercise price, then no adjustment is made to the income statement. Many employee share option schemes contain conditions that must be met before the employee becomes entitled to the shares or options. These are called vesting conditions and could require, for example, an increase in profit or growth in the entity's share price before the shares vest. In this case the vesting condition is the employment condition. $940,000 ($3 million $\times$ 94% $\times$ 1/3) will be charged in the income statement and credited to equity at 30 June 2006.

### Recommendations and conclusion

The above report sets out the recommendations regarding the accounting treatment of the items specified. It is imperative that the recommendations are followed as non-compliance with a single IFRS constitutes a failure to follow International Financial Reporting Standards for reporting purposes.

### Appendix 1

|  | $m | $m |
|---|---|---|
| Present value of obligation at 1 July 2005 (15 ÷ 1.05) | 14.3 |  |
| Provision for decommissioning (95% × 14.3) | 13.6 |  |
| Provision for damage through extraction (5% × 14.3) |  | 0.7 |

Statement of financial position at 30 June 2006

|  | $m | $m |
|---|---|---|
| Non-current assets: |  |  |
| Cost of power station | 100 |  |
| Provision for decommissioning | 13.6 |  |
|  | 113.6 |  |
| Less depreciation (113.6 ÷ 20 years) | (5.7) |  |
| Carrying value | 107.9 |  |

Other provisions:

| | |
|---|---|
| Provision for decommissioning 1 July 2005 | 13.6 |
| Unwinding of discount (13.6 × 5%) | 0.7 |
| | ———— |
| | 14.3 |
| Provision for damage (0.7 ÷ 20 years) (see tutorial note) | 0.1 |
| | ———— |
| | 14.4 |
| | ———— |

**Income statement**

| | $m |
|---|---|
| Depreciation | 5.7 |
| Provision for damage | 0.1 |
| Unwinding of discount (finance cost) | 0.7 |
| | ———— |

A simple straight line basis has been used to calculate the required provision for damage. A more complex method could be used whereby the present value of the expected cost of the provision is provided for over 20 years and the discount thereon is unwound over its life.

*Tutorial note*

*The working for the provision for damage results in an amount of $35,000. After three years the cumulative amount will be $105,000 which rounds to $0.1 million. The above answer recognises this amount in the first of the three years.*

| ACCA marking scheme | |
|---|---|
| | *Marks* |
| Oil contracts | 4 |
| Power station | 7 |
| Operating leases | 5 |
| Proposed dividend | 3 |
| Share options | 4 |
| Effective communication | 2 |
| | —— |
| Total | 25 |
| | —— |

## 3 KESARE GROUP

(a) Under IFRS, an asset or liability is recognised if it meets the definition of such in the Framework document. The definitions refer to the right to receive or the obligation to transfer economic benefits as a result of a past event. The accounting model used to account for deferred tax is based on the premise that the tax effects of transactions should be recognised in the same period as the transactions themselves. The reality is, however, that tax is paid in accordance with tax legislation when it becomes a legal liability. There is an argument, therefore, that deferred tax is neither asset nor liability.

The temporary difference approach is based on the assumption that an asset will ultimately be recovered or realised by a cash inflow which will enter into the determination of future taxable profits. Thus the tax payable on the realisation of the asset should be provided for. It is argued that it would be inconsistent to represent that the asset can be recovered at its carrying value whilst ignoring the tax consequences.

Similarly for a liability carried in the statement of financial position, there is an implicit assumption that the liability will ultimately be settled by a cash outflow. The outflow will enter into the determination of tax profits and any tax deduction allowable will effectively be an asset. As above, it would be inconsistent to recognise the liability while ignoring the tax consequences of its recognition.

Conceptually there is a weakness in this approach as only one of the liabilities, that is tax, is being provided for and not other costs which will be incurred, such as overhead costs. The principal issue in accounting for deferred tax is how to account for the future tax consequences of the future recovery or settlement of the carrying amounts of the assets and liabilities.

(b)

| | Fin Stats | Adjusts to Fin Stat | Adjusted Fin Stats | Tax base | Temporary difference |
|---|---|---|---|---|---|
| | $000 | $000 | S000 | $000 | $000 |
| PPE | 10,000 | | 10,000 | 2,400 | 7,600 |
| Goodwill | 6,000 | | 6,000 | 6,000 | N/A |
| Other INCA | 5,000 | | 5,000 | 0 | 5,000 |
| Financial assets | 9,000 | 1,500 | 10,500 | 9,000 | 1,500 |
| | | | | | |
| Total NCA | 30,000 | 1,500 | 31,500 | | |
| | | | | | |
| Trade receivables | 7,000 | | 7,000 | 7,500 | (500) |
| Other receivables | 4,600 | | 4,600 | 5,000 | (400) |
| Cash and equivalents | 6,700 | | 6,700 | 6,700 | N/A |
| | | | | | |
| Total assets | 48,300 | 1,500 | 49,800 | | |

| | Fin Stats | Adjusts to Fin Stat | Adjusted Fin Stats | Tax base | Temporary difference |
|---|---|---|---|---|---|
| | $000 | $000 | $000 | $000 | $000 |
| Long term borrowings | 10,000 | (400) | 9,600 | 10,000 | 400 |
| Deferred tax | 3,600 | | 3,600 | 3,600 | – |
| Employee benefits | 4,000 | 1,000 | 5,000 | 5,200 | 200 |
| Current liabilities: | | | | | |
| Current tax | 3,070 | | 3,070 | 3,070 | – |
| Payables | 5,000 | | 5,000 | 4,000 | (1,000) |
| Total liabilities | 25,670 | 600 | 26,270 | | 12,800 |
| Share capital | 9,000 | | 9,000 | | |
| Other equity | 4,500 | 1,500 400 | 6,400 | | |
| Retained earnings | 9,130 | (1,000) | 8,130 | | |
| | 48,300 | 1,500 | 49,800 | | |

| | $000 |
|---|---|
| Temp diffs re deferred tax liabilities ((14,700 × 30%) | 4,410 |
| Temp diffs re deferred tax assets (1,900 × 30%) | (570) |
| Deferred tax provision required at 30 June 2006 | 3,840 |
| Deferred tax provision b/fwd at 1 July 2005 | 3,600 |
| Increase in deferred tax provision for the year | 240 |

Comments:

(i) The financial assets at fair value through other comprehensive income should be valued at fair value with the increase going to equity ($1.5 million).

(ii) The bond should be split into its equity and liability elements as per IAS 32, with a reduction in the liability and transfer to equity of $400,000.

(iii) The defined benefit plan should recognise in full the consequences of the rule change as required by IAS 19 (revised). This amounts to past service costs where future benefits paid be increased based upon past years of service. Thus the employee benefit liability will be increased by $1 million, and retained earnings will be reduced by the same amount.

(iv) As the development costs have been allowed for tax already, it will have a tax base of zero. Goodwill is measured as a residual and, therefore, the impact is not measured under IAS 12.

(v) The accrual for compensation will not be allowed until a later period and, therefore, will reduce the tax base relating to trade and other payables.

| ACCA marking scheme | | | |
|---|---|---|---|
| | | | *Marks* |
| (a) | Quality of discussion | | 2 |
| | Framework | | 1 |
| | Temporary difference | | 2 |
| | Liability | | 1 |
| | Weakness | | 1 |
| | Maximum | | 7 |
| | | | |
| (b) | Adjustments: | Financial assets at FV through OCI | 2 |
| | | Convertible bond | 2 |
| | | Defined benefit plan | 2 |
| | | Property, plant and equipment | 1 |
| | Deferred tax: | Goodwill | 1 |
| | | Other intangibles | 1 |
| | | Financial assets | 1 |
| | | Trade receivables | 1 |
| | | Other receivables | 1 |
| | | Long-term borrowings | 1 |
| | | Employee Benefits | 1 |
| | | Trade payables | 2 |
| | | Calculation | 3 |
| | Available | | 19 |
| | Maximum | | 18 |
| | Available | | 26 |
| | | | |
| Total | | | 25 |

## 4 IFRS

(a) International Financial Reporting Standards (IFRS) were initially developed for the preparation of group accounts of listed companies. The use of IFRS is growing such that in some countries that are building or improving their accounting regulatory framework, IFRS based corporate reports are deemed to be more reliable and relevant than local GAAP reports. In many of these countries IFRS are the statutory requirement for legal entities and, therefore, an implementation issue that has arisen is that the national law has to be reconciled with the requirements of IFRS.

Another implementation issue relates to small and medium-sized enterprises (SMEs) in terms of whether a separate set of standards should be developed and what should be the underlying conceptual and methodological basis for such standards. Effective implementation requires continuous interaction between the International Accounting Standards Board (IASB) and national regulators. The IASB has issued a draft Memorandum of Understanding on the role of Accounting Standard Setters and their relationship with the IASB. It identifies responsibilities that the IASB and other standard setters should adopt to facilitate the ongoing adoption of or convergence with IFRS.

With the increase in the number of entities applying IFRS, the demand for implementation guidance is growing. The International Financial Reporting Interpretations Committee (IFRIC) has been given the task of meeting this demand but there may be a need for additional coping mechanisms as a limited number of interpretations have been issued since the inception of IFRIC.

Variations in translation of IFRS could introduce inconsistency. In some countries the capacity for highly technical translation is low and there may be a conflict with existing national terminology and legislation. Additionally, time lags in the local 'endorsement' process and in translating new IFRS could mean that financial reports may not be consistent with the latest body of standards. Additionally the successful implementation of IFRS will depend upon the robustness of the local regulatory framework. Effective corporate governance practices, high quality auditing standards and practices, and effective enforcement or oversight mechanisms will be required to underpin the IFRS. Often endorsement of the standards is required as part of the implementation process. For example, in the European Union, after IFRS have been issued by the IASB, they must go through an endorsement process before companies listed in the European Union are required to apply them. This process could create standards that differ from those of the IASB.

Implementation of IFRS can have implications for a number of legislative areas. The more complex the regulatory framework, the more problems will arise. There can be tax, price control and company law implications, and certain sectors, such as banking and insurance, may be subject to additional regulation that may require special reporting requirements. Entities may find that they are in breach of existing covenants with lenders where the provision of funding is based on national GAAP ratios. Similarly corporate law may set out the requirements on distribution of dividends and unless the necessary corporate law amendments are made then dividend distributions would be based on national GAAP which might create confusion.

An international mechanism for the co-ordination of enforcement of IFRS is required. IOSCO provides an infrastructure for enforcement with respect to publicly listed companies. IOSCO has put forward proposals for the regulatory interpretation and enforcement of IFRS. On a more local level, the European Union has established the Committee of European Securities Regulators whose role is to improve co-ordination among securities regulators and ensure implementation of legislation in the European Union.

The complex nature of IFRS and the sheer volume of standards make the task of implementation difficult. The standards are deemed to be 'principles based' and this may lead to inconsistencies of application, particularly in countries without a critical mass of experienced accountants. Most accountants will have been trained to apply domestic accounting standards, and where there are options in IFRS, then it is likely that the accounting practice closest to their National GAAP will be chosen. Similarly IFRSs utilise fair value measurement extensively and market information is required to more accurately reflect the value. The nature of this market information will vary around the world. If market information is not available, an alternative source can be obtained by simulating a hypothetical market or by using mathematical modelling. Experience of such techniques will vary worldwide, and this experience will be variable in such areas as actuarial estimation, impairment testing, and valuing share based payments. The concepts set out in IFRS may be new to some accounting professionals and may be difficult to grasp.

(b) Under current accounting practice the objective of acquisition accounting is to reflect the cost of the acquisition. To the extent to which it is not represented by identifiable assets and liabilities (measured at their fair value), goodwill arises and is reported in the financial statements. These exposure drafts adopt a different perspective and require the financial statements to reflect the fair value of the acquired business. The recognition of the acquired business at fair value will mean that any existing interest owned by the acquirer before it gained control will be re-measured at fair value at the date of acquisition with any gain or loss recognised in the income statement.

The proposals treat the group as a single economic entity and any outside equity interest in a subsidiary is treated as part of the overall ownership interest in the group. As a consequence, transactions with minority shareholders are to be treated as equity transactions. No gain or loss will be recognised in the income statement. Accounting for business combinations has to date been based on the 'parent entity' concept where the extent of non-controlling interests and transactions with non-controlling interests are separately identified in the primary financial statements.

It is also proposed that goodwill is to be recognised in full even if control is less than 100%. IFRS 3 currently requires that goodwill arising on acquisition should only be recognised with respect to the part of the subsidiary undertaking that is attributable to the interest held by the parent entity.

Costs incurred in connection with an acquisition are not to be accounted for as part of the cost of the investment but will be charged in the income statement. There will also be changes to the way in which some assets and liabilities acquired in a business combination are recognised and measured. The draft IFRS requires assets and liabilities acquired to be measured and recognised at fair value at the acquisition date. Currently estimated fair values are used and guidance was given as to how to measure 'fair value' in the current standard. This guidance often resulted in the measurement of assets and liabilities in a manner which was inconsistent with fair value objectives.

| ACCA marking scheme | | |
|---|---|---|
| | | *Marks* |
| (a) | Subjective | 18 |
| (b) | Subjective | 7 |
| | | —— |
| Total | | 25 |
| | | —— |